ECONOMICS TODAY— THE MACRO VIEW

Second Edition

15-23

ECONOMICS
THE MACRO

Roger LeRoy Miller

Professor of Economics   Department of Economics
and Associate Director
Center for Studies in Law and Economics

University of Miami

TODAY–VIEW

Second Edition

Canfield Press San Francisco
A Department of Harper & Row, Publishers, Inc.

New York   Hagerstown   London

We gratefully acknowledge the following sources for information
and quotations used in the biographical sketches:

Newsweek Magazine
U.S. News and World Report
Fortune Magazine
New York Times
Times Magazine
Business Week
Who's Who in America
Time Magazine
Current Biography
The Nation
The New Republic

The New York Review of
  Books
Harpers
Science
Webster's American
  Biographies
Encyclopedia Brittanica Book
  of the Year 1973
American Economic Review
Ralph Nader Congressional
  Report, 92nd Congress

This book was set in Melior by Computer Typesetting Services.
The editors were Gerald Papke and Eva Marie Strock; the
designer was Paula Tuerk; the graphic illustrations were
done by Axya Art; the cover was designed by Michael
Rogondino; the index was prepared by Carol Talpers.
Nick Keefe supervised production.
The printer and binder was W. A. Krueger Co.

Economics Today — The Macro View

Harper & Row, Publishers, Inc.
10 East 53rd Street
New York, NY 10022

Library of Congress Cataloging in Publication Data

Miller, Roger LeRoy.
    Economics today, the macro view.

    Includes the chapters dealing with macroeconomics
from the author's Economics today, 2d ed.
    Includes bibliographies and index.
    1. Macroeconomics I. Title.
HB171.5.M6425 1976   339   75-40361
ISBN 0-06-3854 60-0

76 77 78 79 80   10 9 8 7 6 5 4 3 2 1

Contents in Brief

UNIT ONE

GETTING STARTED

UNIT TWO

THE AMERICAN ECONOMY AND ITS PROBLEMS

UNIT THREE

INCOME AND EMPLOYMENT DETERMINATION MODELS   **175**

UNIT FOUR

THE INTERNATIONAL SCENE   **303**

Detailed Contents

UNIT TWO

UNIT THREE
INCOME AND EMPLOYMENT DETERMINATION MODELS   175

Preface

To the Instructor

Today there are indeed few people who would not agree that economic issues rank at or near the top of the list of problems confronting Americans. There is no news telecast, newspaper edition, or weekly news magazine that does not report on some new economic datum which shows that either things are getting worse or things are getting better. Those "things" obviously have something to do with the rates of inflation and unemployment, the length of food stamp lines, the number of individuals still on welfare rolls, the amount of racial discrimination still being practiced, the cost of cleaning up the air, or the handling of corporate profits.

Many, if not most, of the current social issues are involved with economics in some way or another. However, for students to understand and apply economic reasoning to social issues, they must have a solid foundation in economics. *Economics Today—The Micro View* was written both to provide that necessary foundation and to demonstrate the application of economic reasoning to the problems around us.

The Theory-Issue Interface

Economic reasoning requires a knowledge of basic theory. The eighteen chapters in this book present that basic theory. However, the successful application of any theory requires continued demonstration of its usefulness. The eighteen issues in this text serve that purpose; the issues are the topical applications and extensions of the theory presented in the chapters. Additionally, the issues provide an important component of the pedagogue's tool kit: a source that will generate interest among the students and stimulate discussion.

Economics Today—The Macro View is a flexible theory-issue text that lends itself to a variety of teaching uses. For example, many instructors find that their lecture time is best spent explaining the theory contained in the chapters while letting the students test their understanding of the theory by reading and perhaps discussing the issues associated with it. Other instructors use the opposite technique: class discussion centered only on the issues, with reading assignments to take care of the theory.

Organization of the Text

Unit One begins with an issue that discusses the scarcity society. Little actual theory is presented in this issue; the idea is to start students in their study of economics with a pressing problem always in the news. The rest of Unit One presents foundation materials for the study of economics at both the macro and micro level, including chapters on the science of economics, how different systems solve the economic problem, and supply and demand.

Unit Two presents some necessary background materials to the income and employment models that follow in Unit Three. International materials as well as the topics of growth and development are covered in Unit Four.

Other Characteristics of the Text

In addition to its use of issues and its organization around those issues, the text offers six other useful features.

Biographical Sketches

Generally, the biographies consider living economists and industrial leaders. These sketches are presented for their intrinsic interest (students like to know what economists and economics are all about) and as historical background of what was involved in the policymaking at the national level.

Definitions of New Terms

All new economic terms are introduced into the text by bold type. At the end of each chapter and issue there is a glossary of definitions for these particular words. Also, in the index, page numbers indicating where these defined words appear in the text are shown in bold so students can immediately find the definitions of terms that are unclear to them.

Chapter Summaries

Chapter summaries are presented in a point-by-point format that allows for quick review of the preceding materials.

Questions for Thought and Discussion

There are selected questions for thought and discussion after every chapter and issue. Most of these questions are designed to elicit discussion either among the students themselves without the aid of an instructor or during classtime with the instructor's guidance.

Numerical Problems

Where appropriate, a numerical problem is presented as the last Question for Thought and Discussion. Answers to these problems are in the *Instructor's Manual.*

Selected References

There are selected references following each chapter and issue for those students who wish to further research any topic in the book. These references were selected with the students in mind. No specialized journal articles or books that would be understandable only to a trained economist are given; specialized references are included in the *Instructor's Manual.*

Teaching Aids and Supplements

Economics Today—The Macro View is part of an entire teaching package that includes the following five items:

Instructor's Manual

The *Instructor's Manual* presents an outline of each chapter and issue from which lecture notes can be drawn as well as additional comments for further points of discussion or additional lecture. There is a list of free materials when applicable; the instructor can send for these free materials and hand them out in class. Also included are extensive selected references for further research by the instructor, and, in some cases, films (and addresses) that relate to the topic discussed in the specific chapter or issue. As mentioned, there are answers for those problems that are at the end of certain Questions for Thought and Discussion in the text.

Student Learning Guide

The accompanying *Student Learning Guide,* written by Professor Lee Spector of S.U.N.Y. at Buffalo, started in a rather odd way. Spector asked himself what sort of materials students would need if they wanted to learn economics on their own. Starting from this unusual premise, Spector has written a truly different study guide: It not only provides tests of whether students are understanding the material, but it also gives substantial help to those students who are having trouble. Consequently, this supplement is called a learning guide, rather than merely a study guide. Included in this guide are such helpful features as learning objectives, hints on how to study the material, alternative explanations of difficult material, glossaries, and both pre- and posttests.

Independent Study Modules (ISMs)

A complete and heavily pretested audio/graphic learning system is available to instructors who have available classrooms or student learning centers that are equipped with tape playback facilities. These unique materials were independently developed in conjunction with the use of the first edition; they were further refined for the second edition by their authors, James Mason, Mike Melvin, and Craig Justice. The ISM package includes a total of thirty separate cassettes, fifteen for the macro view and fifteen for the macro view. Besides the graphic packets and cassette tape materials, there are self-tests that can be used in a programmed-learning manner.

The weekly ISM materials can be used in a variety of ways. One way is as a substitute for one lecture period. ISM materials can also be used to reinforce a full lecture schedule on an assigned or even a voluntary basis. The emphasis of the system tends toward integrating it with chapter theory while giving specific examples of problems that are different from those in the text.

We have found from extensive field testing that the ISM supplements develop positive responses to learning economic theory by the students. Students have a greater appreciation of the opportunity to learn the complex material objectively at their own individual pace. The instructors who have used the system contend that students come to lectures better prepared and with positive expectations.

Test Bank

The test questions, of which there are approximately 1,000, are quite different. They evolved from the audio/graphic learning system (ISM) developed by Mason, Melvin, and Justice. The test bank consists of both graphic and verbal multiple-choice questions that are divided by degree of difficulty. They are subdivided as to whether they treat concepts, problem solving, or institutional materials. There are also references to the page number in the hardcover *Economics Today*, to which students may be referred to if they get any incorrect answers.

Transparency Masters

All the important graphs and charts are available in a set of transparency masters that are free to adopters.

The Second Edition

This edition of the text does not merely contain a few updated tables and graphs. Rather, I wanted to completely reorganize and redo sections of the text to increase its usability as a teaching device. To that end I have added fourteen new issues and eliminated those that seemed less interesting to today's students. The new issues are more serious and perhaps less ephemeral than those eliminated. Additionally, a great deal of the theoretical materials have been completely redone. In particular, the simplified Keynesian income and employment determination model is discussed in a more complete and easily learned manner. A number of materials were eliminated from the second edition because of their after-the-fact limited use by adopting professors.

Although not complete, the following summary indicates some of the substantial changes or additions to this second edition:

1. Inclusion of a brief appendix on reading and working with graphs, useful for those students who are unfamiliar with the techniques (Appendix A).

2. Expanded explanation of why the production-possibilities curve is bowed outward (Chapter 2).

3. Inclusion of elasticity in one basic supply-and-demand chapter (Chapter 3), which is, however, subdivided into Parts A and B; elasticity is treated exclusively in part B. Thus instructors who wish to postpone a discussion of elasticity have a definite cut-off point.

4. Stress on the distinction between relative and absolute prices when presenting the laws of supply and demand (Chapter 3). Chapter 3 includes an enumeration of determinants of demand other than price and numerical examples of how actual price elasticities can be calculated.

5. Application of supply and demand to one particular illegal activity—Prohibition—in Issue I-4.

6. Completely revised presentation of national income accounting presenting the expenditure and income approaches (Chapter 4).

7. A more complete presentation of unemployment, including duration of unemployment and hidden unemployment (Chapter 6).

8. An expanded presentation of stagflation (Chapter 7).

9. Greater distinction is made between anticipated and unanticipated inflation as well as the effects of the two different kinds of inflation on the wealth position of debtors and creditors (Chapter 7).

10. Expanded presentation of determinants of planned investment; stress on the difference between planned and actual values of aggregate variables.

11. Inclusion of a brief appendix on the accelerator (Appendix B).

12. Inclusion of T accounts to explain the multiple expansion of the money supply (Chapter 11).

13 Inclusion of numerous new biographical sketches and the updating of those retained from the first edition.

14. Fourteen new issues, including issues on the scarcity society, national priorities, the effects of unemployment compensation on the rate of unemployment, indexing, public service employment, subsidizing commercial banks, problems with short-run stabilization, the threat of international competition, and flexible exchange rates and worldwide inflation.

I received numerous comments from many adopters while preparing the second edition; these comments aided me greatly in improving the text and its supplemental materials. I welcome further comments on what is included in this edition. This edition, as with the first, is also available in the hardcover *Economics Today* and has a companion paperback volume: *Economics Today—The Micro View.*

Roger LeRoy Miller
Coral Gables

Cross-Listing of Chapters and Issues in *Economics Today*, *Economics Today—The Macro View*, and *Economics Today—The Micro View*

ECONOMICS TODAY	ECONOMICS TODAY—The Macro View	ECONOMICS TODAY—The Micro View	ECONOMICS TODAY	ECONOMICS TODAY—The Macro View	ECONOMICS TODAY—The Micro View
Issue I-1	Issue I-1	Issue I-1	Chapter 17		Chapter 5
Chapter 1	Chapter 1	Chapter 1	Chapter 18		Chapter 6
Issue I-2	Issue I-2	Issue I-2	Issue I-18		Issue I-6
Chapter 2	Chapter 2	Chapter 2	Issue I-19		Issue I-7
Issue I-3	Issue I-3	Issue I-3	Chapter 19		Chapter 7
Chapter 3	Chapter 3	Chapter 3	Issue I-20		Issue I-8
Issue I-4	Issue I-4	Issue I-4	Issue I-21		Issue I-9
Chapter 4	Chapter 4		Chapter 20		Chapter 8
Issue I-5	Issue I-5		Issue I-22		Issue I-10
Chapter 5	Chapter 5		Issue I-23		
Issue I-6	Issue I-6		Chapter 21		Chapter 9
Issue I-7	Issue I-7		Issue I-24		Issue I-11
Chapter 6	Chapter 6		Issue I-25		Issue I-12
Issue I-8	Issue I-8		Chapter 22		Chapter 10
Chapter 7	Chapter 7		Issue I-26		Issue I-13
Issue I-9	Issue I-9		Chapter 23		Chapter 11
Issue I-10	Issue I-10		Issue I-27		Issue I-14
Chapter 8	Chapter 8		Issue I-28		Issue I-15
Chapter 9	Chapter 9		Chapter 24		
Chapter 10	Chapter 10		Issue I-29		
Issue I-11	Issue I-11		Chapter 25		Chapter 12
Issue I-12	Issue I-12		Issue I-30		Issue I-16
Chapter 11	Chapter 11		Chapter 26		Chapter 13
Issue I-13	Issue I-13		Issue I-31		Issue I-17
Chapter 12	Chapter 12		Issue I-32		Issue I-18
Chapter 13	Chapter 13		Chapter 27		Chapter 14
Issue I-14	Issue I-14		Issue I-33		Issue I-19
Chapter 14	Chapter 14	Chapter 16	Chapter 28		Chapter 15
Issue I-15	Issue I-15		Issue I-34		Issue I-20
Chapter 15	Chapter 15		Chapter 29	Chapter 16	
Issue I-16	Issue I-16		Issue I-35	Issue I-17	
Chapter 16		Chapter 4	Chapter 30	Chapter 17	Chapter 17
Issue I-17		Issue I-5	Issue I-36	Issue I-18	Issue I-21

To the Student

Whether you are taking economics as a general course in a liberal arts education or, more specifically, as the foundation for further study of economics and/or business, the textbook you use can hopefully make the course more rather than less enjoyable. My comments should make the book a more useful aspect of the course you are now taking. Note, however, that my comments are secondary to the way your instructor wishes you to use the text.

The issues complement the theoretical points discussed in the chapters. Many of you may find that a quick first reading of the issues without attempting a thorough grasp of points not understood completely will be a good introduction to the particular topics at hand. Then, a quick reading of the appropriate theoretical chapter is in order, with a more careful later rereading of those points not understood. Finally, if the issue is skimmed again, any aspects of the theory not yet mastered will become apparent. Alternatively, first you can handle the theoretical chapters in more detail so you can find out, upon the initial reading of the issue, whether the application of theory is understandable.

This second edition includes a large number of new issues that have been included so you will keep abreast of the changing events in our economic world. Ideally, you will find the currency of these issues helpful in mastering the application of analysis to the real world.

For review, there are self-contained graphs, definitions of new terms, chapter summaries, and, in some cases, actual numerical or graphical problems that may be assigned by your instructor (who has the answers in the *Instructor's Manual*). You can, after having read all the text, go over one or more of the reviewing devices. If you want to do additional study on a particular topic, selected references are listed at the end of each chapter and issue.

An entirely new *Student Learning Guide* has been prepared for this edition. The guide not only reinforces the concepts and analysis presented in the text, it also helps you master particularly difficult aspects of economics without further help from your instructor or a tutor. In this sense, the *Student Learning Guide* is a self-contained learning program.

I sincerely hope you will become interested in the economic issues of our times, not in spite of, but with the help of, your textbook.

R. L. M.

Acknowledgements

The First Edition

The following people were responsible for critically commenting on the manuscript during its formation, writing, and rewriting. To them I owe my gratitude but certainly do not hold them responsible for any remaining errors:

John R. Aidem, Miami-Dade Junior College
Glen W. Atkinson, University of Nevada
Charles A. Berry, University of Cincinnati
Warren L. Coats, Jr., University of Virginia
Conrad P. Caligaris, Northeastern University
Ed Coen, University of Minnesota
Alan E. Ellis, De Anza College
Grant Ferguson, North Texas State University
Peter Frost, University of Miami
Martin D. Haney, Portland Community College
Timothy R. Keely, Tacoma Community College
Norman F. Keiser, California State University at San Jose
E. R. Kittrell, Northern Illinois University
John L. Madden, University of Kentucky
John M. Martin, California State University at Hayward
E. S. McKuskey, St. Petersburg Junior College
Herbert C. Milikien, American River College
Jerry L. Petr, University of Nebraska at Lincoln
I. James Pikl, University of Wyoming
Richard Romano, Broome Community College
Augustus Shackelford, El Camino College
Howard F. Smith, California Polytechnic State University at San Luis Obispo
William T. Trulove, Eastern Washington State College
Robert F. Wallace, Washington State University
Henry C. Wallich, Yale University
James Willis, California State University at San Jose
Shik Young, Eastern Washington State College

The Second Edition

Many first edition adopters were asked for specific comments on what changes they wanted in the second edition. These comments were taken into account when the revised Contents were made. An additional set of reviewers was then able to comment on the proposed changes in the second edition. All the following people participated in writing a review or answering a questionnaire:

Frank Emerson, Western Michigan University
Claron Nelson, University of Utah
Mike Ellis, North Texas State University
John Rapp, University of Dayton
E. L. Hazlett, Kansas State University
Travis Wilson, De Kalb Community College
Nicholas Grunt, Tarrant County Junior College
Glen Marston, Utah State University
Daniel Joseph, Niagara Community College
J. M. Sullivan, Stephen F. Austin State University
E. D. Key, Stephen F. Austin State University
Wylie Walthall, College of the Alameda
G. Jeffry Barbour, Central Michigan University
Ralph T. Byrns, Clemson University
James Mason, San Diego Mesa College
Robert P. Thomas, University of Washington
Mike Melvin, San Diego Mesa College
Craig Justice, Chaffey College
George Spiva, University of Tennessee
Barry Duman, West Texas State University
G. B. Duwaji, University of Texas at Arlington
Bruce Kimzey, New Mexico State University
Larry Ross, Anchorage Community College
Lee Spector, State University of New York, Buffalo
Maryanna Boynton, California State College, Fullerton
Demos Hadjiyanis, College of St. Thomas
David Jones, College of St. Thomas
Terrence W. Kinal, College of St. Thomas
Herbert Milikien, American River College

Before I started working on the second edition, Ronald Reddall of Allan Hancock College prepared a detailed, page-by-page critique of what was included in the first edition. My admiration for his tenacity is great.

The following people made submitted detailed comments on drafts of the second edition. These reviewers were crucial in providing me with needed criticisms of my preliminary drafts of this edition. My admiration for their ability is unbounded.

Thomas Borcherding, Simon Frazer University
Raburn M. Williams, University of Hawaii
G. Hartley Mellish, University of South Florida
Thomas Curtis, University of South Florida
James Foley, University of Miami

I especially wish to thank Richard O. Sherman, Jr., of Ohio State University for his detailed participation in this project from the very beginning of the second edition. His comments were of immense help to me.

The biographies were skillfully developed by John Cobb. The issue (and occasional chapter) photographs were taken by Susan Vita Miller, who understood the concept of opportunity cost so well that she did not want to do the job jointly with me. Her photographs were all taken with a Nikon F-2.

R. L. M.

ONE

GETTING STARTED

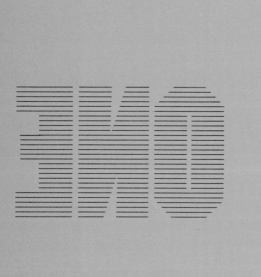

ARE WE RUNNING OUT OF EVERYTHING?

Can We Preserve Our Way of Life?

Americans have grown used to enjoying the highest living standard of any country in the entire world. But perhaps our way of life has become too wasteful and we can no longer take its preservation for granted. We are in an era of shortages, and scarcity seems to plague not only the American economic landscape but also that of just about every other country today. It was just a few years ago that a congressional survey of 258 major industries showed that 245 of them believed they confronted shortages of at least one commodity vital to their business. In fact, Honeywell, Bell & Howell, Utah International, and Stokely-Van Camp indicated that they were short of almost everything they needed. The list became impressive: 108 firms could not get an adequate supply of petrochemicals; 106 could not get all the steel they wanted; 74 said that they faced shortages of aluminum; and 62 lacked a sufficient supply of copper. All in all, the 245 corporations listed a **shortfall** of some 64 vital commodities.

The Shortage Society

The number of items considered in short supply began to grow rapidly after the first couple of years in this decade. By 1974, large companies were seeking alternatives for practically everything. General Foods was looking for a sugar substitute, Clorox was looking for a soda ash replacement to use in bleach, Alcoa decided to stop producing household aluminum foil, and Del Monte Corporation could not purchase enough glass for jars, fiberboard for boxes, or tin plates for cans.

The Energy Shortage That Started It All

People first became acutely aware of serious shortages throughout our economic system when the Persian Gulf oil-producing nations decided to boycott the United States in the fall of 1973. At the time, it was feared that the shortfall of petroleum products—mainly gasoline and heating-fuel oil—would greatly disrupt our economy. Indeed, some politicians and many concerned scientists told

us that because we had been profligate in the use of energy in the past, we now had to pay for our sins. Many spokespeople assumed that the scarcity of petroleum products would last indefinitely, even after the embargo was lifted, so they prescribed expensive long-run policies for research and development to make the United States self-sufficient in energy by 1980. They also exhorted the American people to change their basic life-style in order to conserve precious energy resources. In fact, some observers went so far as to state that the energy crisis suffered by Americans was "good." Why? Simply because it brought us to our senses, made us aware of our dependence on foreign sources for a vital resource, and showed us how wasteful our life-style had become.

Next on the list of actual and potential shortages that loomed large in the eyes of American consumers was food.

The Impending Food Crisis

In the 1950s, 1960s, and early 1970s, the United States was plagued with a problem that might be quite foreign to most of you reading this text. The American agricultural industry, the most productive in the world, produced not shortages but surpluses—year in and year out.

In fact, the surpluses became so embarrassing that the United States government at one time was dumping wheat into the Gulf of Mexico. Naturally, our less-developed neighbor nations, with untold numbers of undernourished individuals, found such activity appalling.

We obviously have solved the surplus problem—perhaps even for good. Thanks to unanticipated problems with agriculture throughout the world, shortages, not surpluses, are the order of the day. For a while, the specter of bread lines, similar to those for gasoline that occurred only a few years ago, seemed to be a real one. In fact, the Community Nutrition Institute of Washington stated that "sooner, but probably reluctantly later" the United States government would be forced to ration food. It's hard to believe, but the Los Angeles police force has been trained to handle riots that might occur over food shortages in this country.

If we look at what has happened to world grain reserves, we can get an idea of how serious the problem really is. In recent years the world has had to draw down its grain reserves with increasing frequency. This happened noticeably in 1966 and 1967 and has become much more pronounced in this decade. The number of days of grain reserves have been falling, on the average, since the early 1960s. Where we will go from here is indeed a serious question to be answered.

A study by the Ford Foundation came up with a proposal for a world food reserve, with the United States contributing a large amount but not 100 percent. This would be keeping in line with what the United States

government has done in the past because since 1954 this country has given away, under Public Law 480, $25 billion worth of grain to developing countries.

At a world food conference sponsored by the United Nations and the Food and Agricultural Organization a few years ago, 135 nations met to consider long-term measures to improve world food production. At the time this conference was meeting, an estimated 10,000 people a day were dying from starvation or diseases related to hunger. One of the attempts at the conference was to form a new system of international grain reserves similar to that proposed by the Ford Foundation. The international system would establish an emergency food aid bank and an agency to administer $5 billion worth of annual farm assistance. The con-

cern of the United States—far and away the largest producer of food —was that the burden of holding surpluses for the whole world would fall to it.

Our Dwindling Mineral Resources

When we look at mineral resources we find the same perplexing scenario—increasing shortages. Just look at Table I-1.1. Here we list some of the better-known and critical nonrenewable natural resources and the approximate number of years it will take to use up known worldwide reserves. Assuming no recycling, it is clear that we will one day run out of nonrenewable natural resources, no matter how slowly we use them. The problem, according to many, is that we are going to run out of critical natural resources in the very near

Table I-1.1

When Will the Day of Reckoning Arrive for Natural Resources?

By using a projection based on an ever-increasing rate of growth of consumption of nonrenewable natural resources, it is possible to predict how many years we have left before we exhaust today's known global reserves of these resources.

RESOURCE	WHEN KNOWN WORLDWIDE RESERVES WILL RUN OUT
Aluminum	31 years
Copper	21 years
Lead	21 years
Manganese	46 years
Mercury	13 years
Natural Gas	22 years
Petroleum	20 years
Silver	13 years
Tin	15 years
Zinc	18 years

Source: U.S. Bureau of Mines, *Mineral Facts and Problems,* Washington, D.C.: Government Printing Office, 1970, and D. L. Meadows et al., *Dynamics of Growth in a Finite World,* Wright-Allen Press, 1974.

future. Hence, we will be faced with increasingly disruptive shortages throughout the world economy, as well as in our own.

Some Proposed Solutions to Shortages

What can be done about the shortages that have been observed in the last few years? We have already touched on some long-term proposals for the energy crisis, including increased research and development for new energy sources and policies that would change our energy-consuming life-style. There are also numerous proposals for fixing limits on the amount of energy each person can use. These limits might come in the form of an allotment per individual or per family. Each family might, for example, be allotted a certain number of gallons of gasoline per month and would not be allowed to consume any more. This process is generally known as **rationing.** It was used during World War II for gasoline and other scarce commodities. At that time, ration coupons were given out and had to be used to purchase gas.

For the agricultural crisis that may occur, proposed solutions again draw heavily on improved production techniques to allow America, and indeed even underdeveloped countries, to dramatically increase their food production. However, there have been many suggestions to reduce the demand for food in years to come by drastically curtailing population growth, particularly in those countries where, if growth were to continue at current relatively high rates that cause the population to double every 20 years, there would hardly be enough room for every citizen to stand (let alone sit) by the year 2500.

With respect to nonrenewable natural resources, numerous conservation schemes have been suggested. These include limiting the extraction of certain nonrenewable resources so that we can lengthen the amount of time in which they will be available. Such a rationing, or allocation, procedure presumably would guarantee our grandchildren a continuing supply of such resources as natural gas and copper.

At issue, then, is really the question of whether we can continue our current American life-style, that is, whether we can keep consuming large quantities of many items that have been or threaten to be in very short supply. Americans represent only 6 percent of the world's population but consume more than 30 percent of the world's nonrenewable resources. The implication is that unless we are superbly successful in improving technology so we can simultaneously use fewer resources and increase the output of others, we will have to reduce our standard of material well-being.

The Other Side of the Story

Not all observers of the shortage situation in the United States and elsewhere agree with this doomsday analysis. In fact, if we examine what happened during past periods when energy was scarcer, we can get some inkling of the forces that may be acting to cure the current shortage problem. Perhaps ours will not become a society of empty market shelves and frustrated consumers.

Another View of Energy Shortages

When the supply of petroleum was temporarily reduced a few years ago, there was great expectation of chaos. Many commentators predicted freezing homes and automobiles abandoned for want of gas. There were indeed problems for motorists who, in some sections of the country, had to wait hours in line to get their gasoline, but in many sections of the country motorists did not have to wait at all. The heating-fuel situation too was bleak but not catastrophic. The Denver schools had to close for lack of fuel oil, and some houses did not have enough heat, but massive freezing did not occur. In fact, at the end of the so-called crisis, the amount of fuel oil in inventories of oil companies was greater than at any other time in the history of the United States. How could that have occurred during such a crisis?

For one thing, a powerful force was causing consumers of fuel oil to lower their thermostats, to close their windows, and to take all sorts of measures to reduce their total heating bills. That powerful force was a gradual, but nonetheless significant, rise in the price of heating oil.

At that time, the Federal Energy Office (now called the Federal Energy Administration) was allowing the price of fuel oil to be raised several cents a month. Several cents does not sound like much, but after a number of months, the price to consumers of fuel oil had risen approximately 50 to 70 percent over levels that prevailed the previous year. At the higher relative price, consumers voluntarily conserved fuel oil. (The publicity campaign waged by government officials to get Americans to use less fuel may also have had an effect.)

What we found out was that the "required" amount of fuel oil was related, at least partially, to how much consumers had to pay for it. When they had to pay more, they decided that they could live in a house at 68 degrees instead of 72 degrees, thereby freeing income that would otherwise have gone to paying higher fuel bills. The same thing happened with gasoline, but not as dramatically. In the first place, the Federal Energy Office did not allow the retail price of gasoline to rise as sharply, relative to the price charged in the previous year, as the Office had done for fuel oil. Nonetheless, within less than a year, the price of gas at the pump had risen and consumers had reacted—by cutting their consumption of gasoline by almost 10 percent. (Again, it could be argued that exhortations from government officials to Americans to drive less and to obey gas-saving lower speed limits were at work here. Speed limits, however, may have only been obeyed where there were enforcement efforts.)

Basically, then, the other view of shortages and increased scarcity indicates that after a while shortages may work themselves out because the products in short supply will sooner or later end up costing more and consumers will decide to conserve on those relatively more expensive items. And those who provide the items—the suppliers—will also react to the higher prices, but in the opposite direction. They will be willing to expend more effort and money to find ways to produce more in order to benefit from such higher prices. An understanding of how consumers and producers react when the cost of short-supply items rises is basic to understanding the other view of the supply of minerals in the world.

World Mineral Supplies

Refer to Table I-1.1. The second column is based on the assumption that known global reserves will run out simply because we will consume them all. But what do known global reserves really mean? Those reserve

---

Table I-1.2

The Amount of Minerals Contained in 1 Cubic Kilometer of Average Crustal Rock

The physical quantity of minerals contained in the earth's crust is indeed staggering and gives some idea of the extent of resources physically available.

RESOURCE	AMOUNT OF MINERALS CONTAINED
Aluminum	2,000,000,000 tons
Iron	1,000,000,000 tons
Zinc	800,000 tons
Copper	200,000 tons

Source: D. B. Brooks and P. W. Andrews, "Mineral Resources, Economics Growth, and World Population," *Science,* July 1974, vol. 185, no. 4145, p. 13.

we have seen, that as the relative price of a mineral goes up, the amount of proved reserves goes up also. Witness what happened with petroleum. We have more proved reserves today than we had in 1930, even though we have consumed a tremendous quantity of petroleum during that 45-year period.

Who Is Right?

Are we facing a shortage society? Must we suffer an inevitable decline in the quality of life, or will things work themselves out? In other words, will Americans respond to inevitable higher prices of items in short supply by consuming less and will industry respond to those higher prices by finding better ways to produce and by finding substitutes for the items in short supply?

Do not try to formulate your answer quite yet. Wait until you have gone through some of the economic theories presented throughout this book. Then come back to this introductory issue to see how you react to the problems posed.

figures are based on the amounts that would be taken out of the earth, given the current state of the arts, that is, technology, and given the current profitability of mining those amounts. But that current profitability certainly must, in part, be related to the price that those minerals can bring in the marketplace. Look at Table I-1.2. Here we show how many tons of some important minerals are contained in a single cubic kilometer of average crustal rock. If we were to multiply the numbers included in Table I-1.2 by the surface area of the earth that would, on the average, contain those amounts of minerals, we would come up with quantities of physical reserves many, many times those listed in any mineral tables. The reason we do not use those numbers is because at today's prices it would not be profitable to mine them, for at today's prices, only "proved" reserves are profitable to mine. We might expect, and indeed

Definitions of New Terms	**Shortfall:** The difference between some estimated physical requirement for a commodity and its presumed physical availability. **Rationing:** Any method used to allocate scarce goods and services. In popular speech, rationing refers to any scheme in which a central authority allocates a commodity.

Selected References

Brooks, D. B. and P. W. Andrews, "Mineral Resources, Economic Growth, and World Population," *Science,* vol. 185, no. 4145, July 5, 1974.

Brown, Lester R., *In the Human Interest,* New York: W. W. Norton, 1974.

Heilbroner, Robert L., *An Inquiry into the Human Prospect,* New York: W. W. Norton, 1974.

Meadows, Dennis et al., *The Limits to Growth,* Washington, D.C.: Potomac Associates, 1972.

Mishan, E. J., *Technology and Growth,* New York: Praeger, 1970.

Olson, Mancur and Hans H. Landsberg (eds.), *The No Growth Society,* New York: W. W. Norton, 1973.

What Economics Is All About

Are we running out of food? Are we running out of energy? Are we running out of copper? These were the questions posed and partially analyzed in the introductory issue of this book. No one will deny that such problems are the crucial dilemmas facing our modern world. These and other modern-day problems, such as the urban crisis, overpopulation, pollution, and economic growth, will be our concern throughout the book. They are all areas of study in which you will be able to apply the tools of economic analysis.

Economic issues continue to be examined in the press, on radio and television, and in the halls of Congress. And the future will probably see even greater emphasis on economic issues and on the economic aspects of some supposedly noneconomic issues that have become worldwide problems. But before we can understand its relevance, we have to explain what economics is all about. The easiest way to begin is to relate the subject matter of economics to the scarcity society outlined in Issue I-1.

Scarcity, Economic Goods, and Free Goods

Economics and **scarcity** go hand in hand. We very loosely used the word scarcity in Issue I-1. What do we mean by scarcity? To begin with, we have always faced a problem of scarcity and always will, no matter how abundant natural resources are. If we didn't live in a world of scarcity, you wouldn't have to read about or even think about the economic aspects of anything because there wouldn't be any economic aspects. Scarcity presents us with a problem: How do we allocate the available resources to all the competing demanders; how do we make choices among limited alternatives? There are many people in competition for scarce goods and services, and even if they decided not to compete, they would still face the problem of how the available resources were to be allocated among members of society. So you see, it doesn't really matter what one's moral or political attitudes are. Everybody can love everybody else and want to help everybody else, but the decision still has to be made: Who gets what, how much, when, and by what means? Economics, then, attempts to answer such questions because it is concerned with the *allocation of scarce resources.* If a resource is not scarce, that is, if it is not an **economic good,** then economics has little to say about it.

There are, of course, some things around that are free. We call them **free goods,** as opposed to scarce, or economic, goods. Not many are left. Old economics textbooks used to call air a free good, but that is really no longer true because in many cities pollution makes air unfit to breathe. In many mountain areas clean air is still a free good (once you are there); you can have all of it you want, and so can anybody else who bothers to hike up to where you are. You and anybody else who hikes there do not have to worry about how free goods, including air and running water in many wilderness areas, should be or have to be allocated among competing demanders. There is no scarcity involved. Who is interested in free goods, then? Certainly not economists. Perhaps physicists, hydrologists, biologists, and chemists are interested in free air and water, but the economist steps in only when the problem of scarcity arises, as it does in cities, and people become concerned about allocating the scarce resource. We have seen throughout our history that as population and production increase over time, many "free" goods become "economic" goods, such as land for mining, water, and air for industrial uses, and water for hydroelectric power.

Exchange and Choice

Since individuals live in a world of scarcity, they are unable to obtain all that they might desire to have, even in our own country, the richest nation on earth, where people have a relatively high level of material well-being. We have unlimited wants, but we must make choices among the limited alternatives available to us. Economics is about these choices. You have the alternative of spending time reading this book or spending time in the student union having fun with your friends. You must make a choice because you are up against the problem of scarcity. In this particular case, the scarce good happens to be your time (and this resource is scarce no matter how rich you may be).

When you start trading with other individuals, choices arise because you have to pick among alternative *exchanges* that you could make. We know that people have been exchanging things since the beginning of time. For example, archeologists tell us that during the Ice Age, hunters of mammoths in the Great Russian steppe were trading for Mediterranean shells.

Voluntary and Involuntary Exchanges

In general, we will be talking about voluntary exchanges among individuals and nations. By necessity, every voluntary exchange has to make both parties in the exchange think they are better off: Exchange is mutually beneficial. If it were not, individuals and nations would not bother with it.

However, involuntary exchanges do occur, and some are pretty unpleasant for the losing parties. You find involuntary exchanges in situations where coercive power is used to alter another person's or nation's behavior. For example, when black persons were captured and shuttled aboard intolerably crowded slave ships going to the New World, they were forced to submit to a new economic arrangement whereby they provided labor power to their owners and in turn were given the necessities of life (barely that much in many cases). When individuals are robbed, they too are engaged in an involuntary exchange. Although it is true that the robber might present you with a choice to minimize your loss—you volunteer your money or your life—you are still a victim of coercive power and not in a choice situation to freely make up your mind about what to exchange and what not to exchange.

Markets—Where Exchanges Take Place

You and I make voluntary exchanges all the time. We usually do it by way of an intermediary good called money, but we could—not as easily, of course—trade things for things instead of using money to facilitate this trade. You exchange the purchasing power implicit in the price of this book for the book itself. If you hadn't used money, and we were in fact involved in a system of **barter,** you might have had to exchange a couple of records or another book to get this one. But the fact remains that you are always engaged in these sorts of exchanges whether or not you use money.

Voluntary exchanges take place in what we call a **market.** Markets are institutions that aid in the process of exchange by allowing communication between potential buyers and potential sellers of goods and services. This is the underlying function of all markets, no matter how primitive or sophisticated they might be. For example, in the formally structured New York and American Stock Exchanges, stockbrokers can immediately put potential buyers and potential sellers in touch with each other. The New York and American Stock Exchanges are highly centralized in terms of this function. At the other extreme are very decentralized, informal markets for such services as tutoring, babysitting, occasional home repair, and gardening. You can probably think of many other decentralized, informal markets that you often use.

The reason individuals turn to markets to conduct economic activities or exchanges is because markets reduce the costs of exchanging. These costs are generally called **transactions costs** because they are associated with transacting economic exchange. Certainly, the transactions costs in the most highly organized markets are relatively small. Take the example of the New York Stock Exchange. It is quite easy to obtain immediate information on the price of listed stocks and how many have been bought and sold in the last several hours, what the prices were the day before, and so on.

Generally, the less organized a market, the higher the transactions costs. We will see that no market can completely eliminate transactions costs, but some markets do a better job than others. And, as information-dissemination activity becomes less costly, transactions costs have fallen. Think how costly, in terms of time and money, it used to be for someone living in California to find out the price of stocks being sold in New York when our communications network was not as extensive as it is now.

Exchanges and Specialization

At first, Robinson Crusoe didn't exchange anything with anyone. And even though he had the problem of allocating his time and effort, he never had to worry, at least in the beginning, about making a choice between alternative exchanges with *other* individuals. Few of us, however, live in a Robinson Crusoe economy; we live in societies where many individuals with many different types of productive talents wish to engage in exchanges to make themselves better off. Herein lies the essence of economics and exchange. No one person makes a car or a house, or even a bushel of wheat. There is **specialization** in all our operations as producers of things or services because each of us undertakes only one or very few of the steps required to bring a commodity from its natural-resource state into the hands of the individual who ultimately uses that commodity. Robinson Crusoe was on a deserted island; most of us are not. Most of us specialize in doing one thing or another. Most of us do not attempt to be self-sufficient because if we did, we would be very poor indeed.

Just think about it. How well off could you be if you had to provide all your own food, shelter, clothing, recreation equipment, and so on? Look at an individual state. How well off would the residents of Delaware be if they could not obtain goods from other states but had to be self-sufficient?

It is fairly easy to figure out how any one individual can decide what he or she should specialize in doing. If the individual wants to be as well off as possible, he or she will apply productive talents to endeavors that yield the highest rewards. To figure out what you can do comparatively better than others, all you need analyze are your alternatives. In our society, where money is used, the easiest way to find out which productive endeavors give you the highest rate of return for your time spent working is by seeking out the job you can actually perform that yields the highest income or highest command over goods and services which you would like to consume. (We must add to this any nonmonetary returns received from a job.) Once this is accomplished, then specialization takes place. It is when individuals specialize, and then make exchanges, that material well-being is at its greatest, given the available amount of scarce resources. This is not a new idea, but it was made quite famous when the father of modern economics, Adam Smith, demonstrated the benefit of specialization in his famous pin example:

One man draws out the wire, another straightens it, a third cuts it, a fourth points

it, a fifth grinds it at the top for receiving the head; to make the head requires two or three distinct operations; to put it on is a peculiar business, to whiten the pins is another; it is even a trade by itself to put them into the paper.[1]

Now, making pins this way allowed 10 men without very much specialized skill to make almost 48,000 pins "of a middling size" in a day. One worker, toiling alone, could have made perhaps 20 pins a day; therefore, 10 workers could have produced 200. Specialization, or the *division of labor,* as Smith liked to call it, allowed for an increase in the output of the pin factory from 200 to 48,000! Not only did the pin factory become more productive through specialization, by combining workers' talents and making 48,000 pins rather than a mere 200 per day, but workers became better off: Their wages could now reflect their much higher rate of output, and they could buy more goods and services with the relatively higher wages.

A Simple Example of Specialization

Perhaps another example will help convince you that specialization allows for a greater amount of goods to be obtained from a given amount of resources. For if you are not convinced, you will never think economics is very important because, as a science, it rests on this fact: Individuals desire to specialize and then exchange because in so doing they have found that they can be materially better off.

Look at Table 1-1. Here we show total output available for two productive workers in a small world where they are the only individuals. At first, they do not specialize; rather, each works an equal amount of time, 8 hours each day,

[1] Adam Smith, *An Inquiry into the Nature and Causes of the Wealth of Nations,* 1776.

Table 1-1 Before Specialization

Here we show the relationship between Ms. Jones' and Mr. Smith's daily work effort and the production of granola and ice cream. When Ms. Jones works on her own without specializing in any one activity, she devotes 4 hours a day to granola production and 4 hours a day to the production of ice cream. For her efforts, she obtains 2 pounds of each. On the other hand, Mr. Smith, again not specializing, will produce in the same two 4-hour periods 3 pounds of granola and 1 pound of ice cream. Their total output will be 5 pounds of granola and 3 pounds of ice cream.

DAILY WORK EFFORT	MS. JONES
4 hours	2 lb granola
4 hours	2 lb ice cream
	MR. SMITH
4 hours	3 lb granola
4 hours	1 lb ice cream

Total = 5 lb granola, 3 lb ice cream

Table 1-2 After Specialization

If Ms. Jones specializes in the production of ice cream, she can produce 4 pounds for every 8 hours of daily work effort. Mr. Smith, on the other hand, specializing in the production of granola, will produce 6 pounds. Their grand total of production will be 6 pounds of granola and 4 pounds of ice cream, a pound more of both goods than before they specialized.

DAILY WORK EFFORT	MS. JONES
8 hours	4 lb ice cream
	MR. SMITH
8 hours	6 lb granola

Total = 6 lb granola, 4 lb ice cream

producing granola and ice cream. Ms. Jones has the talent and chooses to produce 2 pounds of granola in 4 hours of work and an additional 2 pounds of ice cream with the additional 4 hours. Mr. Smith has the talent and chooses to produce 3 pounds of granola in his first 4 hours of work but only 1 pound of ice cream in his second 4 hours. The total amount that the two can and choose to produce without specialization is 5 pounds of granola and 3 pounds of ice cream.

Now look at what happens when they specialize. We see, in Table 1-2, that after specialization, when Ms. Jones spends all her time making ice cream, she can produce 4 pounds (since she produces 2 pounds in 4 hours). Mr. Smith, on the other hand, spending all his time making granola, produces 6 pounds (since he can produce 3 pounds in just 4 hours). The total output of this two-individual world has

now increased to 6 pounds of granola and 4 pounds of ice cream, an increase of 20 percent. Amazing, right? With the same two people using the same amount of fixed resources (no cheating was allowed), the total output of this little economy increased from 5 pounds of granola to 6 pounds, and from 3 pounds of ice cream to 4 pounds. Obviously, Ms. Jones and Mr. Smith would be better off (in a material sense) if they each specialized and exchanged between themselves. Ms. Jones would exchange ice cream for Mr. Smith's granola, and vice versa. (Our discussion, of course, has not taken into account the *disadvantages* of specialization—monotony and drudgery in one's job.)

After specialization, each individual would be doing what he or she could do *comparatively* better than the other. This leads us to the concept of **comparative advantage.**

Comparative Advantage

Specialization through the division of labor, as outlined in Smith's famous example of pin making and in our example of granola and ice cream production, rests on a very important fact—different individuals, communities, and nations are indeed different, at least when it comes to the skills of each in producing goods and services. In our simple two-person example, if these persons had been exactly the same in every respect, and therefore could do every job equally well, there would have been no reason for specialization since total output could not have been increased. (Go back to Table 1-1 and make Mr. Smith equally productive in producing both granola and ice cream, and then see what happens to our example after specialization.)

In fact, people are not uniformly talented. Even if they were, even if an individual or a nation had the talent to do *everything* better (for example, by using fewer resources, especially person-hours), individuals and nations would still want to *specialize in the area of their comparative advantage.* A good example involves former President William Howard Taft. Before he became President, he was probably the country's fastest stenographer. He might have been at the same time the country's best typist, best violin player, and best everything else, but he decided to become President when elected because that was where his comparative advantage lay. Had he declined the Presidency to remain a stenographer, the cost to him of that action would have been tremendous.

To continue the example, consider the dilemma of the president of a large company. He or she can type better than any of the typists, file better than any of the file clerks, drive a truck better than any of the truckdrivers, and wash windows better than any of the window washers. That just means that the president has an absolute advantage in all these endeavors. However, his or her comparative advantage lies in managing the company, not in doing the aforementioned tasks. How is it known that that is where the comparative advantage lies? The answer is quite easy: The president is paid the most for being president, not for being a typist or a file clerk or a window washer or a truckdriver for the company. The same is true of the simple two-person economy we previously discussed. If someone were paying Ms. Jones and Mr. Smith, Mr. Smith would obviously be paid more to specialize in producing granola rather than ice cream. In fact, he could figure that out all by himself. To get 1 more pound of ice cream, he would have to give up 3 pounds of granola. However, for Ms. Jones to get 1 more pound of ice cream, she only has to give up 1 pound of granola. She, therefore, has a comparative advantage in producing ice cream, and he, therefore, has a comparative advantage in producing granola, because in both cases the cost of *not* producing the other commodity is lower.

Opportunity Costs

We have a term for the cost of not doing something. That term is **opportunity cost,** defined as the *value of the highest forgone alternative.* What is the opportunity cost of Ms. Jones's making one more pound of ice cream? It is 1 pound of granola. What is the opportunity cost for Mr. Smith if he makes one more pound of ice cream? It is 3 pounds of granola. Since the opportunity cost of producing ice cream is lower for Ms. Jones than for Mr. Smith, Ms. Jones has a comparative advantage in producing ice cream. A useful way of looking at comparative advantage is to understand that it exists whenever opportunity costs are different for producing different things.

But the concept of opportunity cost is much broader and will be used more extensively in the rest of this book. What is the opportunity cost of sitting in an economics lecture? Since you are not working at some income-producing job, you do not have the opportunity to spend one more hour on the job and get one more hour's worth of pay. However, you have available other opportunities, such as playing tennis, or swimming, or reading a book for another class, or drinking coffee in the student union, or listening to records. The fact is you have numerous alternatives available to you, and you can measure the opportunity cost of an economics lecture by figuring out the value you place on the highest alternative among your available choices. Thus, the opportunity cost of your time is equal to its highest alternative use value. Hence, opportunity cost is sometimes called *alternative cost*.

Economics As a Science

Economics is a social science and, as such, shares many techniques and shortcomings with the other social sciences. Each of the social sciences is a special area of inquiry, but these areas overlap to some degree. These sciences are "social" to the extent that they deal, in the final analysis, with human behavior.

Assumptions

All sciences rest on some body of assumptions that form the basis for theories or hypotheses or *models*. A model is merely a simplified, interrelated set of ideas about how the world works. A sociologist will develop a theory or model to explain why a certain event occurred or why a certain subsector of the population acts in a specific way. A political scientist will develop a theory to explain why a nation acted in the way it did vis-à-vis an enemy. We can hope that the political scientist's theory can be used to predict (both forward and backward in time) what will happen in a similar situation in other countries. Of course, this is exactly the same thing that a physicist or biologist does.

Many people have the idea that in some real sense physics is a more exact science than economics, sociology, or psychology. This is an oversimplification of the differences between these sciences. Physics is the study of physical phenomena. Physicists hypothesize theories and test them either by running experiments or by observing physical phenomena in the real world. Economists examine the behavior of individuals and groups of individuals. Just as physicists build theories or models, so too do economists. Both are empirical sciences. One problem in economics is that well-controlled experiments are difficult to set up. Economists must usually be content with observing what has happened in the past in order to test theories that they have devised.

All theories rest on givens, or axioms, or assumptions. However, many students balk at the assumptions used in economists' models. In fact, that is what originally got us into this section. Implicitly, we have used the assumption that individuals prefer to have more than less, that individuals can be assumed to run their lives so as to maximize their ability to consume goods and services. Generally, we call this assumption *utility maximization*—where utility refers to satisfaction. In the following pages we will adhere to a narrower assumption, **wealth maximization.**

The Role of Assumptions

It may be true that the assumption of wealth maximization on the part of individuals is an oversimplification. But everything is a simplification in any explanation of what has happened. If it were not simplified, we would not be able to do anything with it; we would never be able to generalize from the particular to the whole and would therefore never be able to

predict anything. If a theory or hypothesis is so complex that it can refer only to a very specific situation, it cannot be used to analyze or predict what will happen in any other situation.

The assumption of wealth maximization generates the hypothesis that as the profitability increases in a specific area of economic endeavor, resources will flow into that area. And, conversely, if profitability is relatively low in a specific area, resources will flow out into other areas.

If you do not like the assumption that people are out to better themselves economically, that does not mean you will still not want to use it in your economic analysis, because what you would like to be able to do is predict how people will react to changes in their environment. If you can predict and analyze tolerably well using a model based primarily on an assumption of wealth maximization, you would not want, on moral grounds, to discard the assumption. This does not mean that social scientists are amoral but simply that, as scientists, they have to be very careful not to mix ethics with analysis. Some social scientists do become social reformers, but any successes they are able to effect are based on their knowledge of how people behave *in fact,* not on how they think people *should* behave.

The Complexity of the World

Because we have a finite capacity for reasoning and for understanding and because our brains can only hold a finite amount of data. we sometimes oversimplify and make assumptions that do not take everything into account when we analyze any situation. Economists have a tendency to leave out political, sociological, and psychological aspects when looking at any particular problem. This doesn't mean they consider those aspects irrelevant—indeed, more and more researchers are engaging in what are called interdisciplinary approaches to social science. However, only occasionally will we in this book step out of the economist's shoes into those of another social scientist. We are analyzing the economic events that have occurred and will occur in the United States and elsewhere.

Definitions of New Terms

Economics: The social science that is concerned with the way in which our limited resources are allocated—among alternatives today and also between today's uses and future uses. Economics involves making choices.

Scarcity: A condition that exists whenever all individuals taken together desire or want more of anything than exists. Scarcity forces us to make choices among limited alternatives.

Economic Good: Any good that is scarce; any good for which the quantity demanded exceeds the quantity supplied at a zero price.

Free Goods: The opposite of an economic good; any good for which additional quantities will yield no additional satisfaction to individuals.

Barter: A system of exchange in which a person trades one economic good directly for another economic good without the use of money.

Market: An institution that aids in the process of exchange. In any given market for any given good, the price of that good tends toward equality after transportation expenses and quality differences are accounted for.

Transactions Costs: All costs associated with engaging in economic exchange. Transactions costs include the cost of obtaining and disseminating information, the cost of initiating and policing contracts, and so forth.

Specialization: The act of dividing up productive activities among individuals, regions, and nations such that no individual is self-sufficient but rather specializes in certain productive activities and trades with others. Also called division of labor.

Comparative Advantage: A production advantage that arises out of different relative efficiencies in producing particular goods and services. Whenever opportunity costs are different for different individuals or different regions for doing the same productive activity, the one with the lowest opportunity cost will have a comparative advantage.

Opportunity Cost: The value of the highest forgone alternative; sometimes called alternative cost.

Chapter Summary

1. We live in a world of scarcity, which causes us to make choices among competing alternative uses of the scarce resources around us. Whenever we must make choices we are concerned with economics.
2. Economists study economic goods, that is, those which are scarce and those for which alternative competing uses exist.
3. Economics concerns itself mainly with voluntary exchanges and with the way in which individuals choose which exchanges to make from among alternative possibilities.
4. In a system without money as a medium of exchange, a barter system, in which goods are exchanged for goods, occurs.
5. Exchanges take place in a market, which is merely an institution that reduces transactions costs and allows for prices of similar products to tend toward uniformity.
6. Individuals have a comparative advantage in productive activities that yield a higher reward to them than to other people. Concentrating on this area leads to specialization or the division of labor.
7. As long as opportunity costs are different for different individuals, each individual will have a comparative advantage in some area and will be able, therefore, to benefit by specialization and trade.
8. The opportunity or alternative cost of an activity is the value of the highest forgone alternative. It tells an individual or a society the true cost of any action, whether that cost be implicit or explicit.
9. In any science a model is built based on a body of assumptions that can never be proved or disproved. The validity of that model or theory can be put to question, however, if that model or theory consistently predicts incorrectly.

Questions for Thought and Discussion

1. Can you think of any physical truths that are not theories?
2. What actions in your life do not have transactions costs?
3. Have you experienced the use of models in other social sciences, such as sociology or psychology?
4. Why do individuals specialize? What are some of the costs associated with specialization?
5. Do markets require for their existence that individuals engage in exchange through the intermediary good called money?

Selected References

Boulding, Kenneth E., *Economics As a Science*, New York: McGraw-Hill, 1970.
Maher, John E., *What is Economics?*, New York: Wiley, 1969.
Mundell, Robert A., *Man and Economics*, New York: McGraw-Hill, 1968, chap. 1.

Reading and Working with Graphs

Every day you read something containing a graphic display of an idea. For example, you probably have seen graphs showing the rapid rise in the cost of living or in taxes. We call those *descriptive* graphs because they are a means of describing some phenomenon that has occurred in our economy. The same is true of graphs that show how much unemployment there is over time, how fast the American standard of living has risen over time, and so on. Most students have little difficulty in understanding such diagrams.

However, when we move from the realm of descriptive diagrams to what we call *analytical* graphs, some confusion may arise. An analytical graph is merely a graphic representation of a theory or model. The theories and models that we discussed abstractly in the previous chapter can be presented in three different ways: in words, in equations (mathematically), or in graphs. We will present most of our theories with only words, but a lot of them can be more easily understood if they are also presented graphically. (We'll leave the mathematics for a more advanced course.) For those of you who have had little experience with graphs, this appendix should put you at ease so that, starting in Chapter 2, our graphic explanation of economic theories will not seem so foreign. As you will see, a graph may not be worth a thousand words, but it is certainly worth quite a few.

A Basic Graph

We have set out a graph in Figure A-1. It is merely two heavy lines denoted X for the horizontal one and Y for the vertical one. We have divided each into equal parts 10 units long. Each of the parts is numbered 1 through 10. In geometry, the horizontal axis or bottom line in the graph is called the X axis; the vertical one is the Y axis.

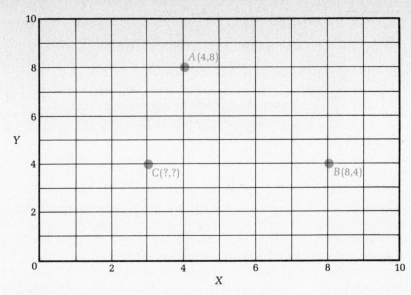

FIGURE A-1

The resultant criss-crossed graph resembles a sea captain's nautical chart, and in fact, if you had studied navigation, such a graph wouldn't be at all foreign to you. You would label the horizontal lines as latitude and the vertical lines as longitude. If somebody gave you a position, such as 38° longitude and 54° latitude, you would merely seek out the point on your nautical charts where the 54° latitude line intersected the 38° longitude line. We're not working with latitude and longitude, however, but with an abstract X and a Y. Later the X and the Y will be replaced by other things, like prices and quantities, interest rates and the amount of credit, and all the other things we study in economics. Right now, let's see if you can find the point at which X is equal to 4 and Y is equal to 8. That shouldn't be hard, and in fact we have labeled that point A. After the A we have put in parenthesis 4,8. This is a standard notation to show the coordinates of the point A. One other point is shown on the diagram also. It is labeled B, and its coordinates are 8 and 4, just the reverse of the above, meaning that it is a point where X is equal to 8 and

Y is equal to 4. We have also put in a point C. Can you find the coordinates of point C?

Charts or graphs using axes like those presented in Figure A-1 are generally used to show how one quantity of something varies with another. In Table A-1, we have shown a set of numbers giving the relationship between X and Y. That set of numbers is then plotted in the graph labeled Figure A-2. Here the resultant line or curve slopes downward from left to right. We say then that the two variables are inversely related. As X increases, Y decreases; and as X decreases, Y increases. (How would a positive relationship look?)

Charts or graphs are not limited to one curve or line. Figure A-3 shows the results of two relationships, one direct and the other inverse. The inverse one slopes downward, just as in the graph in Figure A-2, but the direct relationship slopes upward.

The Numbers on the Axes

We were careful in the first three diagrams to have both the X and the Y axes numbered

X	2	3	4	5	6	7	8	9	10
Y	10	9	8	7	6	5	4	3	2

TABLE A-1

exactly alike. This is not always the case. In fact, it would be impossible to number most axes exactly alike because we would be talking about two different variables. In descriptive graphs the variable on the horizontal, or X axis, is usually time in years, whereas the variable on the vertical axis might be the price level, standard of living, taxes, or something else. You must carefully label clearly on your graphs what the axes represent. You also have to pick a scale, and the scale will depend on the range over which you are graphing something. If you have a graph that is taking up, say, 2 inches of space on either axis and you want to graph a relationship between the price level and time for a period of, say, 10 years, the scale will be much different than if you take the same graph and put on the relationship between the cost of living and time over a period of 150 years. In the latter graph, you would have to have

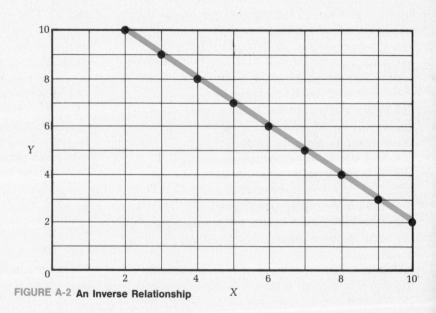

FIGURE A-2 **An Inverse Relationship**

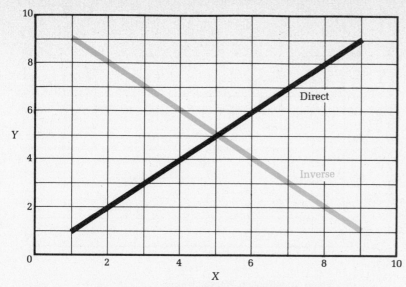

FIGURE A-3 **A Direct and An Inverse Relationship Shown on One Graph**

much smaller spaces between each year than in the former graph. There is no way to know ahead of time what your scale should be until you actually get to a graphic problem. Figures A-4 and A-5 show two possible scales that can be used for two separate problems using the same size graphs. Figure A-4 presents the historical relationship between time, labeled T on the horizontal axis, and the median family income in the United States for a 6-year period.

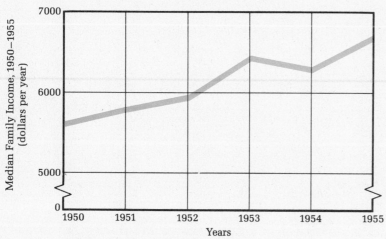

FIGURE A-4 **Median Family Income 1950 to 1955**

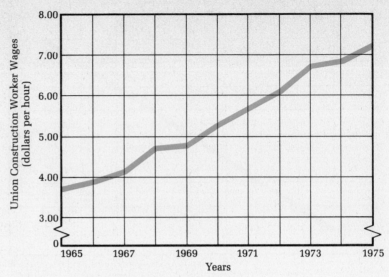

FIGURE A-5 **Union Construction Worker Wages**

Note that the vertical axis which used to be labeled Y is now labeled income, and everything is expressed in dollars. Now look at Figure A-5. Here we plot the average hourly pay for construction workers over an 11-year period. Again, the horizontal axis is time but the scale is different. The vertical axis is dollars, but it is labeled average wage, and of course its scale is vastly different than the one for the vertical axis in Figure A-4.

Does Money Mean Happiness?

HOW IMPORTANT IS MATERIAL WELL-BEING?

The Difficulty of Measuring Happiness

It is difficult, if not impossible, to measure how happy people are. Because happiness is a subjective state, there are no objective criteria that we can use to assess it. We simply have to ask people how they feel. Nonetheless, many of us hold common conceptions concerning what makes people happy. One common myth, probably partly based on idealized notions of the "simple life" or on Judeo-Christian teachings, is that the poor are really happier than the rich. However, we find out that no studies have given much support to the existence of "happy poverty."

An Opinion Poll

The American Institute of Public Opinion a number of years ago asked Americans whether they would rank themselves "very happy," "fairly happy," or "not very happy." They grouped the interviewees by income, level of education, sex, age, and other categories related to economic and social status.

The 1969 results were striking: 56 percent of those interviewed who had incomes in excess of $15,000 considered themselves to be "very happy." On the other hand, not even 30 percent of those in the income range of $3,000 and under considered themselves to be "very happy." Looked at another way, those who responded that they were "not very happy" numbered a mere 4 percent among the higher-income group but represented over 13 percent in the very low-income group.

Another Study Confirms

A study published under the auspices of the National Opinion Research Center confirms these findings: "To those who have the attributes that go with positions higher in the social structure, such as higher education and income, also go the psychic rewards of greater happiness.[1] The study suggested that there is a high correlation between level of income and general feelings of happiness.

[1]Norman M. Bradburn, *The Structure of Psychological Well-being*, Chicago, Ill.: Aldine, 1969, p. 226.

Other Factors Affecting Happiness

Now income per se is not really what we are talking about. Nobody has ever concluded from such poll results that individuals become happier simply because they have more income. Rather, happiness probably increases with income because higher income allows individuals to consume more goods and services. Note also that these goods and services do not necessarily have to be only big cars and fancy houses. They can include better health care, better diet, more education, more travel, more cultural activities, and freedom from worry, from overwork, or from working at boring jobs.

It is thus somewhat misleading to say that income itself leads to happiness. Rather, it is what income buys that may be causing the individuals' poll responses to indicate that they are happier when they have higher levels of income. In fact, when the pollsters asked more detailed questions of those being interviewed, they did indeed find out that happiness was highly correlated with such factors as health and family relationships. Note, though, that health is highly correlated with level of income because higher-income individuals spend more resources on better diet and medical care and are generally more educated so that they are aware of what is appropriate for improved health.

Comfort to the Economist

Since "more is better than less" is a key assumption in economists' theories and since much of what economists concern themselves with is the individual's quest for better material well-being, it is perhaps some comfort to know that there is an empirical correlation between higher levels of income and how happy individuals perceive themselves to be. At the very least, we can be sure that material well-being plays some role in people's happiness.

Questions for Thought and Discussion

1. "Since it is virtually costless to dispose of undesired wealth, the question whether or not more income leads to more or less happiness does not seem like a very meaningful line of inquiry." Analyze this statement.
2. Is it possible to measure happiness objectively?

How Different Systems Solve the Economic Problem

The basic economic problem reared its head in the first issue of this book. Whether you consider nature stingy or generous, you must agree that human beings never have all they could conceivably desire. They have unlimited wants, and decisions therefore have to be made about who gets what and how much. The way such decisions are made depends on the economic and social system in which one is operating. We will look at the two major economic systems operating today—**capitalism** and **socialism**—and consider two of their real-world variants, American capitalism and Soviet socialism. Issue I-3 will provide a closer view of the Chinese method of solving the economic problem.

We will start the discussion by describing the output capabilities of any one nation, whether it be capitalist, socialist, or communist. In this way we can consider the connection between economic systems and the concepts of scarcity and opportunity costs, which were introduced in Chapter 1.

Society's Choices

Scarcity, or the limitation of the total resources needed for producing the different things which individuals and nations want, means that choices must be made between relatively scarce items. This can be easily demonstrated by use of a graph. (If that word scares you, go back to Appendix A.) To make the analysis simple, we'll look at a nation's production alternatives between, say, hamburgers and textbooks. Of course, this is an unrealistic example in the sense that no nation would produce only hamburgers and textbooks. It would be more realistic to talk about a nation's choice between military and civilian goods, agricultural and manufactured goods, and so on.

The Numbers

Table 2-1 shows five distinct alternatives for our hypothetical society. Notice that a *trade-off* occurs in each. To move from no hamburgers to 1 billion hamburgers, our economy must suffer a reduction of 10 million textbooks. The trade-off here, then, is between 1 billion hamburgers and 10 million textbooks. This trade-off, which changes as you go down the rows in Table 2-1, always means diverting resources away from textbook production and into hamburger production to get more hamburgers. We are assuming that the full resources available in the economy—labor, machines, natural materials, technology—are being used, so that the production alternatives in Table 2-1 represent the maximum technologically feasible alternatives there are.

Putting the Numbers onto a Graph

Let's see what happens when we turn the numbers in Table 2-1 into a graph. Look at points *A*, *B*, *C*, *D*, and *E* in Figure 2-1. The result is what we call the **production-possibility frontier,** a fancy name given to a graphical

depiction of a simple fact of life: In a full-employment economy, to produce one good you must direct resources from and therefore give up something of another good. All economic systems face this trade-off.

Note that the axes in Figure 2-1 are labeled with a time dimension, in this case "per year," because we have to specify the time during which the production of hamburgers or textbooks is going to take place. Certainly, the numbers would change if we were talking about production over a 10-year period rather than a 1-year period. After all, production occurs day in and day out. It is what we call a **flow,** as opposed to a **stock.** The number of textbooks waiting at your local bookstore we call a stock, but we refer to the production of textbooks over a year as a flow. When we draw a graph or talk about, for example, production and consumption, we have to specify the time period. Usually, it is a year if it is not specified.

Inefficiency and Underemployment

Look at point *U* in the production-possibilities frontier in Figure 2-1. What does it represent? It either represents a point of inefficient use of available resources in producing textbooks or represents a situation of less than full employment, or *underemployment,* in which workers as well as machines are idle. The problems of being inside the production-possibilities frontier are discussed in greater detail in later sections of this book.

Why the Production-Possibilities Frontier Is Bowed Outward (the Law of Diminishing Returns)

If you look at the curve *ABCDE* in Figure 2-1, representing the production possibilities for an economy, you will see that it is bowed outward.

Table 2-1 Alternatives Available

Here, the alternatives available to our society are hamburgers and textbooks. One alternative is to produce no hamburgers and 100 million textbooks. At the other extreme, we have no textbooks to read but 4 billion hamburgers ready to eat. In between the two extremes are several other alternatives open to this economy; each involves a trade-off and the diversion of textbook resources to the production of hamburgers.

	HAMBURGERS	TEXTBOOKS
A	0	100 million
B	1 billion	90 million
C	2 billion	70 million
D	3 billion	40 million
E	4 billion	0

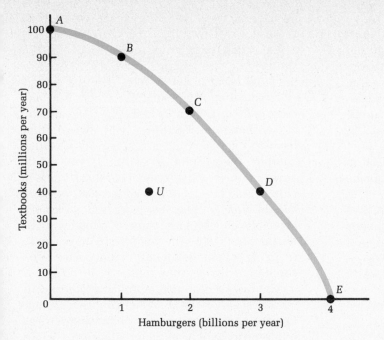

That is not an accidental shape but a graphic representation of a law which is a true in all economies. Briefly, the bulge shows that it is increasingly expensive to shift productive resources out of one good into the other. To see how relatively more expensive it becomes, let's go back to Table 2-1.

When we are producing no hamburgers, we can produce 100 million textbooks. If we shift just enough resources out of textbook production to increase hamburger production by 1 billion, we sacrifice only 10 million books. But how about at the other end of the scale? What about going from the production of 3 billion hamburgers per year to the production of 4 billion? Again, we have an increase of only 1 billion hamburgers, but now that increase costs us 40 million books. In other words, there is an increasing opportunity cost as we increasingly shift production from one activity to another.

What explains this increasing opportunity cost? First, the factors of production are specialized; that is, some resources are just plain better suited for producing one good than another. Resources are better combined in one way for producing, say, hamburgers and in another way for producing, say, textbooks. A compromise, to keep costs to a minimum, is therefore chosen. Thus, as resources shift from textbook production to hamburger production, the appropriate proportions of resources used for textbooks must be more or less employed for hamburgers. Hence, increasing costs and diminishing returns.

Second, we have the **law of diminishing returns.** The easiest way to understand this law, which we will meet over and over again, is to consider two broad categories of goods. Instead of hamburgers, we'll talk about all food products, and instead of textbooks, we'll talk about all manufactured goods.

This is what we do in Figure 2-2. We've merely redrawn Figure 2-1 with different labels on the axes. When we reduce the production of manufactured goods we shift workers from manufacturing into agriculture. We are going to assume here that workers are the only *variable input* to consider. The *fixed input* in the production process for agriculture is land.

At first, when we shift workers onto land there is lots of it around, and the increase in agricultural production is great. This can be seen by looking at the movement from A to C on the production-possibilities curve. All we had to give up in terms of manufacturing goods was the amount AB, and we got the amount BC in agricultural goods in return. However, look what happens on the next round. Again we have given up an amount, CD, which is just equal to the previous amount, AB, of manufacturing goods, but lo and behold, the increase in agricultural output is a far cry from BC. It is much smaller, actually only DE. This is what we would expect. We can get only a *diminish-*ing amount of extra output when we successively add equal units of our variable input to a fixed amount of some other input. In our simple case, the variable input is workers, and the fixed input in agricultural pursuits is land.

Think of specific examples where you add more and more variable input to a fixed amount of another input. Suppose you owned some farmland and had 100 workers. If you added another 100 workers, do you think you would double output? If you're not sure, ask yourself what would happen if you added 4000 workers. Would your output be increased 40 times? Probably not, because some of those workers would start getting in the other workers' way, reducing the amount of output that each worker could contribute to the total.

The law of diminishing returns is generally operative everywhere. When you start producing, the law may be one of increasing returns, but returns will eventually diminish. Sometimes it is only after you add a considerable number of equal doses of the variable input

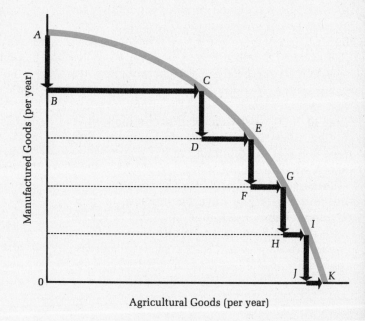

FIGURE 2-2 **The Law of Diminishing Returns**

This production-possibilities curve between agriculture and manufactured goods can be used to demonstrate the law of diminishing returns. What we do is start at point A, where we have no agricultural goods and all manufactured goods being produced. We now reduce the production of manufactured goods from A to B and shift those productive resources into the agricultural sector. The increase in agricultural production is relatively large—B to C. Now we reduce manufacturing production again by the same amount as before so that CD is equal to AB. What is our possible increase in agricultural goods? Only DE, which is certainly smaller than BC. The same is true throughout the rest of the graph. As we shift equal amounts of productive capacity from manufacturing to agriculture, we obtain smaller and smaller increases in agricultural output. This diminishing incremental increase can be attributed to the fixity of land, one kind of input.

that diminishing returns set in and you get the bowed-out production-possibilities curve depicted in Figures 2-1 and 2-2. The curve is a reasonable and accurate representation of the trade-offs facing any economy.

But who decides at which point on that curve to operate? The answer depends on where one is because the economic system determines how and by whom that decision is made. Let us now ask the question, "What is an economic system?"

What Is an Economic System?

Any economic system must deal with the following fundamental questions: What is to be produced? How is it to be produced? Who is to receive what is produced? In analyzing economic systems, we will keep these fundamental questions in mind.

We might formally want to characterize an economic system as all the institutional means through which national resources are used to satisfy human wants. By institutions we mean principally the laws of the nation, but we may also mean the habits, ethics, and customs of the citizens of that nation.

It should be obvious that all economic systems are artificial; none of them is God-given or sent from the stars. All economic institutions are just what human beings have made them,

and when modifications of laws and other institutions occur, they are made by human beings: the judges, workers, government officials, consumers, and legislators are the ones who change, destroy, create, renovate, and resuscitate economic institutions.

These institutions are flexible and continually undergo change. After all, in the Middle Ages we had a feudal system. In the sixteenth and seventeenth centuries, mercantilism was the dominant system. After mercantilism came laissez-faire capitalism. The history of economic systems is one of constant change.

Alternative Economic Systems

One possible way of comparing alternative economic systems is to look at how decentralized their economic decision-making processes are. We can see in Figure 2-3 that on the extreme right-hand side is pure free-enterprise capitalism, where all economic decisions are made by individuals without government intervention. On the extreme left-hand side of the scale we see pure command socialism, where most economic decisions are made by some central authority. Somewhere in between would be the mixed economic systems such as we have in the United States and in the United Kingdom. The closer we go to a pure capitalist system, the less political centralization there is, and vice

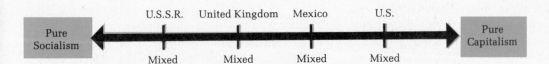

FIGURE 2-3 **Scale of Decentralization**
On the extreme right-hand side of the diagram we find pure capitalism, which no country follows. On the extreme left-hand side is pure socialism, which again no country follows. In the middle are all the mixed economies in the world. The U.S.S.R., the United Kingdom, Mexico, and the United States are shown, with the United States closer to capitalism, of course, than any of the others.

versa. Some economists like to distinguish economies according to whether or not they are planned, that is, whether or not the economy is a (political) **command economy** or a decentralized economy.

Four questions must be answered when analyzing different economic systems, and the answers to these questions indicate the attributes that each system has. If we want to know how any given economic system works, we must find out:

1. Who is permitted to own which items of wealth?
2. What kinds of incentives are presented to people to induce them to produce?
3. What forces determine the individual benefits that people get from producing?
4. Which lines of economic activity may individuals engage in on their own initiative and which lines are forbidden? What are individuals allowed to do with the proceeds of permitted activities?

Let's take a look at capitalism in theory and see how its economic institutions answer these four questions.

Capitalism in Theory

The theoretical concept of capitalism is usually associated with the father of laissez-faire[1] economics, Adam Smith, who wrote *The Wealth of Nations* in 1776. Smith described a system in which the government had little to do with economic endeavors other than enforce contracts between people. Individuals pursued their own self-interest and in so doing—according to his doctrine of the "invisible hand"—maximized the income and social welfare of the nation. Capitalism in its purest form may never

[1]The French phrase translates loosely as "let alone."

have existed, even though classical writers sometimes described theoretical capitalism as if it did exist.

Difference between Capital and Capitalism

At the outset, we should be careful to distinguish between *capital* and *capitalism*. In this book, *capital* has been used in two senses: One is *money* capital, and the other is *physical* capital. Money capital is a claim on resources, and business firms have to raise money capital either by borrowing, selling shares of stock, or using their own savings. Firms use the proceeds of those efforts to purchase physical capital for the production of goods and services that they later sell, hopefully for a profit. "Capital" can refer both to artificial things and to natural, tangible things that are not directly used in consumption. Capital goods assist in the production of other capital goods and of consumption goods. Obviously, every economic system, regardless of its label, has some sort of physical capital, if only the land on which individuals work.

To define capitalism, we must look to the economic institutions that characterize it and how these institutions answer the four questions we have posed. We shall use the following definition:

Capitalism is an economic system in which individuals privately own productive resources and possess the right to use these resources in whatever manner they choose, subject to certain (minimal) legal restrictions.

Notice here that we used the term *productive resources* rather than *capital*. This takes into account not only machines and land but also labor services. We see, then, that the definition of capitalism includes (at least implicitly) the right of individuals to use their talents in their own best interest. One of the most fundamental economic institutions in a capitalist system is that of private **property rights.**

Private Property

The ownership of property under a capitalist system is usually vested in individuals or in groups of individuals. That is, the state is not the owner of all property, as in some other systems which we might come up with in theory. In the United States, the government does own certain pieces of property, but in general we live under a system of private property rights. Private property is controlled and enforced through the legal framework of laws, courts, and police. Under capitalism, individuals have their property rights protected; are usually free to use their private property as they choose, as long as they do not infringe on the legal property rights of others; and are usually allowed to enter into private contractual agreements that are mutually satisfying.

These statements really apply to the realm of pure capitalism. In our **mixed capitalist system,** the government often intervenes in contracts between individuals, even when their private property is concerned. In some states, even if someone is willing, you cannot lend him or her money at an interest rate that exceeds a stipulated maximum. In some industries, you could not go to work for a wage rate below a specified minimum, even if you were willing to do so. You are prevented from using your private property—your personal labor services—in any manner that you see fit.

Under capitalism, the existence of private property rights makes the owners of productive resources the controllers of those resources. Exchanges of these resources are made between property owners who are largely private persons rather than government officials, bureaucrats, or politicians. Moreover, in a private property system, any accumulation of wealth that you as an individual amass throughout your life belongs to you and to no one else. You can decide who will get that accumulation of wealth upon your death. In fact, inheritance rights are a key aspect of capitalism in its purest form, for they provide an incentive for accumulation and conservation of wealth and thereby help keep the system going. In the United States there are taxes on inheritance, but there are few restrictions on how inherited wealth can be distributed.

Free Enterprise

Another attribute of a purely capitalistic system is free enterprise, which is merely an extension of the concept of property rights. Theoretically, free enterprise allows individuals to freely select economic activities for whatever resources they own and to seek whatever occupation they want; there are no restrictions. In the United States, however, people are not generally free to go into any occupation they wish. Try to become a doctor without first getting admitted to a medical school. Try to become a plumber without getting admitted to the plumbers' union.

Free enterprise is probably another way of stating laissez-faire. In a free-enterprise capitalistic system (at least in theory), productive resources are generally supposed to be directed toward their best uses. Presumably, workers will go where they can make the most money and, therefore, contribute the most to the social product.

The Price System

The way productive resources generally are directed to their best uses is via changing prices. We therefore talk about a price, or market, system in which just about everything that is exchanged has its price. There are virtually no legal restrictions on the prices for permitted goods or services. Prices are set only by the market forces that we will describe in Chapter 3, when we talk about supply and demand. Briefly, it is the interaction between buyers and sellers in a marketplace that results in changes in the prices of goods and services; prices, then, reflect *relative* scarcities.

The Role of Government

Even in a purely capitalistic system, there is still a role for government, for someone has to enforce private property rights. The government protects the rights of individuals and businesspersons to keep private property private, to keep the control of the property vested with the owners. Even the father of free enterprise, Adam Smith, described in some detail the role of government in a purely capitalist system. He talked about the need for government in providing national defense and in eliminating monopolies that would restrain trade.

American Capitalism

If America had a pure capitalist system, the economic problem would be solved forthrightly within the context of that system. Scarce goods would be allocated according to who wanted them most, evidenced by each individual's willingness to pay the market price for each item in question. In essence, individuals would vote in the marketplace with their dollars. When a good became relatively scarce, its price would rise, thus causing some consumers to cut back in their purchases of that good but at the same time encouraging some suppliers to increase their production of that good. Resources would seek out areas in which they yielded the highest reward. Individuals would not be restricted in seeking employment where they obtained the highest wages.

Restrictions in the American System

The American brand of capitalism, however, is not pure. All resources, for example, do not flow to areas where they yield the highest rewards for their private owners. There are numerous restrictions on economic activity in the United States by both government bodies and private organizations. Government restrictions make our system of capitalism a mixed one in which some elements of centralization or command by a political body enter into decisions on where resources should go, how they can be used, and who should get them. Moreover, the private sector in the economy obtains some of its goods and services—including fire and police protection and education—from the government. And most income-maintenance schemes are devices whereby some taxpayers put money into the general coffers so that that money can be redistributed to other individuals, not as a payment for services but rather as a gift, or income transfer.

Competition and Capitalism

In the purely capitalist system envisioned by Adam Smith, competition would always prevail. However, in the mixed American system it does not because some large firms control entire markets. Two well-known industries have no competition: the telephone company and the electric company. It has been argued that to a lesser extent large companies in the steel, aluminum, and rubber industries prevent competition.

In brief, although the American version of capitalism is based on free enterprise and private property rights, there are many exceptions. We cannot always be safe in applying the model of pure capitalism to our own country in order to answer the question "How is the economic problem solved?" Often, political decisions enter into the solution, and we must take these into account—especially when we try to understand how noncapitalist countries solve the economic problem. Most of these countries have systems that operate under some form of socialism.

Socialism in Theory

A socialist economy is often called a command economy because there is an authority, somebody in the government, who commands the means of production, such as land and machines. One of the most prevalent features in any theoretical socialist system is the attempt to redistribute income. The government will typically use its taxing powers to reduce inherited wealth and large incomes. Socialist systems usually have larger welfare services provided by the collective purse of the government than do even mixed capitalist systems.

Socialism As a Movement

"Socialism" usually refers to a movement that aims to vest in society, rather than in the individual, the ownership and management of all **producer goods** (capital goods used in any large-scale production). When we call socialism a movement, we imply that there exist organizations and programs at work to transform socialistic ideals into some concrete economy in which certain property rights—specifically property rights in producer goods—are vested in "society as a whole." However, to speak of "society as a whole" is to assume the continued existence of some form of *organized* society, that is, a society organized on "democratic" principles.

If the ownership of the means of production were vested in a group of people whose actions did not reflect the wishes of the masses, that would not be ownership by "society as a whole." Essentially, if the ownership and management of producer goods are to be vested in society as a whole, then the decisions concerning the use of those goods will be made "directly" by society rather than by individuals. Socialism as a movement, then, is really concerned with transferring decision-making powers from individuals to society. Most theories of socialism assume that this transference of power takes place only for large-scale, not for small-scale, production. Land and tools used personally by their owners, for example, are not usually subject to decision making by "society as a whole." Also implicit in the theoretical definitions of socialism is that a socialist economy will lead to increased output for the nation as a whole.

Economics—the Core of Socialism

Obviously, the heart of socialism is economic. The central issues include who should have the property rights in producer goods, who should make decisions about the use of these goods, and how income should be distributed once it is created. To be sure, around this central economic core there will be political, social, religious, and other types of issues. In fact, many of these issues seem to loom larger than the economic ones in current discussions of socialism. The central problem, however, is how to alter society's methods of producing, distributing, and consuming economic goods. We know—and socialists do not deny—that a change from a capitalistic system to the institutions necessary for a socialistic system will also entail many social, philosophical, religious, and even psychological changes.

Key Attributes

Perhaps we can best isolate the key attributes of a socialistic system by seeing how it answers the four questions outlined previously.

1. Although individuals are allowed to own many items of wealth, in a socialist system the government owns the major productive resources, such as land and capital goods. Individuals can own consumer goods and consumer durables, but they are not allowed to own factories, machines, and other things that are used to produce what society wants.

2. People are induced to produce by wage differentials. However, taxation of large incomes to redistribute income does reduce some of the incentives to produce a lot.

3. The forces that determine the reward people get from producing are usually set by the state, not by the market. That is, the government, rather than supply and demand, determines people's wage rates and who should be paid what in government-owned and operated factories.

4. In a socialist system, individuals are allowed to enter only certain endeavors. They cannot, for example, set up their own factories. They cannot become entrepreneurs or capitalists, for the state controls such enterprises.

This summary explanation of socialism is purely on the theoretical level. The real-world varieties of socialist systems seem to have only one thing in common: Their governments control more factors of production than do capitalist governments. We should not underestimate the importance of control of resources either because in many cases controlling resources is more important than owning them. In socialist countries such as the Soviet Union, ownership of resources is widely dispersed but very centrally controlled. In other socialist countries, such as Yugoslavia, both control and ownership of resources is widely dispersed because workers in individual factories largely control those organizations by assuming management functions. In the United States, both ownership and control of resources are widely dispersed, too, but government controls fewer factors of production.

Since we have taken a look at American capitalism, let's now take a look at Russian socialism and compare that system with socialist theory.

Russia Today

In the Soviet Union, the state owns almost all the factors of production. Workers receive wages, and they can choose what they want to spend their lives doing. However, Soviet citizens do not have as much geographic mobility as American citizens do, and they have to ask permission to take a job in another region or in another industry. They usually receive permission to move to a place where they think they can make higher wages; in fact, the current system now tries to attract workers to different locations by a system of wage differentials.

In the past, physical quotas were set for factories, but they caused too many problems: Factories would put out numerous items, all of poor quality, just to meet the physical quota. The typical Soviet factory is now generally evaluated according to some overall concept of profitability. The government does not measure profitability in the same way a factory in the United States measures it, but it is moving in that direction. Within the factory itself, the managers—in addition to getting a better-than-average paycheck—obtain special benefits that workers are not allowed to have, such as travel expenses, perhaps a car, and other privileges. This is a centralized system, and although there seems to be a change toward more and more decentralization, there is a continuous hierarchy within an individual firm and within economic life itself. Right now there are regional economic councils, above them a council of ministers, and beyond that, planners who decide which industries should do what.

Resource Allocation

Remember that in the United States, resources flow to where their relative rates of return are highest. If the highest rate of return is in making consumer goods, then resources will flow into making consumer goods. Individuals more or less decide how much should be saved and invested, how much put away and not consumed. And the amount of saving that the whole economy actually engages in follows these individuals' decisions.

Such is not the case in the Soviet Union. Generally, the planners decide how many of the economic resources available should be used in producing what consumers want, as opposed to producing what we'll call *capital equipment*—machines and the like. After the Bolshevik Revolution of 1917, there was a distinct drop in the amount of production that went to satisfy consumer wants. In fact, one of the reasons Russia grew so rapidly is that it spent a large amount of its resources in *capital formation* so it would have a higher level of living in the future.

Until recently very little market information was used to determine which consumer goods should be produced. The obvious result: lots of things in short supply and other things oversupplied or never bought at all. Today, however, central planners realize that when consumer goods are not purchased, production should be slowed down and that when goods are in short supply, production should be increased. Russian planners are even starting to engage in marketing surveys to see what consumers really want.

The Problem of Coordination

Since the Soviet Union is a command economy, it faces a fundamental problem of coordination. Even if a central plan mandates a 20 percent increase in steel production, planners must take additional steps to ensure that there are sufficient supplies, raw materials, and capital and labor for such an increase in steel output. For example, if the iron-mining industry does not achieve its quota, the desired goal for steel production will not be met. You can imagine what problems there might be in coordinating such economic endeavors nationwide.

Central planners somehow have to make sure that each of over 200,000 industrial enterprises in Russia today receives resources in correct amounts and at the right time to keep production moving smoothly. Millions, if not billions, of planning decisions must be made, and they are all interrelated. Mathematicians and computer experts have come up with advanced techniques to help the planners cope with such massive problems of coordination. For example, they analyze the relationship between inputs and outputs in different sectors of the economy and put their estimates into what are called input-output tables. The information in these tables tells planners how much input they require to change a specific output in a specific industry. This is one way they can avoid bottlenecks.

The planning techniques used in the Soviet Union are certainly too complicated to go into in this brief discussion. We know that priorities are established, with heavy industry given special status as a "leading link" and consumer goods assigned a lower priority. We also know that Soviet planners depend on large reserves or inventories of, for example, ball bearings, so that bottlenecks will be avoided. In any event, to get a command economy working, there is an enormous administrative problem.

The Economic Problem Is Universal

By now you should be convinced that the economic problem—scarcity—is common to all economic systems; only the solutions differ. Most of what we will discuss in the remaining pages of this book centers on the American capitalist system and a number of other mixed capitalist systems throughout the world. However, do not be surprised to find that you can apply the analysis you learn for our system to totally different systems—particularly to systems in which the assumption of individual wealth max-imization is valid. Few economists would find it invalid. However, those visiting the Chinese mainland believe, to some extent, that this assumption is inappropriate for analyzing the behavior of Chinese citizens. This is such a fascinating possibility that we treat it in the following issue.

Capitalism: An economic system in which individuals privately own productive resources and can use them in whatever manner they choose, subject to certain legal restrictions.

Socialism: An economic system in which producer goods for large-scale production are owned and controlled primarily by the state.

Production-Possibility Frontier: The line (or set of points) showing the boundary between that which can and that which cannot be produced at a moment in time, given the available resources in the community. At any point on the production-possibility frontier it is impossible to produce more of one good without producing less of another.

Flow: Those variables that are defined per unit time period. For example, income is a flow that occurs per week, per month, or per year.

Stock: The quantity of something, as measured at a point in time, for example, an inventory of goods and a bank account. Stocks are defined independently of time although they are assessed at a point in time.

Law of Diminishing Returns: A proposition stating that after some point, if all factors of production save one are fixed, an increase in that one variable input will yield a less-than-proportionate increase in output.

Command Economy: An economic system in which the central political authority allocates scarce resources.

Property Rights: Legal rights in property. We usually talk about private property rights where individuals have control over the use and disposal of whatever they legally own.

Mixed Capitalist System: A system that combines private property ownership with the ownership and control of certain aspects of the economy by government authorities.

Producer (Capital) Goods: Goods used in the production of other goods. Machinery and buildings are often called producer goods.

1. Every economic system must solve the economic problem of allocating scarce resources. In every economic system trade-offs must be made between producing one set of goods and services as opposed to an infinite number of other sets.

2. We can graphically show the concept of a trade-off by using a production-possibilities curve. At any point along that curve, society's resources

are being fully utilized. No point outside the curve is possible, and at any point inside the curve, underemployment of resources is implied.

3. The production-possibilities frontier is bowed outward for a number of reasons, the most obvious being that some resources are better suited for the production of particular commodities than other resources.

4. The law of diminishing returns is also operating. According to this proposition, after some point, less-than-proportionate increases in output will occur when one factor of production is increased in use.

5. An economic system deals with the questions of what should be produced, how should it be produced, and who is to receive what is produced. An economic system is a set of institutions that guides individuals in their use of resources. All economic systems are artificial.

6. We can look at the spectrum of systems in terms of how centralized (in a political sense) economic decision-making processes are. The United States has a less centralized economic system than the U.S.S.R.

7. It is important to distinguish between capital and capitalism. All economies have capital, but in a capitalist system individuals privately own productive resources and possess the right to use these resources in whatever manner they choose subject to certain legal restrictions.

8. A key aspect of a capitalistic system is the right to own private property and producer goods for large-scale production.

9. The capitalist system is sometimes called the free-enterprise system. This is merely an extension of the concept of private property rights. In a free-enterprise system, individuals can freely select economic activities for whatever resources they own.

10. American capitalism is certainly not a system of pure capitalism. Central authorities control and generate some resources throughout the economy.

11. In general, a socialist economic system is defined as one in which the major resources for production are owned by the state. The socialist system is often called a command economy.

12. In any command economy there is a problem of coordination. How does one coordinate the over 200,000 industrial enterprises in the U.S.S.R. today, for example?

Questions for Thought and Discussion

1. Since the means of production are owned by the state in a socialist system, would you expect to find less antisocial business behavior in the form of pollution in a socialist system?

2. The Soviet Union uses large amounts of capital. In one sense, is the Soviet Union capitalistic?

Selected References

Balinky, Alexander, *Marx's Economics: Origin and Development*, Lexington, Mass.: D. C. Heath, 1970.

Bornstein, Morris and Daniel R. Fussfeld (eds.), *The Soviet Economy*, 4th ed. Homewood, Ill.: Irwin, 1974.

Is There a New Breed of People on the Mainland?

CHINA TODAY

The Early System under Mao

One of the economic systems in the world that is most different from ours in the United States is in mainland China. Since Mao took power, the country has become a model of collectivist economic planning and operation. The differences between that system and ours are so significant that it is worthwhile to describe them in some detail.

Maoist Economics

The main features of the Chinese economy include public ownership of all industries, agricultural cooperatives, communes, and massive central planning. The state makes all the decisions regarding investment versus consumption, how labor should be supplied to different sectors of the economy, and the prices of various goods and services. In the Chinese economy, there is always full employment. Although in theory workers have complete freedom to change jobs, there are internal policy regulations and particular quota systems that prevent complete job mobility. For example, university students are generally assigned their future positions while still in school.

The Planning Operation

After taking power in 1949, the communists under Mao Tse-tung devised plans to help put their devastated country back onto the road to economic prosperity. The first Five Year Plan was instituted in 1952. It stressed investment in heavy industry, retention of small-scale and handicraft industries, and a land-reform policy that took land from wealthy Chinese and gave it to poor peasants. Farms were also collectively organized. In 1958, the second plan was put into effect. It started out with the so-called Great Leap Forward, a plan by Chinese economic policymakers to increase individual output by over 25 percent per year and develop heavy industry even more rapidly than they had in the previous 5 years. The plan called for labor to be used more intensively in order to reduce underemployment of the labor force. Instead of directing all heavy industrial plants from the central government, there was to be some decentralization—in the sense that local managers would have more control over what their plants bought and sold and what production methods would be used.

From the very beginning, there were unexpected and tragic consequences of the Great Leap Forward. The program was, in a word, too ambitious. Many goods were being produced that were not really wanted in the economy, and many large-scale irrigation projects that were undertaken were poorly planned and managed. The result was often a complete fiasco. Steel was being made by many unskilled workers in unsafe, often quite primitive production environments. Often the steel produced was of such poor quality that it could not be used.

A food shortage began to develop. Many workers had been transferred from agriculture to the city to help in the great industrial expansion program. The consequence was too little production of food. Finally, the much needed New Economic Policy was instituted.

The New Policy

The leaders of China finally realized that agriculture had to be built up before rapid industrialization could be attempted. The only way that urbanization can occur is for productivity in the agricultural sector to rise fast enough to allow those who stay in agriculture to feed those who go to the city. The Chinese leaders finally realized this. Agriculture then became the foundation of the entire economy.

One of the most interesting aspects of the agricultural program in China is a system of communal farming in which work teams are essentially self-governing and the workers are paid work points (providing a daily income of less than $1 today in American purchasing power). In a communal system, the workers live together on the same site where they work. However, not all the communes worked out well, and we found fewer and fewer communes being started even after the Great Leap Forward.

Growth in the Chinese Economy

The most recent estimates we have for real economic growth in the Chinese economy are indeed surprising. They show that mainland China has grown much faster than we originally thought. For example, the average annual GNP growth rate from 1952 to 1957 was a whopping 19.2 percent per year. If we look at Figure I-3.1 we see that the index of gross output of Chinese industrial production started at 100 in 1952 and ended up at almost 1000 in 1971. The annual growth rate for this period is about 12 percent per annum.[1] Some economists who

[1] Thomas G. Rawski, "Chinese Industrial Production, 1952 to 1971," *The Review of Economics and Statistics,* vol. 55, no. 2, May 1973, p. 169.

have visited mainland China contend that the reason this tremendous rate of economic growth was possible was that there are "new men and women" on the mainland who are different from the workers in the United States. In the following section we discuss the attributes of this new breed of people as outlined by Professor John W. Gurley.[2]

Goals of the New Men and Women

It appears that Maoists believe that the principal aim of a nation should

[2] John W. Gurley, "The New Man in the New China," *The Center Magazine,* vol. 3, no. 3, May 1970, pp. 25–33.

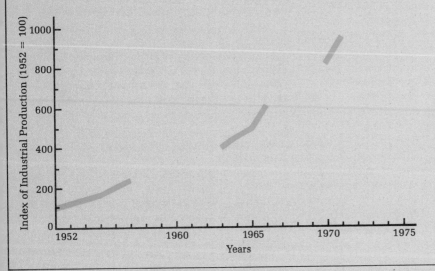

FIGURE I-3.1 Chinese Industrial Production

Starting with an index of 100 for the year 1952, Chinese industrial production has grown at an average annual rate of about 12 percent a year (data for certain years were not available). (*Source:* T. G. Rawski, "Chinese Industrial Production, 1952–1971," *The Review of Economics and Statistics,* vol. 55, no. 2, May 1973, p. 169, Table 1.)

Photo by H. Cartier, Magnum

be not only to raise the level of material welfare of the population but also to develop the full human being. That is, each person in the economy should develop his or her creative powers (on an egalitarian basis).

In the United States we place a very high social and economic value on education, particularly higher education. The same is true in Maoist China, but the emphasis is a bit different: The aim of education is not just to make individuals more productive but to shape their values as communist citizens. Ideology, then, is a large part of each individual's education process.

There is a tendency toward nonspecialization in Maoist China—just the opposite of what has happened in the United States. Adam Smith once said specialization was determined by the extent of the market. In China, even though the market is huge, there is a tendency to despecialize workers so that there is no upper echelon of leaders, experts, authorities, and technicians. It appears, then, that Maoists are willing to pursue the goal of transforming workers into communist men and women, even if it means some slowdown in short-run economic growth.

However, as we have seen in Figure I-3.1, the slowdown is not at all apparent. According to Maoist thought, the elimination of specialization will increase workers' willingness to work hard for social rather than individual goals. Moreover, despecialization allows workers to get a broader view of the world around them because they are forced to participate in numerous production processes. The cost to the worker is struggle. According to Mao, "Unprincipled peace [gives rise] to a decadent philistine attitude. . . ." Progress, then, must be made by struggling with the world around oneself. One of the struggles is, of course, the same old Marxist class conflict: the proletariat versus the bourgeoisie.

Serving the Proletariat

According to social thinkers and decision makers in the new China, every individual must be devoted to the masses rather than to his or her own economic and personal ends. In other words, workers should be

Photo by Marc Riboud, Magnum

We have already noted the tremendous economic development in communist China. More impressive than that, however, is the conclusion Professor Gurley made:

> The basic overriding economic fact about China is that for 20 years she had fed, clothed, and housed everyone, has kept them healthy, and has educated most. Millions have not starved; sidewalks and streets have not been covered with multitudes of sleeping, begging, hungry, and illiterate human beings; millions are not disease ridden. To find such deplorable conditions one does not look to China these days but, rather, to India, Pakistan, and almost anywhere else in the underdeveloped world. These facts are so basic, so fundamentally important, that they completely dominate China's economic picture, even if one grants all of the erratic and irrational policies alleged by her numerous critics.[3]

What is important, according to Gurley, is that communist China is engaged in a social and economic experiment in which there is an attempt to develop industrially without dehumanization. The Marxist-Leninist goal is that eventually a communist man or woman will emerge in a classless society where every person works according to his or her ability and consumes according to his or her needs.

Is there a new breed of people

[3] Ibid., p. 31.

willing to serve the world proletariat. This differs little from the standard Communist Party line, "workers of the world, unite." The worker will work hard for the community or the nation rather than for his or her own selfish goals. To this end, Maoists deemphasize all material incentives because these lead to the decadence of bourgeois capitalist societies. Hence, workers must be disciplined and selfless. There must be unity. This is the aim of all teachings throughout mainland China.

Deemphasizing Careers

In keeping with the view that individuals should not specialize, Maoists have tried to eliminate the distinction between the city and the country. Consequently, most people who work in the city have to spend time farming in the country. Each person thus becomes a well-rounded communist man or woman, not a person who specializes in some specific type of career. And to avoid creating a hierarchy of bureaucrats and experts, much decision making is done by "the masses." This involves establishing new industries in rural areas even though the economic environment may not be the most favorable in those areas. The growth of cities as cultural and industrial centers has been discouraged for some time now. This, of course, imposes a loss in real output on the New China. But "So what," say the Maoists. "We are after the development of the communist man. And whatever development we have will be equitable, even if it is relatively inefficient."

Photo by Rene Burri, Magnum

in communist China? According to Professor Gurley, yes. One expert's account on the subject is hardly enough to answer the question, but it does give us a beginning. The Maoists claim that within each person numerous powers exist that can be released by proper ideological and economic planning. According to Gurley, "If [the Maoists] are right, the implications for economic development are so important that it would take blind men on this side of the Pacific to ignore them."

Time will tell.

Questions for Thought and Discussion

1. After reading this issue, do you think there is a new breed of people in China?
2. Is it possible to separate the social from the economic experiment in communist China?
3. Why do you think China isolated itself for so many years? Could this have been important for allowing the formation of the new men and women?

Selected References

Crook, F. W., "Collective Farms in Communist China," *Monthly Labor Review,* March 1973, p. 45ff.

Eckstein, Alexander et al., *Economic Trends in Communist China,* Chicago: Aldine, 1968.

Galenson, Walter and Nai-Ruenn Chen, *The Chinese Economy under Communism,* Chicago: Aldine, 1969.

Hoffman, Charles, *Work Incentive Practices and Policies in the People's Republic of China, 1953–65,* Albany, NY: State University of New York Press, 1967.

Richman, Barry M., *Industrial Society in Communist China,* New York: Random House, 1969.

Wheelwright, E. L. and Bruce McFarlane, *The Chinese Road to Socialism,* New York: Monthly Review Press, 1970.

Some Economic Tools: Demand, Supply, and Elasticity

PART A: DEMAND AND SUPPLY

Market pricing makes up a good part of everyday activity in all countries. Crucial to understanding market pricing are the forces that underlie the determination of prices. Why does 1 pound of peanuts cost, say, $1, but 1 pound of macadamia nuts cost $3? Why does a steel worker earn, say, $10 an hour and a store clerk only $4 an hour? The only way to find out why the **relative price** of some things in our economy is high and that of other things is low is to understand what demand and supply are all about. We will first look at demand, then at supply, and finally put together the two concepts to show how prices are determined. After that, we will talk about some properties of demand and supply.

The Law of Demand

A commonsense notion of "demand" is simply "how much people want of something." You have a certain demand for records, Big Mac's, and textbooks, and so do I. In our analysis, however, we have to be careful about how we use that term because it can be confused with desire or want. Our desires, or wants, are unlimited; our demand for a particular scarce resource has to be limited because each of us has a limited income and therefore faces a personal scarcity problem. Since we all have limited incomes, we must solve our economic problem by allocating our incomes to various classes of expenditures. And here the pricing mechanism and **the law of demand** come into play. Since economic goods are provided to us only at a positive price (except where governments or other institutions provide the scarce resource at a zero price), it follows that none of us can completely ignore the price of things we buy. It also generally follows that at a higher relative price an individual will purchase less of most items. Why? Simply because if that person were to attempt to purchase the same quantity at a higher relative price than at a lower relative price, he or she would necessarily run out of income and be unable to buy the same quantities which could be bought at lower relative prices. Some people will decide that at a higher price a certain good, say, French fries, is just not worth it because they have to give up too much of other things they buy, such as Big Mac's and Cokes.

The Law in Words

The law of demand can now be stated succinctly:

> At higher (relative) prices, a lower quantity will be demanded than at lower (relative) prices, *ceteris paribus*.

Notice our use of "relative" before "prices." That's an important distinction to make when you want to study the demand for an individual commodity. Otherwise, you will get confused with problems involving all prices changing simultaneously in an up or down direction. Also notice that two funny Latin words were added at the end of the law of demand. *Ceteris paribus* simply means all other things are held constant. The reason we put it in the law of demand is fairly straightforward: All we are looking at is the relationship between prices and quantities demanded. Since we ignore, for the moment, all the other things which determine the demand for a good or service, we have to assume that all other things, such as income and the price of substitutes, do not change along with the relative price of the good or service in question.

The law of demand is not a law in the legal sense. Rather, it is a tendency that we commonly observe in the world around us, and it seems to accurately describe how individuals do behave when faced with a higher relative price for any commodity, *ceteris paribus*. After all, there are substitutes for most things that we buy, and if the price of those substitutes has not gone up, some of us will want to purchase them instead of paying a higher price for the alternative. If the price of butter goes up relative to the price of margarine, many households will sacrifice butter in favor of margarine.

The Law in Numbers

Let's take a hypothetical demand situation to see how the inverse relationship between the price and the quantity demanded looks. What we will do is consider the quantity of French fries demanded by American college students per year. Without stating the time dimension, we could not make any sense out of this demand relationship because the numbers would change if we were talking about the quantity demanded per month or per decade.

Look at Table 3-1. Here we show the price per constant-quality bag of French fries. Notice the words *constant quality*, which take care of the problem of varying quality in adding up all the bags of French fries that are sold, or could be sold, every year. After all, you would not count as equally valuable a bag of half-cooked, soggy fries and a bag of perfectly done, crisp ones sold at the same price.

What we see in Table 3-1 is that at a price of 10¢ per bag, 10 million bags would be bought by American college students each year, but at a price of 50¢ per bag, only 2 million would be bought. This reflects the law of demand. Table

Table 3-1 Demand Schedule for French Fries by American College Students

Column 1 presents the price per constant-quality bag of French fries. Column 2 presents the quantity demanded by American undergraduates, again measured in constant-quality bags per year of French fries. The last column merely labels these various price-quantity demanded combinations. Notice that as the price goes up, the quantity demanded per year falls.

PRICE PER CONSTANT-QUALITY BAG	QUANTITY DEMANDED OF CONSTANT-QUALITY BAGS PER YEAR	COMBINATION
$0.10	10 million	E
0.20	8 million	D
0.30	6 million	C
0.40	4 million	B
0.50	2 million	A

3-1 is also called a **demand schedule** because it gives a schedule of alternative quantities demanded per year at different prices.

The Law in Graphic Terms

We saw in Appendix A how tables expressing relationships between two variables can be represented in graphic terms. To do this here, we need only construct a graph that has the price per constant-quality bag on the vertical axis[1] and the quantity measured in constant-quality bags per year on the horizontal axis. All we have to do is take combinations A, B, C, D, and E from Table 3-1 and plot those points in Figure 3-1. Now we connect the points with a smooth line, and voilà, we have a **demand curve.** It is downward sloping to indicate the

inverse relationship[2] between the relative price of French fries and the quantity demanded per year by American undergraduates. Our presentation of demand schedules and curves applies equally well to all commodities, including toothpicks, hamburgers, textbooks, credit, and labor services.

Demand, of course, is only one side of the picture. The other side is supply, which we will now consider.

The Law of Supply

To derive a supply relationship for French fries, we can simply go back to the production-possibilities curves that we derived in Figures 2-1 and 2-2 on pages 27 and 28. We recreate that curve in Figure 3-2. On the horizontal axis we have French fries, and on the vertical axis we have all other goods. Now we measure equiva-

---

[1] Since we are really interested in the relative price of French fries, the vertical axis should be labeled "price for French fries/the price of other goods," not merely dollars and cents. The way around this problem is to standardize the units of all other goods so that a unit of all other goods costs exactly $1. Then, what we are showing on the vertical axis is essentially the relative price of French fries.

[2] An inverse, or negative, relationship (or correlation) is one in which an increase in one variable means a decrease in the other. A positive relationship (or correlation) is one in which the variables move in the same direction; an increase (or decrease) in one causes an increase (or decrease) in the other.

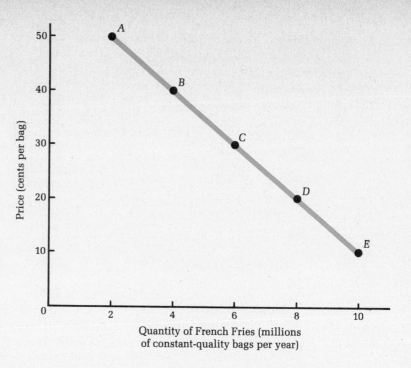

FIGURE 3-1 The Demand Curve for French Fries

We measure the quantity of French fries in millions of constant-quality bags per year on the horizontal axis and the price per constant-quality bag on the vertical axis. We then take the price-quantity combination from Table 3-1 and put them in this diagram. These points are *A*, *B*, *C*, *D*, and *E*. When we connect the points, we obtain a graphic representation of a demand schedule. It is downward sloping to show the inverse relationship between quantity demanded and price.

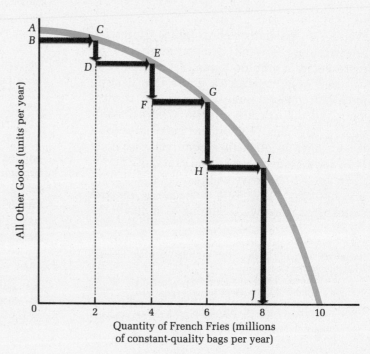

FIGURE 3-2 The Increasing Cost of Producing French Fries

Here we show a production-possibilities curve for all other goods and French fries. On the horizontal axis we measure French fries per year in millions of constant-quality bags, and on the vertical axis we give an unspecified measure of the production of other goods per year. Notice that as we increase French fry production by equal increments of 2 million bags per year, the reduction in the production of other goods becomes greater. As we move, for example, from 0 to 2 million French fries produced per year, the reduction of the output of other goods is only *AB*, but when we increase production by another 2 million, from 2 to 4 million French fries, the output of other goods falls by *CD*, which is greater than *AB*. We say, then, that because of the law of diminishing returns, opportunity cost rises as we increase French fry production.

lent units of French fries on the horizontal axis. As we go from zero to 2 million fries, we have to give up the quantity *A-B* of all other goods. Now, when we go from 2 to 4 million bags of fries, we have to give up the quantity *C-D* of all other goods.

The Law in Words

We continue this throughout the range of our experiment and find, not surprisingly, that as we attempt to produce more and more French fries, the opportunity cost of shifting productive resources into French fries production increases. What does this mean? Simply that for suppliers of French fries to be induced to supply more, and hence to incur higher opportunity costs, they must be paid more; that is, the only way to obtain a higher quantity supplied is by offering a higher price to suppliers. We see then that **the law of supply** is as follows:

> At higher (relative) prices a larger quantity will be supplied than at lower (relative) prices, *ceteris paribus*.

The Law in Numbers

We see this in our hypothetical **supply schedule** presented in Table 3-2.

The Law in Graphic Terms

We can easily convert the supply schedule presented in Table 3-2 into a **supply curve,** just as we earlier created a demand curve. All we do is take the price-quantity combinations from Table 3-2 and plot them in Figure 3-3. These we have labeled *F* through *J*. Now we connect them with a smooth line, and again we have a curve. This time it is upward sloping to show the *positive relationship* between price and the quantity supplied. Again we have to remember that we are talking about quantity supplied per year and measured in constant-quality units.

Now we are ready to put demand and supply together to answer the question, "How are prices determined?"

Putting Demand and Supply Together

Let's combine Tables 3-1 (the demand schedule) and 3-2 (the supply schedule) into Table 3-3. Column 1 shows the price; column 2 the quantity supplied per year at any given price; column 3, the quantity demanded. Column 4 is merely the difference between columns 2 and 3, or the difference between the quantity supplied and the quantity demanded. In column 5 we label those excesses as either an excess quantity demanded or an excess quantity sup-

Table 3-2 Hypothetical Supply of French Fries

At higher relative prices suppliers will be willing to supply more French fries. We see, for example, in column 1 that at a price per constant-quality bag of 10¢, only 2 million bags will be supplied, but at a price of 50¢ per bag, 10 million will be forthcoming from suppliers. We label these price-quantity combinations in the third column.

PRICE PER CONSTANT-QUALITY BAG	QUANTITY SUPPLIED OF FRENCH FRIES (MEASURED IN CONSTANT-QUALITY BAGS) PER YEAR	COMBINATION
$0.10	2 million	F
0.20	4 million	G
0.30	6 million	H
0.40	8 million	I
0.50	10 million	J

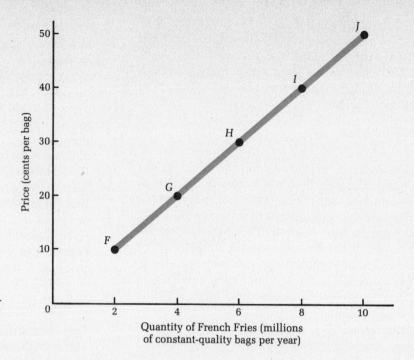

FIGURE 3-3 Supply Curve for French Fries

The horizontal axis measures the quantity of French fries supplied expressed in constant-quality bags per year. The vertical axis, as usual, measures price. We merely take the price-quantity combinations from Table 3-2 and use them as points F, G, H, I, and J. Then we connect those points to find the supply schedule for French fries. It is positively sloped, demonstrating the law of supply: At higher relative prices, a larger quantity will be forthcoming.

Table 3-3 Putting Supply and Demand Together

Here we combine Tables 3-1 and 3-2. Column 1 is the price per constant-quality bag, column 2 is the quantity supplied, and column 3 is the quantity demanded, both on a per year basis. The difference is expressed in column 4. For the first two prices, we have a negative difference; that is, there is an excess quantity demanded, as expressed in column 5. At the price of 40¢ or 50¢ we have a positive difference; that is, we have an excess quantity supplied. However, at a price of 30¢, the quantity supplied and the quantity demanded are equal, so there is neither an excess quantity demanded nor an excess quantity supplied. We call this price the equilibrium, or market clearing, price.

(1) PRICE	(2) QUANTITY SUPPLIED PER YEAR	(3) QUANTITY DEMANDED PER YEAR	(4) DIFFERENCE (2)–(3)	(5) EXCESSES
$0.10	2 million	10 million	−8 million	Excess quantity demanded
$0.20	4 million	8 million	−4 million	Excess quantity demanded
$0.30	6 million	6 million	0	Market clearing price = equilibrium
$0.40	8 million	4 million	4 million	Excess quantity supplied
$0.50	10 million	2 million	8 million	Excess quantity supplied

plied. For example, at a price of 10¢, there would be only 2 million bags of French fries supplied, but the quantity demanded would be 10 million. The difference would be a negative 8 million, which we label an excess quantity demanded. At the other end of the scale, a price of 50¢ per bag would elicit a 10 million quantity supplied, but quantity demanded would drop to 2 million, leaving a difference of 8 million, which we call an excess quantity supplied.

Now, do you notice something special about a price of 30¢? At that price, both the quantity supplied per year and the quantity demanded is 6 million bags of French fries. The difference then is zero. There is neither an excess quantity demanded nor an excess quantity supplied. Hence, this price, 30¢ is very special. It is called the **market clearing price**—it clears the market of all excess supply or all excess demand. There are no willing demanders who want to pay 30¢ but are turned away from hamburger stands, and there are no willing suppliers who want to provide French fries at 30¢ but who cannot sell all they want to sell at that price. The market clearing price is also called the **equilibrium price,** or price at which there is no tendency for change. Demanders seem happy with the quantity they are buying at that price; suppliers seem happy with the amount they can sell at that price.

Perhaps we can better understand the concept of an equilibrium, or market clearing, price by looking at the situation graphically. What we want firmly established is the understanding that in the market, a good or commodity will tend toward its equilibrium, or clearing price, and once that price is reached, unless something else happens, the price will remain in effect.

Supply and Demand in One Graph

Let's combine Figures 3-1 and 3-2 into Figure 3-4. The only difference now is that the hori-

zontal axis measures both the quantity supplied and the quantity demanded per year. Everything else is the same. The demand curve is now labeled DD; the supply curve SS. We have labeled the intersection of the supply curve with the demand curve as point E, for equilibrium. That corresponds to a price of 30¢, at which both the quantity supplied and the quantity demanded per year is 6 million. There is neither excess quantity supplied nor excess quantity demanded. Point E, the equilibrium point, always occurs at the intersection of the supply and the demand curves. Now let's see why we said that this particular price is one toward which the market will automatically tend to gravitate.

What if we were at a price of 10¢, where the quantity supplied was 2 million and the quantity demanded was 10 million. Demanders of French fries would find that they could not buy all the French fries they wanted at that price. We can surmise what would happen. Some demanders would sneak around the back of the hamburger stands and offer the owners a tip or a gift to get the French fries they wanted to buy. This would effectively raise the price received by the owner, and he or she could then be induced to supply a larger quantity (remember that the supply curve slopes upward). We would move from point A toward point E.

The process would indeed come to a halt when the price reached 30¢ per bag. The hamburger stand owners would not be getting any more orders for fries than they could handle, and French fry eaters would be able to buy all the French fries they wanted to buy at the going price of 30¢. We would move from a situation of excess quantity demanded at a price of 10¢ to a situation of no excess quantity demanded at a price of 30¢.

Now let's repeat the experiment with the price at 50¢ per bag. We draw a horizontal line at 50¢ to find out what the quantities de-

FIGURE 3-4 **Supply and Demand on One Graph**

The intersection of the supply and demand curves is E. It occurs at a price of 30¢ per constant-quality bag of fries, and at point E there is neither an excess quantity demanded nor an excess quantity supplied. At a price of 10¢ the quantity supplied will only be 2 million bags per year, but the quantity demanded will be 10 million. The difference is excess quantity demanded at price 10¢. There are forces that will cause the price to rise, so we will move from point A up the supply curve to point E, and from point B up the demand curve to point E. At the other extreme, 50¢ elicits a quantity supplied of 10 million, with a quantity demanded of 2 million. The difference is excess quantity supplied at a price of 50¢. Again, forces will cause the price to fall, so we will move from points Y and Z down the demand and the supply curves to the equilibrium point, E.

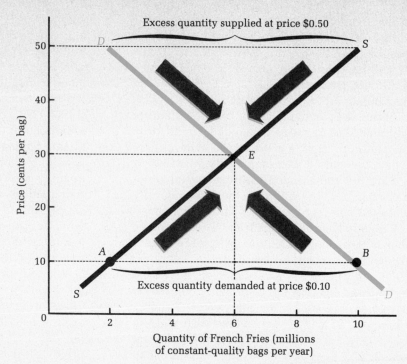

manded and the quantities supplied are. As can be expected, the quantity demanded has fallen and is now only 2 million bags per year, but the quantity supplied has risen greatly, to 10 million. There is one simple way for that excess quantity supplied to be eliminated. All that has to happen is for the price to fall from 50¢ to 30¢. As the price falls, that is, as the hamburger stand owners start offering French fries as a special to get rid of the excess quantities they want to supply consumers, consumers will indeed demand a larger quantity. The process will stop again at the equilibrium, or market clearing, price of 30¢.

Movements Along the Curve

Take note that when we dealt with a change in the relative price of French fries, we moved along curves which do not themselves change because the law of demand and the law of

supply are stated in such a way that the only thing that matters is the price. Hence, when there is a price change, the quantities supplied and demanded change also. We move to a different price-quantity combination in Table 3-3 or Figure 3-3. The table remains the same, as do the curves.

Shifting the Curves

If price determines *quantities* demanded and supplied, what causes changes in the curves and in the demand and supply schedules? The subtle difference here is important, as we will now see.

Shifting Demand   How would we represent a dramatic increase in the quantity of French fries demanded at *all* prices because of a medical discovery that French fry consumption caused longer life? We could surely not move along the demand curve presented in Figure 3-4. What we have to do is *shift* the curve outward or to the right to represent an increase in demand, that is to say, an increase in the quantities demanded at *all* prices. We do this in Figure 3-5. The demand curve has shifted from *DD* to *D'D'*. Take any price, say, 30¢. Originally, before the great medical discovery, the quantity demanded was 6 million bags per year. After the discovery, however, the new quantity demanded is 10 million bags per year. Thus, we have witnessed a shift in the demand for French fries. We could use the same argument when discussing a shift inward, or to the left, of the demand curve for French fries. This might happen, for example, in the case of a medical discovery that French fry con-

sumption actually shortened life. We can list very briefly some obvious determinants of demand, that is, some factors which will cause the demand curve to shift:

1. *Changes in income* At higher incomes individuals generally buy more of most commodities.
2. *Tastes* A change in tastes, say, for miniskirts as opposed to maxis causes the demand curve to shift for both types of skirts.
3. *The price of substitutes* As the price of butter goes up, the demand schedule for margarine shifts upward, and vice versa.
4. *The price of complements* As the price of one item used together with another goes up, the demand schedule for the other will shift downward. For example, if the price

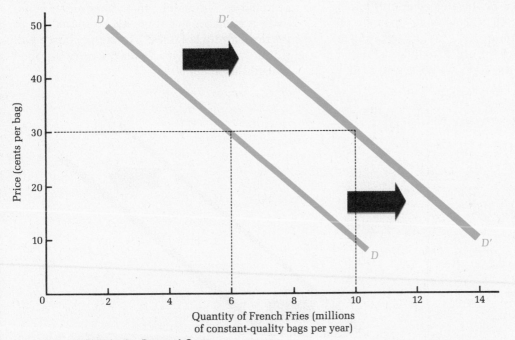

FIGURE 3-5 A Shift in the Demand Curve

If the relative price of French fries changes, we move along a given demand curve. However, if some factor other than price changed, the only way we can show its effect on the quantity demanded is by moving the entire demand curve from *DD* to *D'D'*. We have assumed in our example that the move was precipitated by a medical discovery showing that French fry consumption led to longer life. That meant that at *all* prices a larger quantity would be demanded. For example, at a price of 30¢, instead of 6 million bags per year being demanded, 10 million would be demanded.

of tennis balls went to $50 apiece, the demand curve for tennis rackets would undoubtedly shift inward (that is, decrease).

5. *Expectations* If the relative price of a good is expected to go up in the future, consumers may buy more of it now than they would otherwise buy. If the relative price of a good is expected to fall in the future, consumers may buy less of it than they would otherwise.

Shifting Supply Similar analysis can be applied to the supply curve. A change in price will cause a movement along a stable curve. However, anything that affects the entire supply schedule will shift the curve. Just take an example: If a new method of cooking French fries reduces the cost of cooking them by 98 percent, competition among sellers to produce more will shift the supply schedule of French fries outward to the right, as we see in Figure

3-6. At a price of 30¢, the quantity supplied was originally 6 million per year, but now the quantity supplied will be 9 million per year. Why? Simply because suppliers will now supply more at all prices because their cost of supplying French fries has fallen so dramatically.

The opposite case will make the point even clearer. Suppose that a new potato bug sneaks in from Iceland in somebody's backpack and that, within a matter of months, it has reproduced and destroyed 80 percent of the potato crop. When raw French fry makers go to buy potatoes, they will find an incredibly reduced supply. All of them—in competition, of course, with other businesspersons who want to sell potatoes in other markets—will bid up the price of potatoes. Ultimately, then, hamburger stand owners will have to pay greatly increased prices for raw, cut-up potatoes. The supply curve will shift inward. At all prices the quantity supplied will fall dramatically.

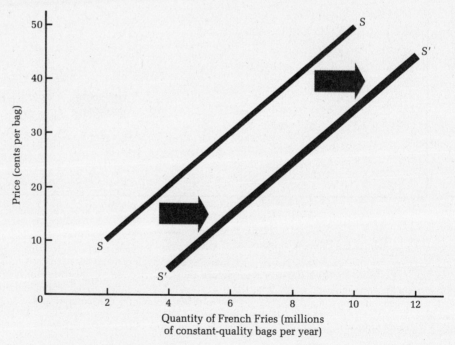

FIGURE 3-6 A Shift in the Supply Schedule

If the price changes, we move along a given supply schedule. However, if, for example, the cost of production of French fries were to fall dramatically, the supply schedule would shift outward from SS to S'S' so that at all prices a larger quantity would be forthcoming from suppliers.

The factors affecting the position of supply curves are fewer than those affecting the position of demand curves. The cost of production basically determines the position of supply curves. Anything that affects the cost of production will therefore move a supply curve in or out. It is mainly technology and resources that affect the cost of production. Any technological improvement in the means of production or decline in resource prices will shift a supply curve outward. However, changes in the prices of other goods can also shift a supply curve for a product. A decline in the price of corn, for example, may cause a farmer to offer more wheat for sale at all possible prices. Expectations concerning the future price of a product also determine the position of the current supply curve. And lastly, if more and more new firms enter the industry, the supply curve will also shift outward.

We cannot overstress the importance of distinguishing between a movement along the curve, which occurs only when the price changes, and shifts in a curve, which occur only with changes in factors other than price. You should always ask yourself which situation you are analyzing:

If the price changes, we move along a curve; if something else changes, we shift a curve.

PART B: ELASTICITY

Price Responsiveness

When we talked about changes in the quantity demanded or supplied, we always talked in terms of prices. Now the question before us is "By how much will quantities demanded or supplied change as the price changes?" To figure this out, we must determine exactly *how responsive* demanders and suppliers are to changes in price. We would like to come up with a way to measure such *price responsiveness* and a way to talk about different degrees of price responsiveness. Do consumers change their spending habits a little or a lot when the price of gasoline goes up by 10 percent? Do suppliers change their production decisions greatly or hardly at all when the price of corn goes down by 10 percent?

We will look first at the demand side and then at the supply side.

Price Elasticity of Demand

If the price of French fries goes up by 1 percent, what will be the percentage reduction in the quantity demanded? If we can figure out the answer to that question, we will indeed come up with a numerical idea of what price responsiveness actually means. The technical term for price responsiveness is the **price elasticity of demand,** where the term elasticity is just the economist's way of saying responsiveness. A simple definition of price elasticity, which we will call e, will be the following:

$$e = \frac{\text{percentage change in quantity demanded}}{\text{percentage change in price}}$$

Here, we are comparing a change in the quantity demanded with a change in the price, and we have to express such comparisons in terms of percentage changes, not absolute changes. After all, the units of measurement of price are different from the units of measurement of quantity demanded. Moreover, if we tried to express price responsiveness in terms of absolute changes, a change in scale would give us a different number each time. By using percentages, we ignore problems of scale.

We have not indicated it in our definition, but by now it should not surprise you to learn that elasticity of demand will always be negative because the law of demand states that at higher prices, smaller quantities will be demanded, and vice versa. In other words, the change in price is always in the opposite direction to that of the change in the quantity demanded. We will not put the negative sign in front of our demand elasticities, but you should always keep in mind that *they are implicitly negative.*

Let's see if we can compute the elasticities from Table 3-1. We are going to have to use a modified form of our elasticity formula because we are measuring price changes over such a large range. What we have to do is essentially get an average percentage change of both price and quantity. We do that by computing the percentage change in price as follows:

$$\frac{\text{Percentage}}{\text{change in price}} = \frac{\text{actual change in price}}{\text{av. of higher and lower price}}$$

We will do the same thing to compute the average percentage change in the quantity demanded. Using the data in Table 3-1, let's look at the numerical calculation of elasticity, *e*, presented in Table 3-4. Here we see that the computation of elasticity ranges from 3 down to 0.33. What does that mean? Simply that at very high prices for French fries, such as between 50¢ and 40¢ a bag, a 1 percent decrease in price will elicit a 3 percent increase in the quantity demanded. At the other extreme, at relatively low prices for French fries, say, between 20¢ and 10¢ per bag, the elasticity of minus 0.33 means that a 1 percent reduction in price will elicit only a one-third of 1 percent increase in the quantity demanded.

Different Kinds of Elasticities

We have names for the varying ranges of price elasticities, depending on whether a 1 percent change in price elicits more or less than a 1 percent change in the quantity supplied.

1. *Elastic demand* We call any price elasticity of demand in excess of 1 an **elastic demand.**

Table 3-4   Numerical Calculation of Price Elasticity of Demand for French Fries

Column 1 is the quantity demanded at different prices. Column 2 is the change in the quantity demanded. In other words, we merely subtract the smaller from the larger quantity. In each case, the change is 2 million bags per year. Column 3 is the price per bag, and column 4 is the change in the price, which happens to be 10¢ in each case. Columns 5 and 6 are the average quantities and prices. Column 7 presents an approximation of the price elasticity of demand, *e*.

(1) Quantity (Q)	(2) Change in Q	(3) Price (P)	(4) Change in P	(5) $\frac{Q_1 + Q_2}{2}$	(6) $\frac{P_1 + P_2}{2}$	$e = \dfrac{\text{change in } Q}{(Q_1 + Q_2)/2} \Big/ \dfrac{\text{change in } P}{(P_1 + P_2)/2}$
2		$0.50				
4	2	0.40	$0.10	3	$0.45	$2/3 \div 0.10/0.45 = 3$
6	2	0.30	0.10	5	0.35	$2/5 \div 0.10/0.35 = 1.4$
8	2	0.20	0.10	7	0.25	$2/7 \div 0.10/0.25 = 0.714$
10	2	0.10	0.10	9	0.15	$2/9 \div 0.10/0.15 = 0.333$

A 1 percent change in price causes a greater than 1 percent change in quantity demanded. Candidates for elastic-demand sections of our demand schedule in Table 3-1 are obviously an *e* of 3 and an *e* of 1.4.

2. *Unitary elasticity of demand* In this situation, a 1 percent change in price elicits exactly a 1 percent change in the quantity demanded.

3. *Inelastic demand* Here, a 1 percent change in price elicits a less than 1 percent change in quantity demanded. An elasticity of 0.33, as in the last line of Table 3-4, represents a situation of **inelastic demand.** In brief, a 1 percent change in price causes a less than 1 percent change in quantity demanded.

Extreme Elasticities

There are two extremes in price elasticities of demand: One is total unresponsiveness, which is called a *perfectly inelastic demand* situation,

and the other is complete responsiveness, which is called an unlimited, infinite, *perfectly elastic demand* situation.

We show perfect inelasticity in Figure 3-7. Notice that the quantity of French fries demanded per year is 8 million, no matter what the price. Hence, for any percentage price change, the quantity demanded will remain the same, and thus the change in the quantity demanded will be zero. Look at our formula for computing elasticity. If the change in the quantity demanded is zero, then the numerator is also zero, and anything divided into zero is zero too. Hence, perfect inelasticity.

At the opposite extreme is the situation depicted in Figure 3-8. Here we show that at a price of 30¢, an unlimited quantity of French fries will be demanded. At a price that is only slightly above 30¢, none will be demanded. In other words, there is complete, or infinite price responsiveness here, and hence we call the

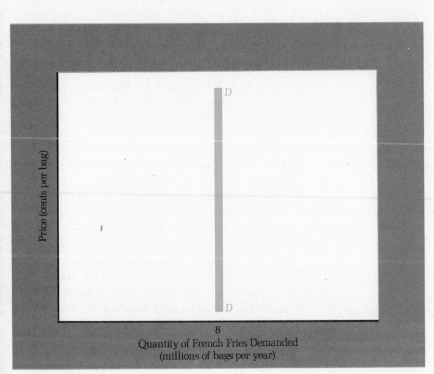

FIGURE 3-7 Price Unresponsiveness for French Fries

If people had to have their fries no matter what the price, the demand schedule would be represented by a vertical line, *DD*. Here consumers demand 8 million bags of fries per year no matter what the price. The elasticity of demand in this case is zero. We say that the demand is perfectly inelastic.

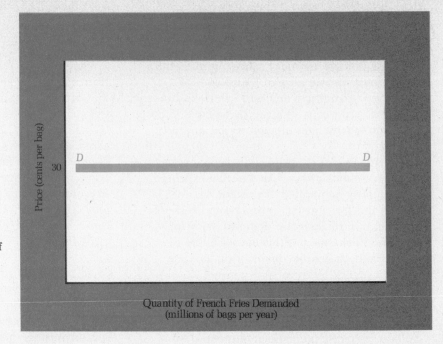

demand schedule in Figure 3-8 infinitely elastic.

All demand-schedule elasticities lie between the two extremes. We present, for example, in Table 3-5 demand elasticities for selected goods. None of them is zero, and the largest one is 4.6—a far cry from infinity. Remember, again, that even though we are leaving off the negative sign, the inverse relationship between price and quantity demanded makes it implicit.

Price Elasticity of Supply

The price elasticity of supply is defined in exactly the same way as the price elasticity of demand. However, supply elasticities are generally positive because the law of supply indicates that at higher prices larger quantities will be forthcoming from suppliers. Our definition of the price elasticity of supply, s, is the following:

$$s = \frac{\text{percentage change in quantity supplied}}{\text{percentage change in price}}$$

To compute the price elasticity of supply from the data in Table 3-2, for example, or from the supply curve in Figure 3-3, we would have to use the same approximation presented for computing the price elasticity of demand. Rather than having the numbers worked out for you, go back to Table 3-2 and compute the price elasticities of supply.[3]

Just as with demand, there are different types of supply elasticities. They are similar in definition. If a 1 percent increase in price elicits a greater than 1 percent increase in the quantity supplied, we say that at the particular point in question on the supply schedule, supply is elastic. If, on the other hand, a 1 percent in-

---

[3]Starting with the lower prices, you should end up with 1.0, 1.0, 1.0, and 1.0.

Table 3-5 Demand Elasticity for Selected Goods

Here we have obtained the estimated demand elasticities for selected goods. All of them are negative, although we have not shown a minus sign. For example, the price elasticity of demand for onions is 0.4. That means that a 1 percent increase in the price of onions will bring about a 0.4 percent decrease in the quantity of onions demanded.

	ESTIMATED ELASTICITY
Food Items:	
White potatoes	0.3
Green peas, fresh	2.8
Green peas, canned	1.6
Tomatoes, fresh	4.6
Tomatoes, canned	2.5
Other Nondurable Goods:	
Shoes	0.4
Stationery	0.5
Newspapers and magazines	0.1
Gasoline and oil, short-run	0.2
long-run	0.7
Durable Goods:	
Kitchen appliances	0.6
China and tableware	1.1
Jewelry and watches	0.4
Automobiles, long-run	0.2
Tires, short-run	0.6
long-run	0.4
Radio and television receivers	1.2
Sports equipment, boat,	
pleasure aircraft, short-run	0.6
long-run	1.3
Services:	
Physicians' services	0.6
Legal services	0.5
Taxi	0.4
Rail commuting	0.7
Airline travel, short-run	0.06
long-run	2.4
Foreign travel, short-run	0.7
long-run	4.0

Sources: H. S. Houthakker and L. D. Taylor, *Consumer Demand in the United States, 1929–1970,* Cambridge, Mass.: Harvard University Press, 1966; U.S. Department of Agriculture, 1954.

crease in price elicits a less than 1 percent increase in the quantity supplied, we refer to that as an inelastic supply situation. If the change in the quantity supplied is just equal to the change in the price, then we talk about unitary elasticity of supply.

We show, in Figure 3-9, two supply schedules, *SS* and *S'S'*. Can you tell at a glance, without reading the caption, which one is infinitely elastic and which one is perfectly inelastic?

As you might expect, most supply schedules exhibit elasticities that are somewhere in between the range of zero to infinity.

Elasticity and Slope

It is important not to look at the slope of a demand curve as representative of its elasticity because the slope of a curve on a diagram can be easily changed merely by changing the scale of the axes. Remember from our initial discussion of elasticity that we had to abstract somehow from scale problems. We did this by expressing elasticity as a ratio of *percentage* changes in quantity demand over *percentage* changes in price. There is no way of picking up such information from the slope of a straight-line demand curve. As a matter of fact, the measured elasticity along, for example, a normal, or downward-sloping, straight-line demand curve goes from infinity to zero as we move down the curve. The only time we can be sure of an elasticity by looking at a curve is if that curve is either perfectly horizontal or perfectly vertical.

The Long and the Short of Elasticities

Elasticities do not come out of the blue. In almost all cases, the only way we can discover the elasticity of demand or supply for a particular good is by looking at what actually hap-

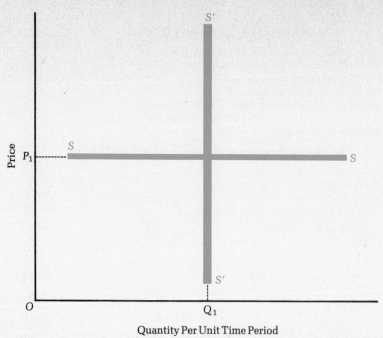

FIGURE 3-9 **The Extremes in Supply Curves**

Here we have drawn two extremes of supply schedules. *SS* is a perfectly elastic supply curve. *S'S'* is a perfectly inelastic one. In the former, an unlimited quantity will be forthcoming at the price P_1. In the latter, no matter what the price, the quantity supplied will be Q_1. An example of *S'S'* might be the supply curve for fresh fish the morning the boats come in.

pened in the marketplace in the past. That is, we have to look at real numbers which show us changes in quantities after there were changes in prices. Realizing this, we see that there are probably going to be different measures of elasticity for different time spans. One would assume, for example, that a change in the price of the good will elicit a smaller change in the quantity demanded and supplied *immediately after* the price increase than it would, say, after 1 year. One should distinguish, therefore, between *short-run* and *long-run* elasticities. Short-run elasticities are measured during the period immediately following the price change when people and firms don't have time for *complete* adjustments. Long-run elasticities are measured after people and firms have had time to adjust completely. In fact, we usually find that the demand schedule for a good in

question will pivot and become more elastic if more time is allowed for adjustment.

Demand

Let's take an example. Suppose the price of electricity goes up 50 percent. How do you adjust in the short run? You can turn the lights off more often, you can stop running the stereo as much as you used to, and so on. Otherwise it's very difficult to cut back on your consumption of electricity. In the long run, though, you can devise methods to reduce your consumption. Instead of using electric heaters, the next time you have a house built you will install gas heaters. Instead of using an electric stove, the next time you move you will have a gas stove installed. You will purchase fluorescent bulbs because they use less electricity. The longer you have to figure it out, the more ways

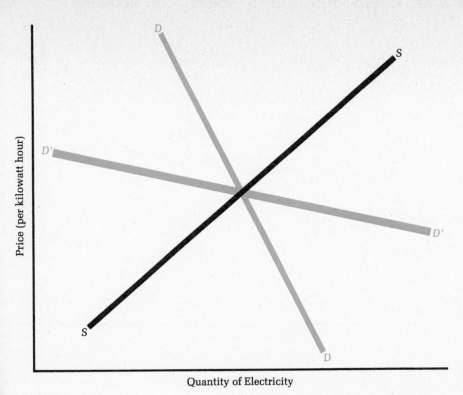

Price (per kilowatt hour)

Quantity of Electricity

FIGURE 3-10 **Short- and Long-Run Demand Curves for Electricity**

Here we have shown a supply schedule for electricity, *SS*. We have assumed that in the short run it is difficult to adjust to a change in the price of electricity. The demand schedule is therefore relatively inelastic, as shown by *DD*. However, as time goes on, adjustments can be made more easily. The demand schedule becomes relatively more elastic and pivots around to *D'D'*. In general, the longer the time allowed for adjustment, the more elastic demand will become.

you will find to cut electricity consumption. We would expect, therefore, that the short-run demand for electricity would be highly inelastic, as exhibited by *DD* in Figure 3-10. However, the long-run demand curve may exhibit much more elasticity, like *D'D'* in Figure 3-10.

Supply

The same holds for the supply curve. In the short run, the supply of umbrellas may be fairly inelastic because there are only several manufacturers and they would run into increasing costs per unit of production if they tried to expand their production rate very rapidly. However, in the long run, more and more firms can enter the market. They might be almost as efficient as existing firms. The long-run supply curve for umbrellas may nearly be the horizontal line *S'S'* in Figure 3-11. In fact, it has been asserted that in the long run, the supply curve for most manufactured goods is quite elastic because of the possibility of many new firms entering the market.

Once you distinguish between long-run elasticities and short-run elasticities, you will not be surprised to find that people's responsiveness to an increase in price is not very large immediately after the price change. As people learn to adjust and adapt to new methods of satisfying their wants, their responsiveness to the price increase will become larger. That is, the long-run elasticity of demand will be much larger than the short-run elasticity.

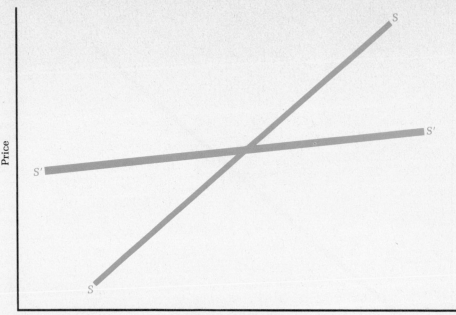

FIGURE 3-11 Short- and Long-Run Supply of Umbrellas

Here we assume that in the short run, the supply schedule for umbrellas is SS. However, if given a long enough time to adjust—that is, if given enough time for new firms to develop and more plants to be built—the supply schedule may pivot around to S'S', which is almost a horizontal line.

Definitions of New Terms

Relative Price: The price of a commodity compared to the price of another commodity or a group of other commodities.

The Law of Demand: The law that states that the quantity of a good or service varies inversely with the price.

Demand Schedule: The relationship between the prices for which a good can be purchased and the respective quantities demanded at those prices.

Demand Curve: A line showing the demand schedule. The demand curve shows the maximum price at which a given quantity will be demanded.

The Law of Supply: The law that states that the quantity of a commodity supplied is directly related to its price.

Supply Schedule: The relationship between the various quantities that will be forthcoming from suppliers at different prices.

Supply Curve: A line showing the supply schedule. The supply curve represents the minimum price at which a given quantity will be forthcoming.

Market Clearing Price: The price of a good or service at which the market is cleared; that is, the quantity demanded equals the quantity supplied.

Equilibrium Price: Another term for the market clearing price or the price at which the quantity supplied equals the quantity demanded.

Price Elasticity of Demand: The price responsiveness of the demand for a commodity. The price elasticity of demand is defined as the percentage change in quantity demanded divided by the percentage change in price.

Elastic Demand: A characteristic of a demand curve in which a given percentage change in price will be met by a larger percentage change in the quantity demanded in the opposite direction.

Inelastic Demand: A characteristic of a demand curve in which a given change in price will be met by a less-than-proportionate change in the quantity demanded in the opposite direction.

Chapter Summary

1. It is important to distinguish between the relative price of goods and services and their absolute price. During a period of rising prices, such as we are now experiencing in the United States, almost all prices go up, although some go up faster than others.

2. The law of demand is one of the most fundamental propositions in economics. It merely states that at a higher relative price individuals will purchase less of most commodities, and at a lower relative price they will purchase more.

3. When stating the law of demand we must be careful to add the phrase *ceteris paribus,* which means all other things held constant.

4. When discussing the law of demand (and supply), we must be careful to talk in terms of constant-quality units of the commodity in question. In other words, we have to correct for quality differences.

5. The law of demand can be seen in the demand schedule, which shows the relationship between the prices and quantities of an item purchased per unit time period. In graphic terms, the demand schedule is shown as a demand curve that is downward sloping.

6. To derive a supply curve or supply schedule, we can construct a production-possibilities curve, where we see that at a higher rate of production of one commodity, a higher opportunity cost is incurred. To induce producers to supply more, they must be paid more to cover these higher opportunity costs.

7. The supply curve is generally a positively sloped line, showing that at higher prices more will be forthcoming from suppliers. Again, we must talk in terms of constant-quality units of measurement and we must specify a time period for our analysis.

8. Where the demand and supply curves intersect, we find the equilibrium or market clearing price at which the quantity demanded equals the quantity supplied.

9. It is important to distinguish between a movement along a demand or supply curve and a shift in one of those curves. Whenever the relative price changes, we move along the curve. However, if something else changes, such as income, preferences, or population, then there is a shift in one or both of the curves.

10. We measure the price responsiveness of consumers to a change in the relative price of a commodity by use of the price elasticity of demand, which is defined as the percentage change in the quantity demanded divided by the percentage change in price.

11. The price elasticity of demand is always negative; this follows from the law of demand.

12. Price elasticity of demand can range from zero (perfectly inelastic demand) to a negative infinity (perfectly elastic demand). Most demand curves have price elasticities somewhere in between these two extremes.

13. Elasticity of supply is measured similarly to the elasticity of demand. In general, however, it is a positive number. Supply price elasticities can range also from zero to positive infinity. A zero price elasticity of supply indicates that there is a fixed quantity available no matter what the price. An infinite price elasticity of supply indicates that an unlimited quantity will be forthcoming from suppliers at a particular price.

14. The slope of a demand curve does not indicate its elasticity. Price elasticity is a ratio of percentage change in quantity demanded to percentage change in price. The slope of the curve, however, can change depending on the units chosen on the horizontal and vertical axes.

15. Both demand and supply price elasticities are greater in the long run than in the short run.

Questions for Thought and Discussion

1. If the price of economics textbooks went up by 100 percent, is there any way you could adjust your purchase of them?

2. Why is it important to distinguish between relative and absolute prices?

3. Can you think of exceptions to the law of demand?

4. Can you think of exceptions to the law of supply?

5. What is the difference between demand and quantity demanded?

6. What is the difference between supply and quantity supplied?

7. Why is the supply curve generally upward sloping?

8. If the price of a commodity is set below the equilibrium price, what would you expect to occur?

9. "The price of margarine has nothing to do with the price of butter." Evaluate this statement.

10. Is it possible for all price elasticities of demand to be less than 1, that is, inelastic?

11. Can you think of any commodities that have a perfectly inelastic supply? Does the time period allowed for adjustment affect your answer?

12. If it is true that the price elasticity of the demand for heroin is, indeed, very low—if not zero—what happens when the government mounts a program to decrease the quantity of this illegal drug in the United States?

13. Use the following hypothetical demand schedule for marijuana to answer the following questions:

Quantity Demanded/week	Price/oz	(Elasticity)
1000 oz	$ 5	
800	10	
600	15	
400	20	
200	25	

(a) Using the above demand schedule, determine the elasticity of demand for each price change (Example: when price changes from $5 to $10, quantity demanded changes from 1000 to 800 oz, so the elasticity of demand is ⅓ or 0.33).

(b) The data given in the demand schedule would plot as a straight-line demand curve. Why is demand more elastic the higher the price?

Selected References

Henderson, Hubert, *Supply and Demand,* Chicago: The University of Chicago Press, 1958.

Watson, Donald S., *Price Theory and Its Uses,* 3d. ed., Boston: Houghton Mifflin, 1972, chaps. 2 and 3.

Illegal Activities

PROHIBITION IN RETROSPECT

Applying Supply and Demand

We all know that illegal activities, including gambling, prostitution, and drug abuse, go on all the time despite legislation against them. Various estimates of the market value of all illegal activities taken together are around $50 billion for an average year.

What is interesting about illegal activities from an economic point of view is what happens because of their illegality. In this issue, we use the analysis of supply and demand that we developed in Chapter 3 to look at an actual case study in illegality: Prohibition.

Alcohol Prohibition

In 1808, Dr. Billy F. Clark met with citizens in Saratoga County, New York, who were opposed to hard liquor. Together, they organized the first American Temperance Society. At their second convention in 1836 they added beer and wine to their list of opposed intoxicants. In the 1850s, 12 states enacted dry laws, but most of these were repealed by 1900. The temperance forces then started to gain real momentum, and

by 1909, 5 states had again gone dry. By 1919, 29 states had adopted prohibition. On August 1, 1917, the Senate approved submitting the Eighteenth Amendment to the states. This amendment, along with the Volstead Act, was the fruit of temperance efforts.

Finally, on January 17, 1920, the Eighteenth Amendment to the United States Constitution was put into effect. It prohibited "manufacture, sale or transportation of intoxicating liquors within, or the importation thereof into, or exportation thereof from the United States . . . for beverage purposes." The Eighteenth Amendment, therefore, was a legislative attempt to eliminate the *supply* of alcoholic beverages.

We know, though, that there are two sides to every coin: No law is effective without enforcement, and Congress was aware of this. In 1919, while the Eighteenth Amendment was being ratified by the various states, the National Prohibition Act, or Volstead Act, was passed to enforce the amendment. This 73-section act tried to prevent trade in liquor by making it illegal to "manufacture, sell, barter, transport, import, export, deliver, furnish or possess any intoxicating liquor." Legislation therefore had also attacked the

demand side of the alcohol question by making possession illegal.

The days of speakeasies, the Feds, and Al Capone were quickly upon the nation. Admittedly, hindsight is always better than foresight, but economists would nevertheless have been able to predict many of the events that occurred during the Prohibition era. They would have used the simple concepts of supply and demand along with an analysis of the risks involved in transacting illegal business. As an introduction into the workings of economics, let's take a look at the supply and demand for liquor.

From the Supply Side

Before the passage of the Eighteenth Amendment, business people entered into the liquor business if they thought as large a profit could be made in distilling, importing, exporting, wholesaling, or retailing alcoholic beverages as could be made in some other line of commercial endeavor. Take, for example, the cost involved in distilling and wholesaling bourbon. A bourbon distillery usually consists of distilling, blending, and bottling plants; each plant contains highly specialized equipment such as stainless steel tanks (where the mash is heated to convert starch to sugars), cypress wood fer-

menting vats, large patent or column stills, and new charred white oak barrels for aging.[1] The owner has to pay for all this equipment and also must pay employees at least the amount they could earn by working for someone else in a similar job.

When the bourbon manufacturer goes to sell the product to wholesalers or even to retailers, if the manufacturer wants to eliminate the middleman, the bottles of whiskey must be provided with fancy labels that customers can use to identify this particular brand of spirits. The manufacturer has to package the trademarked bottles of bourbon in cartons so that they can be transported to the buyer. In order to make wholesalers, retailers, and the public aware of this particular product, the

[1]Old Carolina moonshiners assert that one can get by with considerably less equipment: a copper pot and worm, a section of garden hose, and some fruit jars, at a minimum. Suggested also is a rifle.

manufacturer also has to spend money on some sort of advertising. When wholesalers and retailers demand the product, the manufacturer either has to rent delivery trucks or purchase trucks. The manufacturer then has to pay the wages of the drivers. To guard against losses due to theft or accident, the manufacturer needs to purchase some form of insurance.

Before Prohibition, firms supplied an estimated 100,000 tax gallons a year at the going price of alcohol. At this price, it was not profitable for firms to expand their production of spirits. But what happened to the supply of whiskey when producing and selling it became illegal? We all know that the whiskey well did not dry up, despite the attempts of Congress to eliminate the source. Legislation against the manufacture, importation, and sale of alcohol merely changed certain aspects of the supply of that greatly demanded product. After prohibition, the cost of manufacturing and selling alcohol

suddenly shot up. For example, any distiller faced the possibility of a stiff fine or jail sentence if he were caught continuing his production process. From 1920 to 1930 alone, property worth over $136,000,000 in appraised value was seized by federal prohibition agents (71 of whom were killed while performing their duties).

One way to minimize the risk of being caught was to extend payoffs to the police and officials who were charged with preventing the illegal manufacture and sale of alcohol. In December, 1921—only 1 year after the start of Prohibition—about 100 federal agents in New York City were dismissed for the "abuse of permits for use of intoxicants." One New York speakeasy proprietor estimated that about 30 percent of his operating costs went for protection money to law enforcement agencies. Of course, it was no longer possible to buy insurance against economic losses from theft and accident. Apparently, the only insurance against theft was to pay off organized crime —the Mafia. Indeed, the Mafia's take in any individual's business dealings with alcoholic beverages was rumored to be substantial.

Briefly, as manufacturing and distributing spirits became illegal the cost of doing business increased. The amount of alcohol businesspersons were willing to supply at any given price thus had to decrease.

From the Demand Side

Even though the purchase and consumption of spirits became illegal after the passage of the Volstead Act, the demand for intoxicating beverages did not disappear. Before

Prohibition, the demand for alcohol was dictated, at least in part, by people's *preferences*, their *incomes*, and the *prices* they had to pay for what they wanted to drink. Let's look at the aspect of price first.

We all know that the price of any product or service represents what we have to give up in order to purchase it. Give up what? you might ask. Someone buying a fifth of bourbon in 1918 would have to give up $2 of purchasing power over other goods and services that were then being sold. For the price of a single fifth of bourbon, our whiskey drinker could have bought perhaps 12 bottles of beer, or 2 steak dinners, or 5 passes to the movies, or 6 new ties. The list of alternatives for the $2 purchase was large indeed. The higher the price, the more you have to give up of all other things; so you usually find that when the price of a commodity is high, you buy less of it. This is true for legal as well as illegal goods and services. Before Prohibition, the higher the price of alcohol, the less of it was sold. After Prohibition, the same relationship continued to hold.

When discussing the price of anything, we should be aware of the different qualities of the same product that can be purchased at any time. Before and after Prohibition, different qualities of alcoholic beverages could be bought. Connoisseurs could perhaps tell the difference, and those who desired high-quality alcohol were willing to pay a higher price. Those who were not so insistent upon high quality purchased cheaper spirits of a lesser quality.

Income was one of the other determinants of how much alcohol was purchased before Prohibition. Usually, the higher people's income is, the more goods and services they demand. For some, when income goes up even a little bit, the quantity demanded jumps a lot. For others, even when incomes goes up a lot, the quantity demanded doesn't change much at all. Historically we have seen that as incomes have been rising, per capita consumption of spirits has increased even more.

A third determinant of the demand for alcohol is preference. It is always correct to state that tastes determine what people buy. If I happen to prefer alcohol very very much, I may decide to forgo purchasing a large amount of other goods and services in order to satisfy my urge to drink. Even if my income is very small, I may demand a much higher quantity than, say, a multimillionaire who doesn't want to buy alcohol but who can obviously "afford" many times over what I could consume. Economists have very little to say about what determines taste. We have not come up with any generally accepted body of theory that explains how people form preferences, and consequently this text makes no attempt to present

FIGURE I-4.1

There has been a steady rise in liquor consumption since 1954. Because this graph shows total consumption rising faster than population (the line is steeper), per capita consumption is increasing. Can you explain why so much liquor was consumed in 1946? *(Source: Adapted from The Liquor Handbook, New York: C. Frank Jobson, 1969.)*

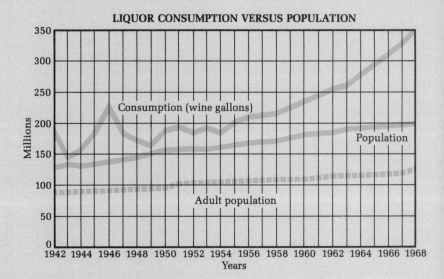

LIQUOR CONSUMPTION VERSUS POPULATION

a theory of preference formation. It's a fascinating topic, but one that few economists feel competent to discuss. Economists can assume that tastes remain constant, and then they can ask what happens if the price goes up or the income goes down. In this manner we are able to develop a usable theory that tells us what to predict in the future.

When Prohibition made consumption of alcohol illegal, certain of the determinants of the demand for spirits changed drastically. Costs that were unknown before Prohibition suddenly faced the potential drinker. When bourbon was legal, manufacturers advertised openly the various qualities that could be found in each individual product. The prices of different brands were well known and widely publicized. The courts upheld trademark laws, so consumers were fairly certain that a particular brand they bought was made by the same manufacturer. If the product was of high quality the last time it was purchased, it would probably be of the same quality the next time. Any manufacturers attempting to sell low-quality alcohol would not be successful in such a situation unless they lowered their price accordingly to induce buyers to buy their "inferior" product.

When Prohibition came, there was no more advertising. Brand names were not as numerous as before, and the possibility of fraudulent use of a brand name was now very high. A distiller couldn't very well go to the authorities to complain about some other bootlegger using his brand name. In a phrase, the cost of information about prices and quality went up drastically after alcohol production and consumption became illegal. So, even if the price of a fifth of bourbon had remained the same, the actual cost to drinkers would still have gone up because they could not be sure about what they were buying. In fact, they risked the possibility of blindness or even death from drinking bootlegged liquor. Since information was so difficult and costly to come by, bootleggers could get away with producing an occasional batch of lethal bourbon and still stay in business—something that would have been much more difficult before Prohibition. Competitors would have made sure that consumers found out about such behavior, even if bourbon drinkers didn't take the time to inform themselves.

Another cost to imbibers was the risk of being involved in a speakeasy raid. After all, consumption of spirits was illegal, even though the authorities did not arrest all whiskey drinkers during the Prohibition period. In its first 10 years, the enforcement of the National Prohibition Act resulted in about 550,000 arrests. One might ask which people were most likely to be caught in a speakeasy raid. Who were the people least able to find out about the best whiskey? Or, who were the people most likely to pay intermediaries to go to Canada to purchase high-quality Canadian whiskey? Obviously, we would not be surprised to learn that richer whiskey drinkers ended up with consistently high-quality bourbon and did not run a very high risk of being jailed for consuming it. As we shall point out on numerous occasions in this book, when the cost of information goes up, the people who suffer the most are usually those who are less well off. The poor are usually the ones who pay the most for our attempts to legislate morality.

The Final Outcome

What would economists predict as the final outcome? Would the price of liquor go up? Would the quantity demanded go down? Would society be better off? Very few things can be said with certainty in economics. However, predictive and analytical statements can be made with a high degree of reliability if qualifications are tacked on. We know that the cost of providing alcohol went up during Prohibition because of the risk of jail sentences or fines, the price of paying off the police or the Mafia to stay in production, and the difficulty of product differentiation in a market where open advertising was forbidden. Hence, if everything else had remained the same, we could state that the higher costs of production and distribution would have resulted in higher prices for alcoholic beverages, and smaller quantities of alcoholic beverages would have been demanded than before.

Everything else didn't remain the same, though. On the demand side, the implicit cost of purchasing spirits went up due to higher information costs and the possibility of being jailed or fined. In this case, if everything else had remained the same, less alcohol would have been demanded. We assume, for the moment, that income and preferences did remain the same. We see then that we could have predicted a *lower quantity both supplied and demanded* of alcohol after the passage of the Eighteenth Amendment.

A Graphic Analysis

It's fairly straightforward to translate our verbal analysis into a graph. We do that in Figure I-4.2, where we show the demand and supply of alcoholic beverages before and after prohibition. The "before" situation is represented by curves *DD* and *SS;* the "after" situation, by curves *D'D'* and *S'S'*. If our analysis is correct, what happened after prohibition was a shift of the supply curve inward because of the increased risk to the supplier, among other things. The shift in the demand curve inward is less certain. Presumably, because of

the stigma attached to the illegality of drinking, a lower quantity would be demanded at all prices, and hence the shift inward to *D'D'*. But demanders were rarely if ever punished like suppliers, so that the shift inward of the supply curve probably predominated. The market clearing, or equilibrium, price would rise from P_L to P_I because that is the price at which the relevant supply and demand curves intersect. That is to say, it is the forces underlying demand which yield these two market clearing prices. After prohibition, a smaller quantity would be both supplied and demanded at a higher price. Remember that we have to be talking in terms of constant-quality units per time period. In our case, we can talk about a constant-quality liter of alcoholic beverage per year.

The Case of Completely Inelastic Demand

What if the demand for alcoholic beverages were perfectly inelastic, as shown in Figure I-4.3? The decrease in supply from *SS* to *S'S'* would merely result in a higher price, but the quantity demanded would remain the same.

Was Society Better Off after January 16, 1920?

We cannot determine whether society was better off after January 16, 1920. People whose values included strictures against liquor were probably better off just knowing that the Eighteenth Amendment and the Volstead Act had been passed. If, in fact, the quantity of alcohol con-

FIGURE I-4.2 The Effects of Prohibition

We show the original supply and demand curves for alcoholic beverages as *SS* and *DD*. The equilibrium is established at their intersection, *E*. The market clearing price when alcoholic consumption is legal is P_L. Now prohibition comes into effect. The supply schedule shifts up to *S'S'*, and the demand schedule, presumably, shifts down to *D'D'*. A new intersection occurs at *E'*. The market clearing price after prohibition is now P_I, which is greater than P_L.

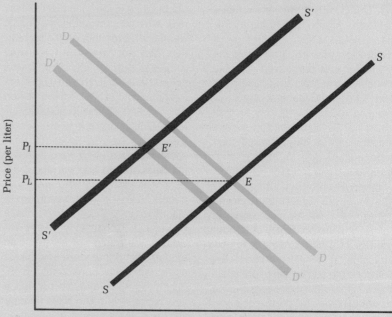

Quantity of Alcoholic Beverages (measured in constant-quality liters per year)

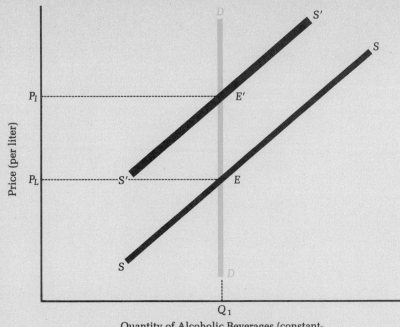

Price (per liter)

P_I - - - - - - - - - - - - - - - - - - - E′

P_L - - - - - - S′ - - - - - - - E

S′

S

D

S′

D

S

Quantity of Alcoholic Beverages (constant-
quality liters per year)

Q_1

FIGURE I-4.3 An Inelastic Demand for Alcoholic Beverages

What if the demand for alcoholic beverages were completely inelastic? Before prohibition, the intersection of the supply curve, *SS*, and the demand curve, *DD*, is at *E*, with a legal market clearing price of P_L. Now prohibition comes into effect, raising the cost of doing business and shifting the supply curve to *S′S′*. The new intersection occurs at *E′*, with a market clearing price of P_I. However, the quantity demanded does not fall, as in the example depicted in Figure I-4.2. Rather, it stays the same at Q_1 because of the inelastic demand for alcoholic beverages. This is certainly a possibility, but it isn't very probable. After all, at some point some demanders of alcoholic beverages will seek less expensive substitutes.

sumed actually declined during Prohibition, these same people could have felt even more satisfied. If less consumption of spirits led to higher productivity, less social unrest, fewer barroom brawls, and so on, we could count these effects as benefits.

As for the costs to society, we must include the resources spent on increased law enforcement, court proceedings, and keeping people in prison. Also, we must not overlook the alcohol drinker's loss of happiness caused by the smaller amounts

he or she could drink. This is not an exhaustive list of the costs and benefits to society. To determine whether or not society benefited by Prohibition, we have to deal, in the final analysis, with value judgments.

Questions for
Thought
and Discussion

1. Why would you expect the price of a product to be higher when that product is illegal than when it is legal?
2. Some observers contend that more alcoholic beverages were consumed during Prohibition than before or after. If this is indeed true, how can you explain it?
3. What are the characteristics of an illegal good that distinguish its market from that of a legal good?
4. Who gains from making a good illegal? Who loses?

Selected
References

Severn, William, *The End of the Roaring Twenties: Prohibition and Repeal,* New York: J. Messner, 1969.
Sinclair, Andrew, *Era of Excess: A Social History of the Prohibition Movement,* New York: Harper & Row, 1964.

TWO

THE AMERICAN ECONOMY
AND ITS PROBLEMS

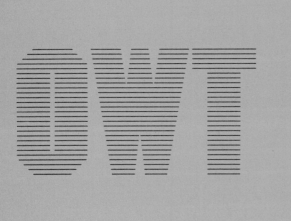

Measuring the Economy's Performance: National Income and Product

The American economy is gigantic and complex. It is composed of millions of businesses and even more millions of households. Workers do millions of different jobs, and there are innumerable ways households can spend their income. In this chapter, and in several following chapters, we will be concerned with **macroeconomics.** The study of macroeconomics entails the study of aggregates, that is, the total values of certain variables, such as income, employment, unemployment, and the like, for the entire economy. Macroeconomics concerns itself with the issues of unemployment and rising prices, whereas **microeconomics** concerns itself with the behavior of individual households, firms, and markets.

To study the aggregates in our economy, we have to both identify and define them. We also have to be able to measure the aggregates. This is where the study of **national income accounting** comes into play because it involves attempting to measure things like national income and its components, which we will discuss throughout this chapter and in the issue that follows. In addition, economists as scientists cannot know whether their theories are worthwhile and accurate until they test those theories with actual data.

Additionally, policymakers need information on our economy's performance in order to implement any given economic policy. This information may consist of such things as the unemployment rate, the rate of price rises (inflation), and changes in the total production of the economy. There are several ways that we can go about measuring total production and total income for the entire nation. Let us first see how production and income are related.

National Income ≡ National Product

What would a good definition of **national income** be? If you answered "The total of all individuals' income," you would be right. But all income is actually a payment for something, whether it be wages paid for labor services, rent and depletion to owners of natural resources, or interest and depreciation to owners of capital; therefore, national income is better defined as the total *cost* of producing the entire output of *final* goods and services.

Now what would your definition of **national product** be? Wouldn't it involve the aggregate of everything that was produced? Yes, it would. National product, then, can be formally defined as the total monetary value of all national output of final goods and services. National income, on the other hand, consists of the receipts from the sale of all the products comprising national output. National income must always equal national product, and this is what is illustrated by Figure 4-1. It shows the **circular flow of income** and product in any economy.

The Circular Flow of Income and Product

The concept of a circular flow of income involves two very simple principles: (1) In every economic exchange the seller receives exactly the same amount that the buyer spends, and (2) expenditures and resource payments flow in the opposite direction to products and to the services used to make those products (factor services).

In the simple economy presented in Figure 4-1, there are only two participants: businesses

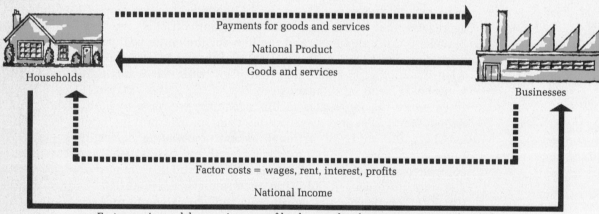

Payments for goods and services

National Product

Goods and services

Households

Businesses

Factor costs = wages, rent, interest, profits

National Income

Factor services = labor services, use of land, control and management, use of capital

FIGURE 4-1 **Circular Flow of Income, Or Why National Income ≡ National Product**

This diagram shows a simple, two-sector economy comprised of just households and businesses. Households sell their factor services to businesses in return for which they obtain wages, rent, interest, and profits, which are called factor costs. This is national income. On the top of the diagram, we see that businesses provide households with goods and services (products) in return for which businesses receive payments. The broken lines are money flows, and the solid lines are real flows—goods and factor services. The nation's flow of output in the upper half of the diagram must equal the nation's flow of income in the lower half. (Actually, profits act as the residual, or balancing, item that brings about this identity.)

and households. It is further assumed that firms sell their entire output immediately to households and that households spend their entire income immediately on consumer products. Households receive their income by renting out whatever factors of production they own, such as labor services.

There are a number of things that may puzzle you about the simplified circular-flow-of-income diagram in Figure 4-1. We have listed profits as a factor cost. The commonsense view is that profits are not part of the cost of producing goods and services, but profits are indeed a part of this cost because the owners of capital anticipate being rewarded for providing that capital. Their reward is profit. If there were no expectation of profit, some owners would consume their stock of capital rather than invest it. That is why we consider profits a cost of doing business.

We have obviously simplified the world by leaving out the government sector, the foreign sector, taxes, investment, and depreciation. We will explain these elements in this chapter. Now let us try to get a clearer picture by looking at the makeup of the most widely used measure of total, or aggregate, economic activity: **gross national product.**

Gross National Product

Gross national product (GNP) represents the total money value of the nation's annual final product, or output. We will formally define GNP as the total market value of all final goods and services produced in an economy during a year period. We must specify a time period when we refer to any measure of a flow. We discussed the distinction between stocks and flows in Chapter 2, but it is worthwhile to mention it again. A nation produces at a certain rate, and you receive income at a certain rate.

It might be at a rate of $5,000 per year or $50,000 per year. In any event, the income you receive is a flow. You must contrast this with, for example, your total accumulated savings, which is a stock measured at a point in time, not across time. Implicit in just about everything we deal with in this chapter, and throughout the rest of the macroeconomic section of the book, is a time period—usually a year. All the measures of national product and income are specified as rates measured in billions of dollars per year.

As we have noted, GNP measures the value of *final* output; it ignores intermediate goods, or goods used up entirely in the production of final goods, because to include them would be to double-count. The way to understand this is to define GNP as the total of all *value added* at each stage of production. We can see what "value added" means by looking at Table 4-1. Here we show the respective sales values and values added at each stage in the production of a donut. You can see that the value added is equal to the sum of all incomes generated from the production of that donut. Those incomes are equal to profit, wages, rent, and interest.

There are two different ways of computing gross national product: the **expenditure approach,** in which we add up the dollar value at current market prices of all final goods and services produced by the nation's economy, or the **income approach,** in which we add up all the national income, including wages, interest, rent, and profits. Let's first look at the so-called expenditure approach.

Deriving GNP with the Expenditure Approach

How do we spend our income? As households or individuals we do that through consumption expenditure (C), which falls into three catego-

Table 4-1 **Sales Value and Value Added in Cents Per Donut at Each Stage of Production**

(1) STAGE OF PRODUCTION	(2) SALES VALUE	(3) VALUE ADDED
Stage 1: Fertilizer and seed	$0.01	$0.01
Stage 2: Growing wheat	0.02	$0.01
Stage 3: Flour milling	0.04	0.02
Stage 4: Donut baking	0.10	0.06
Stage 5: Donut retailing	0.15	0.05
Total sales value	$0.32	Total value added $0.15

Stage 1: A farmer purchases a penny's worth of fertilizer and seed that are used as factors of production in growing wheat.

Stage 2: The farmer grows the wheat, harvests it, and sells it to a miller for 2¢. Thus, we see that the farmer has added 1¢ worth of value. That 1¢ represents income paid in the form of rent, wages, interest, and profit by the farmer.

Stage 3: The flour miller purchases the wheat for 2¢, and adds 2¢ to the value added; that is, there is 2¢ for him as income to be paid as rent, wages, interest, and profit. He sells the ground wheat flour to a donut baking company.

Stage 4: The donut baking company buys the flour for 4¢ and adds 6¢ as the value added. It then sells the donut to the final retailer.

Stage 5: The donut retailer sells fresh hot donuts at 15¢ apiece, thus creating additional value of 5¢.

We see that the total sales value resulting from the production of one donut was 32¢, but the total value added was 15¢, which is exactly equal to the retail price. The total value added is equal to the sum of all income payments, including payments to rent, wages, interest, and profit.

ries: **durable consumer goods, nondurable consumer goods,** and **services.** Durable goods are arbitrarily defined as items that last more than a year; these include automobiles, furniture, and household appliances. Nondurable goods are all the rest, such as food and gasoline. Services are just what the name suggests, medical care, education, and the like.

You should be aware of the fact that there are some goods and services which do not pass through the marketplace. For example, food grown on the farm for household consumption by the farmers' families is certainly a consumption expenditure, but it does not show up in the usual way. In fact, government statisticians have to estimate it to put it into gross national product. Additionally, the implicit rental value[1] of owner-occupied homes is also estimated and put into personal consumption expenditures (rental payments on apartments and the like are automatically included).

Government Expenditures

In addition to personal consumption expenditures, there are government expenditures on goods and services (G). Generally, we value

[1]If you own a home, you do not actually pay rent. However, whatever you would have to pay to some other owner of that same house is called the implicit rental value.

goods and services at the price at which they are sold. But many government goods and services are provided at no direct cost to the consumer. Therefore, we cannot use their market value when computing GNP. The value of these goods is considered to be equal to their cost. For example, the value of a new road is considered to be equal to its construction cost and is included in the GNP for the year it was built.

Gross Private Domestic Investment

Now we come to an expenditure that we haven't yet talked about—**investment** (I) on the part of business firms. We have to be careful when using the term "investment" because it has one meaning in everyday life but has another when it refers to the national economy. You know that an investment occurs when you buy a stock or a bond or a piece of property. However, from our national-accounting point of view, that is not an investment but merely a *transfer* of asset ownership among individuals. For our purpose here, we will define investment as the addition to or replacement of physical assets that can add to the productive capacity of the nation. Investment, therefore, includes new capital goods, such as factories and machines. It also includes newly built housing since the consumption of the shelter provided by a house lasts for a long time after it is built. Note the new housing is the only good bought by consumers that is included in *"I."* Investment also includes changes in **inventories.** Inventories are defined as finished goods a firm has on hand for sale at a later date. An inventory is a stock concept that is measured at a moment in time. The investment aspect of inventories is the flow to or from that stock, that is, any increase or decrease in it over time.

The Foreign Sector

To get an accurate representation of gross national product, we must include the foreign sector, which we treat at length in Chapter 14. We, as Americans, purchase foreign goods called imports. The goods that foreigners purchase from us are our exports. To get an idea of the increase in total expenditures from the foreign sector, we subtract the value of our imports from the value of our exports to get net exports for a year:

Net exports = total exports − total imports

To get an idea of the relationship between C, G, and I, just look at Figure 4-2. Here we show gross national product, personal consumption expenditures, government purchases, gross private domestic investment, and net exports from 1929 to 1975.

Note that when we sum up the expenditures of the household, government, business, and foreign sectors, we get GNP, which is sometimes called GNE, or gross national expenditure.

Getting Rid of the Gross

We have used the terms gross national product and gross private domestic investment without really indicating what "gross" means. The dictionary defines it as "without deductions," as opposed to "net." Deductions for what? you might ask. Deductions for something we call **depreciation** is the answer. In the course of a year, machines and structures wear out as they are used in the production of national product. For example, houses deteriorate as they are used, and machines need repairs or they will fall apart and stop working. Most capital, or durable, goods, if not all, therefore suffer a form of depreciation. Expenditures on repairs and other means of replacing the existing capital stock are often netted out of gross national product to arrive at a figure called **net national product** (NNP), which we define as:

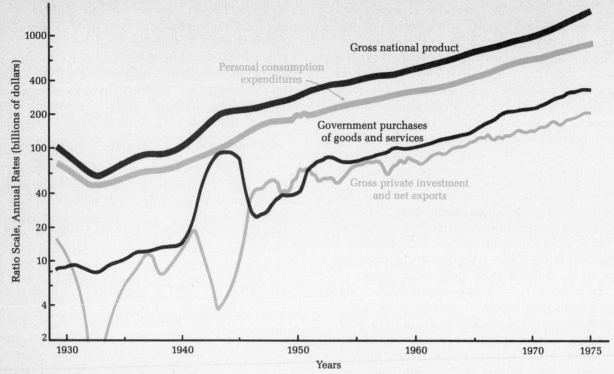

FIGURE 4-2 **GNP and Its Components**

Here we see a time-series display of gross national product, personal consumption expenditures, government purchases, and gross private domestic investment with net exports for the years 1929 to 1975. (*Source:* U.S. Dept. of Commerce. Data for 1975 are preliminary.)

NNP = GNP − depreciation (capital consumption allowances)

Depreciation is also called a capital consumption allowance because it is the amount of the capital stock that has been consumed over a year. Two other ways of defining NNP are:

NNP = C + gross I + G + net exports − depreciation

NNP = C + net I + G + net exports

Net investment measures changes in our capital stock over time and is positive nearly every year. Since depreciation does not vary dramatically as a percentage of GNP, you will get a similar picture about what is happening to our economy by looking at either one—NNP or GNP.

Let us now turn to the second approach of calculating GNP.

GNP with the Income Approach

We can calculate GNP in terms of the flow of costs or payments that firms make in order to produce the things they sell to households. We previously defined national income as the total amount of national factor payments to the owners of the factors of production that are utilized. Stated in other words, national income is the total income earned by the owners of resources who put their factors of production to work. Using this approach we have four categories:

1. *Wages* The most important category is, of course, wages, including wages and salaries and other forms of labor income, such as income in kind, incentive payments, and so on. We also count Social Security taxes (both the employees' and the employers' "contributions").
2. *Interest* Here, interest payments do not equal the sum of payments for the use of money capital in a year. Rather, interest is expressed in net rather than in gross terms. In other words, the interest component of national income is the difference between interest paid by the domestic business sector and interest received by that sector from all other sectors (plus the net interest received from other countries).
3. *Rent* Rent is all income earned by individuals for the use of their real (nonmonetary) assets, such as farms, houses, and stores. As we stated previously, we have to include here the implicit rental value of owner-occupied houses. Also included in this category are royalties received from copyrights and patents and things like oil and gas wells.
4. *Profits* Our last category includes total gross (pretax) corporate profits and so-called proprietors' income. Proprietors' income is that income earned from the operation of unincorporated businesses, which include sole proprietorships, partnerships, and producers' cooperatives.

These four components, added together, give us national income at factor cost. To get gross national income, which will then be equal to gross national product, we have to add two other components: **indirect business taxes** and depreciation.

Indirect Business Taxes

Excise taxes, sales taxes, and property taxes incurred by businesspersons make up what are called indirect business taxes. Think of it this way: Businesses are actually acting as the government's agent when they collect a sales tax. They collect it from you and turn it over to the government. The tax is a business expense, but the real burden is likely to be on the customer, who pays a higher price. Because of this, such indirect taxes are included in gross national income as a cost item.

Depreciation

Just as we had to look at depreciation in figuring out why NNP differed from GNP, to go from net national income to gross national income, we must add depreciation. Depreciation can be thought of as that portion of the current year's GNP which is used to replace physical capital consumed in the process of production. Since somebody is paid to do the replacement, depreciation must be added as a component of gross national income.

The last two components of GNP are called nonincome expense items.

Look at Table 4-2. Here we show a comparison between gross national product and gross national income for 1975. Whether you decide to use the expenditure point of view or the income point of view, you will come out with the same number. There are sometimes statistical discrepancies, but they are usually extremely small.

Now let us consider the other variants of GNP and GNI.

Table 4-2 Gross National Product and Gross National Income, 1975 (in Billions of Dollars Per Year)

By using the two different methods of computing the output of the economy, we come up with gross national product and gross national income, which are, by necessity, equal. One viewpoint is through expenditures, or the flow of product; the other viewpoint is through income, or the flow of costs.

EXPENDITURE POINT OF VIEW—PRODUCT FLOW		INCOME POINT OF VIEW—COST FLOW	
Expenditures by Different Sectors:		National Income (at Factor Cost):	$1,168
Household sector		Salaries/wages	
Personal consumption expenses	$ 938	All salaries/wages and supplemental compensation to employees	886
Government sector		Rent	
Payments for goods and services	339	All rental income of individuals plus implicit rent on owner-occupied dwellings	27
Business sector		Interest	
Gross private investment—domestic	147	Net interest paid by business	72
Foreign sector		Profit	
Net exports—goods and services	9	Business, professional, and farm income Corporate profits before taxes deducted	97
		Expenses not classified as income	265
		Indirect business taxes	138
		Depreciation (capital consumption allowance)	127
Gross national product	$1,433	Gross national income	$1,433

Source: U.S. Department of Commerce, preliminary data, 2d quarter.

The Rest of National Income Accounting

Table 4-2 shows the remaining components of the national income accounts. We have already defined gross national product and net national product. The difference is depreciation, or capital consumption allowances.

National Income

We know that net national income represents the total market value of goods and services available for both "consumption," used in a broader sense here to mean "resource exhausting," and net additions to the economy's stock of capital. NNP does not, however, represent the income available to individuals within that economy because it includes indirect business taxes, such as sales taxes, which we talked about in the last section. We therefore deduct these indirect business taxes from NNP to arrive at the figure for all factor payments to resource owners. The result is national income, or NI.

Personal Income

National income does not actually represent what is available to individuals to spend because some people obtain income for which they have provided no concurrent good or service and others earn income but do not receive it. In the former category are mainly recipients of **transfer payments** from the government, such as welfare, food stamps, and the like. These payments represent shifts of funds within the economy by way of the government, where no good or service is rendered in exchange. For the other category, income earned but not received, the most obvious examples are undistributed corporate profits that are plowed back into the business, contributions to social insurance, and corporate income taxes. When transfer payments are added and when income earned but not received is subtracted, we end up with **personal income,** or PI.

Disposable Personal Income

Everybody knows that you do not get to take home all your salary. To get **disposable personal income,** DPI, subtract all personal income taxes from personal income. This is the income that individuals actually have available for consuming or not consuming (saving).

We have completed our somewhat complicated rundown of the different ways GNP can be computed and of the different variants of national income and product. What we have not yet even touched on is the difference between national income measured in this year's dollars and national income representing "real" goods and services. This is an important distinction to make, especially now that we have significant increases in all prices every year.

Correcting GNP

If an eight-track stereo tape costs $5 this year, 10 tapes will have a market value of $50. If next year they cost $10 each, the same 10 tapes will have a market value of $100. There will have been no increase in the total quantity of tapes, but the market value will have doubled. Apply this to every single good and service produced and sold in the United States and you realize that GNP, measured in "current" dollars, may not be a true indication of economic activity. After all, we are really interested in variations in the real output of the economy. What we have to do, then, is correct GNP (and just about everything else we look at) for changes in overall prices. Basically, we need to generate an index which approximates the changes in overall prices and then divide that estimate into the value of output in current dollars to get the value of output in what are called **constant dollars.** This price-corrected GNP is called *real* GNP. Current price indices in the United States are compiled by the Department of Labor, Bureau of Labor Statistics, and have a 1967 base year. We present, in Figure 4-3, deflated, or price-corrected GNP (real GNP), with a base year of 1967. In Chapter 7, when we talk about inflation and how to measure it, we will go into some detail about the actual price indices used in the United States. However, correcting for prices is not the only analytical problem we should be concerned with. Another one involves how many people there are to share in GNP.

Per Capita GNP

If "real" GNP over a 10-year period went up 100 percent, you might immediately jump to the conclusion that the material well-being of the economy had increased by that amount. But what if, during the same period, population increased by 200 percent? Then what would you say? Certainly, the amount of GNP per person, or per capita, would have fallen, even though total deflated, or real, GNP would have risen. What we must do to account not only for price changes but also for population

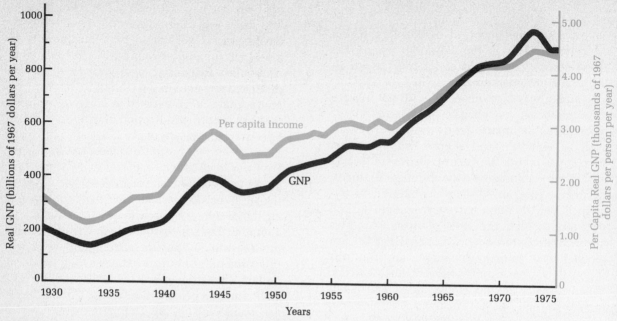

FIGURE 4-3   **GNP and Real Per Capita GNP over Time**

Here we see real GNP from 1929 to 1975 expressed in constant 1967 dollars. That is, the base year is 1967. We also put in the same diagram real GNP per capita, which is merely real GNP divided by the population for each year. *(Source: U.S. Dept. of Commerce.)*

changes is first deflate GNP and then divide by the total population, doing this for each year. This is what we have done in the bottom line of Figure 4-3. We show deflated, or real, GNP per capita in the United States over a 40-year period. If we were to look at certain underdeveloped countries, we would find that in many cases even though real GNP has risen over the past several decades, real GNP per capita has remained constant because population growth ate up all the gains in total output.

The difficulties in using GNP as an indicator of social well-being do not end here. In fact, there has been a running battle over the use of GNP statistics when recounting the material gains of our economy. What else is wrong with this measure, and what should be done to correct it? That is the topic of our next issue.

Definitions of New Terms

Macroeconomics: The study of economic aggregates, their movements, and the causes of their movements. In other words, the study of the economy as it functions as a whole.

Microeconomics: The study of the behavior of the individual economic agents in our society.

National Income Accounting: The science of measuring the theoretical concepts used in the study of macroeconomics. Specifically, national income accounting involves attempts at measuring national income and its components.

National Income: The total payment or cost to the economy of producing the entire output of final goods and services.

National Product: The total dollar value at current prices of all the final goods and services that are produced in a 1-year period.

Circular Flow of Income: The schematic representation of how real goods and services move among firms, households, and the government and the resulting receipts and payments from these movements.

Gross National Product (GNP): The total market value of all final goods and services produced by the entire economy in a 1-year period.

Expenditure Approach: A way of computing GNP by adding up the dollar value of current market prices of all final goods and services; to be contrasted with the income approach.

Income Approach: A way of measuring GNP by adding up all components of national income, including wages, interest, rent, and profits.

Durable Consumer Goods: Goods, used by consumers, that have a life span, that is, goods which endure and can give utility over a longer period of time.

Nondurable Consumer Goods: Goods, used by consumers, that are used up more or less immediately.

Services: Commodities purchased by consumers that do not have physical characteristics. Examples of services are those purchased from doctors, lawyers, dentists, repair personnel, housecleaners, and educators.

Investment: The creation of new capital goods, such as factories and machines, that can yield production and hence consumption in the future. Also included in this definition are changes in business inventories.

Inventories: The stock of finished goods that a firm holds over from one period to another.

Depreciation: Reduction in the value of capital goods over a 1-year period due to physical wear and tear and also to obsolescence.

Net National Product (NNP): GNP minus depreciation.

Indirect Business Taxes: All business taxes except the corporation tax on profits. Indirect business taxes include sales and business property taxes.

Transfer Payments: Payments to individuals for which no goods or services are exchanged in return. Examples are food stamps, unemployment benefits, and Social Security benefits.

Personal Income (PI): The amount of income that households actually receive before they pay personal income taxes.

Disposable Personal Income (DPI): Personal income after personal income taxes have been paid.

Constant Dollars: Dollars expressed in terms of purchasing power using a particular year as the base or standard of comparison.

1. National income accounting is the science (and art) by which economists attempt to statistically measure the variables with which they are concerned in their study of macroeconomics.

2. In any economy, there is a circular flow of income because every economic exchange involves a seller of a product or service who receives a payment in return. Thus, goods and services flow in one direction, and payments flow in the other direction.

3. One of the most often used concepts in national income accounting is gross national product, which is defined as the total market value of all *final* goods and services. The stress on "final" is important to avoid the double counting of so-called intermediate goods that are used in the production of other goods.

4. We can compute GNP by using the expenditure approach or the income approach. In the former, we merely add up the dollar value of all final goods and services, and in the latter we add up the payments for all those goods and services, or wages, interest, rent, and profits.

5. It is difficult to measure the market value of government expenditures because generally government-provided goods are not sold at a market clearing price. We have used the device of valuing government expenditures at their cost to include them in our measure of GNP.

6. It is important to realize that investment does not occur when there is merely a transfer of assets among individuals; rather, it occurs only when new productive capacity for the future is generated, such as when a machine is built to be used later.

7. Part of our capital stock is worn out or becomes obsolete every year. To take account of the expenditures made merely to replace such depreciation, we subtract depreciation from GNP to come up with net national product or NNP.

8. GNP has a number of components, including personal income, disposable personal income, and so on.

9. To correct for price changes, we deflate GNP in terms of constant dollars to come up with real GNP. To take account of rising population, we then correct for population and come up with real GNP per capita.

1. Is it possible to distinguish between final goods and intermediate goods?
2. What would happen if we double-counted when we tried to measure GNP?
3. What is the difference between gross private investment and net private investment? Which measure of investment would you be interested in if you were analyzing the growth of an economy or its potential growth?
4. Why do we include changes in business inventories as part of investment?

5. How could net private domestic investment be negative in 1933? What would happen if net private domestic investment remained negative for many years?

6. The following data are for a hypothetical economy:

$$Consumption = \$400 \text{ Billion}$$
$$Government \text{ spending} = \$350 \text{ B}$$
$$Gross \text{ private domestic investment} = \$150 \text{ B}$$
$$Exports = \$150 \text{ B}$$
$$Imports = \$100 \text{ B}$$
$$Depreciation = \$ 50 \text{ B}$$
$$Indirect \text{ business taxes} = \$ 25 \text{ B}$$

(a) Based on the data, what is the value of GNP? ____ NNP? ____ NI? ____ .

(b) Suppose that in the next year exports increase to $175 B, imports increase to $200 B, and consumption falls to $350 B. What will GNP be in this year? ____

(c) If the value of depreciation (capital consumption allowance) should ever exceed that of gross private domestic investment, how would this affect the future productivity of the nation?

Selected References

Abraham, William I., *National Income and Economic Accounting*, Englewood Cliffs, N.J.: Prentice-Hall, 1969.

Rosen, Sam, *National Income and Other Social Accounts*, New York: Holt, Rinehart and Winston, 1972.

U.S. Department of Commerce, *The Economic Accounts of the United States: Retrospect and Prospect*, Washington, D.C.: U.S. Government Printing Office, 1971.

Does GNP Mean Gross National Promise?

ARE WE MEASURING THE WRONG THING?

National Income Accounting and Human Happiness

The United States Department of Commerce defines GNP simply as "the market value of the output of final goods and services produced by the nation's economy." But critics of the economic situation in the United States define GNP as "gross national promise," indicating that it does not measure what is actually happening in the United States. We can all agree that no measure of a nation's production or output, no matter how perfect, can be used to assess the happiness or satisfaction of its citizens. There is no way we can equate human welfare with either economic goods and services or the satisfaction derived from them. The best we can hope for is a measure of material well-being based on how much the population consumes. After all, it is consumption, not production, that generates satisfaction.

Noting the many deficiencies in GNP and the national income accounts, several economists have suggested that we come up with a better measure to gauge economic growth and improvements in economic well-being. At the end of this issue we will present one such measure.

More Corrections for GNP

In Chapter 4 we saw that several adjustments have to be made in our computation of GNP. Let us now consider some items that are not taken into account by government statisticians.

Do-It-Yourself Activities

When you decide to fix your own car, you engage in the production of a service that is not included in GNP. Had you decided to take your car to a garage, that same service would have been included in GNP because you would have paid a mechanic. Services in the home represent the biggest category under this heading of what is left out of GNP.

Housewives' Services

The value of the services performed by women in the home is substantial,

as can be seen in Table I-5.1. These services range from cooking, to food buying, to being a practical nurse. In fact, if an individual marries a paid housekeeper and that housekeeper leaves the labor force, GNP will fall.

However, the services of non-working husbands or wives are becoming less significant with respect to computing GNP. As more services are contracted for with regular businesses and with individuals selling those services, they become part of GNP (assuming, of course, the income is reported). Cases in point are the purchases of laundry services and convenience foods. Since World War II, the purchase of household activities has increased markedly, so some of the growth in measured real GNP has been exaggerated relative to previous growth before this phenomenon occurred.

Illegal Activities

A large number of illegal activities do not enter into our national income accounts. These include, but are not limited to, narcotics, gambling, bootlegging, and prostitution. Since these activities generate satisfaction, they certainly do contribute to the well-being of the consumers. It is impossible to estimate their total market value, but it is probably in the neighborhood of $50 billion.

Income Never Reported

A number of economic activities generate income that, in principle, should be included in our national income accounts. However, for purposes of tax evasion, some people do not report this income. The general term for this activity is "skimming." It is alleged, for example, that professionals (doctors, lawyers, and so forth), often skim by not reporting a certain percentage of cash payments received from patients or clients.

Measures of Satisfaction

Assuming we were able to include every single economic activity that should be included to measure real GNP, we could come up with a perfect measure of output, or production. However, output does not nec-

Table I-5.1

Value of a Housewife's Services—1974–1975

The market value of housewives' services is not insignificant. In this particular survey, the estimated value per week was $306.82.

SERVICE	HOURS PER WEEK	VALUE OF SERVICE PER HOUR	VALUE OF SERVICE PER WEEK
Nursemaid	44.5	$2.50	$111.25
Housekeeper	17.5	3.50	61.25
Cook	13.1	3.50	45.85
Dishwasher	6.2	2.25	13.95
Laundress	5.9	2.60	15.34
Food buyer	3.3	3.75	12.38
Chauffeur	2.0	4.00	8.00
Gardener	2.3	6.00	13.80
Maintenance "man"	1.7	6.00	10.20
Seamstress	1.3	4.00	5.20
Dietician	1.2	5.50	6.60
Practical nurse	0.6	5.00	3.00
Total	99.6		$306.82

Source: Chase Manhattan Bank of New York. Data are based on updated rates of pay in the New York area for the occupations listed.

essarily equal satisfaction, and a higher level of output may not be associated with a higher level of satisfaction. For example, if output were to increase by 10 percent but population were to increase by 20 percent, the amount of output available per person would fall. As we noted in Chapter 4, we can correct for this problem by dividing real GNP by population to obtain per capita real GNP, but even then we are faced with another problem.

What if the rich get richer and the poor get poorer as GNP grows? Has the general level of satisfaction increased? Many people would say no because the distribution of income, even though we have no way of taking it into account, must surely play an important part in determining the level of satisfaction of society.

And what about leisure? Surely it is a scarce good. As such, it has value and generates satisfaction. Although it has recently leveled off, in the United States, the amount of leisure time has been growing since World War II. Figure I-5.1 shows that the number of hours worked on average fell by some 18 percent from 1943 to mid 1971. This increased leisure certainly has added to our satisfaction, but it is not included in any measure of the national income accounts.

Gross National Pollution

Environmental concern in the 1970s has focused attention on a large deficiency in our measurement of the nation's economic well-being. Numerous critics of the environmental degradation in our nation maintain that our standard definition of GNP is misleading. In fact, some regard GNP as a symbol of everything that is wrong with America. The idea is that if GNP growth were slowed or even halted, economic output would fall but so would pollution. Dr. Arthur F. Burns, Chairman of the Board of Governors of the Federal Reserve System, told Congress that he would like to see GNP adjusted to "take account of the depreciation in our environment." He indicated that there should be a "proper recording of the minuses as well as the pluses." In Burns' opinion, GNP, properly adjusted, would be a good deal lower than it now appears.

FIGURE I-5.1 Average Weekly Hours Worked, 1943–1975

Up until 1970 there was a fairly steady decline in the average weekly hours worked in America. In other words, Americans were enjoying more leisure as their real incomes rose. Recently, however, the trend has leveled off. (*Source:* Bureau of Labor Statistics.)

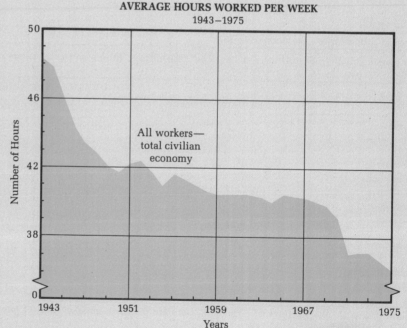

AVERAGE HOURS WORKED PER WEEK
1943–1975

All workers—
total civilian
economy

Number of Hours

Years

The trade-off between production and pollution is represented in Figure I-5.2. On the horizontal axis (output) are measured "good" goods, and on the vertical axis (pollution) are measured "bad" goods. The upward-sloping line is an odd sort of production-possibilities curve: Instead of having to give up more of one good when we produce more of the other, we get more of both. But we are not happy with an increase in the "bad" good.

A proper assessment of economic performance should probably include some type of subtraction for all the damages (expressed in economic terms) done by pollution. Moreover, we probably should not include the cost of pollution abatement in the measure of economic well-being because these services are not desired for their own sake.

Neither is police protection. Most people do not get any direct satisfaction or utility from services that are carried on in order to reduce illegal activities. With regard to our well-being, the inclusion of police protection in the national product is an inappropriate entry. Consider what would happen to our general level of happiness if, all of a sudden, robberies were to increase fivefold: We would need increased police protection; we would have to pay for it with additional taxes; and we would therefore have lower material well-being. The reduction would not show up in the national income accounts because the taxes would be used to pay the salaries of additional police personnel.

Given all the deficiencies in our national income accounts, is it possible to come up with a new measure of GNP? Yes, say two innovating experts in the field, James Tobin (whose biography follows this issue) and William Nordhaus.

MEW: A New Measure of GNP

Professors Tobin and Nordhaus a few years back presented their view of what GNP would look like if it were to actually take account of many of the deficiencies we have outlined. They called it "measure of economic welfare," or MEW. You get MEW by modifying GNP in three ways:

1. Subtracting certain costs or "bads," such as pollution
2. Excluding "regrettable necessities," such as police services
3. Adding activities that are not

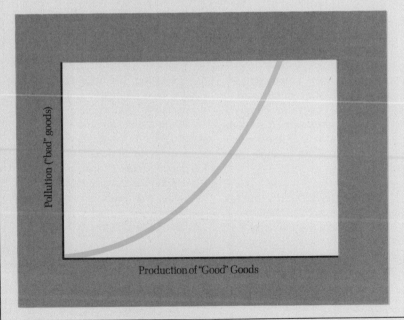

FIGURE I-5.2 The Pollution Costs of Increased Production

This graph represents a peculiar production-possibilities frontier since more "good" goods are associated with more of the "bad" goods—pollution. At very small rates of production, there may be little or no pollution. Nature can handle it in small doses. However, at higher rates of production, more pollution results, increasing even more rapidly than output.

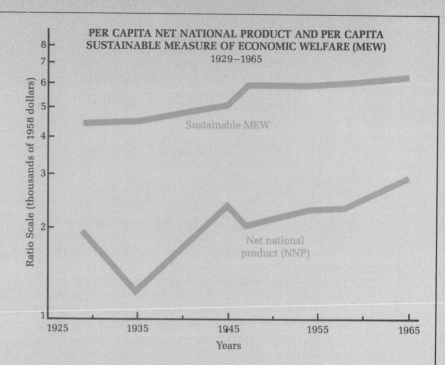

PER CAPITA NET NATIONAL PRODUCT AND PER CAPITA SUSTAINABLE MEASURE OF ECONOMIC WELFARE (MEW)
1929–1965

Ratio Scale (thousands of 1958 dollars)

Sustainable MEW

Net national product (NNP)

Years

FIGURE I-5.3

As we can see, the measure of economic welfare, MEW, is much greater than net national product, NNP. However, the growth rate of MEW is significantly less than the growth rate of NNP.

included in GNP, such as household services, home repairs, and leisure

Figure I-5.3 shows MEW compared with NNP. The results are interesting. MEW has been growing—but at a considerably lower rate (1.1 percent per year) than per capita real GNP (1.7 percent per year).

Using MEW instead of GNP is considered by many to be a step in the right direction. MEW is a good measure of consumption, but it is not, unfortunately, a measure of economic welfare. The two concepts are related, but economic welfare

depends on the amount of total satisfaction that each of us actually receives from our consumption. Nordhaus and Tobin are certainly aware of these problems. The intent and the conclusions of their study are best summarized in their own words:

We recognize that our proposal is controversial on conceptual and theoretical grounds and that many of the numerical expedients in its execution are dubious. Nevertheless, the challenge to economists to produce relevant welfare-oriented measures seems

compelling enough to justify some risk-taking. We hope that others will be challenged, or provoked, to tackle the problem with different assumptions, more refined procedures, and better data. We hope also that further investigations will be concerned with the distribution, as well as the mean value, of a measure of economic welfare, an aspect we have not been able to consider.[1]

[1]William Nordhaus and James Tobin, "Is Growth Obsolete?", in *Economic Growth*, Fiftieth Anniversary Colloquium, vol. 5, New York: National Bureau of Economic Research, 1972, p. 26.

Questions for Thought and Discussion

1. Do you think that the statistical measurement problems in deciding what MEW is are significant? If they are, is MEW still a better measure of economic welfare than GNP?
2. How would your ideal measure of economic welfare be constructed, assuming there were no problems of statistical measurement with any of its components?

Selected References

Goldsmith, Raymond and Christopher Saunders (eds.), *The Measurement of National Wealth,* International Association for Research, in Income and Wealth, ser. VIII, Chicago: Quadrangle Books, 1959.

Lekachman, Robert, *National Income and the Public Welfare,* New York: Random House, 1972.

Economic Growth and Income Redistribution

JAMES TOBIN

Former Member, Council of Economic Advisers (CEA) 1961–1962

When asked to make sacrifices for the defense of their nation, the American people have always responded. Perhaps some day a national administration will muster the courage to ask the American people to tax themselves for social justice and domestic tranquility.

Sentiments such as these appealed to George McGovern during the 1972 campaign when he called upon their author, 54-year-old Yale professor of economics, James Tobin, to help frame a viable economic program that would broaden the candidate's platform. Among the group of McGovern's advisers, Tobin was, in the words of *Time,* "the intellectual giant" and the economist who had "most influenced McGovern personally."

Best known for his schemes for income redistribution through changes in the tax system, former CEA member James Tobin devised for McGovern a negative income tax plan based on his article in *Agenda for the*

Nation, "Raising the Incomes of the Poor" (1968). In that article he proposed that all tax exemptions, exclusions, and standard deductions be eliminated and replaced with a system of taxation whereby every individual making under $2,250 would be reimbursed one-third of the difference by the federal government, and every individual making over $2,250 would pay one-third of the excess in taxes. Such a program could be financed, Tobin thought, through "the normal growth of tax revenues" and government funds freed by peace in Vietnam.

Tobin has written many other articles on income redistribution and economic growth. Aside from his recommendation with William Nordhaus for a new "measure of economic welfare" to replace GNP, the traditional measure of economic growth, Tobin has written on the costs and benefits of faster economic growth. In a 1969 article coauthored with Leonard Ross, Tobin proposed the creation of a "National Youth Endowment" that would make government credit available to the young for educational purposes and shift the burden of cost from parents to the students themselves. More recently, in September 1974, Tobin criticized the Nixon administration's economic policies and called for a new "social contract" to help reduce the rate of inflation. Among other proposals, he suggested that workers' take-home pay could be increased without inflationary consequences by reforming the Social Security tax structure to make it more equitable and progressive.

Educated at Harvard, Tobin worked as an economist for the Office of Price Administration and the War Production Board before joining the Yale faculty in 1950. He served as a consultant to the Board of Governors of the Federal Reserve System from 1955 to 1956. In early 1961, President Kennedy appointed Tobin to the Council of Economic Advisers, where he stayed until August 1962. Like other economists associated with the Kennedy administration, Tobin has been a firm believer in what has become known as the "new economics," which is actually based on the Keynesian idea that economic growth can be stimulated and unemployment reduced by a combination of tax cuts and deficit spending. Tobin discussed elements of this strategy in his 1966 book *National Economic Policy.*

In his latest book, *The New Economics: One Decade Older* (1974), Tobin reassesses the idea of the "new economics" and attempts a qualified defense of the economic policies of the 1960s. Though admitting that the "new economics" was "oversold," he asserts that the economic growth of the early 1960s "did more to lift the incomes of the poor and disadvantaged than any conceivable redistribution program." The "new economics" provided the basis for successful policy through 1965, he believes; "then things began to fall apart." Tobin attributes the federal budget increases and the late 1960s surge in inflation to the Vietnam conflict and the timing of Johnson's tax increase, adding that "the validity of New Economics as science is not impaired but rather reinforced by the fact that bad things happened as predicted when the advice of its practitioners was rejected."

In defending the "new economics" against charges that its policies are inflationary, Tobin says "Our economy, like all others of the modern world, has an inflationary bias. When it operates without socially intolerable rates of unemployment and excess capacity, prices will drift steadily upward." Tobin suggests that the lapse of the "new economics" is only "partial and temporary" and believes it would retain its relevance if a number of fiscal and monetary reforms were adopted.

Government Spending and Taxation

Can you think of any aspect of your life that is not in some way influenced by the government? Almost every time you buy something, the government takes its cut in the form of sales taxes. Almost every time you produce something, the government takes its cut in the form of income taxes. Most of you have had your education provided by the government, and even if you are now going to a private college or university, it may be receiving government grants. This textbook might have been mailed to your college bookstore using the government's postal services. It would be difficult, if not impossible, to make a list of every way that the government influences your life. It seems appropriate, then, for us to spend this chapter finding out about the economic functions of government, the ways in which government spends its revenues, and the ways in which it obtains those revenues. Let us first look at the functions of government in our economy.

The Economic Functions of Government

The complex functions of government can be classified into five broad categories:

1. The provision of public goods
2. The regulation of economic activity
3. The redistribution of income
4. The stabilization of the economy
5. The administration of justice

These categories are not all-inclusive, but they do cover the bulk of government activity. After we have talked about these functions, we will look at the growth of government in our nation.

Providing Public Goods

Until now we have generally talked about private goods, such as French fries, hamburgers, and manufactured commodities. But some other goods—**public goods**—are in a class by themselves. National defense and police protection, for example, are public goods. If you partake of them, you do not necessarily take away from anybody else's share. The principle of exclusion does not apply as it does, for example, to an apple pie because if you eat the pie, no one else can do the same.

Pure Public Goods   We can list several distinguishing characteristics of public goods that set them apart from all other goods.

1. Public goods are usually indivisible. You can't sell $5 worth of our ability to annihilate the world with bombs. Public goods cannot be produced or sold very easily in small units.
2. Public goods can be used by increasing numbers of people at no additional cost. Once a television signal has been emitted, turning on your tube does not cost the TV station anything.
3. Additional users of public goods do not deprive other users from any of the services of the good. If you turn on your radio, no one gets weaker reception because of your action.
4. It is very difficult to charge people for a public good on the basis of how much they use. How does one determine how much any person uses or even values national defense?

Free Riders   This last point leads us to the free-rider problem, in which people either think

that others can take the burden of paying for public goods, such as national defense, or argue that they receive no value from such government services. For example, they will tell interviewers they are unwilling to pay for national defense because they don't want any of it—it's of no value to them. We all want to be free riders when we think we can get away with it.

Look at the problem as it is schematized in Table 5-1. How much national defense will you benefit from if you agree to pay and everyone else also pays? $90,000,000,100. How much will there be if you don't pay but everyone else does pay? $90,000,000,000. If you think everyone else will pay, wouldn't you be tempted to get a free ride?

However you view it, when government steps in, more public goods are provided than would have been provided by the private sector. Since many products and services in our economy are public goods, there is a strong case for the government's financing them. In some cases the private sector might not produce these goods at all.

In our discussion of government-provided goods, do not, however, confuse public goods with government-provided ones. Not all goods financed by the government are public goods, as we have defined them. Furthermore, not all public goods are provided by the government. TV and radio wave emissions are good examples.

Regulating Economic Activity

Another major function of the government is the regulation of economic activities. Governments at federal, state, and local levels are engaged in setting certain prices throughout the economy. Governments regulate the price of electricity, natural gas, and telephone service; they attempt to regulate illegal activities, such as prostitution and narcotics consumption; and

	If you pay	If you don't pay
If everybody else pays	$90,000,000,100	$90,000,000,000
If no one else pays	$100	$0.00

Table 5-1 **Scoreboard for National Defense**

The free rider is the one who will gladly let everyone else pay the bill. If you don't pay your share of national defense but everyone else does, there will still be $90 billion available for the country's defense. Whether you pay or not seems to make very little difference.

they attempt to foster competition by enforcing antitrust laws.

Moreover, the government has attempted to regulate economic activities that generate **negative externalities,** or harmful spillover effects, such as pollution. Government acts in this area by setting standards on air and water quality and by prohibiting certain production methods from being used altogether.

Redistributing Income

A third major government function is the redistribution of income from certain groups of individuals in our society to other groups of individuals. This is generally done through a system of transfer payments, direct payments to individuals who provide no concurrent goods and services to the government. Foremost among these payments are Social Security benefits, veterans' benefits and services, unemployment compensation, and aid to families with dependent children (AFDC). Other types of government transfers include food stamps, public housing, rent supplements, welfare, and medical care payments. Public education can be viewed as an indirect transfer to members of

lower-income groups who receive more benefits from public education than they pay for. We will have more to say about income redistribution in our section on taxes in this chapter.

Stabilizing the Economy

Our economy is presently plagued with the twin problems of unemployment and rising prices. The government, especially the federal government, has taken on the task of attempting economic stabilization, or smoothing out fluctuations in economic activity. The following chapters in this macroeconomic section of our book are all about this task of government. Suffice it to say here that economic stabilization occupies a relatively large amount of government policymaking. To a lesser extent, state and local governments have started considering stabilization as one of their roles also.

Administering Justice

Our legal system is based on the government provision of a police force, courts, and jails. The role of government in such a system has been to enforce private property rights and to prevent, or at least discourage, private individuals from using force in their dealings, whether they be economic or otherwise, with other citizens.

The Growth of Government

Look at Figure 5-1. Here we show the percentage of GNP accounted for by total government purchases at all levels of government—federal, state, and local. Up until the 1930s, government purchases accounted for less than 10 percent of GNP. Today they account for more than 25 percent, and if we look at total government expenditures, which include not only government purchases of goods and services but also

transfer payments, the growth in government is even more startling. This can be seen in Table 5-2, where we also break down the percentage of GNP expended by the three levels of government.

The Components of Government Expenditures

Government is growing; of that there is no question. What is less obvious is where it has grown and, more specifically, which individual components make up total expenditures by governments. Where does government spend most of its revenues? This is a topic we will now look at, first at the federal level and then at the state and local levels.

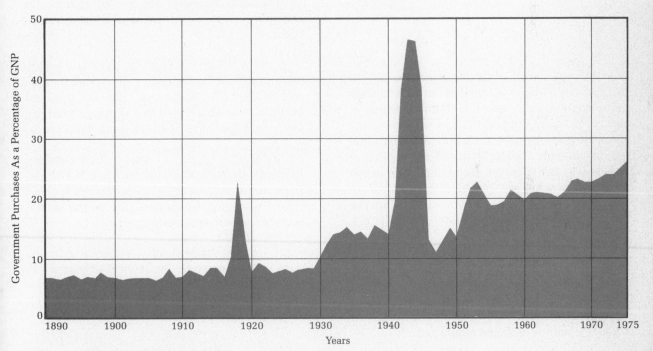

FIGURE 5-1 **Rising Government Purchases**

Here we show government purchases at all levels—federal, state, and local—of goods and services as a percentage of total gross national product. The big jump occurred during World War I, and the upward trend has continued ever since. (*Source:* U.S. Dept. of Commerce.)

Table 5-2 **Outlays of Government As a Percentage of Gross National Product**

This table shows the percentage of GNP accounted for by total government outlays, *including* transfer payments. Upon close examination, we see that although the federal government accounts for the major share of government outlays, the expenditures of both state and local governments are growing also.

YEAR	ALL GOVERN- MENTS	FED- ERAL	STATE	LOCAL
1950	25	15	4	6
1955	28	18	4	6
1960	30	18	4	8
1965	30	17	5	8
1970	34	19	6	9
1975	39	22	7	10

Source: U.S. Bureau of the Census, *Statistical Abstract of the United States*

The Federal Budget

The federal budget is big and is getting bigger. We see in Table 5-3 that Uncle Sam spends over $300 billion a year. The trends in the categories of federal budget outlays are interesting because they show the direction of the national priorities. This is such an important topic that we will cover it in the following issue when we discuss what are and what should be national priorities. Right now we will explain the particular categories enumerated in Table 5-3.

Defense Defense includes all outlays for the military or space program and for foreign affairs. Many critics of defense spending contend that the official government estimate is biased downward because it does not include *all* money spent on defense affairs.

Cash Income Maintenance These programs provide cash benefits, including Social Security benefits to the aged, unemployment compensa-

tion, and public assistance to the poor and disabled.

Helping People Buy Essentials This category includes vouchers or cash that allows individuals to buy *specific* goods and services. The most obvious specific service is medical care for the aged under the various Medicare and Medicaid programs. In addition, this category includes food stamps and housing supplements.

Aid for Social Programs This category includes all the funds that the federal government expends to assist state and local governments in providing such services as education, manpower training programs, community revitalization, and regional development.

Investment in Physical Environment Federal programs in this area are for environmental recreation, water, and transportation development.

Revenue Sharing These programs provide nonearmarked funds to state and local governments. General revenue sharing was initiated in 1972. It is also called tax sharing, whereby states and localities share in the federal taxes.

Direct Subsidies to Producers This category includes all federal programs intended to expand output and/or stabilize income in specific industries, such as in agriculture, the postal service, and maritime shipping.

Net Interest These are interest payments paid to the public on the federal debt and are sometimes called interest payments on the national debt. We discuss the national debt in detail in Issue I-10.

State and Local Expenditures

By far the biggest category in state and local expenditures is education, as can be seen in

Table 5-3 Federal Budget Outlays by Major Category (Fiscal Year 1976)

Here we see the components of the federal budget for 1976. The individual categories are explained in detail in the text. It is obvious, however, that redistribution of income plays an important part in federal activities since cash income maintenance, aid for social programs, and helping people buy essentials added together overshadow any other budget category.

CATEGORY	AMOUNT (IN BILLIONS PER YEAR)	PERCENTAGE OF TOTAL
Defense, space, foreign affairs	$104.9	29.1
Cash income maintenance	118.7	32.8
Helping people buy essentials	42.2	11.7
Aid for social programs	24.4	6.8
Investment in physical environment	23.1	6.4
Revenue sharing	7.2	2.0
Direct subsidies to producers	3.1	0.8
Net interest on public debt	26.1	7.2
Other programs plus financial adjustments	11.6	3.2
Total	$361.3	100.0

Source: Budget of the United States Government, and B. M. Blechman et al., *Setting National Priorities: The 1976 Budget,* Washington, D.C.: The Brookings Institution.

Table 5-4. This should not be surprising since most elementary and secondary education, as well as a good amount of higher education, is provided by public funds. The other significant

Table 5-4 State and Local General Expenditures

The largest category for state and local expenditures is education, mainly for local schools below the college level. The "all other" category accounts for over one-fourth of state and local expenditures, and it includes parks and recreation, fire and police protection, public housing, and so forth.

FUNCTION	FISCAL 1975 (IN BILLIONS OF DOLLARS)
Education	$80.7
Highways	23.0
Public welfare*	27.1
Cash payments	13.4
Medical care	10.0
Health and hospitals	17.6
All other	66.3
Total	$214.7

*Includes items not shown separately.
Source: Tax Foundation, Inc.

categories for state and local governments are public assistance, hospitals, and health. Then come highways and a variety of other items. Note that "all other" general expenditures constitute a large category, absorbing perhaps one-fourth of state and local outlays. It includes parks and recreation, public housing, fire and police protection, public sanitation, and other such goods and services.

Now we know how government revenues are spent, but we have yet to explain how the government gets its revenues. The vast majority of them are obtained by taxation, which has become inevitable for just about everybody everywhere.

Taxation

Governments obtain revenues principally by taxation. There are, however, many ways to tax the public. Income can be taxed, so can wealth, and so can certain types of economic activities. Each tax has its own peculiar attributes, and taxes affect differently the behavior of individuals in our economy. Before we go into a discussion of the specific types of taxes in our system, let's look at several theories of how taxes should be levied.

Theories of Taxation

Should the rich pay more taxes than the poor? Should some types of activities be taxed more heavily than others? What is the "best" tax? These are questions to which philosophers, scientists, politicians, and laypersons have addressed themselves for centuries. The two most popular theories of taxation that remain with us today are based on individuals' ability to pay and the benefits received from government.

Ability-to-Pay Principle

A taxing principle which states that individuals should pay taxes according to their ability to pay has been popular for at least several thousand years. This principle of taxation may be simple to state, but it is certainly not easy to put into effect. We all agree that an individual who earns $20,000 per year is better able to pay taxes than an individual who earns only $2,000 per year. A serious question remains: "How much greater is the first person's ability to pay than the second's?" No one has yet come up with a functionally meaningful way of measuring ability to pay, and the same can be said of the next popular taxing principle.

Benefits-Received Principle

According to this principle, people should be taxed in proportion to the benefits they receive from government services. If they benefit a lot, they should pay a lot; if they benefit little, they should pay only a little. This principle has problems in application, however. First of all, what value do people place on government-provided goods and services? Can we ask them? Our discussion of the free rider suggested some of the problems of asking people what they feel. One way out of this dilemma is to assume that the higher a person's income, the more services he or she receives, and therefore the more value that person obtains from the goods and services provided by the government. Nevertheless, an individual's income is only a crude measure and may not be a good criterion to use for a taxing formula.

Types of Taxes

Without a reliable measure, we cannot say which type of tax we ought to use. All we can do is describe the various types of taxes in terms of the relationship between taxes paid and income. The three main types in all economic systems are proportional, progressive, and regressive.

Proportional Taxation

A proportional system of taxation is just what you would think it would be: As an individual's income goes up, so, too, do taxes—in exactly the same proportion. A proportional tax system is also called a *flat tax*. Taxpayers at all income levels end up paying the same *percentage* of their income in taxes. In other words, if the proportional tax rate were 20 percent, an individual who had an income of $10,000 would pay $2,000 in taxes. An individual making $100,000, would pay $20,000 in taxes, the identical 20 percent rate being levied on both.

Progressive Taxation

Under progressive taxation, the more a person earns, the more he or she pays, just as in a proportional system.

However, the taxes paid, expressed as a percentage of income, go up as more income is earned. In a progressive system, the **marginal tax rate** increases as income increases. Marginal merely means incremental. Thus:

$$\text{Marginal tax rate} = \frac{\text{change in tax bill}}{\text{change in income}}$$

We should compare the marginal tax rate with the average tax rate, which is defined as:

$$\text{Average tax rate} = \frac{\text{total tax bill}}{\text{total income}}$$

The difference between the marginal and the average tax rate can be seen in Table 5-5. Let's take the example in Table 5-5. Say the first $100 in income is taxed at 10 percent, the next $100 at 20 percent, and the third $100 at 30 percent. The average tax rate is always less than (or equal to) the marginal tax rate with a progressive tax system. With a proportional tax system, the marginal tax rate is constant and always the same as the average tax rate.

Table 5-5 **A Progressive Tax System**

The percentage of tax taken out of each additional dollar earned goes up; that is, the marginal tax rate increases progressively with income.

INCOME	MAR-GINAL RATE	TAX	AVERAGE RATE
100	10%	$10	$\frac{\$10}{\$100} = 10\%$
200	20%	$10 + $20 = $30	$\frac{\$30}{\$200} = 15\%$
300	30%	$10 + $20 + $30 = $60	$\frac{\$60}{\$300} = 20\%$

Regressive Taxation We have yet to talk about regressive taxes. Any tax that is regressive takes away a smaller and smaller percentage of additional income as income rises. The marginal rate falls and is below the average rate. As an example, imagine that all revenues of the government were obtained from a 99 percent tax on food. Since we know that the percentage of income spent on food falls as family income rises, we also know that the percentage of total income that would be paid in taxes under such a system would likewise fall as income rose. It would be a regressive system.

Figure 5-2 shows the relationship between the percentage tax rate and level of income for all these tax systems. It is important here to distinguish between the legal, or legislated, tax rate, and what we will call the **effective tax rate.** Taxes are generally levied on a base that does not include all income, as we will see when we talk about the American tax system and its oddities in Issue I-7. The tax bill is determined by multiplying the tax rate times the base. To find the effective tax rate, we merely divide total income into the tax bill. If the effective tax rate so described rises as income rises, the tax is progressive; if it is constant, the tax is proportional; and if it falls, the tax is regressive.

Now we will look at three broad areas of taxation in the United States: income, wealth, and economic activities.

Income Taxes

At the federal level, income taxes are by far the most important source of revenues. Income taxes take the form of either taxes on personal income or income from corporations. Increasingly, states and even some cities are also levy-

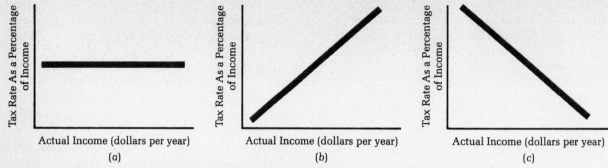

FIGURE 5-2 **Proportional, Progressive, and Regressive Tax Systems**

In (a) we see that the tax rate as a percentage of income remains constant as actual income rises. This, then, represents a proportional tax. (b) illustrates a progressive tax in which the percentage tax rate rises with income. With the regressive tax shown in (c), the opposite is true: As income rises, the percentage tax rate falls.

ing income taxes, but the federal government is still the leader.

Personal Income Taxes

Most of us are aware that the personal income tax system in the United States is progressive.

In Table 5-6, we see part of the 1976 tax schedule. Notice that the marginal tax rate goes up as taxable income rises, even though the rate applicable to the previous lumps of income stays the same. Many students think that someone in a 50 percent tax bracket pays 50 percent

Table 5-6 **Federal Personal Income Tax for a Childless Couple, 1976**

Here we show the different income brackets and the marginal tax rates along with the average tax rates. As you can see, the marginal tax rates go up to a maximum of 70 percent. However, if income qualifies as being "earned," the maximum is 50 percent. All wages are considered earned income, but interest on bonds or dividends from stocks is not.

NET INCOME BEFORE EXEMPTIONS (BUT AFTER DEDUCTIONS)	PERSONAL INCOME TAX	AVERAGE TAX RATE, PERCENT	MARGINAL TAX RATE
Below $ 1,500	$ 0	0	0
2,000	70	3.5	14
3,000	215	7.2	15
4,000	370	9.2	16
5,000	535	10.7	17
10,000	1,490	14.9	22
20,000	3,960	19.8	28
50,000	16,310	32.6	50
100,000	44,280	44.3	60
200,000	109,945	55.0	69
400,000	249,930	62.5	70
1,000,000	669,930	67.0	70
10,000,000	6,969,930	69.7	70

Source: Internal Revenue Service

of his or her taxable income to the federal government. That is not the case, even for an honest taxpayer. Fifty percent may be paid on the last $15,000, for example, but certainly not on all the income.

At the federal level, personal income taxes account for over 40 percent of all federal revenues. We see in Table 5-7 that the federal budget tax receipts show over 45 percent coming from personal income taxes. In the same table, we see that at the state and local level only 20 percent comes from personal income taxes; however, this percentage has been rising.

Progressive Taxation and Income Distribution

Our progressive federal tax system on personal income is usually justified on the basis that it redistributes aftertax income. How effective has the federal government been in altering the distribution of income in the United States? A look at Figure 5-3 suggests that very little has actually changed. We have the same levels of income differences that existed after World War I. We will discuss why so little income redistribution has actually occurred in Issue I-7, when we discuss the ways that individuals can avoid paying taxes.

The Corporate Income Tax

Corporate income taxes account for over 15 percent of all federal taxes collected and for over 8 percent of all state and local taxes collected. Corporations are generally taxed on the difference between their total revenues or receipts and expenses. In 1901, the corporate tax rate amounted to a mere 1 percent of corporate profits, with the first $5,000 a year being exempted. By 1932, this exemption had disappeared and the rate had jumped to 13.755 percent. Since 1950, corporations have had to pay a "normal" tax on the first $25,000 of profit

Table 5-7 **Government Revenues Accounted for by Personal Income Taxes**

During the Depression, individual income taxes accounted for less than 20 percent of federal revenues. Now, however, individual income taxes account for almost 45 percent of federal revenues. The importance of the personal income tax has increased. The same trend is true at the state and local level.

FISCAL YEAR	PERCENT OF FEDERAL REVENUES ACCOUNTED FOR BY PERSONAL INCOME TAXES	PERCENT OF STATE AND LOCAL REVENUES ACCOUNTED FOR BY PERSONAL INCOME TAXES
1927	25.7%	
1932	19.0	
1936	16.7	
1940	15.5	
1944	39.5	
1950	40.7	12.3
1955	45.1	13.0
1960	45.6	14.6
1965	43.8	15.6
1970	45.0	18.1
1975	45.1	20.0

Source: U.S. Department of the Treasury

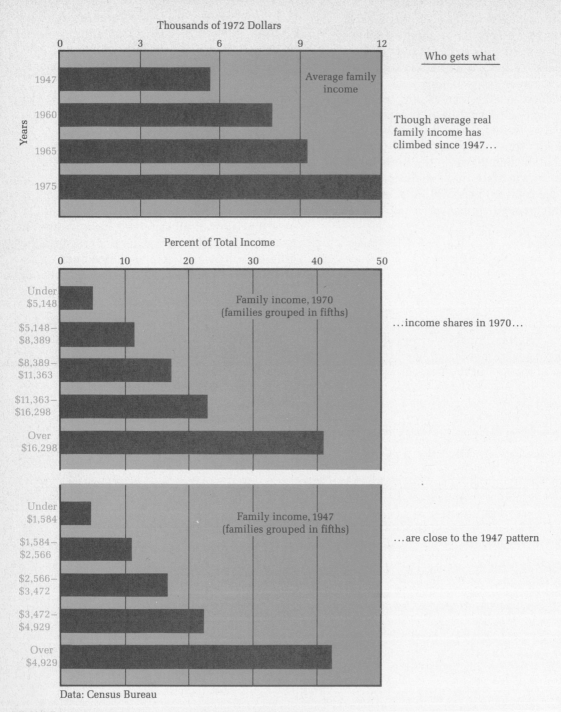

Thousands of 1972 Dollars

Who gets what

Though average real
family income has
climbed since 1947...

...income shares in 1970...

...are close to the 1947 pattern

Percent of Total Income

Data: Census Bureau

FIGURE 5-3 **Income Shares in the United States through Time**

We see that the income shares in 1970 are quite close to the 1947 pattern. After 23 years of rising average incomes, the distribution of income has hardly changed at all in the United States. (*Source: Business Week,* Apr. 1, 1972, p. 56.)

per year, and a **surtax,** or addition to that normal tax, on profits in excess of $25,000 per year. Currently the "normal" tax rate is 22 percent and the "surtax" an additional 26 percent.

Not a Tax on All Profits

It is often suggested that the corporate income tax is a general tax on the income from capital. Remember that income comes from two sources: labor services and capital. In the United States, the income that goes to labor services has remained steady at about 75 percent of national income. The remaining 25 percent is comprised of profits, interest, dividends, and rent. Corporations pay out all the returns to labor in the form of wages, salaries, and special stock options to executives. After the corporation has subtracted all its other expenses, the result is profit. This profit, therefore, represents the income from the capital invested in the corporation (labor has already been paid its income). Therefore, when these profits are taxed, we are really taxing the income from capital.

Granted, the corporation income tax is a tax on the income from capital, but we know that not all income from capital is generated in the corporate sector of our economy. Fully one-half of capital's income comes from the noncorporate sector, for example, from housing and farming. The corporate income tax is, therefore, definitely *not* a general tax on the income from capital. All capital's income generated in the noncorporate sector is taxed at individual marginal tax rates that, on average, are lower than the corporate rate. Additionally, the aftertax profits of the corporation are taxed again when stockholders pay taxes on dividends or capital gains. If you receive $1000 in dividends, you have to declare them (except for the first $100, or $200 if married) as income, and you must pay taxes at your marginal tax rate. Before the corporation was able to give you those dividends, it had to pay taxes on all its profits, including any that it puts back into the company or does not distribute in the form of dividends. Eventually the new investment made possible by those **retained earnings** will be reflected in the increased value of the stock in that company. When you sell your stock in that company, you will have to pay a capital gains tax on the difference between what you sold it for and what you paid for the stock. In this sense, corporate profits are taxed twice.

Do Corporations Really Pay Their Taxes?

Corporations can only exist as long as consumers buy their products, employees make their goods, stockholders buy their stocks, and bondholders buy their bonds. Corporations, per se, do not do anything. They exist only insofar as they have employees, customers, bondholders, and stockholders. We must ask, then, who really pays the tax on corporate income. There is considerable debate on this subject. Some people say that corporations pass their tax burdens to consumers by charging higher prices. Other economists believe that it is the stockholders, the people who pay money to the corporation by buying stocks (shares of ownership), who bear most of the tax. Since the debate is not yet settled, we will not hazard a guess here as to what the correct conclusion should be. Suffice it to say that you should be cautious when you advocate increasing corporation income taxes. You may be the one who ultimately ends up paying the increase.

Taxes on Wealth

Wealth is defined as anything whose value is its ability to produce income in the future. In our tax system, certain types of wealth do not escape the tax collector's eye. These include taxes on property ownership, and on the transfer of ownership, the latter taking the form of estate taxes.

Estate Taxes

Estate taxes account for a mere 2 percent of total federal tax receipts, and about the same percentage for state government receipts. The federal and state system of taxing whatever wealth individuals own when they die is complicated and worthy of entire law school courses for would-be estate lawyers. There are, literally, thousands of ways to reduce potential estate taxes. If you are interested, just look in some of the legal treatises pertaining to this topic in your library.

Property Taxes

Real property has been taxed at the state and local levels for many years. The bulk of proceeds from property taxes goes to financing public education, streets and roads, and public safety facilities. The justice of the property tax, however, has often been challenged. As one student of property taxation once wrote, "The general property tax as actually administered is beyond all doubt one of the worst taxes known to the civilized world." Such were the words of Columbia University Professor Edwin R. A. Seligman in 1911. In colonial days a property tax was essentially a tax on wealth because most people's wealth was involved in farmland, livestock, buildings, and jewelry; today, however, a person's tangible property is not necessarily an index of his or her wealth or of how much income he or she makes. There are numerous other types of intangible property, such as stocks, bonds, savings accounts, mortgages, and so on. For the most part, intangible property is not touched at all by the property tax.

Taxes on Economic Activities

When you go to a store to buy a toothbrush, you usually have to pay a tax. It is called a sales tax, levied on the final sale of goods and services. In some states, certain necessary commodities such as medicine and food are exempted from the general sales tax.

In addition to general sales taxes, there are special sales taxes called **excise taxes.** These are levied on the manufacture, consumption, or sale of such commodities as gasoline and liquor. State governments rely most heavily on sales and excise taxes, in addition to special taxes on the gross receipts of businesses operating in the state. These three taxes on economic activity account for more than 50 percent of state government revenues.

Unemployment and Social Security Taxes

An increasing percentage of federal tax receipts are accounted for each year by taxes (other than income taxes) levied on payrolls. These taxes are for Social Security, retirement, survivors disability, and old-age medical insurance (Medicare). In 1975, the tax was imposed on earnings up to $14,100 at a rate of 5.85 percent on employers and 5.85 percent on employees. That is, the employer matches your "contribution" to Social Security. These taxes and the base on which they are levied will rise in the next decade. People who are self-employed must pay a self-employment tax equivalent to three-fourths of the combined employer and employee rate. These Social Security taxes came into existence when the Federal Insurance Contribution Act (FICA) was passed in 1935.

There is also a federal unemployment tax, which obviously has something to do with unemployment insurance. This tax rate is 0.5 percent on the first $4,200 of annual wages of each employee. It is only the employer who makes the tax payment. This tax covers the costs of the unemployment insurance system and the costs of employment services. In addition to this federal unemployment tax, some states also have an unemployment system and impose an additional tax of about 3 percent, or less, depending on the past record of particular employers. An employer who lays off workers frequently will have a higher state unemployment tax rate than an employer who never lays off workers.

Social Security and unemployment taxes seem to correspond with the benefits principle of taxation since it is the workers who pay the taxes and the workers who receive the benefits from the services made possible by the taxes. Critics of Social Security, however, note that the amount of Social Security taxes paid bears little relation to the payments individual workers receive. In fact, it has been argued that Social Security is a system whereby current workers subsidize retired workers. It is also argued that the system is not an insurance policy because Social Security benefits are legislated by Congress; they are not part of the original Federal Insurance Contributions Act. Therefore, future generations may decide that they do not want to give large Social Security

benefits to retired workers. Even if workers had paid in large amounts into Social Security, they could conceivably be denied the benefits in the form of large Social Security retirement income.

One last point about Social Security and unemployment: Most people think the employer pays part of the tax in the case of Social Security and all the tax in the case of unemployment insurance. This is not generally the case, however. In fact, in the long run, it can be argued that it is the employee who pays the entire tax. In other words, if employers did not have to contribute to Social Security on the behalf of their employees, the employees could now be making just that much more in wages.

Problems with Spending and Collecting

Government spending activities are large and numerous and extensive. How do we decide where government revenues should be spent? That is a problem of national goals and priorities. We turn to that problem in the next issue. Then we go on to look at problems associated with collecting the revenues that governments will spend. This leads us to the explosive issue of taxpayers' legal methods of avoiding taxes.

Public Goods: Goods that are not subject to the exclusion principle; that is, if one person uses public goods, the amount left for use by other persons is not reduced. Public goods are characterized by zero marginal costs once they are produced; they are generally indivisible.

Negative Externalities: The negative spillover effects of activities that harm individuals who are not compensated because no contract was made with the individuals who caused the negative externalities.

Marginal Tax Rate: The tax rate that applies to the last bracket of income earned. It should be contrasted with the average tax rate, which is merely the total tax bill divided by total income.

Effective Tax Rate: Actual taxes paid divided by actual total income.

Surtax: Any tax that is levied in addition to some normal tax.

Retained Earnings: Those earnings that a corporation saves or retains for use in investment in other productive activities. Earnings that are not distributed to stockholders.

Chapter Summary

1. The economic functions of government can be divided into the provision of public goods, the regulation of economic activity, the redistribution of income, the stabilization of the economy, and the administration of justice.

2. Public goods should be distinguished from government-provided goods, which do not have to be public goods. The former are defined as those goods of which additional users can partake at a zero marginal cost. When you turn on your television set, for example, you do not reduce the amount of TV available for other members of the community. The same is true when you use national defense.

3. With most public goods there is a free-rider problem in which individuals, if asked how much they want to contribute to the production of a public good, might usually indicate very little because they believe that others will pay for the provision of that public good.

4. Economic regulation involves the government setting certain prices throughout the economy, regulating illegal activities, and fostering competition by enforcing antitrust laws, as well as attempting to minimize negative externalities such as those caused by pollution-creating production activities.

5. From a macroeconomic point of view, much government activity is involved in stabilizing the economy, that is, attenuating relatively high rates of unemployment and preventing relatively fast rates of inflation.

6. Total government outlays have risen steadily since the end of World War II, expressed as a percentage of gross national product.

7. The federal budget includes expenditures on defense, cash income maintenance, direct subsidies to producers, net interest on the public debt, and others. Most of the state and local expenditures involve education, highways, and public welfare.

8. Government revenues are mainly derived by taxation. The ability-to-pay principle and the benefits-received principle are two principles of taxation.

9. Taxes can be classified as proportional, progressive, or regressive.

1. Would you want to live in a world where there was no government?
2. Do you expect the share of government expenditures in total national income to increase or decrease in the next decade? Why?
3. Sometimes taxes are less than total expenditures by the federal government. Critics then suggest that specific parts of the budget must be cut. Does it matter which part of the federal budget is cut to get it in line with taxes collected?
4. If you were in charge of scrapping our entire taxation system and coming up with an alternative, what principles of taxation would you use and what kind of system would you devise?
5. When you try to decide whether or not you should take on part-time work, do you look at your average tax rate or your marginal tax rate?

Selected
References

Anderson, William H., *Financing Modern Government,* Boston: Houghton-Mifflin, 1973.

Bureau of the Budget, *Federal Budget in Brief,* current ed., Washington, D.C.: U.S. Government Printing Office.

Carson, Robert B. et al. (eds.), *Government in the American Economy,* Lexington, Mass.: D. C. Heath, 1973.

Eckstein, Otto, *Public Finance,* 3d. ed., Englewood Cliffs, N.J.: Prentice-Hall, 1973, chaps. 3–5.

Groves, Harold M. and Robert L. Bish, *Financing Government,* New York: Holt, Rinehart and Winston, 1973.

Pechman, Joseph A., *Federal Tax Policy,* rev. ed. New York: W. W. Norton, 1971.

Young Man at the End of an Era

ARTHUR OKUN

Former Chairman, Council of Economic Advisers (CEA) 1968–1969

When Lyndon Johnson appointed CEA member Arthur Okun to succeed Gardner Ackley as Chairman of the Council in 1968, there was little surprise in the economic and business communities. Despite the fact that he was the youngest man to have ever been appointed chairman, Okun had been an important member of the Council staff since 1964. Yet, because of Johnson's change in plans in 1968, Okun served for only 1 year.

One of the most active of the "new economists" of the 1960s, Okun has been cited as a major force behind the success of Walter Heller's programs in the early part of the decade. It was Okun who did the "slide rule" work behind the 1964 tax cut. His influence was crucial because the cut was planned at a time of large federal budget deficits. As one Washington economist commented, "One of the reasons Heller was so successful was that he had Art Okun on his staff . . . Okun could do anything the whole Treasury could do and on the back of an envelope, if necessary."

Okun studied at Yale University and was serving on the faculty there in graduate economic programs when he joined the Council research staff in 1964. His work to that time had been concentrated in the area of economic forecasting, to which he contributed Okun's law, which relates changes in the gross national product to fluctuations in the rate of unemployment.

After leaving the federal government at the end of the Johnson era, Okun joined the Washington-based Brookings Institution, with which he has been affiliated ever since. From that vantage point he wrote *The Political Economy of Prosperity,* which was published by the Institution in 1970. While discussing the mechanism of the growth-inflation pattern of the mid-1960s, Okun argued that the Vietnam conflict had made broad analysis of the success or failure of the "new economics" virtually impossible. However, he felt that individual policies, like the 1968 tax hike, could be evaluated as conceptual and operational failures.

Okun was very skeptical of the Nixon administration's attempts to develop a workable fiscal policy. Yet, as an important planner of a highly active fiscal program, Okun is appreciative of the shortcomings of such policies. At the 1972 American Economic Association meeting, Okun commented, "Judged by its contribution to generating social welfare, to solve the big social problems, fiscal policy can be regarded as trivial and obsolete."

By the end of the 1960s, Okun felt that the major focus of administration action should be wage and price stability but that a planned recession would be like "burning down a building to get rid of termites." Okun believed that labor costs were the key to controlling inflation, so he became an advocate of wage and price controls, even though he had opposed these measures while he was chairman of the CEA. When the recession did come several years later, Okun noted that wage costs were indeed moderating. "But what a price to pay," he said. "It is like cutting off your hand and being consoled with the thought, 'Well, they cured your eczema.'"

Okun was a persistent critic of President Ford's gradualistic policies to cure the recession. Among liberal economists, he was one of those most afraid that the 1974 to 1975 recession would develop into a depression unless the government took more affirmative action. He was particularly critical of the restrictive monetary policies of Arthur Burns: "The Fed's policy this year [1975] seems to be the marriage-manual approach to monetary ease. Make it last, go slow, stretch it out, and you enjoy it better that way."

What Are Our National Priorities?

HOW SHOULD PUBLIC FUNDS BE USED?

Government and the Problem of Scarcity

We must eliminate poverty. We must give our children better education. We should extend health services to more Americans. We should create more adequate housing for lower-income families.

What do these statements have in common? At least two things: Each is a statement of value, not of fact, and each involves the use of scarce resources. From a purely scientific point of view, there is no way we can argue for or against the reduction of poverty, the improvement of housing, the extension of medical service, or any other social-reform program in our nation. These are not questions that you and I can resolve as scientists or economists. We react to them instead with our hearts, with our own values concerning what is and what is not appropriate for our society.

On the other hand, it does not require any value judgment to state that improvements in nearly all aspects of our economy require the use of scarce resources. This follows from the basic condition that scarcity is a pervasive phenomenon every-where, even in the United States. That means one thing: Whenever the government—federal, state, or local—increases, say, health care services to the poor, we all have to give up something to pay for those increased services. And the government faces a scarcity problem just like you and I do. After all, at any moment in time the total amount of resources in our nation is fixed. If more resources go to the government for use in social-reform programs, less resources are available to the nongovernmental sector of the economy. A fundamental decision must be made concerning the degree to which the government allocates (exhausts) resources in our economy. This is where national priorities come into play.

Setting National Priorities

Because the government faces a scarcity situation, which we might call the government's budget constraint, it must decide on how to allocate its finite resources among competing ends. One way to do this is to set national priorities and goals. We can observe trends in national priorities—even if politicians don't explicitly state them—by looking at what the government does with the tax dollars that it collects.

Trends in Government Expenditures

In Chapter 5 we looked at the budget of the United States Government for fiscal 1976. What we do now in Table I-6.1 is present that same budget by category for 1960, 1970, and 1975. Some fairly dramatic shifts have taken place in terms of *revealed* national priorities, that is, priorities revealed by the changing composition of the federal budget.

Declining Priorities

Some obvious examples of declining priorities make themselves known in Table 1-6.1. National defense, expressed as a percentage of total federal expenditures, fell from 53.7 percent in 1960 to 31.6 percent in 1975. This is a sufficiently important topic for us to devote a separate section to it later.

Another declining category of budget outlays is direct subsidies to producers, which fell from 5.9 percent of the federal budget in 1960 to 1.2 percent some 15 years later. However, compelling data indicate

Table I-6.1

Changing Federal Budget Priorities (Dollar Amounts in Billions)

Here we see some obvious shifts in federal budget expenditures. Defense outlays as a percentage of total expenditures are declining. Income redistribution programs seem to be on the upswing.

CATEGORY	1960		1970		1975 ESTIMATE	
	AMOUNT	PERCENT OF TOTAL	AMOUNT	PERCENT OF TOTAL	AMOUNT	PERCENT OF TOTAL
Defense, space, foreign affairs	$49.5	53.7	$ 87.7	44.6	$ 96.1	31.6
Cash income maintenance	20.6	22.3	46.6	23.7	98.2	32.2
Helping people buy essentials	1.1	1.2	14.2	7.2	33.2	10.9
Aid for social programs	1.3	1.4	10.3	5.3	18.2	6.0
Investment in physical environment	5.4	5.8	9.4	4.8	17.3	5.7
Revenue sharing	0.1		0.5		6.8	2.2
Direct subsidies to producers	4.5	4.9	6.7	3.4	3.7	1.2
Net interest	6.9	7.5	14.4	7.3	22.0	7.2
Other programs plus financial adjustments	2.8	3.0	6.7	3.4	8.9	3.0
Total	$92.2	100.0	$196.6	100.0	$304.4	100.0
Total as percent of gross national product	18.6		20.6		20.9	

Source: Budget of the United States Government, and B. M. Blechman et al., *Setting National Priorities: The 1975 Budget,* Washington, D.C.: The Brookings Institution.

that subsidies are much more widespread than figures in the federal budgets suggest.

Advancing Priorities

The major candidate for receiving greater priority, at the national level at least, is income maintenance. Cash income maintenance grew from 22.3 percent of the federal budget in 1960 to 32.2 percent in 1975. The category "Helping People Buy Essentials" grew from a mere 1.2 percent to over 10 percent in that same period, and aid for social programs grew from 1.4 percent to 6.0 percent. The Department of Health, Education, and Welfare budget

(under which income maintenance, "Helping People," and aid for social programs fall) exceeds the budget of the Department of Defense. At least from these data, it is apparent that our national priorities have shifted away from military expenditures to social and income redistribution programs, such as aid for migrant children, aid to schools in "federally impacted" areas, expenditures for affirmative action employment policies, and so on.

Income Redistribution

A large portion of the federal budget is now going for cash income main-

tenance programs and such aids as food stamps and housing vouchers. Income redistribution, which we have already discussed, involves taxing higher-income individuals and transferring some of their tax dollars to lower-income individuals who perform no particular economic service in return. Have our programs of income redistribution worked? It would be difficult for us to say that they were a smashing success. Just look again at Figure 5-3 on p. 104. There we showed the income shares going to families grouped in fifths for 1947, just after World War II, and 1972. After 2½ decades of rising income and continued efforts to redistribute income, the distribution seems to have remained approximately the same. This evidence seems to suggest that national priorities, even if expressed by changes in federal budget outlays, can, in fact, be thwarted by opposing forces. We will discuss one of these opposing forces in the following issue when we examine the loopholes in our tax system that allow higher-income individuals to reduce their federal tax liabilities by reducing their taxable income.

Defense Spending Declines

We pointed out above that defense spending as a percentage of total federal expenditures fell dramatically in the last decade and a half. There is no doubt that a guns and butter choice exists here. Look at Figure I-6.1. Here we show a typical production-possibilities curve, with production of military goods and services on the vertical axis (guns) and production of civilian goods and services (butter) on the horizontal axis. What we have done over the last 15 years or so is move from a point such as A to a point such as B. We have moved toward the civilian-goods axis.

We can see the real trend in defense spending if we correct for changes in the price level. In Chapter 4, when we discussed GNP and national income accounting, we pointed out that real GNP (that is, GNP corrected for price changes) was the appropriate measure of physical output. The same is true for military expenditures. If we correct military expenditures by the federal government for changes in the price level, the result is the decline shown in Figure I-6.2. Military spending in real terms has fallen dramatically since our withdrawal from Indochina.

The True Cost of the Military

We know in economics that the true cost of anything is equal to its opportunity, or alternative, cost; hence, the direct, recorded outlays of the Defense Department do not include the entire cost of the military establishment to the American people. This was particularly true when we had a system of conscripted military labor, or draft. Involuntary military servitude means forcing individuals

Guns and Butter

It is true: We cannot have more guns and more butter at the same time when we have full employment at the outset. We have shown here a production-possibilities curve. The horizontal axis measures civilian goods, and the vertical axis measures war goods. If we want to have more war goods, we have to sacrifice civilian goods. There is always going to be a trade-off at any point in time. In the long run, however, as we increase our productive capacity, we can have more war goods and more civilian goods. In the United States there has been a fairly recent movement away from war production toward civilian production (shown here as a movement from A to B).

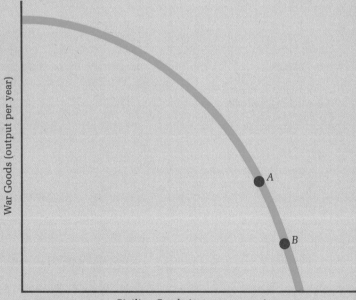

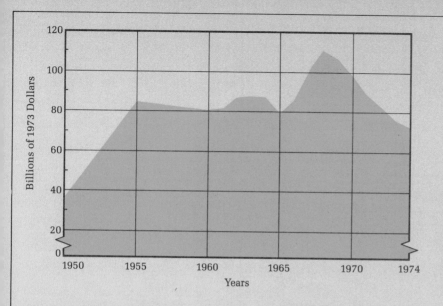

FIGURE I-6.2 Military Spending in Constant 1973 Dollars

The absolute level of military spending in real terms (corrected for inflation) has actually fallen over the last several years. *(Source: U.S. Office of Management and Budget.)*

to work in the military at a lower wage rate than would induce them to join voluntarily. The opportunity (true) cost of those working in the military is measured more or less by what they could be making in the civilian world. Thus, during the draft system the opportunity cost of military labor was significantly higher than the recorded outlays.

Many critics of defense spending contend that there are numerous costs which the public never sees, and therefore we citizens do not know the true size of the military budget. Should the cost to consumers of restrictions on trade with other nations for security reasons be included in the military budget? Should the cost of subsidizing specific industries to maintain strategic capabilities be included in the defense budget rather than in other categories? These are thorny and difficult questions to tackle. We leave them as nothing more than questions for the moment. The general area of subsidization is, however, one on which we can put some numbers.

Government Subsidies

When the government subsidizes a particular economic activity, it either provides the good or service itself to the consumer at a below-cost (in some cases, zero) price, provides ancillary services at below-cost price, or provides credit or a guarantee of same at below cost. Federal subsidy programs are available for economic activities in agriculture, food, medical care, manpower training, education, international trade, housing, natural resources, transportation, and commerce and economic development.

A few years ago there was a massive effort on the part of the Joint Economic Committee (JEC) of the Congress of the United States. They came up with the following conclusion:

Federal subsidies constitute an incredibly diversified and pervasive system of economic assistance to the private economy. Much of the information necessary to understand and evaluate this complex subsidy system is hidden from public scrutiny. Special effort is made to give subsidy programs some other label, such as aid, tax credit, loan, or loan guarantee. In many cases the budgetary costs of these programs are not reported or are incompletely reported in U.S. Budget documents; . . . .

The study went on to estimate that at the beginning of this decade, the cost of federal subsidy programs was of the magnitude of $63 billion per year, but, pointed out the study, "Even these enormous costs do not represent a complete accounting of federal subsidy programs."[1] The JEC's estimate for 1975 was $95 billion.

The authors of this particular study would probably disagree with the statement that direct subsidies to producers are on the downswing. What may be true, according to the Joint Economic Committee, is that an increasingly large number of subsidies are disguised as other types of outlays. It is certainly true that national priorities are all the more difficult to formulate if the na-

tion in fact has no clear picture of how current federal revenues are being expended. The Joint Economic Committee believes that "this absence of facts hides the enormous costs of the overall subsidy system and prevents the evaluation and elimination of inefficient and unfair subsidies."

We can only point out here that more information would allow for a better understanding of our subsidy program and enable us to see whether it coincided with our national priorities. However, as we shall see in Chapter 27, politics is not that simple. There is no such thing as a national consensus that can be accurately determined. We live in a democratic society where the ma-

jority rules. Elected representatives need only obtain 51 percent of the vote either to win or to remain in office. Those who are directly affected by such things as producers' subsidies can readily see the benefits from such subsidies in the form of higher incomes. They therefore form coalitions. Individuals in these well-organized and easily recognizable groups go to great lengths to influence legislation on their own behalf. Thus, it is perhaps only over a very long period of time that the desires of "the public" ever form such a thing as a national consensus which can ultimately work itself around to reordering the national priorities as expressed in the budget outlays of the federal government.

[1]United States Congress Joint Economic Committee, "The Economics of Federal Subsidy Programs," 92nd Congress, First Session, Jan. 11, 1972, Rept. no. 5270–1326, Washington, D.C.: U.S. Government Printing Office, p. 4.

Questions for Thought and Discussion

1. In this issue, changing national priorities have been inferred from changing government expenditure patterns. Can you think of any other way to assess changing national priorities?
2. Is it possible to obtain a consensus from Americans about what national priorities should be? How would you go about obtaining such a consensus?

Selected Reference

Setting National Priorities. Available every year, generally in May, from The Brookings Institution, Washington, D.C.; gives an analysis of each fiscal year's federal government budget.

Fiscal Policy and Trend Analysis

OTTO ECKSTEIN

Former Member, Council of Economic Advisers 1964–1966

The energy and food crises of 1973, economist Walter Heller told a conference of social scientists, had caught economists with their "parameters down." It was a relatively bad year for economic forecasters, and trend predicting, like the economy, seemed to go from bad to worse in 1974. Even Harvard professor Otto Eckstein, an often accurate and longtime respected forecaster of the nation's economic health, misjudged the duration and extent of the 1974 recession.

Using econometric models and information gathered by Data Resources, Inc., of which he is president, Eckstein simulates the effects of government policy alternatives and makes frequent predictions of trends in particular industries as well as the economy as a whole. Though now seen primarily as a skilled forecaster, Eckstein has conducted research on many aspects of the economy, ranging from a 1958 study of the merits of government intervention in water resource development to a recent study showing that the average corporate tax rate has declined from 43.3 percent in 1961 to 35.6 percent in 1973.

A graduate of Princeton and Harvard, Eckstein rose to prominence as an expert in fiscal policy during the early 1960s. He was an important contributor to Kennedy's "Let's get the country moving again" campaign in 1960 and served as a consultant to both the Treasury Department and the Council of Economic Advisers during the Kennedy administration. Drawing on his 1959 work as technical director of the employment, growth, and price-level study for the Joint Economic Committee of Congress, Eckstein suggested a remedy for the recession Kennedy had inherited in a 1961 article, "The World's Dollar and Ours." The government during the Eisenhower years was so concerned over the balance of payments and so afraid of inflation, he said, that the growth rate had declined but without curtailing inflation. The government needed to encourage economic growth in order to generate more profits, which would in turn stimulate business investment. Eckstein advocated a more flexible policy on consumer credit controls and tax revisions, using these as methods to promote economic stability. He argued that the government should launch "an offensive against trade restrictions and export subsidies and against high costs at home" in order to defend the dollar and stimulate the economy.

In September 1964, Lyndon Johnson appointed Eckstein to the Council of Economic Advisers, where he served until February 1966, overseeing the government's wage and price guidelines. During Eckstein's term on the CEA, indications of prosperity were everywhere in evidence: GNP, personal income, corporate profits, and employment all showed increases.

Like many economists associated with the administrations of Kennedy and Johnson, Eckstein has long believed in the necessity for government intervention in some areas of the free market system. He is an advocate of variable tax rates to control unemployment and inflation, not so much in the interests of income redistribution as in the interests of economic stability. In his 1964 book on taxation and government expenditure, *Public Finance,* Eckstein suggested the President might be given standby authority to adjust taxes up or down as conditions warranted. Two years later, he proposed a method Congress could use to achieve the same results.

Since rejoining the Harvard faculty in 1966, Eckstein's views on government economic policy and trends in the economy have been solicited frequently by both public and private interests. He has been a persistent critic of the "tight money" policies of the Federal Reserve Board. In February 1974, he worried that nations would adopt restrictive domestic monetary and fiscal policies aimed at fighting inflation and reducing demand, with high world unemployment as the consequence. A participant in President Ford's 1974 economic summit conference, Eckstein also criticized President Ford's 1975 economic program, seeing it as too conservative and contradictory in its proposed solutions to the recession that began in 1974.

The Rape of the Taxpayer

WHAT DO LOOPHOLES COST THE AMERICAN TAXPAYER?

Taxes and Best Sellers

A few years ago a book appeared across the nation explaining what tax loopholes were: the ways in which taxpayers could legally avoid paying taxes. The author, P. M. Stern, contended that loopholes cost American taxpayers $77 billion every year.[1] Stern entitled tax loopholes "The Rich Welfare Program," presumably because loopholes only benefit higher-income individuals. Even if the annual figure of $77 billion turns out to be an exaggeration, there is little doubt that tax loopholes do exist in our system, and there is even less doubt that such loopholes effectively do much to negate the progressive structure of that system.

Progressive Taxes and Loopholes

You will recall from Chapter 5 on government spending and taxation that, in principle, we have a progressive, personal income tax system. Proponents of progressive income

[1]P. M. Stern, *The Rape of the Taxpayer*, New York: Random House, Vintage Books, 1974.

taxes argue their necessity on many grounds, not the least of which is the goal of redistributing income from the more well-to-do to the less well-to-do. In other words, tax the rich proportionately more than the poor and transfer to the poor some of that income.

If we look at the effective rates of the combined federal, state, and local taxes from the latest detailed study computed by members of The Brookings Institution in Washington, D.C., the result is striking, as can be seen in Figure I-7.1. For the most part, our effective tax system can be described as proportional rather than progressive. The authors of the study from which this information was obtained conclude that the "United States tax system is essentially proportional for the vast majority of families and therefore has little effect on the distribution of income . . . the very rich pay tax rates that are only moderately higher than average."[2] The ability of individuals earning higher income to reduce their taxes

[2]Joseph A. Pechman and Benjamin A. Okner, *Who Bears the Tax Burden?*, Washington, D.C.: The Brookings Institution, 1974.

is a fact of life. It is largely through the use of tax loopholes, or "shelters" as they are sometimes called, that this is accomplished.

Why Congress Legislates Loopholes

Why would Congress ever knowingly legislate a loophole in our tax system that would defeat its progressive nature? The answer is twofold: In the first place, a tax loophole or tax shelter that is applied to a particular type of economic activity or investment will induce individuals and businesses who would otherwise not be interested to undertake that task. As such, a tax shelter affecting, for example, oil drilling, will cause more resources to be devoted to oil drilling than would otherwise have been the case. To the extent that Congress desires to expand such economic activities as, say, oil drilling, an appropriate tax shelter will bring about that result. An argument could be made that it is in society's best interest for certain activities to be encouraged to ensure a larger supply of oil, energy, meat, or eggs.

However, an alternative and perhaps less altruistic view of congressional activity would be that tax loopholes provide a method to reduce the tax liabilities of high-income individuals in our society. Given that

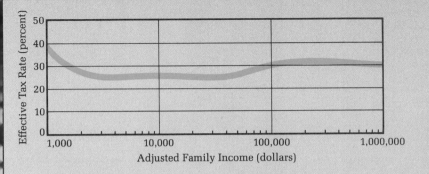

FIGURE I-7.1 Effective Rates of Taxation

We see that there is only a slight amount of progressiveness in our effective tax rates as incomes climb into the higher reaches. To a certain extent, tax rates are somewhat regressive over lower income levels. (*Source:* Joseph A. Pechman and Benjamin A. Okner, *Who Bears the Tax Burden?*, Washington, D.C.: The Brookings Institution, 1974.)

the incentive to influence legislation is directly correlated with the potential benefits, higher-income individuals, who are therefore in higher tax brackets, would be inclined to expend considerable resources seeking special legislation in the form of tax loopholes. This point cannot be overstressed—*a reduction in taxable income benefits the taxpayer directly in proportion to that taxpayer's marginal tax rate.* Perhaps the easiest way to see this is to examine one of the most common tax shelters—tax-exempt state and municipal bonds.

Tax-Exempt Bonds

The tax-exempt status of interest paid to holders of state and municipal bonds is well known to many investors. It is a form of tax shelter in the sense that the interest income which the investor obtains from a tax-exempt bond does not have to be reported on federal income tax returns. Hence, taxable income is reduced by the amount of income received from those bonds for it would otherwise have to be reported to the Internal Revenue Service. Now, what is the benefit to you of

tax-exempt income? You cannot answer that question unless you first determine what your marginal tax rate is. Let's say that it is 50 percent. Every dollar you get in tax-exempt interest from a municipal bond is a dollar on which you will *not* have to pay 50¢ in taxes. Therefore your tax savings from investing in municipal bonds is 50 percent. On the other hand, if your marginal tax bracket is only 20 percent, your tax savings is only 20¢ on every dollar of tax-exempt income.

Bond buyers are aware of this relationship, and what happens is that in their competition to obtain tax savings, that is, tax-exempt income, from these bonds they will bid up the price of the bonds, causing the yields to be relatively low. If you look in the financial pages of a newspaper that gives the yields on tax-exempt bonds and non-tax-exempt bonds of the same quality (risk), you will see that those yields will be different. The yield on the tax-exempt bonds will be lower. Usually, it is lower by between 30 percent and 40 percent.[3] Let's take a specific example. As-

[3]This difference represents the implicit taxes that you pay when buying a tax-exempt bond.

sume that tax-exempt municipal bonds are selling at a price which yields 7 percent per year and that the equivalent non-tax-exempt bond is selling at a price which yields 10 percent a year. Which one should you buy if you had to make the choice?

If you are in a relatively high tax bracket, you should buy the tax-exempt bond, but if you are in a relatively low tax bracket, you should not. Let's say you are again in the 20 percent bracket. If you buy a non-tax-exempt bond yielding 10 percent, the aftertax yield would be 8 percent. Of course the before- and aftertax yield on the municipal bond is the same, 7 percent, because no taxes are paid on the interest. You are obviously better off buying a non-tax-exempt bond and staying out of a tax shelter that benefits only those who are fortunate enough to be in the 50 percent tax bracket. A person in this bracket would not choose your non-tax-exempt bond whose yield is a mere 5 percent, certainly less than the 7 percent net yield on the tax-exempt municipal bond.

This simple example should demonstrate more clearly that it is be-

cause of our progressive tax system that tax shelters are beneficial only to those in higher income tax brackets. This is so because competition among investors drives up the price of tax-sheltered income-earning assets to reflect the tax savings.

The purpose of exempting income from state and municipal bonds was to subsidize state and local governments: The tax-exempt status of these bonds allows such governments to sell their debt (borrow) at a lower interest rate. The subsidy is real and may or may not be desirable, depending on your point of view. However, its distortion of the progressive nature of our tax system is perhaps an unwanted side effect.

The Oil Game

Oil exploration, drilling, and sales are areas of economic endeavor where individuals and corporations can shelter their income. Since the oil depletion allowance has been the most talked about of special tax gimmicks for the oil industry, that is the one we'll discuss first.

Oil Depletion Allowance

We know that the amount of oil found under each successful well is eventually going to be depleted by the pump put over it. Instead of having to pay taxes on all the income, owners of producing wells used to be able to choose a special tax program whereby they were allowed a

percentage oil depletion allowance (a deduction) when computing their taxes. All businesspersons who buy machines are allowed to deduct the cost of *depreciation* on the machine. For example, if General Motors buy a $1 million bumper maker and the bumper maker is going to last 10 years, then every year GM can deduct part of the purchasing price of that machine from their income. This is done in such a way that by the end of 10 years they have deducted the entire purchase price from their income. This procedure is called *cost depreciation*. It is allowed because a percentage of the value of the machine is presumably used up each year while it is producing. Any legitimate cost deduction like this means the company has to pay fewer taxes. Obviously, businesspersons, if given

the choice, would prefer as much depreciation as possible because that would mean valuable tax savings.

A businessperson who was pumping oil out of the ground could—instead of using cost depreciation—deduct 22 percent of the value of the oil from his or her income every year.[4] Now, you might be asking yourself why an oilperson would prefer a 22 percent depletion instead of the regular depreciation that other

---

[4]Oil depletion allowances for major oil companies were curtailed by 1975 legislation, which set a 3-year phase-out schedule. Small independents, however, retained the tax saving on the first 2000 barrels per day.

businesspersons use. One way of looking at it is to realize that if you pay $1 million for a machine, the most you can depreciate is $1 million. Suppose that an oil well costs $1 million but the oilperson opted for percentage depletion. That person ended up being able to deduct more than $1 million because the 22 percent of gross wellhead revenue depletion allowance was used year in and year out until the well was actually depleted. Twenty-two percent of the total amount depleted may far exceed the actual amount that was spent constructing the well or purchasing the mineral rights.

Dry Holes

There are other tax advantages bestowed on the oil industry. Let's look at oil exploration. We know that not all oil wells drilled are gushers. In the United States, probably only 20 percent are. But, of course, the only way to find out if you have a successful well is to drill. You may get a dry one. If you are going out to drill for oil, you have to expect that part of your costs will be spent on dry holes. Thus, in the United States, the true cost of finding one producing well includes the cost of drilling perhaps four dry ones.

The laws laid down by Congress in our tax code allow oilpersons to deduct all the costs of dry wells from other income. If you were a doctor, for example, who had invested money in oil exploration, you could deduct the full cost of all dry holes from your doctoring income. If your marginal tax bracket is 50 percent, every dollar you spend on a dry hole ends up costing you only 50¢.

IDCs

Even for successful wells, about 70 percent of the costs can be deducted from other income because 70 percent of the cost of drilling a successful well is considered **intangible drilling costs** (IDC). These costs include expenses such as labor (as opposed to pipe), and all such IDCs are deductible in the year they are incurred. Thus, an oil company can plan its annual budget so as to pay zero taxes without planning to drill merely dry wells.

Capital Gains

In addition to percentage depletion and the dry-hole tax provisions outlined above, all exploration firms that sell successful wells are required to pay only the capital gains rate on the difference between the selling price and the total calculated cost of the wet well. (Remember that the costs of dry holes have already been deducted from other income.) Here the oil explorers get a double benefit. They can use the lower capital gains tax rate on the income from selling the gushers and still get the benefits of a higher tax-savings kickback by applying the cost deduction of dry holes to their other income, which is necessarily taxed at the higher-than-capital-gains rate.

Depletion allowances, deducting the cost of dry holes from other income, and capital gains concessions end up hurting the economy because they cause "excessive" use of resources in oil development. For example, investors would find and have found it profitable to spend $3 worth of resources to recover $2 worth of

oil. This is an inefficient use of our scarce resources.

You Can Lose Money in Tax Shelters

If you were Liza Minelli, Barbara Walters, Bob Dylan, Andy Williams, or Senator Jacob Javits, you would have learned a few summers ago that tax shelters are not always what they are cracked up to be. The so-called summer star-spangled swindle involved not only the above-mentioned luminaries but some 2000 other wealthy investors, including the President of the First National City Bank. They sank an estimated $100 million into an oil-drilling tax shelter called Home Stake Production Company. They all lost their shirts.

Obviously, then, not all tax shelters earn their investors a positive rate of return. The purpose of a tax shelter is to *show* a loss, for tax-accounting purposes, over a period during which the investor is in a relatively high income tax bracket. The ultimate purpose of a tax shelter is not to lose money but to eventually make a positive rate of return on the venture over a period of years. If someone were to offer you a tax shelter that only promised tax deductions, you would usually not be very interested. Say an oil-drilling scheme will allow you a 100 percent tax deduction on your investment, so you put in $10,000 and that year are allowed to deduct from gross income (in arriving at taxable income) $10,000. Even if you are in the highest tax bracket, your tax saving will not give you your money

back and certainly not allow you to have a positive rate of return. Eventually, the investment must make income or you won't even get your original outlay back, let alone any compensation for letting somebody else use your money.

Tax Shelters and Opportunity Costs

It would be a long list indeed if we were to write down every single tax shelter or loophole that exists in our system. They are all basically the same: a method of generating deductions so that taxable income is reduced, thereby reducing one's tax liability to the federal government. Tax shelters are involved in the purchase of professional athletes' contracts, Broadway plays, motion pictures, railroad tank cars, eggs, cattle, apartment buildings; the list goes on and on. All the shelters taken together constitute a reduction in revenues to the United States Treasury. However, that reduction is probably somewhat less than the number we gave in the beginning of this issue, the annual $77 billion estimated by P. M. Stern.

The reasons are fairly straightforward. In the first place, purchasers of tax-exempt municipal bonds do not walk away with no income reduction. After all, if the yield on tax exempts is 30 percent lower than non-tax exempts, those who buy tax exempts are implicitly paying a tax of 30 percent. More important, it would be unrealistic to assume that upper-income individuals would, in fact, make as high an income as they now make if they were actually assessed for taxes in a truly progressive manner. Many of these high-income-earning individuals would opt for "the purchase of" more leisure since its price, or opportunity cost, would fall if they really only netted 30 percent of their income. What is the cost of forgoing a dollar's earnings? Not a dollar, but only 30¢. The opportunity cost, then, of not working is equal to the aftertax income that could have been earned. And when effective tax rates go up, the opportunity cost of not working goes down, and hence less work is performed. What would this mean for the government? Certainly we could not call those tax savings that upper-income individuals get a "raid" on the United States Treasury of $77 billion per year. If all those tax shelters were eliminated, $77 billion in additional taxes would not be reaped by the United States Treasury because the individuals now taxed at a higher rate would most certainly work less and earn lower gross and therefore taxable incomes.

Other Costs of Tax Shelters

Be that as it may, the loss to the United States Treasury is probably small compared to the sum of two additional costs: (1) the amount of resources used to obtain special legislation in the form of tax shelters, and (2) the resources that are squandered in tax-sheltered economic activities merely for the purpose of obtaining tax-sheltered income. The latter cost usually refers to an inefficient use of our available resources. In other words, if tax shelters were eliminated, fewer resources would be used in the now tax-sheltered investments and more resources would be used in other activities where they would have higher economic value.

An Alternative

Opponents of tax shelters contend that they subsidize the wealthy and cause an inefficient use of re-sources. As an alternative to tax shelters, they offer explicit subsidies to appropriate industries. For example, explicit subsidies to state and local governments (of exactly the same amount as the implicit subsidy they are now receiving as a result of the tax-exempt status of their bonds) would both save the United States Treasury billions of dollars and restore some of the progressiveness to our tax system, if that, in fact, is deemed desirable.

The same is true for tax-shelter-type subsidies to industries such as oil drilling and cattle raising. If Congress deems it desirable to increase production in a particular industry, let the subsidy be direct, say these observers, and eliminate the implicit subsidies in the form of special tax gimmicks. Politicians and their constituents would have the numbers laid out on the table so that more conscious decisions could be made about the social desirability of giving special treatment to particular industries.

Definitions of New Terms	**Percentage Oil Depletion Allowance:** The percentage of the value of oil that is taken out of the ground which is allowed to be deducted from income before taxes are paid. **Intangible Drilling Costs:** Mainly the labor costs of drilling a successful well. These can be deducted from other income.
Questions for Thought and Discussion	1. Why do you think tax shelters get written into legislation? 2. Given our progressive system of taxation, who benefits the most from tax shelters? 3. How is it possible to lose money in tax shelters?
Selected References	Stern, Philip, *The Rape of the Taxpayer,* New York: Random House, 1973. U.S. Congress, Joint Committee on the Economic Report, *Federal Tax Policy for Economic Growth and Stability,* Washington, D.C.: U.S. Government Printing Office, 1956.

Changing Business Conditions and Unemployment

Business activity in the United States has been moving ahead since this nation's economic life began. As we will see in this chapter, however, business activity has zigzagged rather than sloped smoothly upward. Studies of this movement are studies of the **business cycle,** the ups and downs that recur in our economy. Each of us personally feels the effects of inflation, unemployment, and other economic conditions that rise and fall with fluctuations in the business cycle. In this chapter we examine the nature of business cycles and consider several theories about why they occur. Using this information, we then move on to a detailed analysis of unemployment and its causes.

The Business Cycle and Business Activity in the United States

If we measure deviations from the upward trend line in overall business activity (real GNP) in the United States, we get an interesting picture. Figure 6-1 shows clearly that although American business cycles have been recurrent, they have varied greatly in intensity. The most obvious of the "downers" in Figure 6-1 (pages 128–129) falls a full 50 percent from the trend line. That was the period of the Great Depression, when, for a while, one out of every four Americans in the labor force was unemployed. The most visible of the "uppers" were the World War II boom and the prosperous period covering most of the 1960s. In fact, during the later 1960s, after the boom continued without interruption for 104 months, economists and government officials alike began to consider the whole concept of the business cycle old-fashioned. It seems that the history of business ups and downs had finally come to an end. Even the Department of Commerce, in November 1968, saw fit to change the title of its monthly publication from *Business Cycle Developments* to *Business Conditions Digest.*

As it turned out, the elimination of business ups and downs just wasn't in the cards because along came the recession of 1969 to 1970. Since then the American economy has been faced with the twin problems of unemployment and inflation, and students of the American economy are back to studying the ups and downs of business activity, that is, the business cycle.

Phases in the Business Cycle

As the name implies, a business cycle is an up-and-down motion in the economy's activity (real GNP) that takes place over time. Its fluctuations affect such aggregate variables as output, employment, income, and the price level. If we were to consult an *idealized* business cycle model, it would look like the one presented in Figure 6-2, in which the horizontal axis measures time, in years, and the vertical axis is a measure of business conditions.

There are four specific phases in an idealized business cycle, and we use these same phases to describe what happens in real-world business activity. The difference, of course, between an idealized business cycle and the actual ones is that the real world's changing conditions are not so neatly periodic and predictable. For example, real-life recessions do not come with unvarying intensity every X number of years, with boom time in between because actual business cycles and their phases are not periodic. The four phases depicted in the idealized model are nevertheless useful concepts and are fairly straightforward:

Recession This is the downward phase of business activity. Real income, employment, and output are decreasing. Business and consumer pessimism is prevalent.[1]

[1]A depression is an *abnormally* severe recession. Very high rates of unemployment persist. Very few businesspersons or consumers feel that the economic outlook is rosy. We have had very few true depressions in this country compared to the number of recessions.

Bottom or Trough The low point in business activity.

Recovery This is the upward phase of the cycle. All aggregate variables, such as output, employment, and real income, are rising. Consumer and business optimism are rising.

Boom This is the uppermost point of the cycle, generally associated with tight labor markets, that is, low unemployment, rising output and real income, and in addition, inflationary pressures as the economy approaches its capacity.

Indicators of Business Activity

In the real world we have indicators of business activity that either coincide with, lead, or lag behind the business cycle. These indicators are published by the Department of Commerce in *Business Conditions Digest.* Let's go to Figure 6-3 to see what they look like. Figure 6-3 shows the *leading, coincidental,* and *lagging* indicators from the period 1965 to 1975. Notice how well the leading indicators predicted the recession of 1969 to 1970. Some examples of leading indicators are the average work week for production workers, the average weekly overtime hours by production workers, the index of net business formation, new orders for machines, and changes in business inventories. Examples of coincident indicators are current dollar GNP and personal income, retail sales, unfilled orders, and an index of help-wanted advertising. Examples of lagging indicators are the unemployment rate, spending on new plant and equipment, labor costs per unit of output, and consumer installment debt outstanding.

Economists who are interested in predicting business activity in the United States sometimes rely on leading indicators for their information. However, economists attempting to predict the future of the price level, unemployment, con-

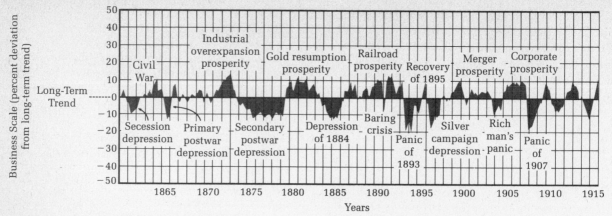

FIGURE 6-1 **Business Activity in the United States**

Here we see the ups and downs of business activity in the United States from before the Civil War until today. The prosperity during the 1960s, which was uninterrupted for almost 10 years, was the longest period of sustained rise in business activity that we have ever had. The ups and downs in business activity are measured as a percentage change compared to the long-run trend in the United States. (*Source:* Cleveland Trust Company.)

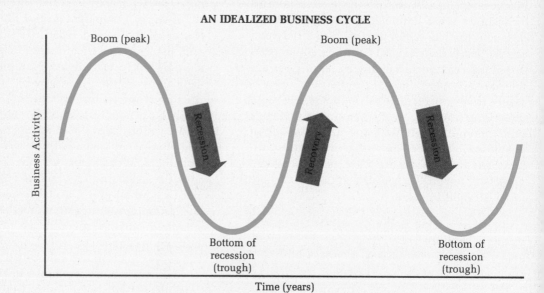

FIGURE 6-2

The diagram shows that in an idealized business cycle there is first a boom period toward the end of the recovery, then a sliding off into recession and/or depression, which eventually bottoms out and another recovery begins.

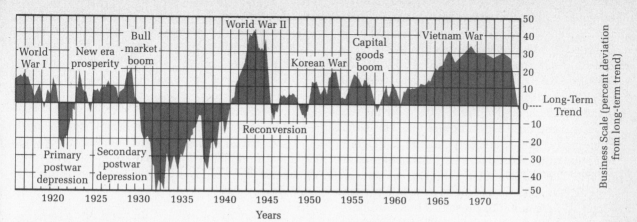

FIGURE 6-1 *(cont'd.)*

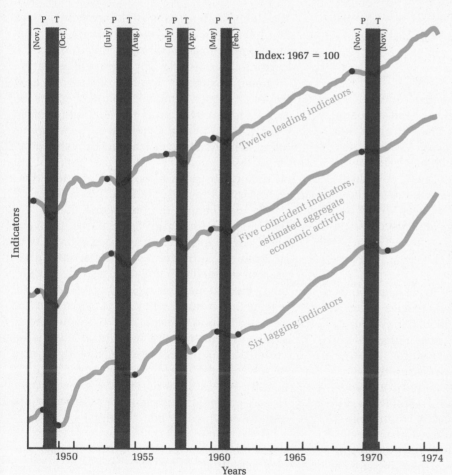

FIGURE 6-3 **Leading Coincidental and Lagging Indicators**

Changes in leading business indicators usually signal the turns of the business cycle, but not always. Coincidental indicators move concurrently with business activity. On average, leading indicators peak about 5 months before the peaks in business activity. Lagging indicators usually turn down about 3 months after business activity has done so. *(Source: U.S. Bureau of the Census, Business Conditions Digest.)*

sumer spending, and other aggregate variables use much more sophisticated techniques. These forecasting techniques are usually based on a theory about how income is determined. The first step is to collect data for the relevant variables, such as past rates of change of prices, unemployment, and output. The next step is to feed these data into a computer. The computer analyzes the data, using an income-determination model based on a particular economic theory. The success of the theory, of course, depends on its ability to make accurate predictions. We are going to present a basic modern theory, or income-determination model, in the following unit. For now, we will see how some older theories of the business cycle—including Marx's theory—described it.

Earlier Business-Cycle Theories

In any field of study there have been as many theories as there have been theorists, and this is also true for the business cycle. We will look at a few of the theories that have stood out above all the others because of their popularity or success. Three theories that used to be popular based their predictions on very dissimilar things: sunspots, innovation, and psychology.

The Sunspot Theory

In the late nineteenth century, some economists believed that sunspots caused changes in business activity. Inane as this theory may sound, it did have some scientific basis. Sunspots affected the weather, and the weather affected the output of farmers. Since agriculture was such a large part of business activity, a change in agricultural output would affect overall business conditions. Historically, there was a fairly high correlation between sunspot cycles and agricultural cycles, but, unfortunately for the theory's advocates, the correlation seemed

to disappear just as the theory was gaining ground. The **sunspot theory** would have been a very useful predicting tool had the relationship between weather and business activity held, since we can *predict* sunspot activity accurately. Given the high accuracy of that prediction, the link to business activity could have been quite useful. Meteorological data would have led to sunspot prediction, which would have enabled weather prediction, which finally would have allowed business-activity prediction.

The Innovation Theory

We all know about some of the great *inventions* that have been made—the cotton gin, the telephone, and many others. An invention is the creation of something new. Once the invention is made, businesses have to figure out how to use it. That's where *innovation* comes in. We define innovation as the adaptation of an invention to actual production techniques. Many inventions never lead to innovations because they are never put to use; think about all the unsuccessful home inventors with their gadgets piled high to the basement ceiling.

The idea behind the **innovation theory** was that innovations caused fluctuations in investment, which ultimately caused ups and downs in business activity. As soon as one entrepreneur decided to innovate (use an invention), many businesspersons would hop on the bandwagon. In so doing, they'd also invest in the new production process, and we would see a rise in overall business activity as all this investment took place. Soon the new investment rage would die down, and aggregate business activity would slow down as a consequence. Hence, sporadic innovations would cause ups and downs in economic activity.

There is an important difference between the innovation theory and the sunspot theory. Sunspot activity is predictable; however, we don't know how to predict *when* innovations will occur. *After the fact*, we can hypothesize which ones caused the particular "take off" in economic activity, but we wouldn't have known beforehand what to predict. The innovation theory is therefore useful for *explaining* cycles, but not for *predicting* the *timing* of them.

The Psychological Theory

The **psychological theory** holds that the psychological reactions of businesspersons to changes in political, social, and economic events result in business-activity cycles. These decision makers ride waves of optimism, depending on the prospects for peace or war, on new discoveries of natural resources, and on many other factors.

Many stock market analysts maintain that swings in stock prices are due to psychological factors. The psychological theory may indeed prove useful in explaining stock market waves. Be careful, though: A dip in the stock market doesn't always precede a recession. In fact, one astute observer noted that the stock market has predicted nine of the last five recessions!

Marx's Theory of the Business Cycle

One of the key analyses offered by Marx in his economic works was his theory of the exploitation of laborers by capitalists. Marx came up with the notion of *surplus* value. In his theory, he pointed out that workers spend part of every working day earning the costs of maintaining themselves and their families. These are, in fact, their subsistence wages. The rest of the day it appears that they work without payment, creating for the capitalist some sort of surplus value, a source of wealth and profit for the capitalist class. In other words, in Marx's world the value of any good or service was directly proportional to the amount of labor used to

make it. That means that the worker will work all day to make, say, $50 worth of shoes, but will only be paid, say, $30. The difference is surplus value, and it accrues to the capitalist. It is this small group of lucky capitalists—that is, those who happen to own capital—who are able to garner this surplus. The reason the workers will not get more is because they supposedly only "require" wages that allow them to subsist. And because of an ever-increasing **reserve army of the unemployed** who seek work, the capitalists have always available to them a ready work force to exploit.

Economic Crises

According to Marx, the accumulation of capital would inevitably create contradictions. He predicted that as more and more things were produced and economic development continued, the reserve army of the unemployed would become depleted. Wage rates would have to rise. But capitalists would seek to increase their profits by introducing more sophisticated production equipment and techniques. Eventually, however, capitalists would no longer be able to sell their increased output because of deficient demand. Unemployment would result, thus reducing purchasing power. This would lead to a recession and depression. Marx saw continuous cycles of recessions and depressions in the capitalist economy, but these were different from the ones we've talked about in this book.

Business Cycles

Marx's theory of the business cycle describes the explosion and collapse of capitalism and the eventual revolution of the workers' class. He predicted that the rate of profit would fall in the long run. Industrial power would become increasingly concentrated in fewer and fewer monopolistic firms. Wealth also would become concentrated in the hands of fewer and fewer capitalists. Laborers would become more and more exploited as production became more and more capital intensive. Eventually, the workers of the world would unite and revolt. The whole system would be overthrown, and a more rational socialist economy would prevail:

> The revolt of a working class, a class always increasing in numbers and discipline, united, organized by the very mechanism of the process of capitalist production itself. Centralization of the means of production and socialization of labor at last reach a point where they become incompatible with their capitalist integument. This integument is burst asunder. The knell of capitalist private property sounds. The expropriators are expropriated.[2]

Marx's views caused considerable debate. His theories are still highly regarded by many economists, but his predictions about revolution in industrial capitalist societies have proved incorrect. His views on the inevitability of rising unemployment also have not been proved correct. Unemployment is still a problem in this country and elsewhere, but it seems to be more one of a cyclical nature rather than a secular increase in the percentage of the labor force that is unemployed. Let us now see how unemployment is measured and what different types of unemployment exist.

Unemployment

One of the major consequences of faltering business activity is the ensuing unemployment, particularly of workers, but also of other factors of production (resources). Unemployment has so many costs—in human suffering, in loss of dignity, in loss of savings—the list goes on and

[2]Karl Marx, *Das Kapital,* vol. 1, Moscow: Foreign Language Publishing House, 1961, p. 163.

on. That is why policymakers in our economy closely watch the unemployment figures published by the Department of Labor's Bureau of Labor Statistics. Unemployment is thought to be a social evil that must be kept at an "acceptable" level. We can see from Figure 6-4 that unemployment in the United States has been very low at times—1.2 percent in World War II—but has been intolerably high at other times—almost 25 percent at one point during the Depression.

How Is It Measured?

The Bureau of Labor Statistics, in cooperation with the United States Bureau of the Census, takes monthly surveys in an attempt to estimate unemployment rates. The government statisticians have designed a sampling method to collect the data. They have divided the country into almost 2000 primary sampling units, which generally consist of single counties or groups of counties with contiguous boundaries. They have further refined the sampling technique to take account of population density, rate of growth, percentage of minority groups, and principal industries. Out of each of these areas, called *strata,* statisticians, using demographic data available for all sample units, select one of the sampling units to represent that entire group. Then, within the unit, they randomly select a certain number of individual households and contact these households during each monthly survey. The households contacted change over time, so that no biases creep into the responses by those interviewed. All in all, the 1100 or more employees who go out into the field sample 50,000 households each month.

To be classified as unemployed, a person must meet the exacting official criteria. According to the definition used by the Bureau of the Census, an unemployed worker is a person who (1) did not work at all during the survey week but was looking for work and was available for work; or (2) was waiting to be

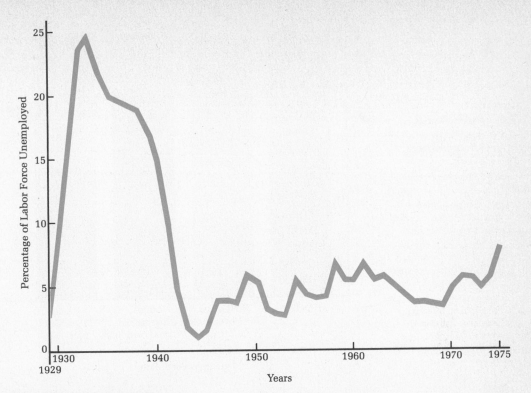

FIGURE 6-4 Unemployment in the United States
Unemployment has varied in the United States from a low of 1.2 percent of the civilian labor force at one point during World War II to almost 25 percent at the depths of the Great Depression. As can be seen, the cyclical variations in unemployment are irregular. (*Source:* U.S. Dept. of Labor, Bureau of Labor Statistics.)

called back after being laid off; or (3) was waiting to report to a new job within the next 30 days and was not in school; or (4) would have been looking for work but was temporarily ill.

The unemployment rate reported by the government lumps together everyone who meets these qualifications. However, the survey does reveal some interesting profiles on unemployed workers. For one thing, it allows us to distinguish between voluntary and involuntary unemployment.

Voluntary Unemployment

It's hard to imagine that unemployment may be voluntary, but a look at Figure 6-5 may change your mind. The unemployed include quite a few individuals who have been neither laid off nor fired. Among the unemployed are those who quit their jobs, those who are looking for first jobs, and those who have decided to "reenter the labor force" after being out of it. At least three-fourths of the unemployment among youths and more than half the unemployment among females is voluntary. However, the unemployment rate determined by government sampling does not tell us how long unemployed individuals, whether they became unemployed voluntarily or involuntarily, remain unemployed. In fact, official statistics, by failing to take certain factors into account, can either overestimate or underestimate unem-

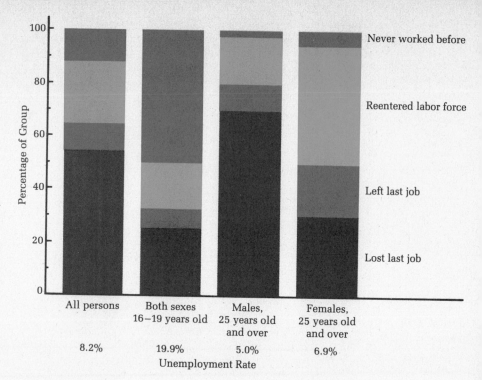

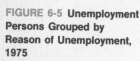

FIGURE 6-5 Unemployment Persons Grouped by Reason of Unemployment, 1975

It would appear that a lot of unemployment is actually voluntary. Those included in the voluntary category are those who have either quit their job, are looking for first jobs, or have "reentered the labor force" after having been a "nonparticipant." At least 44 percent of all unemployment in 1975 fell into these three categories. (*Source:* U.S. Dept. of Labor, Bureau of Labor Statistics.)

ployment rates. They can err on the upside by ignoring duration of unemployment. And duration of unemployment is an important factor that relates to our study of the business cycle.

The Business Cycle and the Duration of Unemployment

Look at Figure 6-6. It shows total unemployment broken down into three categories: people remaining unemployed for less than 5 weeks; from 5 to 14 weeks; and for 15 weeks or more. Actually, the average duration of unemployment is closely associated with the business cycle. In 1969, for example, at the end of the 1960s boom, the average duration of unemployment had fallen to a low of 8 weeks. However, as the recession set in, the average duration

of unemployment rose. In fact, much of what is seen as an increase in the unemployment rate is really a reflection of an increase in the average duration of unemployment. After all, if the *same* percentage of the labor force becomes newly unemployed each month, but all of a sudden those who are unemployed take several weeks *longer* to find a new job, survey results will show an *increase* in the unemployment rate. This suggests that care should be taken in interpreting monthly statistics that show slight variations in unemployment rates. Chances are that relatively small variations in the average duration of unemployment will fully account for these slightly inflated unemployment rates.

On the other side of the coin, official unemployment rates may seriously *underestimate*

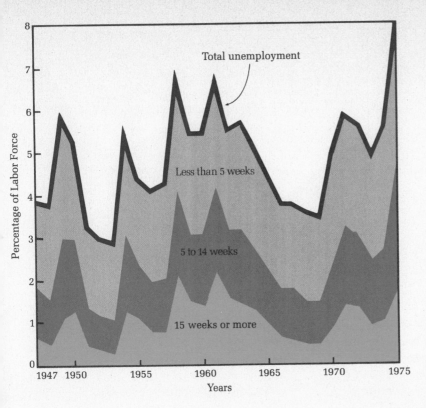

Percentage of Labor Force

Total unemployment

Less than 5 weeks

5 to 14 weeks

15 weeks or more

1947 1950 1955 1960 1965 1970 1975

Years

FIGURE 6-6 **Unemployment Rates by Duration**

A very small percentage of the labor force that is unemployed at any given moment has actually been unemployed for 15 or more weeks. A rise in the unemployment rate often is merely reflecting an increase in the average duration of unemployment. (*Source:* U.S. Dept. of Labor, Bureau of Labor Statistics.)

the true rate of unemployment—particularly during periods of recession and depression—by not taking into account hidden, or disguised, unemployment.

Hidden Unemployment

A number of observers of the unemployment scene believe that official unemployment rates are biased downward because of the criteria used in the survey. To be marked down as unemployed, a person must be out of work yet looking for a job. But what about all those who would like to look for work but are discouraged? Should they not also be included in the unemployed category? This is a question we cannot answer. However, we do know that when Bureau of Labor Statistics personnel in-

terview individuals not in the labor force, they find there are several different reasons for this. Individuals indicate that they are not in the labor force because they think they will be unable to find a job or no jobs are available; an employer will turn them down because they are either too young or too old; or they lack sufficient education or training. If we lump together all these individuals and call them "discouraged" workers, we can see how evident the phenomenon of discouraged workers is in Figure 6-7. In any event, when individuals hold such attitudes, they drop out of the labor force and no longer look for a job—yet official surveys do not count them as unemployed.

In each case, however, the labor-force participation rate will fall for that potential worker's whole group. For example, every mid-

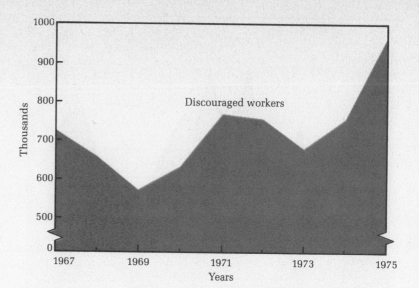

FIGURE 6-7 **Discouraged Workers**
There are many reasons why individuals want a job but are not looking. These reasons include thinking that jobs are not available, thinking that employers will not hire them because they are too old or too young, and so forth. *(Source: U.S. Dept. of Labor, Bureau of Labor Statistics.)*

dle-aged black male who drops out of the labor force lowers the rate of participation for all middle-aged black males. The labor-force participation rate is merely the percentage of available individuals of working age who are actually in the labor force. We show in Figure 6-8 total male and female labor-force participation rates over time. Notice that the male labor-force participation rate has been falling gradually over the past three decades, whereas the female participation rate has been rising gradually.

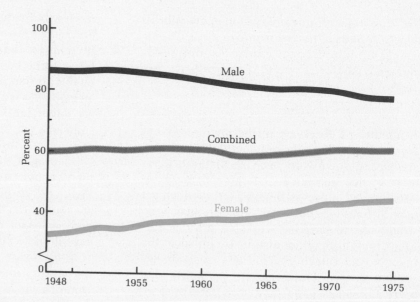

FIGURE 6-8 **Labor-Force Participation Rates by Sex**
The combined labor-force participation rate has increased slightly in recent years. However, over the same period, the male participation rate has fallen, and the female rate has risen. *(Source: U.S. Dept. of Labor, Bureau of Labor Statistics.)*

The Major Types of Unemployment

Unemployment has been categorized into four basic types: frictional, cyclical, seasonal, and structural. You often hear about these different types of unemployment, so you might want to know what they mean.

Frictional Unemployment

Here are the unemployment estimates for 1976: Of the 92 million Americans in the labor force, more than 10 million will have either changed or taken new jobs during the year; about 1 in 20 workers will have quit, been laid off, or been fired every single month; another 5 percent will have gone to new jobs or returned to old ones. In the process, more than 17 million persons will have reported themselves unemployed at one time or another. What we call **frictional unemployment** is the constant flow of individuals from job to job and in and out of employment. We know that some frictional unemployment cannot and probably should not be eliminated. (Notice that the "should" here is a value judgment.) To eliminate frictional unemployment, we would have to prevent workers from leaving their present jobs unless they had already lined up jobs elsewhere where they would start working immediately. It might be difficult for some workers to line up a better job while having to work at their current one. Besides, a complete elimination of frictional unemployment would probably reduce the rate of growth of our economy. One important source of advances in productivity is the movement of workers from sectors of the economy where labor productivity and wages are low to sectors where productivity and wages are high. The search for better job offers is the process by which workers discover areas where their productivity is highest—that is, where they can make the most income. Nonetheless, frictional unemployment can be reduced by getting better information about alternative sources of jobs and available workers.

The level of frictional unemployment determines our definition of "full" employment. If we assert that frictional unemployment is 4 percent of the labor force, then that is what we call full employment. And when governmental officials change their minds and say that full employment should be redefined as 5 percent rather than 4 percent unemployment, they are really saying that labor mobility, knowledge of job opportunities, and so on have changed so as to cause an increase in frictional unemployment. We really don't know how the magic number of 4 percent ever came into being. Perhaps the switch to 5 percent as our goal of "full" employment simply means that the government has learned better ways to estimate frictional unemployment.

Cyclical Unemployment

Cyclical unemployment is related to the business cycle. In fact, cyclical unemployment is defined as unemployment associated with changes in business conditions—primarily recessions and depressions. The way to lessen cyclical unemployment would be to reduce the intensity, duration, and frequency of ups and downs of business activity. Economic policymakers attempt, through their policies, to reduce cyclical unemployment by keeping business activity on an even keel.

Seasonal Unemployment

Seasonal unemployment is just that. It comes and goes with seasons of the year in which the demand for particular jobs rises and falls. Construction workers often can work only during the warmer months in northern climates. They are seasonally unemployed during the winter. Resort workers usually can only get jobs in resorts during the summer season. They, too, become seasonally unemployed during the winter; the opposite is true for ski resort workers. There is little we can do to reduce seasonal unemployment. It is unlikely that employers will begin to develop production techniques to allow, say, construction workers to work during winter months. For one thing, the costs would be prohibitive.

Structural Unemployment

Presumably, there have been structural changes in our economy that cause some workers to become permanently unemployed, or at least unemployed for a very long period of time. Structurally unemployed persons are usually those who simply can't find *any* job they can do. **Structural unemployment** has also been associated with **technological unemployment**—that is, unemployment resulting from the increased use of labor-saving machines.

Unlike cyclical unemployment, structural unemployment is not caused by the business cycle, although the business cycle may affect it. And unlike frictional unemployment, structural unemployment is not related to the labor mobility that occurs when workers move from low-productivity to high-productivity sectors of the economy. Rather, structural unemployment results when the demanding public no longer wants to buy an individual's services and instead of going through retraining, that individual persists in his or her search for employment with "obsolete" skills. According to theory, some of these people eventually will go into new industries. More often than not, in most urban settings this is precisely what happens. However, in some settings this does not happen. Often people refuse to move. They sit and wait for times to improve. The result is a kind of permanent depression in some geographic areas due to labor immobility.

The problem is widespread. Structural un-employment is not merely a matter of locale; it is something you carry with you if there is no demand for your skills. For example, vast numbers of blacks came to the northern cities from southern agricultural areas where they were structurally unemployed. In the cities blacks are now called "hard-core unemployables" because they have no skills that fit into the market demand. Usually, when these people are employed, it is in service jobs (like working in a car wash), and they are frequently the first ones to be hit by a business cycle. Although it may make very little difference to the person you're talking to, you can present a complex economic question by asking: "Are you cyclically or structurally unemployed?" It is sometimes hard to tell, but basically structural unemployment can be cured only by developing new skills for a changed market. For this reason, structural unemployment is a much tougher problem than the one brought on by simple cyclical swings.

One more point needs to be made: Don't assume that structural unemployment is a problem only for those with little formal education. Any time you specialize in something, you run the risk of having the market turn against you. Highly educated men who can build supersonic transports or rockets that go to the moon are in precisely the same jam when their demand (in this case, government) falls away. They are unemployed and must retrain. Much West Coast unemployment among so-called aerospace engineers in the early 1970s was very close in cause and cure to the problems of Appalachia.

It is interesting to note that worry over structural unemployment was quite intense during the 1950s but almost melted away to nothing during the 1960s. When the GNP growth rate finally increased in the 1960s, nobody spoke of structural unemployment as a problem. This leads one to be a little wary about the entire concept of structural unemployment.

Reducing the Suffering

In the United States we have a system of unemployment compensation that transfers income to those individuals who are unemployed and who qualify. This is one way of reducing the loss of income associated with unemployment. However, critics of unemployment compensation contend that such transfer payments, in spite of their positive benefits, have perverse results. How could this be? In Issue I-8 you will see why.

In Issue I-8 you will see why.

Definitions of New Terms

Business Cycle: A recurrent fluctuation in general economic activity. Business cycles usually are observed in such aggregate variables as gross national product and employment.

Sunspot Theory: A business-cycle theory according to which sunspots were believed to affect weather, which in turn affected agricultural output and, therefore, general business conditions.

Innovation Theory: A business-cycle theory attributing changes in business activity to the development of innovations that businesspersons can adopt to increase profits. Presumably once the innovation is successful, other businesspersons jump on the bandwagon, thus causing a rise in investment, which causes a rise in overall business activity. Later, investment peters out and investment activity goes down.

Psychological Theory: A theory which holds that business cycles are caused by the psychological reaction of businesspersons to changes in social and political events, as well as economic events, which cause changes in business activity.

Reserve Army of the Unemployed: In Marxian terminology, the unemployed workers, whose numbers will grow as workers become more and more exploited by the capitalist classes.

Frictional Unemployment: Unemployment associated with frictions in the system that may occur because of the imperfect information which exists.

Cyclical Unemployment: Unemployment resulting from business recessions that occur when aggregate demand is insufficient to create full employment.

Seasonal Unemployment: Unemployment due to seasonality in demand or possible supply of any particular good or service.

Structural Unemployment: Unemployment resulting from fundamental changes in the structure of the economy. Structural unemployment occurs, for example, when the demand for a product falls drastically so that workers specializing in the production of that product find themselves out of work.

Technological Unemployment: Unemployment caused by technologically superior equipment replacing labor in specific tasks.

1. The United States has a history of ups and downs in its business activity. Economists have tried to characterize these ups and downs by using business-cycle theories.

2. The business cycle is a recurrent up and down in economic activity. An idealized business cycle is periodic; that is, it goes up and down at regular intervals. No business cycles in the United States have been so regular. We therefore need a more sophisticated theory to predict turning points in economic activity.

3. There have been many business-cycle theories, including the sunspot theory, the innovation theory, the psychological theory, and Marx's theory of the business cycle. None of these theories are really used today. They have been supplanted by more modern theories.

4. Unemployment in the United States is composed of four types: frictional, seasonal, structural, and cyclical. It is difficult to discern what part of total unemployment is composed of any one of these four categories.

5. Frictional unemployment is caused by the temporary inability of workers to match their skills and talents with available jobs. Frictional unemployment could not be eliminated without passing a law that required employers never to fire a worker and that required employees never to quit a job unless they could go immediately to a new one.

6. Structural unemployment occurs when the demand for a product falls off abruptly. We have observed structural unemployment lately in the aerospace industry. Structural unemployment is often referred to as technological unemployment—that is, it occurs when machines put men or women out of work.

7. The hard-core unemployed are usually defined as undereducated members of particularly prominent minority groups. The hard-core unemployed are not necessarily unemployed because of structural reasons. They may be unemployed because of government legislation, discrimination in the labor market, and certain restrictive hiring practices on the part of unions.

8. The duration of unemployment in the United States varies dramatically over the business cycle. As business conditions worsen, the average duration of unemployment lengthens. As business conditions strengthen, the average duration of unemployment falls.

1. Why do you think the government would like to be able to predict the business cycle?
2. We have referred to unemployment only in terms of the labor force. Are there other unemployed resources in the United States during business recessions?
3. The United States Department of Labor defines unemployed people as those who are seeking work but have not found any. Do you agree with this definition?
4. Can you think of ways to reduce frictional unemployment?

Selected
References

Chandler, Lester V., *America's Greatest Depression: 1929 to 1941*, New York: Harper & Row, 1970.

Economic Report of the President, various issues, Washington, D.C.: U.S. Government Printing Office.

Gordon, R. A., *Economic Instability and Growth: The American Record*, New York: Harper & Row, 1974.

——, "How Obsolete Is the Business Cycle?", *The Public Interest*, Fall 1970, pp. 127–139.

Moore, Geoffrey H., *How Full is Full Employment?*, American Enterprise Institute of Public Policy Research, study no. 14, Washington, D.C., July 1973.

Does Unemployment Compensation Cause Unemployment?

DOES OUR SYSTEM HAVE A BUILT-IN INCENTIVE FOR NOT WORKING?

Helping Out the Jobless

The last chapter discussed unemployment in detail but made only passing reference to its costs to the unemployed. Now we will take a closer look at those "costs." During the depths of the Great Depression, the Roosevelt administration attempted to help out the unemployed with a system of unemployment compensation. We described it in Chapter 5, when we reviewed certain aspects of our tax system. Briefly, employers are required by state governments to collect a payroll tax whose proceeds are used to provide unemployment compensation benefits or "insurance" when employees become unemployed. Not all employees are eligible for unemployment compensation, but somewhere in the neighborhood of 60 percent to 70 percent of the work force is covered. Average unemployment compensation payments per week were 67 dollars in 1975. The average, however, doesn't tell the whole story because there are wide variations among the states. In addition to the wide variations in weekly benefits, the states also differ on the maximum number of weeks that an eligible employee is entitled to draw benefits. The national maximum for this was 65 in 1975.

The unemployment insurance system now in effect has remained essentially unchanged since its inception in the 1930s. However, since World War II there has been a marked increase in the unemployment rate. Since the end of the war, annual unemployment rates have averaged in excess of 4.5 percent. In only one postwar year did the unemployment rate go below 3 percent of the labor force. Some observers contend that a structural shift in the economy has caused the rate of unemployment to go up: Increased complexity and "friction" have made it more difficult for workers who are out of a job to find appropriate employment.

Other observers disagree with this explanation of why average rates of unemployment have risen over the past few decades. They argue that what we are seeing is the "new" unemployment—joblessness induced by a combination of our unemployment compensation system and our system of taxes and transfers. What on earth could they be talking about? The analytics are quite simple because they hinge upon the notion of opportunity cost, which we have discussed on several occasions.

The Low Opportunity Cost of Not Working

Recall from Chapter 5, when we talked about taxation, and from Issue I-7, when we discussed tax shelters, that the opportunity cost of not working was the forgone aftertax income. If an individual's aftertax income is $5 an hour and the individual becomes unemployed, the opportunity cost of being unemployed is then $5 per hour for each normal workday. Otherwise stated, the cost of leisure is the aftertax income forgone by not working.

What would the law of demand tell you about the quantity of leisure demanded if the opportunity cost of not working—leisure's price—were to fall? The quantity would rise. What does that mean? It means that some individuals will be induced by a lower price of leisure to accept unemployment more readily (that is, demand more leisure). What would lower the opportunity cost of not working? Unemployment compensation payments.

Look at Figure I-8.1. Here we show a downward-sloping demand

Issue I-8

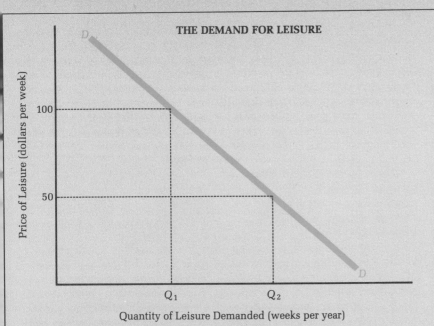

THE DEMAND FOR LEISURE

Price of Leisure (dollars per week)

100

50

D

D

Q₁   Q₂

Quantity of Leisure Demanded (weeks per year)

FIGURE I-8.1

The demand for leisure (not working) is related to its price. Its price, however, is basically an individual's aftertax income because when the individual stops working—that is, "buys" leisure—her or his opportunity cost is the aftertax income loss. We see that when aftertax income is $100 per week, the quantity of "leisure purchased" measured in weeks per year will be Q_1; however, if unemployment compensation makes up for $50 of the weekly aftertax income loss, then the price of leisure will be reduced to $50 per week, at which price the larger quantity, Q_2, will be purchased.

curve for leisure, where leisure is measured in weeks per year. A week of leisure is, of course, synonymous with a week out of work. The vertical axis shows the price per week of leisure. Let's assume that a worker is faced with the following choice: A job can be taken that yields $100 per week in take-home pay. If the job is not taken, the worker pays the price, for each week of leisure, of $100. At that price, the worker would demand a quantity of leisure, Q_1. However, if unemployment compensation of $50 per week were paid to this worker, the opportunity cost of not working would fall from $100 per week to $50. At the lower price of $50 per week, a larger quantity of leisure, Q_2 would be demanded per year. These are the simple demand analytics demonstrating how unemployment compensation will

increase the number of people choosing not to work.

But this is not the end of the story because unemployment compensation is often coupled with other benefits (food stamps, health insurance, and so on) that are lost when a worker goes *back* to work. What we want to determine now is the effective tax rate that is applied to an unemployed worker's potential income if that unemployed worker were to accept a job.

The Benefits of Unemployment

When workers become unemployed, they not only receive unemployment compensation but also are relieved of paying income and Social Security

taxes. Moreover, many may be eligible for food stamps, rent supplements, and even additional welfare payments. We will now look at the taxes one can avoid by being out of a job and accepting tax-free unemployment compensation. We will use the example given in an article by Professor Martin Feldstein of Harvard University.[1]

Consider a worker in Massachusetts in 1971. This worker has a wife and two children. If he remains employed all year long, he earns $500 a month, or $6,000 per year. The wife earns $350 per month, or a total of $4,200 per year if she works all year long.

What happens if the man be-

[1]Martin Feldstein, "The Economics of the New Unemployment," *The Public Interest*, no. 33, Fall 1973.

comes unemployed for 1 month? He obviously loses $500 in *gross* (before-tax) earnings. What does he lose in *net* (take-home) income? His federal income tax is reduced by $83. His Social Security payroll tax is reduced by $26. His Massachusetts state income taxes are reduced by another $25. The total tax reduction is $137. Now unemployment compensation comes into play to give him 50 percent of his gross wage, plus a dependence allowance of $6 per week for each child, totaling a tax-free $302 per month.

When working, his gross income was $500, but his take-home pay was $366. His take-home pay now is $302 because that is what unemployment compensation benefits total. For each month of unemployment (leisure), this man has a reduction in spendable income of only $64.

The Effective Marginal Tax Rate

In the above example, net income falls by $64 when 1 month of unemployment occurs. That means that net income, expressed as a percentage of gross income, falls by about 13 percent, implying an effective marginal tax rate on work effort of 87 percent. Go back to Table 5-6. Can you find 87 percent on that table? No, you cannot. The highest marginal tax rate that the highest income individuals have to pay in this economy is 70 percent, but for the low-income individual who might be eligible for unemployment, the effective marginal tax rate is higher than that paid by the most wealthy. Looking at this man's wife, we can

calculate the effective marginal tax rate to be over 93 percent. And in Massachusetts during the year for which the example was taken, if the family had had three children instead of two, the family's net income actually would have been higher if the woman had remained unemployed for 3 months than if she had worked for that period!

These startlingly high effective marginal tax rates certainly indicate a disincentive effect that may encourage workers to remain unemployed longer than they might otherwise be. After all, look at how much leisure they can buy for each week of unemployment and at what a low price. If we were to be more thorough in our example and include other transfer benefits that would be lost when an unemployed worker becomes employed—food stamps, housing supplements, and so forth—the effective marginal tax rate in many cases for low-income individuals would in some states exceed 100 percent. These individuals must see this, and not a few of them will realize that it pays to remain unemployed—particularly when the effective marginal tax rate is, in fact, in excess of 100 percent.

Inverse Seniority

For evidence that tends to confirm our analysis, we need only look at something new in labor agreements. Historically, seniority has been an issue, particularly in union contracts with employers. Those workers who had the most seniority (who had worked the longest) were the last to be fired or laid off. But in several industries, unions have negotiated

recent contracts that include *inverse* seniority provisions: Workers with more seniority have the option of being laid off earlier than other workers and rehired later. This would only be expected to occur if there were positive benefits attached to unemployment. These benefits are, of course, associated with unemployment compensation as well as with other transfer payments for which unemployed workers become eligible. Additionally, the unemployed worker has more leisure time and, in some cases, will invest part of that leisure time actually looking for a better job or "day-lighting" without reporting the income earned.

In a sense, then, unemployment compensation and the tax system, which taken together lead to high effective marginal tax rates, are subsidies to job searching. They allow workers to take longer to search for a job in the hopes of getting a better one than they had, or from which they had been laid off, or have been offered.

Seasonal Unemployment

We mentioned briefly seasonal unemployment in Chapter 6. Seasonal unemployment occurs whenever certain industries do not operate at specific times during each year. During the off periods, they lay off their workers. If no unemployment compensation were given to workers during these periods, employers who hire workers only seasonally would have to pay relatively higher wages to compensate for the anticipated periods of unemployment. However, with unemployment compensation

available, wages to seasonal workers do not have to be as high because these seasonal workers are partially compensated for their unemployment during the slack season. According to Feldstein, "Because the price of unstable labor has been artificially subsidized, employers organize production in a way that makes too much use of unstable employment."[2]

If there were no unemployment compensation, workers would have to be paid more to get them to accept unstable jobs. The differences in pay between stable and unstable jobs would then reflect the fairly certain probability of being laid off and the expected duration of unemployment. On the other hand, employers faced

[2]Ibid., p. 34.

with this wage differential would attempt to reduce unstable employment by many means, including inventory buildup during slack periods and the introduction of new techniques of production, such as improving outdoor work practices so that bad weather would not curtail employment to the extent it does now.

The results of a new unemployment compensation law in British Columbia offer some evidence for this proposition. In 1974 a new law was passed that allowed full unemployment compensation benefits to be paid to workers who had kept a job for a minimum of only 8 weeks. After the law was passed, the worker turnover rates in such seasonal jobs as logging increased 600 percent. After loggers had worked their requisite 8 weeks, many found it in their

interest to go on unemployment. The same was true among seasonal workers in resort areas. Their turnover rate increased dramatically; more workers had to be hired for the same work season than previously because of the increased turnover.

The New Unemployment

The above analysis leads one to conclude that unemployment compensation, coupled with the peculiarities of our tax and welfare system, is responsible for part of our frictional, cyclical, seasonal, and structural unemployment. In other words, there is a new type of unemployment that is induced by unemployment compensation. Feldstein estimates that the current structure of the unemployment compensation system accounts for at least 1.2 percent of the unemployment rate in the United States. That means that out of, say, a 6 percent unemployment rate, "new" unemployment accounts for over one-fifth of it. Studies done for the Canadian economy show similar results. New unemployment in Canada accounts for 1.5 to 2.5 percent of the total unemployment rate. Otherwise stated, a restructuring of the unemployment compensation system could reduce the unemployment rate by 1 percentage point or more. This is not, however, an argument in favor of abolishing unemployment benefits. Rather, it is presented by Feldstein and others as a case for restructuring the system of benefits paid to unemployed workers because so long as there is a strong incentive to remain unemployed, more workers will become and remain unemployed than they would if the benefits of unemployment were reduced.

One cannot immediately jump to the conclusion that just because unemployment compensation may have a serious effect on work incentives, it should therefore be abolished. We have analyzed some of the problems involved in providing benefits to unemployed workers. That is to say, we have deduced the likely consequences of such a system, furnishing some supportive empirical findings. We would need to step into the realm of normative economics to state that unemployment compensation systems should be abandoned, or even modified, for that matter.

Questions for Thought and Discussion

1. Is it possible to create a system of unemployment compensation that does not have a built-in work disincentive?
2. What are some of the arguments that can be used to counter the statistical findings presented in this issue? In other words, is it possible that, in fact, unemployment compensation as currently provided in the United States does not decrease work effort and hence increase the rate of unemployment?

Selected References

Feldstein, Martin S., "The Economics of the New Unemployment," *The Public Interest,* no. 33, Fall 1973.

——, *Lowering the Permanent Rate of Unemployment,* A Joint Committee Print of the Joint Economic Committee, Washington, D.C.: U.S. Government Printing Office, 1973. Also Hearings of the Joint Economic Committee published as *Reducing Unemployment to Two Percent,* Hearings before the Joint Economic Committee, Oct. 17, 18, and 26, 1972, Washington, D.C.: U.S. Government Printing Office, 1972.

Grubel, H. G. and D. Maki, "Real and Insurance Induced Unemployment in Canada," unpublished paper, Simon Frazer University, June 1973.

Sachs, Shelley, "Measuring the Induced Unemployment Rate in Canada," unpublished master's thesis, Department of Economics, Simon Frazer University, August 1973.

Inflation and Stagflation

The persistent increase in the cost of living in the United States has affected all of us. Rising prices now seem as inevitable as death and taxes. We are continually reminded by newspaper and magazine articles that today's dollar is only worth 30 percent of the 1939 dollar. Although prices have not always gone up at a rate of 5 to 15 percent a year, they rose at a compounded rate of almost 1 percent per year from 1867 to the 1960s. The pace of **inflation** (defined as a *sustained* rise in the general price level), however, has not been even.

Inflation and the History of Prices

The erratic behavior of prices is shown in Figure 7-1. After shooting up at a rate of 25 percent per year during and after the Civil War, the price index *fell* at the rate of 5.4 percent from 1867 to 1879. That is equivalent to a halving of the price level in less than 15 years. Farmers and businesspersons during those years of falling prices cried out, strangely enough, for higher prices—*greenbackism* as it was later called. Farmers thought that inflation would cause the prices of the products they sold to rise faster than those of the products they bought. Politicians apparently didn't listen very well, however, for prices kept falling, averaging a decline of 1 percent per year from 1879 to 1897. Prices then rose 6 percent a year continually until a few years after World War I. For a year or so after the war, prices fell drastically and then remained fairly stable until the Great Depression. Wholesale prices dropped at an average rate of 8 percent a year from the stock market crash in 1929 until Roosevelt declared a "banking holiday" in March 1933. Roosevelt's at-

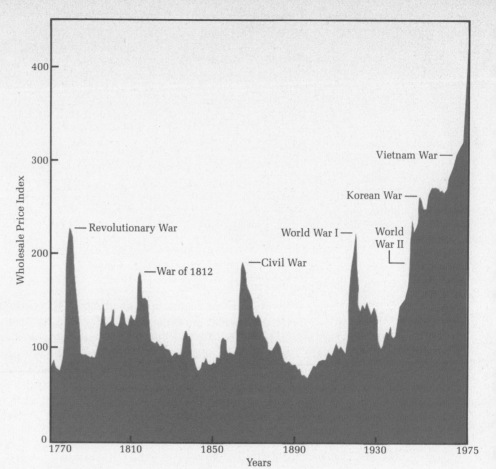

FIGURE 7-1 **History of Prices in the United States, 1770 to 1973**

Here we see the wholesale price index for the past two centuries. Prices have not always been rising, even though the experience of the past few years might lead us to that conclusion. Almost every war in our history has been associated with a rise in the wholesale price index. (*Source:* U.S. Dept. of Commerce.)

tempts to raise prices were moderately successful, and there was general inflation until 1937. Then prices leveled off until the beginning of World War II.

The rate of price increases during World War II was less than it had been during both the Civil War and World War I. The wholesale price index rose 118 percent from August 1939 through August 1948—about 9 percent per year. From 1948 until the mid-1960s, prices remained quite stable except for a jump during the Korean conflict. Since the Vietnam involvement, inflation has accelerated.

Inflation in Other Countries

The United States is not alone in its history of rising prices. Inflation seems to be a worldwide problem. In fact our rate of inflation has been mild relative to inflation in many other countries. Some countries have had waves of hyperinflation that make our wartime episodes look like ripples. In 1939, Hungary had a price index set at 100; by January 1946, it was almost 5,500,000. A half a year later it was 20,000,000,000,000, or 2×10^{13}! This means that a commodity with a 1939 price tag of 100 forints would have cost 5,500,000 forints in January 1946, and by August of the same year it would have cost 20,000,000,000,000 forints. Imagine having to carry a wheelbarrow full of money to the store just to buy a loaf of dark bread!

How We Measure Inflation

If inflation is defined as a sustained rise in the general price level, how do we come up with a measure of the rate of inflation? This is indeed a thorny problem for government statisticians. It is easy to determine how much the price of an individual commodity has risen: If last year a light bulb cost 10¢ and this year it costs 15¢, there has been a 50 percent rise in the price of that light bulb over a 1-year period.

Let's construct a hypothetical price index for light bulbs, using the information in Table 7-1. In the first column we show the year, where year 3 has been singled out as the base year, or period against which all comparisons will be made. Column 2 gives the number of light bulbs sold, and column 3 gives the price per light bulb. The fourth column presents a price index, which is merely the price per light bulb

each year expressed as a percentage of the base year's price. We created columns 5 and 6 to express the output of light bulbs in current dollars, that is, column 2 times column 3, and the value of light bulb output in constant (year 3) dollars. Column 6 is merely a simplification of what real GNP is all about, except here we are talking about "real" light bulbs. All that we have to do to obtain real GNP is correct for price changes, just as we have done in Table 7-1.

Now you should have a little better idea about the difference between *current* dollar or nominal GNP, which is expressed in today's dollars, and *constant* dollar or real GNP, which is expressed in the dollars of some base period. You can see in Figure 7-2 how much of the growth in current dollar GNP has been growth in real output and how much has been due to inflation. The real part was obtained by correcting for inflation as in the above simplified example.

A formal definition of a price index, which may be used for an entire economy, is as follows:

Table 7-1 **Converting the Value of Output in Current Dollars to the Value of Output in Constant Dollars**

We arbitrarily choose year 3 as our base period. We construct a price index in column 4. When we correct for price changes with this price index, we obtain output expressed in constant, year-3 dollars in column 6.

(1)	(2)	(3)	(4)	(5)	(6)
YEAR	PRODUCTION OF LIGHT BULBS	PRICE ($ PER BULB)	PRICE INDEX = EACH YEAR'S PRICE AS A PERCENTAGE OF THE BASE-YEAR PRICE	VALUE OF OUTPUT IN CURRENT DOLLARS (2) × (3)	OUTPUT IN CONSTANT (YEAR 3) DOLLARS (5) ÷ (4)
1	5	$0.10	50%	$0.50	$1.00
2	10	0.15	75%	1.50	2.00
3 = base year	11	0.20	100%	2.20	2.20
4	13	0.22	110%	2.86	2.60

$$\text{Price index} = \frac{\substack{\text{quantities of outputs in the} \\ \text{current year valued at their} \\ \text{current year prices}}}{\substack{\text{quantities of outputs in the} \\ \text{current year valued at their} \\ \text{base-year prices}}}$$

That is exactly the formula we use in column 4 in Table 7-1, except there the price index is for light bulbs only, not the entire economy.

Real-World Price Indices

A number of price indices are used in the United States. They are the consumer price index (CPI), the wholesale price index (WPI), and the implicit price deflator.

Consumer Price Index

The **consumer price index** attempts to measure changes in the average prices of all major categories of goods and services purchased by "typical" clerical workers and urban wage earners. The Bureau of Labor Statistics has its employees go to different parts of the country at regular intervals to buy a "market basket" representative of goods and services people buy in urban areas in the United States. It includes different types of food, clothing, appliances, services, and so on. The prices of approximately 400 different goods and services are currently included in this index. The base year has been rebased arithmetically to 1967. The construction of the current CPI however, involves using relative quantities based on a 1960 to 1961 sur-

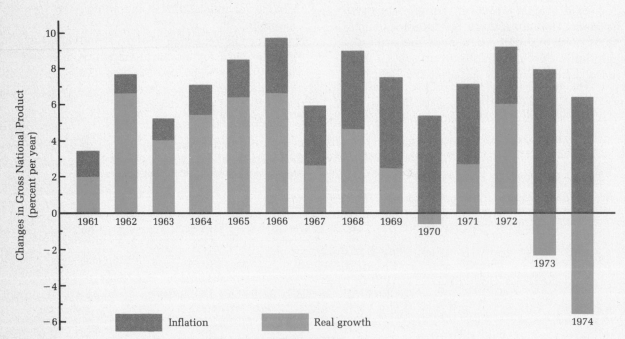

FIGURE 7-2 **How Much Has the Recent Growth in GNP Been Real?**

At various times the rate of growth in nominal GNP has consisted of more or less real growth and more or less inflation, or rise in the price level. In 1970, for example, all the growth was due to inflation. The real growth rate was actually negative in that recession year.

"I see a substantial upswing in the economy by October, but who knows? Maybe it's the Valium talking."

vey of consumer spending habits instead of using the current-year quantities. This saves a lot of time and money on the part of the Bureau of Labor Statistics (BLS) because only new price data have to be collected, expenditure patterns being implicitly assumed unchanged. The BLS updates the quantity computations about every 10 years.

Wholesale Price Index

The **wholesale price index** is similar to the CPI except that it measures changes in the average prices of goods purchased in large quantities by business firms. At present, price quotations are obtained for about 2500 items from producers and manufacturers. No services are included in the WPI market basket. It is calculated in the same manner as the CPI; that is, it employs base-year quantities at current prices and compares them with base-year quantities at base-year prices.

Implicit Price Deflator

The **implicit price deflator,** or GNP deflator, as it is called, is more akin to the original price index we discussed, the one that used current-year quantities at current-year prices compared with current-year quantities at base-year prices. The GNP deflator can be seen as a way of showing the average price level of all final goods and services. We call it a *deflator* because if we divide current dollar GNP by this price index, we get a measure of real or constant dollar GNP. We call it implicit because it is calculated after the fact—after current and real GNP are calculated. As Chapter 4 pointed out, we get today's GNP by adding up the current market value of all final goods and services. Then the dollar value of current output of final goods and services is evaluated at prices prevailing in the base year, which until recently was 1958. The implicit price deflator is then obtained by dividing the former by the latter.

The Accuracy of Price Indices

There is a continuous debate about how accurate the measured price indices really are. Do we have an accurate view of the rate of inflation? We cannot answer that question completely, but we can point out the biases in the price indices that are used.

The first bias has already been mentioned. The CPI and the WPI both use base-year quantities evaluated at today's prices. However, we know from the law of demand that when the relative price of a good goes up, a smaller quantity will be consumed and substitutes will be used in its place. Therefore, too much weight is given to those goods whose prices have risen since the base year relative to other goods; undoubtedly consumers spend a smaller proportion of their income on those relatively more expensive goods than they did in the base year. Nonetheless, the base-year quantities are used throughout the period between surveys on expenditure patterns. This discrepancy imparts an upward bias to both the CPI and the WPI. The opposite is true of the implicit GNP price deflator; since it uses current-year quantities, it has downward bias.

More important perhaps is the bias imparted to all three indices because of improper accounting for changes in quality. At the same nominal price a good is actually cheaper if its quality has been improved. It is difficult for government statisticians to take quality into account. This is also true for the introduction of new products, such as color TVs, that are not included in the market basket of goods because they were introduced after the market basket was made up. These problems probably cause an upward bias in the CPI, WPI, and GNP price deflator.

Theories of Inflation

There are as many theories of inflation as there are inflationary periods in our business history, and we could not hope to cover all of them in this brief chapter. We will limit our discussion to three main theories of inflation.

Quantity Theory of Money and Prices

Perhaps one of the oldest theories of inflation is the **quantity theory of money and prices.** This theory states that the level of prices in the economy is directly proportional to the quantity of money in circulation per unit of output, so that for any given percentage change in the stock of money, [1] there will be an equal percentage change in the price level (output remaining constant). The quantity theory of money comes from the classical equation of exchange.

$$MV = PQ$$

Here we find that M is the money supply, P is the price level, and Q is the output of goods and services. PQ is obviously going to equal output times prices, which is income or GNP. The letter V is called the *income velocity of money*. It is the average number of times per year that a dollar changes hands in purchasing a final good or service. We can define V by juggling the equation of exchange:

$$V = \frac{\text{income}}{\text{money supply}}$$

Let's take an example. Suppose that in 1976 income is \$1.6 trillion and the money supply is \$400 billion. The income velocity of money, V, would equal (\$1.6 trillion)/(\$400 million), or 4. In other words, each dollar would change hands an average of four times a year. We might say, then, that the income velocity of money is a measure of the economy's output per dollar.

The quantity theory of money as expressed by the equation of exchange can, in fact, predict prices if V and Q remain constant. Obviously, any increase in the money supply is going to lead to an increase in the price level. Classical economists did, in a way, think that V and Q were fairly stable.

The evidence shows that the simple quantity theory of money and prices works pretty well for predicting the rate of inflation over a long period of time. For example, Spanish importa-

tion of gold and silver from the New World caused large price increases in Spain and throughout Europe. The discovery of gold in Canada, South Africa, and the United States during the turn of the nineteenth century brought about drastic expansions in the supply of money and rapidly rising prices. However, in the short run, the quantity theory of money and prices as expressed by the equation of exchange does not work too well, mainly because V, the income velocity of money, does not remain constant in the short run. It may move by as much as 30 percent during a 5- to 10-year period.

Demand-Pull Inflation

This theory is summarized by the phrase "too many dollars chasing too few goods." Proponents of the theory of **demand-pull inflation** maintain that the only way we can have inflation (that is, a *sustained* rise in the price level) is for total aggregate demand to exceed the full-employment supply of goods and services at the existing price level. According to the quantity theory just presented, total aggregate demand will exceed the capacity of the economy to satisfy that demand whenever individuals in the economy taken together have too many dollars to spend. This can occur for any number of reasons. Expansionary policies on the part of the government, which we will treat in the following unit, are one of the major reasons cited.

Cost-Push Inflation

The **cost-push inflation** theory of why prices rise has recently reemerged as a popular theory. It attempts to explain why prices rise when the economy is *not* at full employment. Cost-push inflation apparently explains "creeping" inflation and the inflation that the United States

[1] We treat the money supply and its determination in Chapter 11.

experienced during its 1969 to 1970 recession and afterward. There are essentially two explanations of cost-push inflation: union power and big business monopoly power.

Union Power   Many people feel that unions are responsible for inflation. Their reasoning is as follows. Unions decide to demand a wage hike that is not warranted by increases in their physical output. Since the unions are so powerful, employers must give in to union demands for higher wages. When the employers have to pay these higher wages, their costs are higher. To maintain their usual profit margin, these businesspeople raise their prices. This type of cost-push inflation seemingly can occur even when there is no excess demand, even when the economy is operating below capacity at under full employment.

The union-power argument rests on the unions having monopolistic or market power in their labor markets. In other words, some unions are so strong that they can impose wage increases on employers, even when those wage increases are not consistent with increases in the productivity of their labor.

Big Business Monopoly Power   The other variant of the cost-push theory is that inflation is caused when the monopoly power of big business pushes up prices. Powerful corporations are presumably able to raise their prices whenever they want to increase their profits. Each time the corporations raise prices to increase their profits, the cost of living goes up. Workers demand higher wages to make up for the loss in their standard of living, thereby giving the corporations an excuse to raise prices again, and so goes a vicious cycle of price-wage increases.

Who Bears the Burden of Inflation?

Everybody agrees that inflation is a serious problem facing the entire world today. How-
ever, as dispassionate observers of the economic scene, we should be able to measure inflation objectively. It is not enough to note that consumers are hurting because they are facing higher prices. After all, every higher price that someone pays is a higher receipt of income for someone else. Unless higher rates of inflation cause the total physical output of goods and services in the economy (real GNP) to fall, inflation's main effect must be to redistribute income and wealth from certain persons or sectors of the economy to others. We will not discuss in this section how inflation could affect the rate of production of goods and services either at a point in time or over time. That is a point on which few economists agree. However, we can point out, in historical perspective, who has been harmed and who has benefited at the hands of inflation. But, before we can adequately do that, we must distinguish between expected and unexpected inflation.

Expected and Unexpected Inflation

If prices rise by 10 percent next year and everyone fully knew that they would rise by 10 percent, then we call the 10 percent rate of inflation *expected*. However, if, for example, everyone expects prices to rise only at an annual 5 percent rate and, in fact, they end up rising by 10 percent, then we have suffered *unexpected* inflation. This distinction is crucial to understanding inflation's effect on the distribution of income and wealth. This distinction is brought out most clearly in analyzing the redistribution of wealth from creditors to debtors and vice versa during periods of unexpected inflation.

Creditors and Debtors

If you borrow money, you are charged an interest rate that presumably covers the cost of providing you with current purchasing power and gives the lender a profit. Let's assume that there is no inflation and, further, that none is anticipated. The lender charges you 5 percent per year for the use of his or her funds. If you borrow $100, at the end of the year you must pay back $105: $100 principal plus $5 interest.

Consider what would happen, however, if during the year there was a 10 percent rate of inflation. Now you give back the lender $105, but the value of that $105 has fallen by 10 percent. Effectively, then, the lender has lent you $100 and received back about $95 in purchasing power at the end of the year. You, as a debtor, gained; the lender, as a creditor, lost. The reason you benefited and the lender lost is because the inflation was unanticipated. Therefore, we can safely maintain that during periods of unanticipated inflation those who are, on balance, creditors will lose, and those who are, on balance, debtors will gain.

However, if the inflation were fully anticipated, the interest rate that you will be charged will include an inflationary premium which will compensate the creditor for the lower purchasing power of the dollars paid back. There would be no redistribution of wealth from creditors to debtors.

A recent estimate of how much inflation was expected by creditors puts it between one-half and two-thirds of the total inflation rate. That means that interest rates rose enough to compensate for between one-half and two-thirds of the loss in purchasing power of dollars paid back to creditors during the period of rising prices. This still leaves a net transfer of wealth from creditors to debtors. It has been estimated that from 1950 to 1975 this transfer was on the order of two-thirds of a trillion dollars.

Who gained in this situation? We know it was debtors, but who are the debtors? To find out we have to look at the net creditor or debtor status of households and businesses. Generally, the household sector has been a net creditor. That means households have had more assets in savings accounts and banks than they have had liabilities, or debts. Thus, households as

a group lost out during this period because they were net creditors. Businesses and governments gained because they were net debtors.

But what about the various income classes within the household sector? If we look at the net creditor or debtor position of various households, we find that both the very poor and the very rich are net creditors; that is, they have fewer debts than assets. We will discuss the poor and those on fixed incomes in a later section.

Wage Earners

Another group of individuals who lose out during a period of unanticipated inflation are wage earners, whose money incomes rise less rapidly than prices. To the extent that wage earners do not obtain wage increases at least equal to the rate of inflation, there will be a redistribution of income away from this class of individuals. On the other hand, to the extent that inflation is fully anticipated, contracts among wage and salary earners and their employers will take account of this anticipated inflation either explicitly by employing an escalator clause, or implicitly by scheduling nominal wage increases through the contract life.

Inflation and the Poor

It is always argued that inflation hurts the poor, especially those on fixed incomes, such as pensioners, retired persons, disabled people, and the like.

How Inflation Affects Fixed Incomes

However, if we look at the bottom line of Table 7-2, we find that transfer payments, defined as income provided by governments to individuals for which no productive activity is demanded, increased over the two periods studied. In fact, Social Security benefits have risen much faster

Table 7-2 Shifts in Percentage Shares of National Income Due to Inflation, 1950–1973

On average, wages and salaries increased as a percentage of national income during the period 1950 to 1971. However, during the inflationary period of 1972 to 1973, their share actually dropped by 0.4 percent. The reverse was true for corporate profits. Their share of national income fell by 6.2 percent over the period 1950 to 1971, but they rose by almost 1 percent during the 1972 to 1973 period.

INCOME	1950–1971	1972–1973
Wages and salaries	+6.6%	−0.4%
Unincorporated businesses		
Nonfarm	−3.8	−0.1
Farm	−3.7	+0.4
Rents	−1.0	+0.2
Interest	+3.4	0
Corporate profits*	−6.2	+0.7
Transfer payments†	+4.7	+0.1

*After inventory valuation adjustment, before payment of income taxes
†Not a part of national income

Source: U.S. Department of Commerce

than the rate of inflation. Moreover, since 1974 there has been a provision in the benefits system that links these benefits to the consumer price index. As the consumer price index goes up, so too do Social Security benefits without further legislation. It is largely due to this rapid increase in Social Security benefits that we cannot say inflation has hurt the aged more than other groups in society.

The Poor Man's Price Index

It has also been argued that the poor are hurt more than most by inflation. In fact, researchers at the Institute for Research on Poverty at the University of Wisconsin have tried to verify this contention. They have concluded that the prices of the commodities purchased by the poor have risen more rapidly than the general price level. What they have really done is come up with a Poor Man's Price Index.[2] Remember that the consumer price index measures the average change in prices based on the importance of various goods and services for an "average urban" family. This weighting scheme may be inappropriate for those who consume a disproportionate share of items whose price has risen relatively faster than that of other items. This would be true, for example, for medical care services since they have risen much more rapidly than the consumer price index has. The aged spend a disproportionately large share of their income on medical care services, and the consumer price index does not adequately reflect what the rate of inflation has been for them.

It is interesting to note that the price index for poor people rose less rapidly than the government consumer price index over the period from 1953 to 1967. However, if this comparison were extended through the mid-1970s, particularly over the years when the cost of food rose rapidly in comparison to other prices, the opposite would likely be true. That is, the price index for poor people has probably been rising during the first half of the 1970s at a faster rate than the CPI. Thus, the poor would be relatively worse off during this period, even if they received wage gains that took account of "the" rate of inflation as measured by the Bureau of Labor Statistics.

National Income and Inflation

What has happened to the share of national income going to different classes of income earners in our society? If we look at the data

[2] R. G. Hollister and J. L. Palmer, *The Impact of Inflation on the Poor*, sec. II, Madison, Wis.: Institute for Research on Poverty, 1969.

for various subperiods since 1950, we can see quite clearly the varying effects inflation has had on the distribution of income depending on whether inflation had been anticipated or not. We see in Table 7-2 that the percentage of national income going to wages and salaries actually increased by 6.6 percent during the period 1950 to 1971. If you look at Figure 7-1 you will see that during this period the rate of inflation was either effectively nil, or at best grew very slowly until 1965. Then inflation accelerated to a relatively high level at the beginning of this decade. It might be said, then, that in the early period the rate of inflation was more or less expected. At the same time, there was a reduction in the share of national income going to business profits.

However, if we look at the 1972 to 1973 period, just the reverse is shown. Wages and salaries dropped by 0.4 percent in terms of their percentage of national income. Nominal corporate profits went up 0.7 percent. The difference can, in part, be explained by the fact that the inflationary burst in 1972 to 1973 was largely unexpected.[3] Thus, labor incomes did not rise as rapidly as the rate of inflation.

What can we say about who bears the burden of inflation? We have seen that that depends on whether the inflation is anticipated or unanticipated and on which groups are net creditors and net debtors. Moreover, even for those on "fixed" income we must redefine our definition of *fixed* to take account of any increases in benefits such as those that occur with Social Security. That is the only way we can come to a reasonable conclusion about inflation's effects on individuals in our society.

---

[3]But we must be careful here because nominal corporate profits reflected inflationary adjustments in existing inventories, so that at least part of the gain in profits was an illusion.

Unemployment and Inflation

The last chapter pointed out that the business cycle involves ups and downs in both employment and price levels. According to many observers, there is a relationship between unemployment and inflation. If we look at the historical record in the United States and in other countries, we do indeed find some relationship between rising prices and high employment. In fact, we might consider this to be another theory of inflation. Price variation can perhaps be explained through changes in unemployment—low levels of unemployment indicate high economic activity, which puts pressure on wages and ultimately on prices; high levels of unemployment indicate slack economic activity, relatively fewer pressures on wages and prices, and hence less inflation. The policy question that arises is whether or not a definite relationship exists between inflation and unemployment. If there is a trade-off between the two, should we pursue a certain rate of inflation in order to reduce the rate of unemployment?

The Phillips Curve

Almost two decades ago Professor A. W. Phillips discovered that in Great Britain wages rose rapidly when the unemployment rate was declining and rose more slowly when it was rising. He drew a curve showing this relationship, and since the time his article appeared, that curve has been called the **Phillips curve.** Although Phillips' original analysis was in terms of wage rate increases and the unemployment rate, economists have contended that the relationship also holds between price increases and the unemployment rate; there seems to be a close relationship between wage rate change, and consumer price level changes.

We show a hypothetical Phillips curve in Figure 7-3.

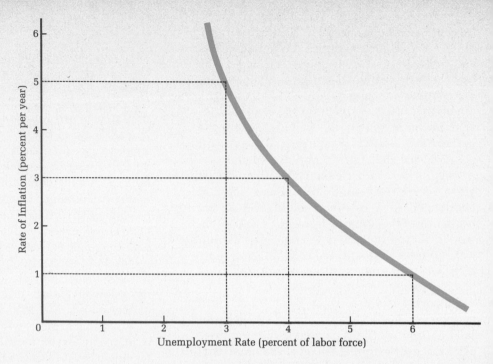

FIGURE 7-3 A Hypothetical Phillips Curve
The Phillips curve shows the relationship between the unemployment rate and the rate of inflation. If we want a 3 percent unemployment rate, we presumably have to live with 5 percent annual inflation. If we don't want to live with 5 percent inflation but only 3 percent, we will have to "buy it" with more unemployment since a 3 percent rate of inflation is associated with a 4 percent rate of unemployment.

The Trade-Off

The implication of Phillips' analysis is that a *trade-off* does exist between unemployment and inflation. Let's look again at our hypothetical Phillips curve in Figure 7-3. If we are at an unemployment rate of 6 percent, and we want to go to an unemployment rate of 4 percent, we have to allow for an increase in the rate of the rise in prices of 2 percent. This poses a dilemma. Inflation is assumed to be an economic "bad" and something that must be avoided. But so too is unemployment. The implication of Phillips' analysis is that one cannot simultaneously have full employment and no inflation; one must make a trade-off. Policymakers must decide what the trade-off should be and walk the line between an "acceptable" amount of inflation and a "tolerable" level of unemployment.

The Phillips curve relationship for the United States has not proved very stable over time. The trade-off numbers seem to be changing, so that policymakers can't really be sure that a given level of inflation will repeatedly allow the same rate of unemployment. The trade-off between unemployment and inflation has become increasingly worse since the mid-1950s. In 1955, for example, a 6 percent unemployment rate implied a 1 percent rate of rise in prices, but the same unemployment rate in 1974 was associated with a 12 percent rate of rise in prices. We will come back later, in our discussion of income-determination models, to the implications of this trade-off, which worsens every year. Here it is sufficient to say that the Phillips curve relationship has not stood up well in its original form. There are now a number of more refined views of what the Phillips curve might look like. These views take into account other variables besides actual rates of inflation and actual unemployment rates.

One of the most important other variables

is individuals' expectations of future inflation rates. The importance of distinguishing between expected and unexpected inflation was covered when we discussed the burden of rising prices and who bears it. The same argument holds when discussing the trade-off between inflation and unemployment.

Unemployment and Inflation Added Together

Almost everybody is convinced that unemployment and high rates of inflation are social evils. We might get a meaningful measure of economic discomfort from combining these two social evils. Arthur Okun of The Brookings Institution and former Chairman of the Council of Economic Advisers constructed such a discomfort index for the economy by combining the unemployment rate and the annual rate of change in consumer prices. Over the last two decades the discomfort index has grown dramatically. This can be seen in Table 7-3. Back in 1955 the discomfort index was only 4.0 percent. The estimate for 1975 was a whopping 15 percent. If we take Okun's index seriously, we must conclude that things seem to have gone awry in the American economy.

Stagflation

The combination of unacceptably high rates of unemployment and inflation has been commonly called **stagflation**—inflationary recessions, or periods when unemployment and inflation increase simultaneously. Economists and policymakers now see that the standard explanations of inflation and recession are no longer valid when both inflation and recession occur simultaneously.

Many policymakers believe that one of the main goals of an economic system should be to generate economic growth. Since we live in an era of continued inflation, the problem facing the nation during the 1970s has become one of preventing economic stagnation without allowing inflation to take off. To fight rising unemployment, or recession, policy tools could be put into effect, but these might increase inflation.

One solution to the problem, which we will talk about in Issue I-10, is wage and price controls. But as we shall see in that issue, controls

---

Table 7-3 An Index of Discomfort

Former Chairman of the Council of Economic Advisers, Arthur Okun, once suggested that we could measure "discomfort." All we need do is add the annual inflation rate and the rate of unemployment. If his measure of discomfort has any accuracy, then the economy is in a much worse position in the 1970s than it was in the previous 15 years.

YEAR	DISCOMFORT INDEX
1955	4.8
1956	7.0
1957	7.3
1958	8.6
1959	7.0
1960	7.0
1961	7.4
1962	6.7
1963	7.3
1964	6.4
1965	6.4
1966	7.2
1967	6.8
1968	8.3
1969	9.6
1970	10.4
1971	9.3
1972	9.0
1973	11.1
1974	16.6
1975	15.0

have not cured stagflation. Economists and politicians, as well as men and women in the street, cannot agree about which evil is the lesser one, unemployment or inflation. At the beginning of the Ford administration, inflation was the number-one enemy. However, within not too many months, recession became the number-one enemy, and all the policymakers were talking about what could be done to lower the rate of unemployment. By the time you read this text, inflation may again have become the number-one evil.

The Use of Models in Policymaking

Is there any way we can change the economic scene? Could we not somehow slow down the rate of inflation and cut out periods of severe cyclical unemployment? These are, of course, the dilemmas and the questions facing policymakers today. These policymakers, in coming up with answers and schemes to alleviate economic suffering, must rely on models. We have already presented several models of price-level determination, but we have yet to present a complete model of income determination. What is it that determines the level of income and output and hence the level of prices? We will turn to this question in the following unit. What we will do is set out the economic variables to be discussed and then construct some simple models of income and employment determination. You will then see what goes into the thinking of economists concerned with keeping our economic ship on an even keel.

Definitions of New Terms

Inflation: A sustained rise in prices.

Consumer Price Index: A statistical measure of the average of prices of a specified set of goods and services purchased by wage earners in urban areas.

Wholesale Price Index: A statistical measure of the average of prices of those commodities that firms purchase from other firms in large quantities.

Implicit Price Deflator: The general price level of all goods and services, found statistically by equating the ratio of GNP expressed in current dollars and real GNP.

Quantity Theory of Money and Prices: A classical proposition which predicts that changes in the price level are directly related to changes in the money supply. The quantity theory of money and prices is based on the equation of exchange.

Demand-Pull Inflation: Inflation caused by the aggregate demand exceeding the full-employment supply of goods.

Cost-Push Inflation: Rising prices caused by rising production costs.

Phillips Curve: A curve showing the relationship between unemployment and inflation. The Phillips curve gives the trade-off between unemployment and inflation.

Stagflation: A period of deficient aggregate demand and rising prices. In other words, a period of both economic stagnation and inflation.

1. The history of the United States has been a history of rising prices, although the rise in the price level has been erratic. It has almost always gone up during war periods. The rate of inflation in the United States is less than in almost all the other countries in the world. Some countries have experienced hyperinflations, where the price level has risen by phenomenal amounts.

2. We measure inflation by a change in some statistical price index. We can use either the consumer price index, the wholesale price index, or the implicit price deflator for GNP.

3. All price indices have biases.

4. There are many theories of inflation. One is demand-pull inflation, which is caused by aggregate demand exceeding the full-employment supply of goods, services, and productive workers. Demand-pull inflation can occur because of overexpansionary monetary and fiscal policy on the part of the government or because of overexpansionary investment activity on the part of individual businesspersons.

5. Cost-push inflation is a theory which asserts that inflation is caused by rising costs. There are two variants on the cost-push inflation argument. One involves union power; the other concerns big business monopoly power.

6. The union power cost-push inflation argument contends that due to the power of unions, employers must give in to union demands for excessive wages. These employers then pass on the higher wages to the consumer in the form of higher prices.

7. The big business monopoly power cost-push inflation argument maintains that powerful corporations are able to raise their prices whenever they want to increase their profits. Each time the corporation raises its prices to increase its profits, the cost of living goes up. Workers then demand higher wages to make up for the loss in their standard of living, thereby giving corporations an excuse to raise prices again.

8. During a period of unexpected inflation, creditors lose and debtors gain because the latter are able to repay debts in "cheap" dollars. Of course, if everybody anticipates rising prices, the interest rate will rise to take account of this future expected depreciation.

9. Anybody who holds cash during an inflationary period loses part of his or her real income as prices rise. The only way to avoid this loss is to not hold any checking account balances or currency in your pocket.

10. Historically, people with fixed incomes have suffered from inflation in the United States because most inflations have been unanticipated.

11. A British economist, A. W. Phillips, found an empirical relationship between the level of unemployment and the rate of wages and prices

in Great Britain. This relationship between unemployment and inflation has been called the Phillips curve. It shows the trade-off between inflation and unemployment.

12. Stagflation occurred in the United States and in many other countries in the world during the late 1960s and 1970s. It is probably the number-one problem of economists.

1. You are a hard-working record store salesperson. You are given a raise of 10 percent at the end of the year. But during that year prices went up 10 percent. Are you any better off because of your raise?
2. People seem to be against inflation today, but they favored inflation in the 1880s. What is different about these two periods?
3. If you are sure that inflation is going to continue, what can you do to protect yourself against it?
4. Are there any groups in society that are helped by inflation? Does your answer depend on whether or not the inflation was anticipated?
5. Why would deflation or falling prices "hurt" lots of people in the United States today? Again, does your answer depend on whether the deflation was expected or unexpected?

Selected References

Brimmer, Andrew F., "Inflation and Income Distribution in the United States," *Review of Economics and Statistics,* vol. 53, no. 1, February 1971, pp. 37–48.

Economic Report of the President, various issues, Washington, D.C.: U.S. Government Printing Office.

Federal Reserve Bank of Philadelphia, Department of Research, *Economics of Inflation,* Philadelphia, 1974.

Lekachman, Robert, *Inflation: The Permanent Problem of Boom and Bust,* New York: Random House, 1973.

Morley, Samuel A., *The Economics of Inflation,* Hinsdale, Ill.: Dryden Press, 1971.

Okun, Arthur M., *The Political Economy of Prosperity,* New York: W. W. Norton, 1970.

Ozaki, Robert S., *Inflation, Recession . . . and All That,* New York: Holt, Rinehart and Winston, 1972.

Would Indexing Help Fight Inflation?

THE USE OF ECONOMYWIDE ESCALATOR CLAUSES

Contracts That Take Account of Inflation

In the last chapter we pointed out several distinct problems associated with inflation. Unanticipated inflation seemed to affect different groups differently, in particular, debtors gain at the expense of creditors who are paid off with cheaper dollars. When we discussed the trade-off between unemployment and inflation, the policy implication was a clear one: Any reduction in the rate of inflation would lead to an increase in the unemployment rate.

A number of economic commentators have recently suggested a way out of these problems. Their solution is to institute widespread *indexing* of the economy. Indexing is nothing more than tacking a cost-of-living escalator clause onto a contract. That would mean, for example, that if you signed a contract to work for $10,000 per year this year and the contract had an escalator clause, you would be guaranteed increases in your nominal wages commensurate with increases in the cost of living. Additionally, you probably would have bargained for an increase in your real wages as well.

Escalator clauses are basically a method by which economic agents can contract in real terms rather than in nominal terms. In the preceding example the contract was for a level or annual growth in a level of real, as opposed to nominal, wages. The inclusion of the cost-of-living escalator clause, or indexing agreement, makes both parties to the contract indifferent to the rate of inflation; this is equivalent to both parties fully anticipating the rate of inflation.

Escalator Clauses Today

At least 50 million Americans are today covered in one way or another by escalator clauses. Under present law those individuals who receive benefits from Social Security are guaranteed increases that match the rate of inflation. This cost-of-living escalator was legislated into Social Security a few years ago. Today there are at least 6 million workers covered by employment contracts that have cost-of-living clauses. Benefits under the federal government's food stamp program are also linked to the rate of inflation. Moreover, it is virtually impossible to ob-

tain a large long-term commercial loan at a fixed interest rate; rather, the interest rate to be paid is specified in relation to some market rate of interest that presumably will mirror the ups and downs in the rate of inflation.

A Short History of Escalator Clauses

Indexing is not a new idea. Back in 1707, a Cambridge don, William Fleetwood, made an attempt to estimate changes in the price level over a six-century period to set a limit on the outside income that holders of fellowships should be permitted to receive in 1707 money, as compared with 1107 money. In other words, he was trying to tie the outside-income limit of fellowship holders to the cost of living. Some 50 years later a form of indexing was used in Massachusetts Bay Colony, and during the same period Oxford and Cambridge Universities in England rented out their land for payments in grain, thus implicitly ensuring against price fluctuations (assuming that the price of grain moved in step with the overall cost of living). Again in England, payment of tithes to the Church was linked to an average of barley, wheat, and oat prices—a form of escalator clause, or cost-of-living index.

In 1886, the English economist Alfred Marshall enthusiastically supported what he called the "tabular standard."[1] Not too many years later the American economist Irving Fisher also came out in favor of the "tabular standard." He was, in fact, successful in persuading a manufacturing company (which he had taken part in founding) to issue securities paying interest (dividends) linked to some sort of cost-of-living index.

After World War I, in the United States changes in the cost of living were given much attention in wage adjustments. However, cost-of-living (escalator) clauses rapidly lost popularity when prices began to drop from their 1920 peaks. Apparently, workers wanted them when prices were rising but not when prices were falling.

The federal government inserted a cost-of-living clause in the Economy Act passed in March 1933. This act authorized the President to make federal salary reductions based on the cost of living.

In the early years of World War II at least 40 percent of all agreements between manufacturers and unions had wage-reopening clauses that permitted wage increases to match any price increases. However, the wartime wage stabilization program suspended most of these reopening clauses from 1942 to the end of the war.

There was little interest in escalator clauses during the 1950s, when prices were fairly stable. By the early

[1] Alfred Marshall, "Reply to the Royal Commission on the Depression of Trade and Industry," 1886, reproduced in *Official Papers by Alfred Marshall*, London: Macmillan, 1926.

1960s only 2 million workers were covered by escalators. This, however, was to rise to over 6 million by the middle of the 1970s, when workers saw their nominal wages lagging behind the double-digit annual increases in the cost of living.

Brazil—A Case Study of Indexing

Brazil is perhaps the one country that has been studied the most for its nationwide indexation. The Brazilians call this a regime of "monetary correction." It started with laws passed in 1964. Basically it involves adjusting the nominal value of such things as mortgage payments, savings account balances, and rentals to take account of changes in the cost of living. The adjustment formulas are based on estimated inflation rates. For example, wage increases are based on an average of *real*, that is, corrected-for-inflation, wages prevailing over the previous 24 months plus prospective increases in productivity and prices. Usually, the measure of the rate of inflation is taken from a general wholesale price index.

Take the example of a savings account. Say that the balance a Brazilian has in a savings bank is 10,000 cruzeiros. Say also that this person is receiving an annual 5 percent rate of interest on that savings account. At the end of 3 months, the cost-of-living increase has been 4 percent. What happens is that the Brazilian's savings account is increased by 4 percent, or 400 cruzeiros. This means that the interest rate being paid on the original account balance

will remain at 5 percent because nothing will have to be subtracted for losses in the purchasing power of that money left in the bank. The savings account is therefore indexed. Its nominal value increases sufficiently so that it does not lose any of its purchasing power.

Another important area where monetary correction is applied in Brazil concerns the value of machines and other items used by businesses. In a period of raging inflation, a machine will increase in nominal market value, even though it is wearing out, because its replacement cost will be rising so rapidly. This increase in the market value of machines and the like was, until the mid-1960s, taxed as part of profits by the Brazilian government. However, since monetary correction was applied to machines and other assets used by businesses, the government has not collected taxes on such fictitious aspects of profits, that is, on the rise in the value of business assets due to general inflation.

According to some observers, the Brazilian indexing experience has proved successful. While the rate of inflation has fallen, the rate of production growth in the economy has risen, and there has been little apparent trade-off between unemployment and inflation. This is not to say; however, that indexing is the cause of the reduced rate of inflation in Brazil; in fact, no one who supports indexing contends that, if adopted, it will reduce the rate of growth of prices. Indexing simply speeds the adjustment to changes in the rate of inflation, *either up or down.*

The Brazilian experience has prompted some economists and

politicians to suggest at least a modified form of indexing for the United States. Let's now look at some of those suggestions, which relate mainly to the government sector.

Indexing in the United States

Proponents of indexing suggest that at the very least our government should put its house in order by indexing its tax system and the way it borrows money from the public.

Indexing Taxes

Remember from Chapter 5 that we have a progressive income tax in the United States. That has important implications during an inflationary period.

Personal Income Taxes What if you had an increase in wages that just equaled the increase in the cost of living? You would probably consider your real standard of living, or real wage rate, unchanged because you would have just been compensated for the rate of inflation. But you would be wrong because if that wage increase put you into a higher income tax bracket, you would have to pay a larger percentage of your gross income in taxes to the federal government. What does that mean? Simply that during periods of relatively rapid inflation, when individuals' incomes are pushed into higher and higher income tax brackets, the percentage of income going to the federal government in the form of individual income taxes will rise without Congress having to legislate this rise.

Also consider the tax-saving benefits of a fixed exemption, say, of $750 per dependent. If you are allowed to exempt $750 of annual income from taxation for each person, including yourself, who depends on your salary, the exemption is worth less every year that the price level rises.

It has also been suggested that the base for calculating capital gains should be corrected for rises in prices. For example, if you bought a share of stock one year and sold it the next year for 10 percent more than what you originally paid for it, right now you would have to pay taxes on all of that 10 percent increase. However, if that 10 percent increase merely reflected a 10 percent rate of inflation, you are being taxed on a fictitious capital gain. The suggestion here, then, is to adjust the base, or "buying price," of capital assets for price-level changes before you figure out the capital gains taxes you must pay. In this simple example, your base would rise by 10 percent, so that the selling price would just equal the buying price (in constant dollars) and you would owe no capital gains taxes.

Essentially, then, indexing personal income taxes would merely take account of rises in the cost of living and hence would not allow the federal government to obtain an increasing share of personal income merely because there were high rates of inflation.

The Corporate Income Tax The corporate income tax would be altered in a similar manner to the personal income tax. The present $25,000 dividing line between the normal tax and the so-called surtax would be increased every year according to the rate of inflation. Capital gains would be altered as mentioned above, and so would some other technical aspects of how corporations are taxed.

Government Bonds

If you purchased a government bond that nominally yields 5 percent a year and the rate of inflation is 5 percent a year, what is your real rate of return? Zero percent. Actually, it is even less than that because presently you will have to pay federal income taxes on the 5 percent a year nominal rate of return. To counter this perverse incentive to savers, it is suggested that government bonds be indexed. This could be done in a variety of ways; however, the most often suggested idea is indexing the principal, that is, the face value of the bond. It would work as follows. If you bought a bond one year for $1,000 and it promised to pay you 3 percent a year, you would, in fact, receive $30 a year in income from that bond; when you redeemed it, you would also get a percentage of the principal equal to whatever the cumulative inflation percentage had been over the ensuing period. If the aggregated inflation had been 50 percent, instead of $1,000, you would get back $1,500. That would mean that your real rate of return would have been 3 percent no matter what the rate of inflation. You would not have to worry about losing out because the rate of inflation exceeded the interest rate being paid.

The Private Sector

Few economists have come out for any obligation on the part of the private sector to index its contracts. Indexing of private contracts has already occurred on a voluntary basis and will continue to occur as long as the rate of inflation remains variable. Some senators have, on occasion, suggested that all wage contracts in the private sector be indexed, but such proposals rarely have been taken seriously.

The Pros and the Cons of Indexing

Opponents of indexing claim that it will remove any pressure to reduce the rate of inflation. If everything were indexed, then no one would

have any incentive to reduce the rate of inflation, or so the argument goes. Still others believe that indexing will have an inflationary impact on the economy. After all, the reasoning goes, every increase in prices will be multiplied many times before there is any halt since it will automatically be spread throughout the economy. Lastly, it has been argued persuasively that, at least with the Brazilian experience, monetary correction leads to more rather than to fewer inequities throughout the economy. Specifically, according to one student of the Brazilian situation, the distribution of income has become more skewed in favor of the upper classes.[2]

On the plus side of indexing are equally compelling arguments. Indexing would allow relative prices to allocate resources naturally—without the distortion due to differential adjustments to our variable rates of inflation. In essence, any rate of inflation would affect the entire economy with equal speed because everything would be indexed to that rate of inflation. But perhaps more

[2]Albert Fishlow, "Indexing Brazilian Style: Inflation without Tears?", *Brookings Papers on Economic Activity*, I, 1974, pp. 261, 282.

important, according to this argument, would be the effect of indexing on the unemployment-inflation trade-off that we outlined in the last chapter. According to the proponents of indexing, if everything were indexed, the rate of inflation would have little impact on the labor market. We could effectively reduce the rate of inflation without paying the relatively high unemployment cost implied by the standard Phillips curve analysis. If one looks at the results in Brazil, one can obtain support for this view: Since 1964, the Brazilian rate of inflation has fallen dramatically, yet the rate of unemployment has beaten the Phillips curve; it has not risen in any systematic manner.

Indexing the government tax system would certainly lead to fewer government revenues unless they were specifically voted by Congress.

Taxpayers' take-home pay in real terms would not shrink just because of the inflation, nor would the real aftertax profits of corporations. The application of indexing to government bonds would give savers an outlet for their savings that would appear extremely attractive relative to other possibilities at the present time. This might encourage more saving and less consumption.

Will We Have More Indexing?

Is a "tabular standard" or "monetary-correction" system in the cards for the United States? Certainly, in the private sector we can safely predict that as inflation continues at historically high and fairly unstable rates, more indexing will occur because it protects both parties to a contract. (Don't forget that indexed contracts have to take account of lower rates of inflation too.) Whether the government will index its tax system is quite another matter. Finally, numerous government officials have suggested the indexing of some government securities, and that suggestion may be a reality by the time you read this.

Indexing has its costs, however, and it is not preferred to a situation of stable prices. After all, with a system of complete indexing, you have to have more contracts written, buy more bookkeepers' time, spend more money on price schedules and their revision, and so on. The economic world preferred by most would be one with stable prices.

Questions for Thought and Discussion

1. Can any argument be made that indexing changes the rate of inflation?
2. Who would gain and who would lose if nationwide indexing became a reality?
3. If the rate of inflation were relatively high but constant, would indexing be necessary?
4. How is indexing related to the difference between anticipated and unanticipated inflation?

Selected References

Jevons, Stanley W., *Money and the Mechanism of Exchange,* 1898 ed., New York: Appleton, pp. 318–326.

Krieger, Ronald A., "Inflation and the 'Brazilian Solution'," *Challenge,* September–October 1974, pp. 42–43.

Organization for Economic Cooperation and Development, Committee on Financial Markets, *Indexation of Fixed Interest Securities,* Paris: O.E.C.D., 1973.

DIRECT ATTEMPTS AT COMBATING INFLATION

The Past As the Future

On August 15, 1971, the United States government, by way of an executive order, froze prices, rents, wages, and salaries for a period of 90 days. This was the first instance in the peacetime history of the United States that wage and price controls had been instituted. These controls were to last, in one form or another, until April 30, 1974.

By now, most individuals are aware of what wage and price controls are—a form of legal limits on certain prices in our economy that have been used in the United States and elsewhere (particularly during wartime) to fight against inflation. Perhaps what many people do not realize is that wage and price controls have a lengthy history that dates back thousands of years.

Controls in Times Past

Price controls were, of course, not new to the American nation. They were first used during the Revolutionary War, and they date back quite a bit earlier than that. We know, for example, that in 1800 B.C. the ruler of Babylonia decreed that anyone caught violating his wage-price freeze would be drowned. It seems that Babylonia endured more than 1000 years of such price fixing. Another example has been cited by historians in A.D. 301. The Roman Emperor Diocletian, in an edict called "Commanded Cheapness," fixed the maximum price on beef, grain, eggs, and clothing and prescribed the death penalty for violators. He also set wage ceilings for teachers, lawyers, physicians, tailors, and bricklayers. But, according to Lactantius, writing in 314, "There was . . . much bloodshed upon very slight and trifling accounts; and the people brought provisions no more to market since they could not get a reasonable price for them; and this increased the dearth so much that after many had died by it, the law itself was laid aside."

In 1636, during the early years of this nation, the American Puritans imposed a code of price and wage limitations. Anyone caught violating the code was considered as bad as "adulterers and whoremongers." Even before the Declaration of Independence, the Continental Congress had set price ceilings. Later, a few states enacted price-control laws. General George Washington complained of excessive rates of inflation, as did others at the time. Sporadic attempts at price controls were highly controversial and certainly not comprehensive. All such efforts were largely abandoned by 1780.

Controls in America during World War II

After starting the huge war production effort in the early 1940s, Congress felt it necessary to pass the Price Control Act of 1942, which established the Office of Price Administration (OPA). The conditions for the implementation of direct controls were, of course, quite favorable. Most citizens were willing to make sacrifices to speed up a successful conclusion of the war.

Regulations During that time, numerous specific price schedules were established. In 1942, Price Emergency Regulation No. 2 noted that rents were climbing too fast for our good health and therefore established rent controls. Price Emergency Regulation No. 3 of October 1942, pointed out that despite regulations, farm prices and wages had moved up, thus forcing continuous amendments and additions to the regulations. By the middle of 1943, the OPA was overhauled: The authority for setting prices was taken away from the main office in Washington and given to the field offices. Advisory committees were appointed; ration books were issued with coupons that allowed you to spend your money only on an amount of the rationed commodity.

By 1944, there were almost 350,000 price control volunteers in addition to about 70,000 paid employees. The banking system was handling 5 billion ration coupons per month by 1944. Wholesale prices in the United States rose only 14 percent from November 1941 to August 1945. By 1946, however, people were no longer willing to make wartime sacrifices. Much of the wartime

price-control machinery was bypassed. It became extremely profitable to break the law.

The Black Market We can analyze the effect of a **black market** by using the supply and demand analysis presented in Chapter 3. Look at Figure I-10.1. Assume that this represents the demand and supply schedule for automobiles at the end of World War II. The equilibrium price would be at P_e, where the demand schedule and supply schedule cross each other. However, the government sets a maximum legal price of P_1. But at that price the quantity supplied by the manufacturers in Detroit would only be Q_s, and the quantity demanded would be Q_d. Obviously, there would be an excess

demand. The actual supply schedule, if the controls were properly enforced at the manufacturing stage, would now be equal to SS'—that is, the supply schedule slopes up until it gets to the intersection with the legal price, at which point it becomes vertical. The intersection of the new supply curve and the old demand curve is at E', or a price of P'_e. The black market price is obtained by customers making under-the-counter payments to retailers and other such gimmicks.

Repressed Inflation After the price controls were lifted in the United States, the wholesale price index jumped 55 percent from August 1945 to August 1948. Some economists maintained that the war

BLACK MARKETS

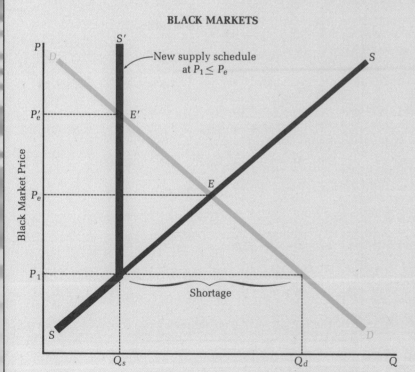

FIGURE I-10.1

The demand curve is *DD*. The supply curve is *SS*. The equilibrium price is P_e. The government, however, steps in and imposes a maximum price of P_1. At that lower price the quantity demanded will be Q_d, but the quantity supplied will only be Q_s. There is a shortage, and black markets develop. The price is bid up in the black market to P'_e because that is where the new supply curve, *SS'*, intersects the old demand curve at *E'*. Black market prices can be obtained by any number of devices, such as under-the-counter payments to retailers.

period was one of *repressed* inflation because total aggregate demand was breaking at the seams while prices were not allowed to rise to cut off part of that demand. (Remember from Chapter 3 what happens when you move *up* the demand curve for goods and services.)

Controls in Other Countries

The United States is not the only modern country that has imposed wage and price controls during both wartime and peacetime. We look at the Dutch experience for an example of such controls.

The Netherlands

In 1945, the Dutch government passed a labor relations act that provided mediators with fairly strong powers to control wages and labor markets. At that time the socialists were in power, and the so-called incomes policy of the early postwar period seemed to be quite effective. Europeans have typically called direct wage controls an *incomes policy* because there is an attempt to maintain people's relative incomes at the same level. More specifically, there is an attempt to maintain the same distribution between the portions of national income that go to capitalists and to workers.

Labor Shortages By 1951 there was a high rate of inflation; with fairly static money wages, real wages (money wages divided by the price level) fell. The situation is shown in Figure I-10.2. On the horizontal axis is the quantity of workers and on the vertical axis is the *real* wage rate, W/P. If W goes up by 100 percent and P goes up by 100 percent, W/P remains the same. We start out in an equilibrium situation where there

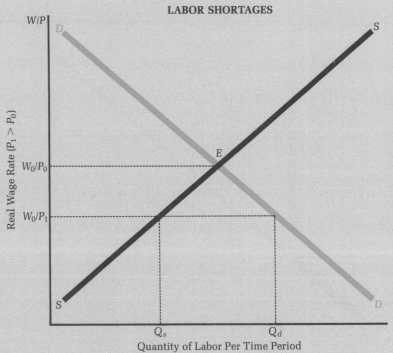

LABOR SHORTAGES

FIGURE I-10.2

The demand for labor is shown as DD, downward sloping as always. The supply of labor is shown as SS. The equilibrium real wage rate (the money wage rate divided by the price level) is established at W_0 divided by P_0 or at E, where the demand and supply curves intersect. Prices have risen in this particular situation to P_1, where P_1 is higher than P_0. At the old nominal wage rate, the real wage rate falls with the higher price level. It falls to W_0 divided by P_1. At that real wage rate, there is an excess demand for workers on the part of employers. The excess demand is the difference between Q_d and Q_s. This is the situation that occurred in the Netherlands following 1951, during their *incomes policy*.

Rather than go into a detailed analysis of their experiences, we refer the interested reader to several studies on European income policies presented in the list of Selected References. The United Kingdom, Sweden, France, West Germany, Austria, Denmark, and a number of other countries have tried over and over again to use wage and price controls to combat inflation. If we judge from casual evidence—whether their rates of inflation are lower with than without an incomes policy—we do not get a picture that would support the use of controls. The same conclusion is generally reached by observers of the American scene. Let's now look at what has happened in the United States over the past decade and a half.

is no excess demand or supply of workers in Holland. That is a real wage rate of W_0/P_0. Now, W_0 is fairly constant because of the incomes policy, but prices are rising. Thus, real wages fall to W_0/P_1, where P_1 is a price level that is greater than P_0. At this real wage rate, the quantity of workers demanded by firms is Q_d and the quantity supplied is Q_s. The excess demand for workers is $Q_d - Q_s$.

Labor shortages inevitably developed, and there was considerable pressure for additional labor resources, especially in industries making a high profit. Employers who had the opportunity to make more money by producing more goods were willing to grant wage increases that exceeded the legal limits. This type of behavior on the part of employers started to undermine the guidelines. There followed a period of prosecutions, fines, and even jail sentences for employers caught offering black market wages.

The Result of Wage Controls The guidelines for wages became increasingly unrealistic throughout the 1950s as the economy of the Netherlands was booming. Finally, in 1959, a more conservative government was put into office. It allowed more flexible limits on wage settlements, and the increased use of collective bargaining was permitted at the industry level. But in 1961 there was a law passed that limited wage increases to increases in productivity. Throughout the 1960s, the government continued to attempt to curtail wage increases, but its ambitious attempts fell into complete collapse by the beginning of the 1970s.

The Rest of Western Europe

The Dutch experience is typical of other Western European countries.

The American Experience

During the past 15 years or so, we have heard subtle and not-so-subtle exhortations from the government to restrain our wage and price demands. These exhortations have taken the form of guideposts and jawboning.

Guideposts

Even during the early 1960s, John Kennedy's Council of Economic Advisers came up with a set of **guideposts** for business and labor; these were rules of the game that would prevent inflation from taking off. In the 1962 *Economic Report of the President,* the Council of Economic Advisers presented a formal statement of guideposts for wage increases. The Council indicated that annual increases should not exceed about 3.5 percent, which was the annual rate of growth of productivity in the economy. The guideposts did not come out of the blue. From 1957 to 1961, every *Economic Report of the President* stressed, in one form or another, that private pricing should be tempered to create stable prices. In other words, restraint on the part of business and workers had been requested. The 1960 *Economic Report* was explicit in stating that wage increases should not exceed the growth in average *national* productivity. Further, the *Report* suggested that price reductions be made in sectors experiencing exceptionally rapid productivity growth since those sectors would be experiencing lower unit labor costs.

Jawboning

The guideposts did not have any legal standing; thus, the only means of enforcement available was public exposure by the Council of Economic Advisers or by the President. This process has been quaintly called **jawboning.** Kennedy did quite a bit of it, getting U.S. Steel, for example, to rescind a price increase in 1962 by making it a national issue. Johnson and Nixon both seemed to be less effective jawboners than Kennedy. In any event, business resented the selective political pressure that the President's Office brought against them, as this seemed to be an extralegal exercise of power.

Eventually, the guideposts broke down. In the President's *Annual Economic Report* of January 1969, the Council of Economic Advisers, although staunchly maintaining the indisputable correctness of the wage-price guidelines, finally admitted that excess aggregate demand pressures had made the guidelines unenforceable—at least for the time being. In that portion of the report, no numerical price and wage guides were set for the coming year.

Controlling Prices and Wages in the 1970s

We started this issue with reference to the first wage and price controls ever instituted in the peacetime history of the United States. They lasted for a period of almost 3 years, taking on various forms, including absolute freezes on wages and prices as well as less-stringent, modified restraints on those same wages and prices.

Did they work? It is very difficult to answer such a question, even after the fact, because we do not know what the rate of inflation would have been had no controls been in effect. The only data we have are data on published prices during the period of control. Let's see what they look like. In Figure I-10.3 we show the rate of change of consumer prices before and after the nearly 3-year period of controls. We notice first that consumer prices were rising at a slower rate just prior to the imposition of the controls than they were during the middle of the control period. We also notice that immediately after the controls were removed, prices started rising at relatively higher rates. This is conflicting evidence. On the one hand, it shows that prices were rising faster during the controls than before, but on the other hand, it shows that prices were rising faster *after* the controls. Perhaps prices were just "catching up" to where they would have been had no such controls been in effect.

The Nitty-Gritty

Everybody who tuned into what was happening during the wage-and-price-control period of the early 1970s knows about the problems that arose. It became literally impossible to effectively control all wages and prices, so the controllers focused on only the most critical prices and wages in our economy. Shortages began to appear not too many months after the controls were put into effect. Whether these shortages can be attributed to the black market variety of price control (exhibited in Figure I-10.1) is an open question because at the same time we had controls, we also had disruptions in normal supplies of such critical materials as petroleum. There was, however, widespread disappointment with wage and price controls, even by its most ardent supporters of earlier years. Apparently, such controls did significant damage to our system of relative prices, so that resources were not being allocated to their most valuable uses.

In spite of these problems, many politicians and economists alike often call for renewed or even more stringent price and wage controls in our economy. The question, then, is "Why would we want wage and price controls?"

Why Controls?

We have a problem of inflation. Few would deny it. We want to stop inflation—at least most of us do. How do we do it? Any solution, of course, has to attack the forces that drive

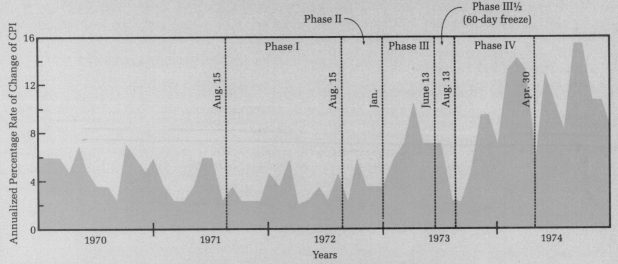

FIGURE I-10.3 Rate of Change of CPI before, during, and after Early 1970 Price Controls
If we look at the annual rate of change of consumer prices, as calculated monthly, we find that the rate of inflation reached a peak prior to the imposition of wage and price controls on Aug. 15, 1971.

inflation. We outlined several theories in the last chapter. They were under two general headings: demand-pull and cost-push. If inflation is in fact of the demand-pull type, then wage and price controls cannot succeed. What they do in such a situation is create shortages and black markets, as we outlined before. However, according to one view, if inflation is of the cost-push variety, wage and price controls can be an effective means of directly dealing with it.

We can further refine this argument, which makes a distinction between those industries where there is a high degree of competition and those dominated by a few firms. John Kenneth Galbraith, for example, has suggested that only the largest, say,

1000, firms in the United States should be subjected to permanent price controls. Such controls would presumably not be necessary for firms selling in more competitive markets. This argument suggests that such permanent price controls are the only way to eliminate price inflation caused by large firms administering relatively high prices.

The Expectations Argument

Is our inflation demand-pull or cost-push? Those who believe it is cost-push believe strongly in wage and price controls; those who believe it is basically demand-pull do not. Both, however, agree that wage and price controls can be effective to

some extent, no matter what the rate of inflation, if such controls alter individuals' expectations about the future change in prices. Otherwise stated, if wage and price controls are a signal to economic agents that wages and prices will be lower in the future, perhaps because the government has decided to institute contractionary policies, then this signal will change people's expectations about what wages and prices they should ask for in the future. Union leaders will not demand a 10 percent increase in wages to take account of an expected 7 percent inflation if they now think that inflation will be only 3 percent. They will demand a lower increase in wages for the next year. Unfortunately, the "expectations" argument cannot be taken too seriously in view of our past experience with controls. Perhaps the first set of controls in 1971 was a signal that prices would rise at a lower rate in the future, and therefore people lowered their price expectations. But today that probably would not be the case; we have a very recent experience that tells us otherwise. Controls did not signal an end to inflation then; therefore, a reimposition of controls will not likely change most individuals' expectations about the future course of prices.

Definitions of New Terms

Black Market: An illegal market that springs up whenever a legal maximum price is set below the market clearing price. Black markets occur during times of extreme price controls.

Guideposts: Official rules to which increases in wages were supposed to adhere during the early part of the 1960s. An official statement of guideposts for wage increases was mentioned in the 1962 *Economic Report of the President*. The Council of Economic Advisers indicated that they should not exceed 3.5 percent, which was the rate of growth predicted in the economy.

Jawboning: "Mouthing" by the President and his advisors against company increases in prices and excessive union wage settlements.

Questions for Thought and Discussion

1. Do you favor wage controls, price controls, or both? Why?
2. Would wage and price controls work if inflation were of the demand-pull type?
3. How do we assess whether or not wage and price controls have worked in a particular country at any particular time?
4. "Price controls cause shortages." Evaluate this statement.

Selected References

Feige, Edgar, L. and Douglas K. Pearce, "The Wage-Price Control Experiment—Did It Work?", *Challenge,* July–August 1973.

Moore, Thomas Gale, *U.S. Incomes Policy: Its Rationale and Development,* American Enterprise Institute, Special Analysis no. 18, Washington, D.C., December 1971.

Pohlman, Jerry E., *Economics of Wage and Price Controls,* Columbus, Ohio: Grid, 1972.

Schultz, George P. and Robert A. Aliber (eds.), *Guidelines, Informal Controls and the Marketplace,* Chicago: University of Chicago Press, 1966.

Sheahan, John, *The Wage-Price Guidepost,* Washington, D.C.: The Brookings Institution, 1967.

THREE

INCOME AND EMPLOYMENT
DETERMINATION MODELS

Consumption, Saving, and Investment

In the last unit we looked at the measurement of economic activity, the role of government, and the problems of unemployment and inflation in the United States. It is now time to construct a model that will help us understand how the levels of income and employment are determined for the national economy. This is known as the *theory of income and employment determination*, or, simply stated, the *theory of income analysis*. The modern theory of income analysis depends on an understanding of consumption, saving, and investment. We touched briefly on the definition of these terms in Chapter 4 when discussing national income accounting. Just to make sure these concepts are understood, we will go over them again. Then we will take a brief look at the classical theory of income and employment, after which an analysis of the determinants of consumption and saving and investment will be presented.

Definitions and Relationships

There are literally only two things you can do with a dollar of income. You can consume it or you can save it. If you consume it, it is gone for good. However, if you save the entire dollar, you will be able to consume it (and perhaps more if it earns interest) at some future time. That is the distinction between **consumption** and **saving.** Consumption is the act of using income for the purchase of consumption goods. **Consumption goods** are those goods that are used up in a very short period of time. Consumption goods are such things as going to movies, food, clothing, and the like. By definition, whatever you do not consume, you save and can consume at some time in the future.

The Difference between Stocks and Flows

It is important to distinguish between saving and savings. Saving is an action that occurs continuously at a particular rate—for example, $10 a week or $520 a year. This rate is called a **flow.** It is expressed per unit of time period, just as we express demand and supply relationships with a time period—usually a year. Implicitly, then, when we talk about saving we talk about a flow or rate of saving. Savings, on the other hand, is a **stock** concept measured at a certain point or instant in time. Your current savings are the result of past saving. You may presently have savings of $2,000 that are the result of 4 years' saving at a rate of $500 per year. Consumption, being related to saving, is also a flow concept. You consume from after-tax income at a certain rate per week, per month, or per year.

Relating Income to Saving and Consumption

If we consider only aftertax or disposable income, we can see the relationship among saving, consumption, and disposable income quite clearly:

Consumption + saving = disposable income

This is called an "accounting identity." It has to hold true at every moment in time. From it we can derive the definition of saving:

Saving = disposable income − consumption

Investment

Investment is also a flow concept. "Investment" as used here differs from the common use of the term. Generally, it's used in relation to the stock market or real estate. However, in macroeconomics, investment is defined as expenditure by firms on things, such as new machines

and new buildings that are expected to yield a future stream of income. It also includes expenditures by households on such things as *new* houses. We must also include in our definition of investment changes in business inventories, a topic we referred to in Chapter 4 when discussing national income accounting. Obviously, if a firm increases its inventory of finished goods, it has accumulated items that are capable of yielding income in the future.

Now do you see why economists do not consider the purchase of a stock or a bond an investment? If you take $100 and purchase someone else's existing shares of stock in a company, you have not made an expenditure that directly creates the possibility of future income in the economy. Rather, you have engaged in a transfer of "paper" assets. You now do not have the $100, and the person who sold you the stocks no longer has the stocks. The $100 allowed you to obtain the ownership rights in those stocks. Wealth has been exchanged; none has been created.

When we refer to the inventory-change component of investment, we see again the clear distinction between stocks and flows. Firms, at any one time, have a certain level of inventories—a stock—of finished goods. However, over time they add to and subtract from those inventories. This net change is the flow of inventories; it is also the only part included in investment.

Who Does the Saving and Investing?

Primarily, it is households who save. Business firms save whenever they retain earnings that are later used for investing in either inventories or new plant and equipment (sometimes called **capital goods**). But on the whole, it is households who do the nation's saving. It is primarily business firms who do the investing. This distinction is crucial in understanding the modern theory of income and employment determination.

Now what happens if households plan a rate of saving that differs from the rate of investment planned by businesses? Don't try to answer that question until you have gone through the rest of this chapter and the following one.

The Circular Flow with Saving and Investment

If you go back to page 74 you will see a highly simplified circular-flow diagram. There is nothing in that diagram about saving and investment. Let's redo it as in Figure 8-1. Here, with two circles, we show two sectors in the economy: the household sector and the business sector. (We'll ignore the government and foreign sectors for the moment.) The flows are somewhat more specific in this figure than they are in Figure 4-1. Saving is funneled into the credit market, which channels the funds to firms that engage in investment expenditures which are added to the consumption expenditures that ultimately determine the demand for goods and services.

Keeping in mind this circular flow of income,

let's look very briefly at the classical theory of income and employment determination.

The Classical Theory and Mr. Say

One school of classical economists believed that a permanent unemployment situation could not exist. This classical theory was based on Say's law of conservation of purchasing power. The law states:

Supply creates its own demand.

The idea behind the law was simple: People produce goods and services so they can use them in the market to buy other goods and services they want. Therefore, Say's law indicates there will always be sufficient aggregate purchasing power in the economy to allow everything that is produced to be demanded. In Say's own words (translated from the French):

The total supply of products and their total demand must, of necessity, be equal, for the total demand is nothing but the mass of commodities which have been produced; a general congestion would consequently be an absurdity.

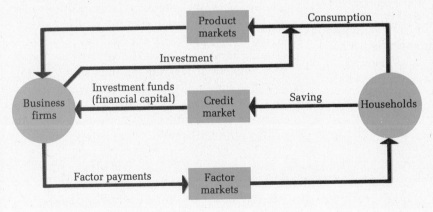

FIGURE 8-1 **The Circular Flow of Income with Investment and Saving Added**

Expenditures can travel from households to product markets in two ways: (1) directly by consumption expenditures and (2) indirectly by investment expenditures. Households do not make investment expenditures directly but rather provide funds via saving that are allocated by the credit market to business firms for investment projects.

By "general congestion," Say meant overproduction, leading to a situation whereby producers would have unwanted, unsold goods in their warehouses. Say's law predicts only temporary periods of excess aggregate supply in the economy, which will be automatically eliminated if prices are allowed to fall.

Say's law still makes some sense in a world of flexible prices. The classical model remains consistent with saving and investment done by different sectors, for example. If there is an excess of saving—that is, a provision for more saving than businesses want to invest—the credit markets would adjust. The price of credit (interest rate) would fall, inducing more investment and also less saving. In other words, no matter how much people save, at some interest rate businesses will borrow those savings to invest in new capital equipment and inventories. The interest rate, which is merely the price of credit, will see to it that saving and investment remain at equal rates. The classical model predicts full employment as a natural tendency. This aspect of the model conflicts with our actual periods of less than full employment and is perhaps the reason why modern economists, particularly in the 1930s, became disenchanted with the classical theory of income and employment determination.

The modern theory places more emphasis on the determination of saving and investment by factors other than the interest rate and the imbalances between the two leading to changes in the level of income and employment. For us to understand that theory, we must look into what determines consumption and finally what determines investment.

Determinants of Consumption and Saving

The major determinant of consumption expenditure is clearly expressed in the 1936 treatise that revolutionized economics: *The General Theory of Employment, Interest, and Money,* written by John Maynard Keynes. Lord Keynes' ideas underpin modern income analysis to an incredible degree. In fact, the modern theory of income and employment is usually called Keynesian. It was Keynes who asserted that to understand how aggregate demand is determined, we have to look at its separate components and how each is determined. According to Keynes, when we look at consumption we find

> ... the fundamental psychological law, upon which we are entitled to depend with great confidence both *a priori* from our knowledge of human nature and from the detailed facts of experience, is that men are disposed, as a rule and on the average, to increase their consumption as their income increases, but not by as much as the increase in their income.[1]

A relationship is suggested here between the planned consumption expenditures of households and their current income. This relationship is called the **consumption function.** Using for the moment only the first three columns of Table 8-1, we will present a consumption function for a hypothetical household.

We see from the table that as disposable income goes up, planned consumption rises also, but by a smaller amount, as Keynes suggested. Planned saving also increases with disposable income. Notice, however, that below an income of $5,000, the planned saving of this hypothetical family actually becomes negative. The more income drops below that level, the more the family either dissaves, going into debt or by using up some of its existing wealth.

---

[1] John Maynard Keynes, The General Theory of Employment, Interest, and Money, London: Macmillan, 1964, p. 96.

Table 8-1 Hypothetical Consumption and Saving Schedules

Table 8-1 presents a hypothetical consumption and saving function. Column 1 presents disposable income from zero to $10,000 per year; column 2 indicates planned consumption per year; and column 3 planned saving per year. At levels of disposable income below $5,000, planned saving is negative. In column 4 we see the average propensity to consume, which is merely planned consumption ÷ disposable income. Column 5 lists average propensity to save, which is planned saving/disposable income. Column 6 is the marginal propensity to consume, which shows the proportion of additional income that will be saved, or the marginal propensity to save.

	(1)	(2)	(3)	(4)	(5)	(6)	(7)
COMBINATION	DISPOSABLE INCOME Y_d	PLANNED CONSUMPTION C	PLANNED SAVING $S \equiv Y_d - C$ (1) − (2)	AVERAGE PROPENSITY TO CONSUME $APC = C/Y_d$ (2) ÷ (1)	AVERAGE PROPENSITY TO SAVE $APS = S/Y_d$ (3) ÷ (1)	MARGINAL PROPENSITY TO CONSUME change in planned consumption (2) $MPC = \dfrac{\text{change in}}{\text{disposable income (1)}}$	MARGINAL PROPENSITY TO SAVE change in planned saving (3) $MPS = \dfrac{\text{change in}}{\text{disposable income (1)}}$
A	0	1,000	−1,000	...	...	...	...
B	1,000	1,800	− 800	1.80	−0.8	0.8	0.2
C	2,000	2,600	− 600	1.30	−0.3	0.8	0.2
D	3,000	3,400	− 400	1.133	−0.133	0.8	0.2
E	4,000	4,200	− 200	1.05	−0.05	0.8	0.2
F	5,000	5,000	0	1.00	0.00	0.8	0.2
G	6,000	5,800	200	0.967	0.033	0.8	0.2
H	7,000	6,600	400	0.943	0.057	0.8	0.2
I	8,000	7,400	600	0.925	0.075	0.8	0.2
J	9,000	8,200	800	0.911	0.089	0.8	0.2
K	10,000	9,000	1,000	0.9	0.1	0.8	0.2

Graphing the Numbers

When we constructed demand and supply curves in Chapter 3, we merely plotted the points from a table showing price-quantity pairs onto a diagram whose axes were labeled price and quantity. We will graph the consumption and saving relationships presented in Table 8-1 in the same manner. In Figure 8-2 the vertical axis measures the level of planned consumption, and the horizontal axis measures the level of actual disposable income. In Figure 8-3 the horizontal axis is again actual disposable income, but now the vertical axis is planned saving. All these are on a dollars per-year basis, which emphasizes the point that we are measuring flows, not stocks.

As you can see, we have taken the income-consumption and income-saving combinations A through K and plotted them. In Figure 8-2 the result is called the "consumption function." In Figure 8-3 the result is called the "saving function." One is the mirror image of the other. Why? Because consumption plus saving always equal disposable income. In other words, what is not consumed is, by definition, saved. The difference between actual disposable income and the planned level of consumption per year must be the planned level of saving per year.

How can we find the rate of saving or dissaving (negative saving) in Figure 8-2? We draw a line that is equidistant between the horizontal and the vertical axes. This line is 45 degrees from either axis. Since it cuts the diagram in half and since we use identical scales for both axes, disposable income is exactly equal to planned consumption at all points along that 45 degree line. Thus, at point F, where the consumption function intersects the 45 degree line, actual disposable income equals planned consumption. Point F is sometimes labeled the break-even income point because there is neither positive nor negative saving. This can be seen in Figure 8-3, as well. The planned annual rate of saving at an actual disposable income level of $5,000 is indeed zero.

Dissaving and Autonomous Consumption

To the left of point F on either Figure 8-2 or Figure 8-3, this hypothetical family engages in dissaving, either by going into debt or selling off its existing assets. The amount of saving or dissaving in Figure 8-2 can be found by measuring the vertical distance between the 45 degree line and the consumption function. This simply tells us that if our hypothetical family temporarily finds its actual disposable income below $5,000, it will not cut back its consumption by the full amount of the reduction. It will instead go into debt in some way to compensate for the loss.

Now look at the point on the diagram where actual disposable income is zero but planned consumption per year is $1,000. This amount of planned consumption, which does not depend at all on actual disposable income, is called "autonomous consumption." In other words, the autonomous consumption of $1,000 is independent of the level of disposable income.

Average Propensity to Consume and to Save

Let's now go back to Table 8-1 and this time look at columns 4 and 5: **average propensity to consume** (APC) and **average propensity to save** (APS). They are defined as

$$APC = \frac{consumption}{disposable\ income}$$

$$APS = \frac{saving}{disposable\ income}$$

Notice that for this hypothetical family, the average propensity to consume decreases as

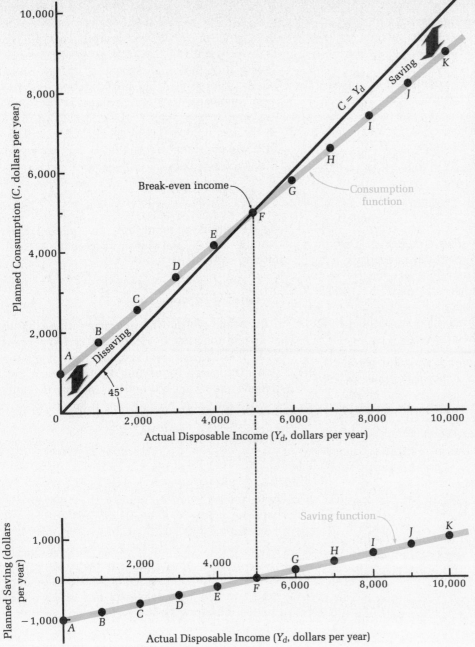

FIGURE 8-2 **The Consumption Function**

If we plot the combinations of disposable income and planned consumption from columns 1 and 2 in Table 8-1, we get the consumption function. Every point on the 45 degree line bisecting this diagram is equidistant from the horizontal and the vertical axes; thus, at every point on it, consumption equals disposable income. Where the consumption function crosses the 45 degree line, we know that consumption equals disposable income and there is zero saving. The vertical distance between the 45 degree line and the consumption function measures the rate of saving or dissaving at any given income level.

FIGURE 8-3 **The Saving Function**

If we plot the relationship between column 1, disposable income, and column 3, planned saving, from Table 8-1, we arrive at the saving function shown in this diagram. It is the mirror image of the consumption function presented in Figure 8-2.

income increases. This decrease simply means that the fraction of the family's disposable income going to saving rises as income rises. The same fact can be found in column 5. The average propensity to save, which at first is negative, finally hits zero at an income level of $5,000 and then becomes positive, never exceeding 1.00.

It's quite easy for you to figure out your own average propensity to consume or to save. Just divide your total disposable income for the year into what you consumed or into what you saved. The result will be your personal APC and APS, respectively.

Marginal Propensity to Consume and to Save

Now we go to the last two columns in Table 8-1. These are labeled **marginal propensity to consume** (MPC) and **marginal propensity to save** (MPS). We have already used the term "marginal." It means "small change in" or incremental or decremental. The marginal propensity to consume, then, is defined as

$$MPC = \frac{\text{change in planned consumption}}{\text{change in disposable income}}$$

Actually, if we wanted to be exact, the word "change" should be replaced by the mathematical symbol Δ (delta). We won't bother with that technicality now, but be aware that marginal generally refers to a small change, and not to just any change.

The marginal propensity to save is defined similarly:

$$MPS = \frac{\text{change in planned saving}}{\text{change in disposable income}}$$

What do the MPC and the MPS tell you? They tell you by what percentage of an increase or decrease in income will change consumption and saving. For example, you have an annual

salary of $8,000. At the end of the year your boss gives you a bonus of $1,000. What would you do with that additional $1,000 in income? If you were to consume $800 of it, then your marginal propensity to consume would be 0.8. By definition, then, your marginal propensity to save would be 0.2 because you would be saving an additional $200 out of the $1,000 bonus. The terms MPC and MPS sound somewhat imposing, but the concepts behind them are, you will probably agree, fairly intuitive. In the example in Table 8-1 the MPC and the MPS are constant; that is, they do not vary with the level of income.

Some Relationships

By definition, consumption plus saving must equal income. This allows us to make the following statements:

1. $APC + APS = 1.00$
2. $MPC + MPS = 1.00$

In other words, the average propensity to consume and save must total 1.00 or 100 percent as well as the marginal propensities. Check the two statements by adding the figures in columns 4 and 5 for each level of income in Table 8-1. Do the same for columns 6 and 7.

Distinguishing between a Movement and a Shift

Take a few minutes to reread pages 50 to 53 in Chapter 3. Here we made a clear distinction between a movement along a supply or demand curve and a shift in either of those curves. This same distinction applies when considering the consumption or saving function. Since the saving function is the reciprocal of the consumption function, let's just talk in terms of movements along, or shifts in, the consumption function.

Look at Figure 8-4. How do we represent the effect on consumption of a rise in actual disposable income of, for example, $2,500 per year, starting from the break-even income at $5,000 per year? We move upward along the consumption function, now labeled C, from point A to point B. Planned consumption per year will increase by the marginal propensity to consume (0.8) times the increase in income, or 0.8 × $2,500 = $2,000; that is, planned consumption will rise from $5,000 to $7,000 per year. The same analysis holds for a decrease in actual disposable income; planned consumption

would fall by 0.8 times that decrease. These represent movements along a given consumption function, C.

How do we represent a decrease in autonomous planned consumption? We do this by shifting the entire consumption function downward by the amount of the decrease. For example, a $500 decrease in the autonomous component of consumption will shift the consumption function C down to C'. Notice that the break-even point moves from point A, or $5,000 to point F, or $2,500. (Verify this for yourself algebraically.) On the other hand, if the autonomous

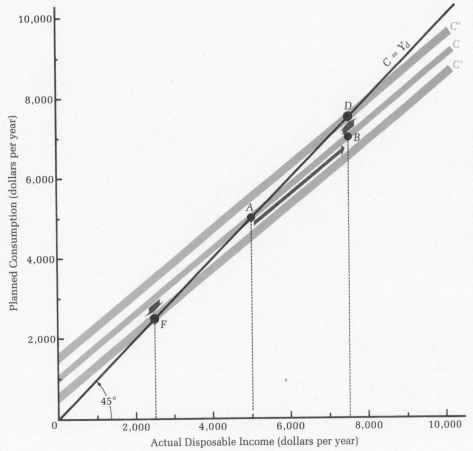

FIGURE 8-4
Distinguishing between Movements Along and Shifts in the Consumption Function
Starting at the break-even income at point A on line C, if actual disposable income increases by $2,500 per year, then we will experience a movement from point A to point B along that consumption function. Planned consumption will go up by a multiple of marginal propensity to consume and the increase in actual disposable income, or by 0.8 × $2,500 = $2,000. Planned consumption will rise from $5,000 to $7,000. On the other hand, if there were a $500 per year decrease in autonomous consumption, the entire consumption function would shift from C to C'. If there were a $500 per year increase in the autonomous component, the consumption function would shift from C to C''.

component of consumption shifts upward, for whatever reason, the consumption function will shift from C to, for example, C''. In this particular case, the autonomous component of planned consumption rose by $500. The new break-even income point, as you can see, is D, or $7,500. Another way of looking at this problem is by realizing that an increase in the consumption function means that at all income levels, more will be consumed than before. A decrease in the consumption function means that at each and every income level, less will be consumed than before.

We can summarize the difference between movement and shift in this way. If disposable income goes up or down, we *move* along a given consumption function to find the change in amount of planned consumption. But if there is a change in the autonomous component of consumption, we *shift* the entire curve. This is called a shift or a change in consumption.

The Historical Record

How does this consumption function hold up against the facts? Figure 8-5 is the historical

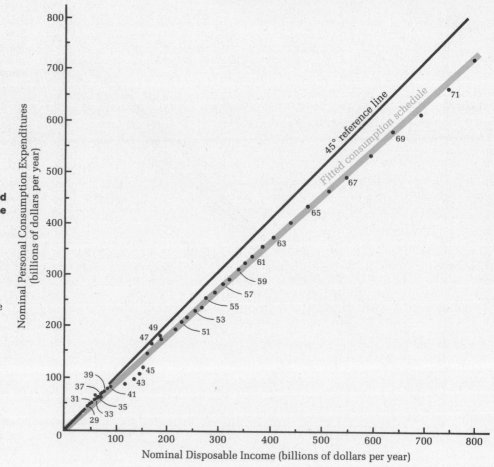

FIGURE 8-5 **Income and Consumption over Time**

Historically, the relationship between consumption and disposable income can be represented by a straight line passing through as many of the points as possible. Notice that the historically fitted crosses the 45 degree reference line at the origin where consumption equals disposable income. (*Source:* U.S. Department of Commerce.)

record for the United States from the Great Depression through 1975. It gives the disposable income for the entire nation and the *actual* personal consumption for the entire country. In a sense, then, this is the aggregate consumption of the United States over time. We have drawn a line to all the dots to show the so-called fitted consumption function. Almost all the points fall to the right of the 45 degree consumption-disposable income reference line, meaning that almost every year, aggregate or national saving was positive. Notice that the fitted consumption function lies above the observed points during the war years because rationing and the unavailability of a number of consumer items during that time. This perhaps encouraged consumers to save even though they might have desired to spend more of their incomes. Also notice that during the Depression there was *dissaving*.

Keynes' theory seems to have been borne out by the empirical evidence. Consumption is greatly dependent on disposable income, and, as income changes, so too does consumption, though by a smaller amount. However, there seems to be a difference between the historical consumption function represented in Figure 8-5 and the hypothetical household consumption function represented in Figure 8-2. In Figure 8-5 there is no autonomous consumption; that is, the consumption function never crosses the 45 degree $C = Y_d$ reference line. In fact, it intersects the vertical axis at zero. How can this be? These two different consumption functions can be reconciled by distinguishing between the short and the long run.

Short- vs. Long-Run Consumption Functions

The historical data show identical marginal and average propensities to consume of about 0.9 since autonomous consumption equals zero. Studies on household behavior, however, reveal significant amounts of autonomous consumption but a marginal propensity to consume that is, on the average, much lower than 0.9. This difference exists because the data, taken at a particular time, reveal the short-run consumption function, as represented in Figure 8-2. The data taken over a 40- or 50-year period, however, give us the long-run consumption function. These results can be explained by the permanent-income hypothesis.

Basically, the **permanent-income hypothesis** holds that consumption doesn't depend on *current* disposable income but rather on some measure of long-run, expected, or permanent income. The long-run may be anywhere from 2 to 3 to 5 years, depending upon people's expectations. According to this theory, consumption will not drop drastically even if, for some reason, people's income falls below what they think their permanent income is. Conversely, consumption will not increase very much even if people's income suddenly jumps above the level they consider permanent.

When we get data on families with different incomes and different levels of spending, we can assume that many high-income people are experiencing those levels of earnings only temporarily, not permanently. On the one hand, their rate of saving appears high because they assume they will not be able to maintain a high spending level when this income goes back to normal. Their rate of consumption, on the other hand, appears to be relatively low. Conversely, many people with low incomes may be at earnings levels that are abnormally low for them, when compared to a higher level they consider to be permanent. These people will probably be saving very little, or spending quite a bit, relative to their current income. Thus, we can imagine plotting a consumption relationship like the one in Figure 8-2. The permanent-income hypothesis would predict such a consumption relationship at any one point in time.

This hypothesis would also be useful in explaining the behavior of, for example, medical students. While they are in medical school, students' consumption expenditures, in general, greatly exceed their actual income. However, this is understandable since the medical student's permanent income will be much higher than the current income. Consumption is geared to expectations of permanent income rather than current levels of income.

This hypothesis also predicts the long-run consumption function found in Figure 8-5 since the permanent-income hypothesis assumes that the marginal propensity to consume is the same in the long run as the average propensity to consume. Proponents of the hypothesis contend that there is no difference between marginal and average propensities to consume if one looks at *permanent* income rather than *current* income. Accordingly, we would not expect to see the rich saving a larger percentage of their income (in the long run) than the poor.

Other Determinants of Consumption

The only determinant of spending in all the theories of consumption presented here is some form of income—whether it be current or permanent. Surely, other things must also help determine the level of consumption and saving in the United States. However, if one could get away with it, one would ignore these other determinants. If one variable—disposable income—were sufficient to predict the yearly level of consumption accurately, then (for the purposes of prediction) it wouldn't matter whether other variables were included. Researchers have found, however, that using just one variable does not yield highly accurate results for all periods of time. Specifically,

economists using the consumption function to predict levels of spending after World War II grossly underestimated what actually happened. After the fact, economists realized that several crucial variables had been left out of the relationship.

Liquid Assets

After World War II, Americans found themselves with a high level of **liquid assets.** A liquid asset is an asset that can be turned into money fairly rapidly and without much loss in value. Obviously, the most liquid asset is money itself. Other liquid assets are government bonds and shares in savings and loan associations. In 1946, many Americans found themselves with a large number of government-issued war bonds. This constituted a ready supply of liquid assets that people now turned in for cash and used to buy goods or services. At the same time, there was no longer a motivation to lend money to the government for the war effort, and consumers began to spend way beyond their regular take-home pay. The result was that the recession which economists predicted after World War II did not materialize.

If we had applied the permanent-income hypothesis to the situation during and after World War II, we probably would have predicted an increase in spending over and above what would have been predicted by just using the disposable-income hypothesis. During the war, people were saving more than they normally would have saved. After the war, this inducement disappeared. The permanent-income hypothesis would predict that after the war people would bring their average propensity to consume up to its normal level. In other words, people would dissave by getting rid of some of the savings they had accumulated during the war.

Expectations

Expectations also play a role in determining how much of their income people are willing to spend. For example, the expectation of future increases in prices may induce consumers to spend more of their current income than they would have spent otherwise. They would try to buy many goods now instead of waiting and paying higher prices in the future. Thus far, these possibilities have not been considered because we haven't really talked about the price level. We've actually been assuming implicitly that the price level remains constant. This, of course, is an unrealistic assumption that we will have to drop if our analysis is to fit the actual situation in the United States today. Expectations is a very subjective concept, however, and it is difficult for economists to come up with a measure of that variable. Therefore, we find it does not appear in many of the numerical studies of the consumption/disposable income relationship in the United States.

Determinants of Investment

Investment, you will remember, is defined as expenditures on new capital equipment and plant and changes in business inventories. As we can see from Figure 8-6, gross private domestic investment in the United States has been extremely volatile over the years. If we were to look at net private domestic investment, that is, investment after depreciation has been deducted, we would see that in the depths of the Great Depression the figure was negative—in other words, we were drawing down our capital stock—we weren't even maintaining it by replacing depreciated equipment.

If we compare investment expenditures historically with consumption and saving expenditures, we find that the latter are quite stable over time but the former are not. Why is this so? The answer is that the investment decisions of business people are based on highly variable, subjective estimates of how the economic future looks. We just discussed the role of expec-

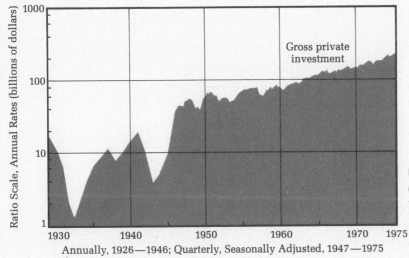

Source: Federal Reserve Bank of St. Louis

FIGURE 8-6 Gross Private Investment

Gross private investment is extremely volatile as shown by the erratic movements in this figure. During the Great Depression it was barely above $1 million, and net private investment was actually negative. *(Source: U.S. Department of Commerce.)*

tation in determining the position of the consumption function. Expectation plays an even greater role in determining the position of the investment function. This could account for much of the instability of investment over time. Given this chronic instability, it is more difficult to derive a satisfactory theory of planned investment expenditures. We do not have the detailed knowledge of the causes of investment that we do of saving and consumption. Nonetheless, we'll make an attempt here to construct an investment function.

The Planned Investment Function

It seems reasonable to assume that the cost of obtaining investment funds to make investment expenditures is an important determinant of investment. Whenever a firm enters the credit market to obtain money capital for investment expenditures, it must pay the market rate of interest. The higher the rate of interest, the greater the cost—whether explicit, or implicit if retained earnings are used—to that firm of undertaking any given investment. Thus, a relatively higher or lower rate of interest cost will sometimes be the deciding factor as to whether or not the project will be undertaken.

It should be no surprise, therefore, that the investment function is the result of an inverse relationship between the rate of interest and the quantity of planned investment. A hypothetical investment schedule is given in Table 8-2 and plotted in Figure 8-7. We see from this schedule that if, for example, the rate of interest is 8 percent, the quantity of planned investment will be $225 billion per year. Notice, by the way, that planned investment is also given on a per-year basis, showing that it represents a flow, not a stock. The stock counterpart of investment is the stock of capital in the economy measured in trillions of dollars at a point in time.

Table 8-2 **Planned Investment Schedule**

The rate of planned investment is asserted to be inversely related to the rate of interest in this hypothetical schedule.

RATE OF INTEREST (PERCENT PER YEAR)	PLANNED INVESTMENT (BILLIONS OF DOLLARS PER YEAR)
5	$300
6	275
7	250
8	225
9	200
10	175

The Elasticity of the Demand for Investment

We talk in terms of interest elasticity in the demand for investment, just as we talked in terms of price elasticity in the demand for goods and services in Chapter 3. We show two extremes in (a) and (b) of Figure 8-8. In (a) we show a completely inelastic planned investment function. This means that regardless of the interest rate, planned investment will be $225 billion per year. In (b) we show a completely or infinitely elastic investment function. Here, at an interest rate of 5 percent, the quantity of investment demanded or planned is infinite; that is, the quantity is infinitely elastic at that interest rate.

Other Determinants of Investment

As with the consumption function, more than one main variable (which is the rate of interest in this case) may be important in determining the investment function. These other variables will have the effect of shifting the investment function up or down. The most important of these are now given.

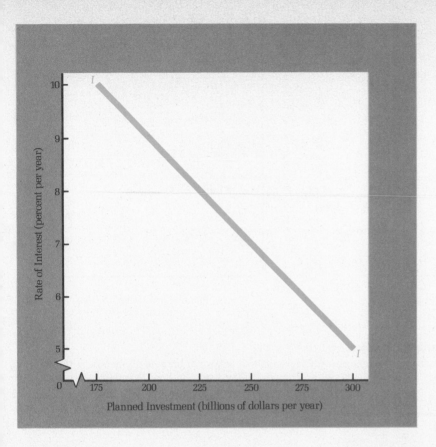

FIGURE 8-7 **Planned Investment**

If we plot the interest rate/planned investment data pairs from Table 8-2, we obtain the investment function, II. It is negatively sloped.

Expectations

Based on expectations as to the future demand for their product, business people may make projections about the future profitability of their investment decisions. If they expect a rosy future for their sector of the economy and for the economy overall, the investment function will shift outward to the right; that is, at each interest rate, more will be invested than before. If they expect the future to be grim, the investment schedule will move inward, to the left, reflecting less desired investment at each and every interest rate.

Cost of New Capital Goods

If the cost of new plant and equipment suddenly were to increase, the decisions of business people as to the amount they should invest might change. In fact, we would expect the investment function to shift inward. The opposite would occur if there were an abrupt, unanticipated fall in the cost of capital goods.

Innovation and Technology

Both improvements in current productive technology and innovations could generally be expected to shift the investment function to the right since both would stimulate a demand for additional capital goods.

Business Taxes

Business people calculate rates of return on investments on the basis of aftertax profits. If

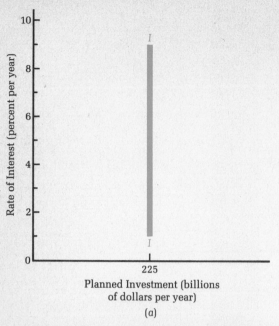

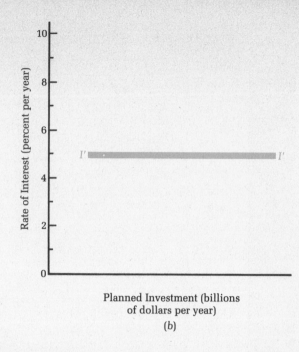

FIGURE 8-8 Two Extreme Planned Investment Functions

In (a) we show a planned investment function that is completely inelastic with respect to the rate of interest. In (b) we show a planned investment function that is completely elastic with respect to the rate of interest at 5 percent per year.

there is an increase in business tax rates, *ceteris paribus*, we expect a shift in the planned investment function inward. If there is a decrease in tax rates, we expect a shift outward.

That completes our discussion of the determinants of investment. To end this chapter, we demonstrate how actual saving must always be equal to actual investment.

The Equality of Saving and Investment

It is often perplexing to students of economic principles to learn that saving must always equal investment. After all, we started this chapter with a statement that those who do the

investing and those who do the saving are different people. How can different people make decisions that always come out alike? To understand the answer, we must look at the difference between planned and actual values. Thus far, we have spoken generally in terms of planned consumption, planned saving, and planned investment. The statement we are making now is in terms of actual saving and actual investment. It is actual values that must be equal—planned values do not have to be.

To better understand this distinction, look at Tables 8-3 and 8-4. Table 8-3 shows the planned rates of production for firms and the planned rates of expenditures for households and firms. We should notice immediately a

Table 8-3 Planned Rates of Production and Expenditures for Firms and Households: Disequilibrium

PLANNED RATE OF PRODUCTION (PER YEAR)		PLANNED RATE OF EXPENDITURE (PER YEAR)	
Consumer goods	$ 900	By households for consumption	$800
Investment goods	100	By firms for new capital goods	100
		By firms for inventory changes	. . .
Total planned production (per year)	$1,000	Total planned expenditures (per year)	$900

discrepancy: Total planned production is $1,000 per year, but total planned expenditures are only $900 per year.

What happens in actuality? The answer lies in Table 8-4. Firms do indeed purchase $100 worth of investment goods that other firms produced that year, and consumers purchase $800 worth of consumption goods for that year. This means that businesses are left with an unplanned inventory increase of $100. Thus, the actual rate of "expenditure" is $1,000, even though the planned rate was only $900. The difference was made up by the residual increase in actual inventories. Firms did not plan to increase their inventories but were forced to do so.

Now you can see why it is important to distinguish between planned and actual values. Now you can see better why actual saving and actual investment must always be equal, by definition.

If we ignore for the moment taxes and government spending, as well as the foreign sector of our economy, we can say that total expenditures ($1,000 in the above example) equal total income (or Y), but we know that total income (Y) is equal to actual consumption expenditures plus actual investment expenditures. Using the symbols C and I for consumption and investment, the equation becomes

$$Y \equiv C + I$$

On the other hand, income can be disposed of in only two ways: by consumption (C) or by saving (S). This must mean that total income is equal to consumption plus saving, or

$$Y \equiv C + S$$

But if this is the case, then I must be equal to S. Note that these terms are applied here to actual consumption, saving, and investment figures.

Table 8-4 Actual Rates of Production and Expenditures for Firms and Households: Equilibrium

ACTUAL RATE OF PRODUCTION (PER YEAR)		ACTUAL RATE OF EXPENDITURE (PER YEAR)	
Consumer goods	$ 900	By households for consumption	$ 800
Investment goods	100	By firms for new capital goods	100
		Unplanned inventory changes	100
Total actual production (per year)	$1,000	Total actual expenditures (per year)	$1,000

Look at the above example and you can see how it works. Planned saving equaled total income ($1,000) minus planned consumption ($800), or $200 per year. But planned investment was only $100. Planned investment did not equal planned saving. After all the cards are dealt, however, we see that actual saving was $200 because households consumed only $800 of the total $1,000 per year of income, but actual investment was $100 a year in capital goods, plus $100 a year in unplanned inventory changes, or a total of $200. Hence, in the end, actual saving equals actual investment. In other words, unplanned inventory changes will always bring actual saving and actual investment into equality. To increase your understanding, you might want to work out some examples similar to the one given in Tables 8-3 and 8-4. To summarize, we note that

1. The actual rate of investment always equals the actual rate of saving.
2. When the planned rate of investment is greater than the planned rate of saving, inventories decrease (unplanned).
3. When the planned rate of investment is less than the planned rate of saving, inventories increase (unplanned).

Now that we have developed a theory of the determinants of consumption, saving, and investment, we have the basis for constructing a model of income and employment determination. This we will do in the next chapter.

Consumption: That which is spent on new goods and services out of a household's current income. Whatever is not consumed is saved. Consumption includes buying food, going to the movies, going to a concert, and so on.

Saving: The act of not consuming all of one's current income. Whatever is not consumed out of spendable income is, by definition, saved. Saving is an action measured over time, whereas savings is an existing accumulation resulting from the act of saving in the past. We usually talk about how much we save out of our paycheck every week or every month.

Consumption Goods: Goods that are bought by households to use up, such as movies, food, and clothing.

Flow: A process that occurs over time, measured in units per unit of time. Income, for example, is a flow, measured in dollars per month or dollars per year.

Stock: An accumulated quantity that exists at a point in time, such as a stock of wealth, the amount of money you have in your savings account today, and so on.

Investment: The spending by businesses on things like machines and buildings, which can be used to produce goods and services in the future. The investment part of total income is that portion which is not consumed this year but rather will be used in the process of producing goods in the future.

Capital Goods: Another name for producer goods, or goods that are used by firms to make other goods.

Consumption Function: The relationship between the amount consumed and the amount earned. A consumption function tells us how much people will consume out of various income levels.

Average Propensity to Consume: Consumption divided by disposable income for any given level of income.

Average Propensity to Save: Saving divided by disposable income.

Marginal Propensity to Consume: The ratio of the change in consumption divided by the change in disposable income. A 0.8 marginal propensity to consume tells us that an additional $100 earned will see $80 consumed.

Marginal Propensity to Save: The ratio of the change in saving divided by the change in disposable income. A 0.2 marginal propensity to save indicates that out of an additional $100 earned, $20 will be saved. Whatever is not saved is consumed. Therefore, the marginal propensity to save plus the marginal propensity to consume must always equal 1.00, by definition.

Permanent-Income Hypothesis: A theory of the consumption function that states that people's desire to spend is a function of their permanent or long-run expected income rather than of their current disposable income.

Liquid Assets: Assets that can be transformed into money quite readily without significant loss of value. The most liquid of assets is, of course, money itself. Government bonds and savings and loan shares are nearly as liquid.

Chapter Summary

1. For analytical purposes, the economy is split up into two sectors: the household sector and the business sector. We assume that these two sectors are entirely separate.

2. The act of saving is an act of not consuming. If you earn $100 in a week and buy food and entertainment and spend on other living expenses equal to $80, you have consumed $80 of your income. The rest you save; you put it in a savings and loan account or something of that nature. Saving is the difference between income and what is consumed. Saving equals what is left over after consumption expenses.

3. We can represent the relationship between income and consumption by a consumption function. A consumption function, in its simplest form, shows that current consumption is directly related to current income. The reciprocal of a consumption function is a saving function. A saving function also shows the relationship between current saving and current income.

4. The marginal propensity to consume shows how much consumption there is out of additional income. We have set the hypothetical marginal propensity to consume at 0.8. That means out of every additional $100 earned, $80 will be consumed and $20 will be saved. The marginal propensity to save is the difference between 1 and the marginal propensity to con-

sume. Otherwise stated, the marginal propensity to save plus the marginal propensity to consume must equal 1.

5. We must be careful to distinguish between the average and the marginal propensities. The average propensity to consume is the amount of total consumption divided by total disposable income. The average propensity to save is the total amount of saving divided by total disposable income for a certain period. The marginal propensities, on the other hand, relate increases in consumption and saving to increases in disposable income.

6. If the marginal propensity to save schedule or consumption function does not start out at the zero point on our typical consumption-income graph, but starts out at some positive subsistence level of consumption, then the average propensity to consume will fall throughout the entire schedule. This falling average propensity to consume implies that rich nations should save more than poor nations and that rich people should save more than poor people. The rich should become richer relative to the poor.

7. There are numerous other theories of the consumption function. One of them is the permanent-income hypothesis, which states that people's desire to consume is a function not of their current income but of their permanent or long-run income.

8. We have discussed one determinant of consumption and saving income. There are also other determinants such as liquid assets and expectations.

9. Investment is done by the business sector of the economy. Investment is the spending by businesses on such things as machines and buildings that can be used later to help produce goods and services which people want to buy for consumption purposes. Investment is the use of resources to provide for future production.

10. Obviously, the only way to provide for future production is not to consume everything today. That means that the only way businesses can invest is for people to save—not consume all their income. Thus, saving must equal investment. This is an accounting necessity that cannot be denied at any time. For investment to occur, households must save some of their income to make resources available for business people to use for investment purposes.

11. There are numerous determinants of investment. We showed the planned investment schedule to be related primarily to the rate of interest. Additionally, investment is a function of changes in expectations, the cost of new capital goods, innovation and technology, and business taxes.

12. After the fact, actual saving must always equal actual investment. This is an accounting identity.

1. The marginal propensity to consume plus the marginal propensity to save must equal 1. Must the average propensity to consume plus the average propensity to save also equal 1?

2. What are some of the reasons people save? Do you ever save? Do you ever dissave?

3. Draw consumption and saving schedules, under the assumption that you consume every last penny of your income.

4. Benjamin Franklin said that a penny saved is a penny earned. Was he right?

5. What do you think would happen to the saving schedule if there was an increased threat of nuclear holocaust?

6. Why does any upshift in the consumption schedule necessarily involve an equal downshift in the saving schedule?

Selected
References

Lekachman, Robert, *The Age of Keynes,* New York: Random House, 1966.

Peterson, Wallace C., *Income, Employment, and Economic Growth,* 3d ed., New York: W. W. Norton, 1974, chap. 4.

Stewart, Michael, *Keynes and After,* Baltimore, Md.: Penguin, 1968.

Income and Employment Determination

Why is the level of income what it is? Why is the resulting level of employment what it is and not lower or higher? To answer these questions, we must construct a model of income and employment determination. To do this, we will first employ the relationships developed in the last chapter to construct an aggregate demand schedule (again leaving out government and foreign dealings). Then we will construct an aggregate supply schedule and from there find out how an equilibrium is set.

Aggregate Demand

The aggregate demand function for the entire economy will ultimately relate everyone's planned expenditures to some variable. The variable we used for the consumption component of **aggregate demand** in Chapter 8 was disposable income. Now we will look at consumption as a function of aggregate or national income. We see this as the C curve in Figure 9-1. Notice that it is now slightly different from the ones we constructed before—here the horizontal axis is now labeled aggregate income. This means that the C function must be shifted downward to account for the amount by which taxes have cut into planned consumption at each level of income. Notice also that we use a C function having an autonomous component. In other words, we are using a short-run, as opposed to a long-run consumption function in this model. Since this model is basically concerned with short-run problems and policies here, this is appropriate.

We add the other component of private aggregate demand: investment spending (I). Instead of using the planned investment function, which relates

FIGURE 9-1 **The Aggregate Demand Function**

If we assume no government, no exports and imports in our model, then planned consumption plus planned investment will equal aggregate demand, all measured in billions of dollars per year. This is represented by the vertical summation of the C line and the autonomous investment obtained from Figure 9-2.

investment to the rate of interest, we will simplify things by considering all investment to be autonomous. The autonomous nature of the investment function is depicted in Figure 9-2. In other words, investment spending is represented by the horizontal distance of the arrow in Figure 9-2 no matter what the level of aggregate annual income. How do we add this amount of investment to our consumption function? We simply shift up the C line in Figure 9-1 by the vertical distance equal to the amount of autonomous investment. That is shown by the arrow in Figure 9-1, which is exactly the same length as the arrow in Figure

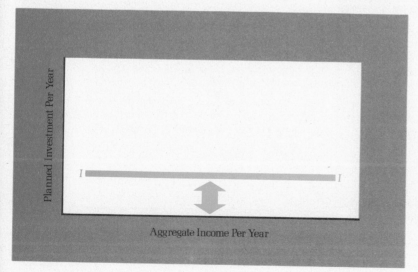

FIGURE 9-2 **The Autonomous Investment Function**

In this simplified model of income and employment determination, we assume that investment spending is autonomous (or exogenous) with respect to aggregate income. It is represented by the vertical arrow, which is exactly the same length as the vertical arrow in Figure 9-1.

INCOME AND EMPLOYMENT DETERMINATION **199**

9-2. Our new line is labeled $C + I$ and is called the consumption + investment line. For the moment it is also our aggregate demand curve because we are leaving out the government and foreign sectors.

Now, to obtain an equilibrium level of aggregate income, we have to find out what the aggregate supply schedule looks like.

Aggregate Supply

Aggregate supply is the total value of all *final* goods and services sold by all firms in the economy. But you'll recall from national income accounting in Chapter 4 that this is identical to national product. Aggregate supply, then, must always equal actual national product.

How does aggregate product or supply vary as actual aggregate or national income varies? The answer is "They are the same!" Remember that national product and national income are identically equal. This is so because the aggregate market value of all final goods and services is, by definition, equal to the actual aggregate factor costs incurred in their production, which is, by definition, equal to aggregate or national income. [In the real world, *gross national product*, (GNP) is the aggregate we use.] It therefore follows that the value of aggregate supply is equal, by definition, to aggregate income.

Thus, the aggregate supply curve is going to be a straight line, as shown in Figure 9-3, that bisects the diagram forming two 45 degree angles.

Now we can establish equilibrium in the goods and services market in our economy: by

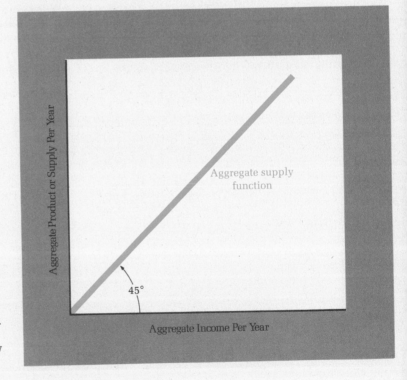

FIGURE 9-3 The Aggregate Supply Function

If we plot aggregate annual income on the horizontal axis and aggregate annual product or supply on the vertical axis, the aggregate supply curve will be a line, every point on which is equidistant from the two. This is because national product and national income are always identical at any and all levels of output.

putting together the aggregate supply curve and the aggregate demand curve on a single diagram.

Finding Equilibrium

What we do is lay out some hypothetical values for aggregate supply, planned consumption, planned saving, planned investment, aggregate demand, and then unplanned changes in inventories.

We are assuming a consumption function with an autonomous component equal to $220 billion per year. As in Chapter 8, the assumed marginal propensity to consume is 0.8 or four-fifths. Thus, planned consumption at an income level of $1 trillion will equal $220 billion plus 0.8 times $1 trillion or $1.02 trillion, as indicated in the first line of column 2 in Table 9-1. The planned saving is negative (in this case, −$20

billion per year). Planned investment in column 4 is assumed to be autonomous at a level of $100 billion per year no matter what the level of national income. Column 5 adds planned consumption and planned investment to get aggregate demand. Ignoring for now the last two columns in Table 9-1, let's plot actual aggregate supply and aggregate demand in Figure 9-4. The horizontal axis measures national income in billions of dollars, and the vertical axis measures consumption and investment in billions of dollars per year. When we plot the consumption function, we obtain the C line as shown. When we add autonomous investment to that C line, we get the C + I line, which is labeled "aggregate demand."

Where do the aggregate demand curve and aggregate supply curve intersect? At point E. Point E is called the "equilibrium point," just as it was in our study of the supply and demand curves for particular commodities. At point E

Table 9-1 **The Determination of Income Equilibrium**

When aggregate demand equals aggregate supply, national income will be in equilibrium. This occurs in our hypothetical example at a GNP level of $1.6 trillion per year. Here, planned saving equals planned investment, and thus unplanned inventory changes are zero.

(1) ACTUAL AGGREGATE SUPPLY (IN BILLIONS OF DOLLARS PER YEAR)	(2) PLANNED CONSUMPTION	(3) PLANNED SAVING	(4) PLANNED INVESTMENT	(5) AGGREGATE DEMAND (2) + (4)	(6) UNPLANNED INVENTORY CHANGES	(7) DIRECTION OF CHANGE IN INCOME
1,000	1,020	−20	100	1,120	−120	Increase
1,200	1,180	20	100	1,280	− 80	Increase
1,400	1,340	60	100	1,440	− 40	Increase
1,600	1,500	100	100	1,600	0	Neither (equilibrium)
1,800	1,660	140	100	1,760	+ 40	Decrease
2,000	1,820	180	100	1,920	+ 80	Decrease
2,200	1,980	220	100	2,080	+120	Decrease

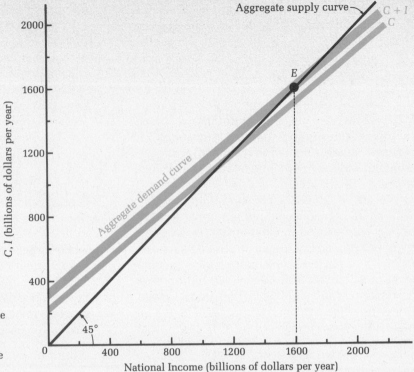

FIGURE 9-4 **The Equilibrium Level of National Income**

The equilibrium level of national income will be established at the output where aggregate demand equals aggregate supply. This occurs where the C + I line intersects the 45 degree aggregate supply curve at point E with an equilibrium level of national income of $1.6 trillion per year.

there is neither an excess aggregate quantity of products supplied (output) nor an excess aggregate quantity of products demanded (spending). This can be seen also in Table 9-1, where aggregate supply at $1.6 trillion is equal to aggregate demand at $1.6 trillion. This figure is called the "equilibrium level of income."

What About Employment?

Now that we've obtained the equilibrium level of income from our aggregate supply and demand model, we would like to know the associated level of employment. This figure depends on the number of employees required to annually produce $1.6 trillion worth of national product. We show a hypothetical relationship between national production and re-

quired employment in Table 9-2. We call it a **production function**, relating input in terms of the number of employees to output in terms of the market value of national product. This relationship is fairly predictable in the short run when the amount of capital and level of technology are fixed.

We see then that at the equilibrium level of annual national income of $1.6 trillion, employment will be 100 million.

What Happens When We Are Out of Equilibrium?

What happens if the level of production is such that aggregate demand exceeds aggregate supply, or vice versa? Let's take two examples and work through the scenario.

Table 9-2 **Production Function**

NATIONAL PRODUCT (IN BILLIONS PER YEAR)	REQUIRED LABOR INPUT (IN MILLIONS OF WORKERS PER YEAR)
1,000	85
1,200	90
1,400	95
1,600	100
1,800	105
2,000	110
2,200	115

Excess Aggregate Demand Let's start with national income at $1.2 trillion. We see in Table 9-1 that at this income level, annual planned consumption will be $1.18 trillion. Adding planned investment, we get an aggregate demand of $1.28 trillion, which exceeds actual aggregate supply by $80 billion. The planned investment of firms exceeds the planned saving of households. In other words, goods and services are being bought at a faster rate than they are being produced. The result of that situation is seen in column 6. Inventories are being drawn down at the rate of $80 billion a year, exactly the rate by which aggregate demand exceeds aggregate supply. As a result, firms will seek to expand their production; they will hire more workers. This will create an increase in income, output, and employment. National income will rise toward its equilibrium level.

Excess Aggregate Supply Now take the opposite situation. National income is at the $2 trillion level. We see from Table 9-1 that at that income level, planned consumption is $1.82 trillion and planned investment is still $100 billion. Aggregate demand (C + I) now equals

$1.92 trillion, which is less than the aggregate supply. In other words, the rate at which households plan to save exceeds the rate at which firms plan to invest. This means that business firms will find their sales less than they had planned. They will accumulate inventories, as we see in column 6, by $80 billion per year. This unplanned accumulation of inventories will cause firms to cut back on their production and lay off workers. The result will be a drop in income, output, and employment toward the equilibrium level, E.

If we look at the mirror images of the consumption and investment schedules, we can get another view of why E is the equilibrium level of income. What we will do is look at the planned investment and planned saving functions. Then we can see clearly how planned and actual saving and investment differ when we are out of equilibrium.

Looking at Saving and Investment

Figure 9-5 shows the planned investment curve as a horizontal line at $100 billion per year. Investment is completely autonomous in this simplified model—it does not depend on the level of income.

The planned saving curve is represented by S. It is taken directly from Table 9-1, which shows planned saving in column 3 and national income in column 1. The planned saving schedule is the reciprocal of the planned consumption schedule, represented by the C line in Figure 9-4. For better exposition, we are looking at only a small part of the saving and investment schedules—outputs between $1.4 trillion and $1.8 trillion.

Why does equilibrium have to occur at the intersection of the planned saving and planned investment schedules? If we are at E in Figure 9-5, planned saving equals planned investment.

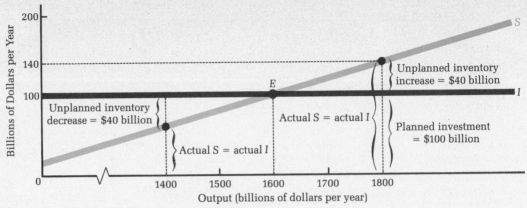

FIGURE 9-5 **Planned and Actual Rates of Saving and Investment**
Only at the equilibrium level of national income of $1.6 trillion per year will planned saving equal actual saving, planned investment equal actual investment, and therefore planned saving equal planned investment. At higher income levels, planned investment will be less than actual investment, the difference being made up of unplanned inventory increases. The opposite is true for all income levels less than $1.6 trillion per year.

All anticipations are validated by reality. There is no tendency for businesses to alter the rate of production or level of employment because they are neither increasing nor decreasing their inventories in an unplanned way.

However, if we are producing at an income level of $1.8 trillion instead of $1.6 trillion, planned investment, as usual, is $100 billion per year, but planned saving exceeds that. It is $140 billion per year. This means that consumers will purchase less of total output than businesses had anticipated. Inventories will now rise by $40 billion, bringing actual investment into line with actual saving. But this rate of output cannot continue for long. Businesses will respond to this unplanned increase in inventories by cutting back production and employment, and we will move toward a lower level of income.

On the other hand, if the national income is $1.4 trillion per year, planned investment continues annually at $100 billion, but at that output rate planned saving is only $60 billion. This means that households will purchase more of the national output than businesses had planned. Business inventories will fall now by $40 billion, bringing actual investment into equality with actual saving. But this situation cannot last for long either. In their attempt to increase inventories to desired previous levels, businesses will increase output and employment, and the national income will rise toward its equilibrium value of $1.6 trillion.

Figure 9-5 demonstrates the necessary equality between actual saving and actual investment. Inventories adjust so that saving and investment, after the fact, are always equal.

The reason we can have a difference between the planned rate of saving and the planned rate of investment is that saving and investment are done by different individuals with different motivations.

The Multiplier

Look again at Figure 9-4. Assume for the moment that the only expenditures included in national income are those for consumption. Where would the equilibrium level of income be in this case? It would be where the consumption function (C) intersects the aggregate supply schedule, which, as we stated before, is at the $1.1 trillion point. Now we add the autonomous amount of planned investment, or $100 billion, and then determine what the equilibrium level of income will be. It turns out to be $1.6 trillion. In other words, adding $100 billion of investment spending increased the equilibrium level of income by five times that amount, or $500 billion.

What is operating is the multiplier effect of changes in autonomous spending. The **multiplier** is the number by which a change in investment, government spending, or taxation is multiplied to get the change in equilibrium income. In other words, any increases in investment or in any autonomous component of consumption will cause a more than proportional increase in income and output. The reverse is also true. To understand why this multiple expansion (or contraction) in the equilibrium level of income occurs, we'll look at a simple numerical example.

We'll use the same figures we used for the marginal propensity to consume and to save. MPC will equal 0.8 or 4/5, and MPS will equal 0.2 or 1/5. Now let's run an experiment and say that businesses decide to *increase* planned investment by $100 billion a year. We see in Table 9-3 that during what we'll call the first round, investment is increased by $100 billion; this also means an increase in income of $100 billion because the recipients of that spending obviously receive the spending as income. Column 3 gives the resultant increase in consumption by households who received this additional $100 billion in income. This, of course, is found by multiplying the MPC by the increase in

---

Table 9-3 **The Multiplier Effect of a $100 Billion Increase in *I***

We trace the effects of a $100 billion increase in investment spending on the level of national income. If we assume a marginal propensity to consume of 0.8, such an increase will eventually elicit a $500 billion increase in the equilibrium level of national income.

ASSUMPTION: MPC = 0.8 or 4/5		
ROUND	INCREASE IN INCOME	INCREASE IN PLANNED CONSUMPTION
1 ($100 B increase in *I*)	$100 B	$80 B
2	$ 80 B	$64 B
3	$ 64 B	$51.2 B
4	$ 51.2 B	$40.96 B
5	$ 40.96 B	$32.768 B
All later rounds	$163.84 B	$131.072 B
Totals	$500 B	$400 B

income. Since the MPC equals 0.8, during the first round, consumption expenditures will increase by $80 billion.

But that's not the end of the story. This additional household consumption will provide $80 billion of additional income for other individuals. Thus, during the second round, we see an increase in income of $80 billion. Now, out of this increased income, what will be the resultant increase in consumption expenditures? It will be 0.8 times $80 billion, or $64 billion. We continue these induced expenditure rounds ad infinitum and, lo and behold, we find that, on account of an initial increase in investment expenditures of $100 billion, the equilibrium level of income has increased by $500 billion. A $100 billion increase in investment spending has induced an additional $400 billion increase in consumption spending for a total increase in GNP of $500 billion. In other words, the equilibrium level of income has changed by an amount equal to five times the increase in investment. We are dealing here with figures much too large for our present economy, but using such large figures enables us to see the multiplier principle more clearly. By the way, this multiplier effect of a change in autonomous spending is a central point in Keynesian macroeconomic analysis.

The Multiplier in Graphical Terms

We can see the multiplier effect more clearly if we look at Figure 9-6. We are looking at only a small section of the aggregate demand and supply diagram we have been using. We start with the equilibrium level of national income at $1.6 trillion. This is the equilibrium given an aggregate demand of $C + I$. Now we increase investment (I) by $100 billion to I'. This shifts the entire $C + I$ curve up to $C + I'$. That is, the aggregate demand curve has shifted vertically upward by $100 billion. Now, aggregate supply

eventually catches up with increased aggregate demand. For each dollar increase in national income, supply has increased by $1, but demand increases by only a fraction of that dollar, that fraction being equal to the marginal propensity to consume or four-fifths. The new equilibrium level of income is established at E' at the new intersection of the new $C + I'$ curve and the aggregate supply curve. The new equilibrium level of income is $2.1 trillion. Thus the increase in income was equal to five times the increase in planned investment spending.

There's an easier way, however, to find the multiplier than by drawing a graph.

The Multiplier Formula

It turns out that the investment multiplier is always equal to the reciprocal of the marginal propensity to save—that is, the marginal propensity to save turned upside down. In our example, the MPC was 4/5; therefore, since MPC + MPS = 1, the MPS was equal to 1/5. If we turn 1/5 upside down, we get 5. Voilà! That was our multiplier. A $100 billion increase in planned investment led to a $500 billion increase in equilibrium income. Our multiplier will always be the following:

$$\text{Multiplier} = \frac{1}{\text{MPS}} = \frac{1}{1 - \text{MPC}}$$

You can always figure out the multiplier if you know either the MPC or the MPS.

When you have the multiplier, the following formula will then give you the change in the equilibrium level of national income due to a change in autonomous spending:

$$\begin{array}{l}\text{Multiplier} \times \text{change} \\ \text{in auton. spending}\end{array} = \begin{array}{l}\text{change in eq.} \\ \text{level of nat'l. inc.}\end{array}$$

The multiplier, as we mentioned, works both

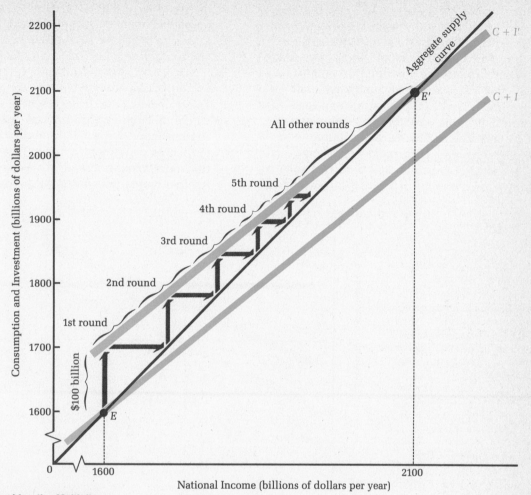

FIGURE 9-6 **Graphing the Multiplier**

We can translate Table 9-3 into graphical terms by looking at each successive round of additional spending induced by an autonomous increase of planned investment of $100 billion. The aggregate demand curve shifts from $C + I$, with an equilibrium level of national income of $1.6 trillion, to a new aggregate demand curve labeled $C + I'$. The new equilibrium level of national income is $2.1 trillion. It is established where aggregate demand equals aggregate supply at E'.

for an increase and a decrease in autonomous spending. In our previous example, if the autonomous component of consumption had fallen by $100 billion, the reduction in the equilibrium level of income would have been $500 billion per year.

The Effects of More Saving

We have talked about movements along schedules and shifts in those schedules. The multiplier effect occurs when there is a shift in the schedule because of a change in autonomous spending. Now we can see, by looking at movements in our schedules, what will happen when there is an increase in the desire to save. In other words, what happens when the autonomous component of consumption falls? It turns out that an increase in thriftiness, that is, a decreased desire to consume, may lead to a *reduction* in the equilibrium level of income.

An individual may feel financially better off because increased thriftiness leads to greater savings and wealth in the future. However, from society's point of view, if all individuals increase their rate of saving, a reduction in output, income, and employment may result. In Figure 9-7(a) the investment schedule is the horizontal line I and the saving schedule is the S curve. Since the equilibrium level of income occurs at the intersection of the saving and investment curves, it occurs here at E, giving an equilibrium level of national income of Y_1. Assume now that all individuals at all levels of income want to save more. This means that they all consume less at all levels of income. In other words, the consumption function shifts

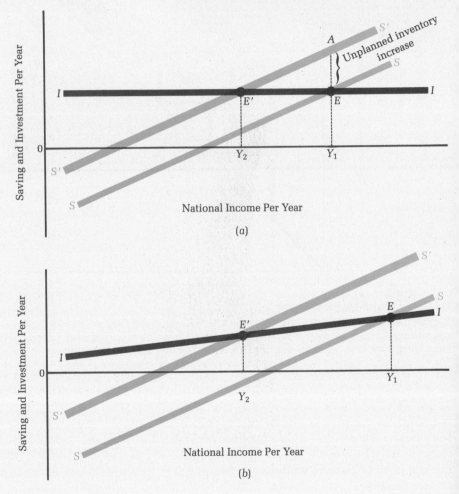

FIGURE 9-7 (a) The Effects of Increased Thriftiness

As all individuals attempt to save more, the saving schedule shifts from SS to S'S'. A new equilibrium is established at a national income of Y_2 per year, which is less than the former equilibrium level of Y_1. Although saving remains the same because investment is a constant, production, output, and employment fall.

(a)

(b) The Paradox of Thrift

If investment is positively related to the level of national income, then the investment function is shown with an upward slope, as II. An increased desire to save on the part of the population will shift the saving schedule to S'S' from SS. The new equilibrium will be established at national income level Y_2, which is lower than the original equilibrium of Y_1. Notice that, even though all individuals want to save more, saving is lower at the new equilibrium than at the old.

(b)

downward and the saving function shifts upward from S to S'. At the old equilibrium level of income Y_1, however, desired or planned saving is equal to the distance from the horizontal axis to A on S'. Now, since firms do not sell as much as they anticipated, they accumulate inventories at a rate equal to the difference between A and E. As they accumulate these inventories unexpectedly, they respond by cutting back production, output, and employment. Because of these cutbacks, income eventually falls to a new equilibrium level of E', where the equilibrium level of national income is now Y_2. You see, then, that as all individuals attempt to save more, the equilibrium level of national income will fall and actual saving will remain unchanged.

The Paradox of Thrift

Now let's examine what has been called the **paradox of thrift.** If investment spending is not autonomous but rather is positively related to the level of national income, an increase in the desire of individuals to save will cause not only a reduction in production, output, and employment but also a reduction in investment and saving. This is an example of the fallacy of composition. What may be good for an individual may not be good for the economy as a whole. The paradox is that as each individual attempts to save more, all individuals taken collectively end up saving less!

We can see the paradox of thrift in Figure 9-7(b). The original saving function is curve SS intersecting the investment function II at point E, yielding an equilibrium national income of Y_1. Now an increased thriftiness occurs on the part of all individuals in the society; at each and every level of income they wish to save more than before. The saving function moves up to S'S'. Eventually, the equilibrium level of

national income is established at the intersection of S'S' and II, or point E', giving an equilibrium level of national income of Y_2. Notice that originally the rate of saving equaled the vertical distance between Y_1 and E and now equals the vertical distance between Y_2 and E'. All individuals have attempted to save and have ended up saving less—hence, the paradox of thrift.

Inflationary and Deflationary Gaps

We have presented in simplified form the modern theory of income and employment determination. We have also pointed out situations where the level of aggregate demand may be greater than, equal to, or less than the level of aggregate supply. If we have some notion of the full-employment level of national income, then we can label the situations. This is what we do in Figure 9-8. We put in the full-employment level of national income at Y_f. In the middle diagram, the $C + I$ or aggregate demand curve intersects the aggregate supply curve exactly at that full-employment level of national income. However, in the top diagram, there is a gap. This is called the **inflationary gap** because aggregate demand exceeds aggregate supply at full employment.

On the other hand, if aggregate demand is less than aggregate supply at full employment, then the difference is called a **deflationary gap;** this is seen in the bottom diagram.

According to proponents of the simplified model we have used here, ways must be found to close the inflationary gap by reducing aggregate demand and the deflationary gap by increasing aggregate demand. Until now we have not really talked about prices changing. In fact, we have implicitly assumed all along that the price level has remained constant. When we

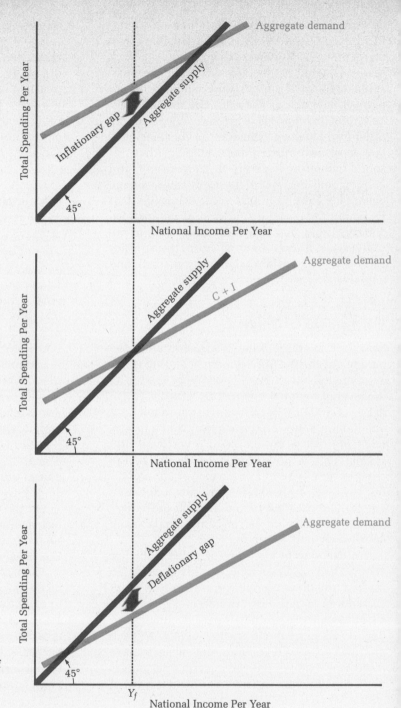

FIGURE 9-8 Inflationary and Deflationary Gaps

Here we show three possible situations. In the middle diagram, aggregate demand and aggregate supply are equal at the full-employment level of national income, Y_f. In the upper diagram, the aggregate demand curve intersects the aggregate supply curve to the right of the full-employment level of national income. The vertical distance between the aggregate demand curve and the aggregate supply curve at the full-employment level of national income is labeled the inflationary gap. In the bottom diagram, the opposite occurs. The aggregate demand curve intersects the aggregate supply curve at less than the full-employment level of national income. The vertical distance between the aggregate demand curve and the aggregate supply curve at the full-employment level of national income is labeled the deflationary gap. (This does not necessarily mean that prices will fall.)

talk about an inflationary gap, however, we refer to a situation where prices are rising, and so we must alter our model slightly to take account of this change.

In the following chapter we introduce the government component into our model and find out how changes in government fiscal policy (spending and taxation) can affect the equilibrium level of national income and help close inflationary or deflationary gaps.

Aggregate Demand: The dollar value of planned expenditures for the economy on all final goods and services per year.

Aggregate Supply: The total dollar value of all final goods and services supplied by firms to the market economy per year.

Production Function: The relationship between input and output. In the short run, if the amount of capital and the level of technology are assumed to be constant, we can use a simplified production function that relates output directly to labor input.

Multiplier: The multiplier is the number by which a change in investment, government spending, or taxation is multiplied to get the change in equilibrium income. The investment or government multiplier is the reciprocal of the marginal propensity to save—in other words, the marginal propensity to save turned upside down. If the marginal propensity to save is 0.2 or 1/5, the multiplier will be 5. A multiplier of 5 means that an increase in autonomous investment or in government spending will increase equilibrium income by a factor of 5.

Paradox of Thrift: A proposition demonstrating that, under certain circumstances, an increase in desired saving will not only lead to a reduction in the equilibrium level of income but also to a reduction in the rates of saving and investment. This concept was first introduced by Bernard Mandeville in the *Fable of the Bees,* 1714.

Inflationary Gap: The gap between full-employment spending and actual spending at full employment. It is usually measured by the vertical discrepancy at full-employment income between the $C + I + G$ schedule and the 45 degree line where spending equals income. The discrepancy is positive.

Deflationary Gap: The difference between actual spending at full employment and the full-employment level of spending. It is usually measured by the vertical discrepancy at full employment between the $C + I + G$ schedule and the 45 degree line. In this case, the discrepancy is negative.

1. When we first construct our aggregate demand schedule, it includes only consumption and investment spending.
2. The aggregate supply curve is merely a 45 degree line along which there is equality between aggregate income and aggregate product.

3. The equilibrium level of aggregate income occurs where the aggregate demand curve intersects the aggregate supply curve (spending = output).
4. To find the level of employment associated with the equilibrium level of income, we require a production function relating national product to required employment.
5. When there is excess aggregate demand, inventories will be drawn down more rapidly than planned. As a result, firms will expand production and, in the process, hire more workers, thus leading to an increase in income, output, and employment.
6. When there is excess aggregate supply, the opposite will occur—inventories will grow unexpectedly, production will be cut, and so too will employment and income.
7. We can look at the entire scenario from the point of view of planned saving and investment, which must be equal at the equilibrium rate of national income. Whenever the actual level of national income exceeds the equilibrium level, there will be an unplanned inventory increase triggering production cuts and layoffs. Whenever national income is less than the equilibrium level of national income, there will be an unplanned inventory decrease calling for increased production and employment.
8. A key aspect of simplified Keynesian analysis is that a change in investment will result in a multiple change in equilibrium income. This multiplier effect of a change in investment is positively related to the marginal propensity to consume. The higher the marginal propensity to consume, the greater the investment multiplier. We find the investment multiplier by first finding the marginal propensity to save (1 minus the marginal propensity to consume) and then turning the marginal propensity to save upside down. A marginal propensity to consume of 0.8 means that the marginal propensity to save is 0.2 or 1/5. Turning 1/5 upside down gives us 5. Thus, the investment multiplier equals 5.
9. If there is an increased thriftiness on the part of individuals, this will lead to a lower equilibrium level of national income. In the situation where investment is positively related to income, increased thriftiness will actually lead not only to a reduction in the equilibrium level of income but also to a reduction in the rate of saving and investment. Hence, the paradox of thrift.
10. If the equilibrium level of national income exceeds the full-employment level, there exists an inflationary gap. If the equilibrium level of national income is less than the full-employment level, there exists a deflationary gap.

Questions for Thought and Discussion

1. Why is the saving schedule the reciprocal of the consumption schedule?
2. Why does the break-even or equilibrium income level remain the same whether we draw the C line or the saving schedule?

3. What do you think the multiplier would be if the marginal propensity to consume were 1.1?

4. People tell you that it is wise to save for the future, but the paradox of thrift indicates that an increase in the rate of saving leads to a reduction in equilibrium income. What gives?

5. What is the difference between planned or desired saving and actual saving? What is the difference between planned or desired investment and actual investment?

6. Answer the following questions based on the table and graph.

National Income (Billions)	Consumption (Billions)
$100	$110
200	200
300	290
400	380
500	470

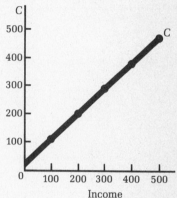

(a) If the linear function $C = a + bY$ describes this consumption function:
  (i)   What is the value of a?
  (ii) What is the significance of a?
  (iii) What is the value of b?
  (iv) What is the significance of b?

(b) If national income in this model increased to $800 B, we would expect C to be _____.

(c) The multiplier consistent with this example is _____.

Selected
References

Dillard, Dudley, *The Economics of John Maynard Keynes,* Englewood Cliffs, N.J.: Prentice-Hall, 1948.

Hansen, Alvin, *A Guide to Keynes,* New York: McGraw Hill, 1953.

Lekachman, Robert, *The Age of Keynes,* New York: Random House, 1966.

Stewart, Michael, *Keynes and After,* Baltimore, Md.: Penguin, 1968.

The Spirit of His Age

JOHN MAYNARD KEYNES

Economist, Cambridge University

The most influential economist of the twentieth century was John Maynard Keynes. During a 25-year period following 1919, he completely revolutionized economics—as a discipline, as an aspect of government policy, and as a way of looking at human society.

Raised in England and educated at Cambridge University, Keynes served as an economic adviser to the British Treasury during World War I. From this position, he was delegated chief economic counsel to the British representatives at Versailles. His distress over the harsh settlement exacted from the Germans inspired *The Economic Consequences of the Peace,* in which he predicted the collapse of the European economy, a prediction that proved tragically correct within 20 years.

During the next decade, Keynes studied interest rates, the gold standard, and the economic future of Europe. At the same time, he built a comfortable fortune in stock market speculation—purchasing on the basis of whim, instinct, and his own calculations, handling his transactions by telephone before getting out of bed each morning.

In 1930, he published *The Treatise on Money,* a book distinguished by a very broad view of economics. It explores the propelling and decelerating forces that seem to act against each other in an economic system.

Keynes' major yardstick of economic health was the rate of investment and capital expansion. In contrast to the classical view, Keynes considered thrift a deadening influence on economic growth: "it is Enterprise which builds and improves the world's possessions . . . if Enterprise is afoot, wealth accumulates whatever may be happening to Thrift; and if Enterprise is asleep, wealth decays whatever Thrift may be doing."

The General Theory of Employment, Interest, and Money was the major accomplishment of this prolific period. It remains the single most influential work of twentieth century economics. Opposing the classical view that employment fluctuates naturally around a "natural" level, Keynes presented a comprehensive approach to the problem of keeping populations working, fed, and housed. Only the maintenance of "effective demand"—that is, the maintenance of a desire for goods and services among people with sufficient income to act on their desire—can keep an economy out of a recession.

With this book, Keynes completely changed the vocabulary and fundamental principles of macroeconomic thinking. The book was greeted at first with confusion and controversy, but it effectively divided the discipline between economists who agreed with Keynes and those who rejected his theories. The division has been institutionalized in the past 40 years; but no matter how carelessly the term is used in the popular media, Keynesian economics remains a concrete school of thought.

Actually, it was Franklin Roosevelt who helped move Keynes' work into the spotlight. Keynes enjoyed a close personal relationship with the American president, and Roosevelt found several aspects of the economist's work that could be applied to the huge task of pushing the American economy out of the Depression.

By the time of his death in 1946, Lord Keynes had seen his theories become the basis of economic policy on both sides of the Atlantic. His close friend and biographer, Roy Harrod, wrote that some might attribute to Keynes a special power beyond the normal range of human capabilities. Keynes, however, had a more modest explanation: "The study of economics does not seem to require any specialized gifts of an unusually high order. Is it not . . . a very easy subject compared with the higher branches of philosophy or pure science? An easy subject, at which few excel! The paradox finds its explanation, perhaps in that the master economist must possess a rare combination of gifts. He must be mathematician, historian, statesman, philosopher—in some degree."

The Acceleration Principle and the Interaction between the Accelerator and the Multiplier

Business investment fluctuates to a much greater degree than does overall business activity. By the nineteenth century, economic observers were quite aware of this fact. By the early twentieth century, the idea had entered the main body of economic theory through the work of J. M. Clark.

The Acceleration Principle

Clark studied fluctuations in railroad traffic and in the orders for new railroad equipment. He noticed, for example, that the level of new car orders was more closely in relationship with *changes* in the level of traffic than in the level of traffic itself. Orders for new cars represent one form of investment by railroads. The empirical work that Clark did with railroads was used as evidence for what is now known as the acceleration principle, or the accelerator:

The level of planned investment varies with *changes* in the level of output rather than with the level itself. Otherwise stated, the level of investment is related to the rate of change of output or sales.

We can see a simple example of the acceleration principle at work in the planned investment of the A & B Water Heater Company. Table B-1 shows the relationship between the company's investment and sales.

(1)	(2)	(3)	(4)	(5)	(6)	(7) = (5) + (6)
			A & B WATER HEATER COMPANY			
YEAR	SALES (MILLIONS OF $ PER YEAR)	REQUIRED STOCK OF MACHINES (MILLIONS OF $)	ACTUAL STOCK OF MACHINES (MILLIONS OF $)	REPLACEMENT INVESTMENT (MILLIONS OF $ PER YEAR)	NET INVESTMENT ON NEW CAPITAL (MILLIONS OF $ PER YEAR)	GROSS INVESTMENT (MILLIONS OF $ PER YEAR)
1966	10	5	5	1	0	1
1967	12	6	5	1	1	2
1968	14	7	7	1	1	2
1969	16	8	8	1	1	2
1970	16	8	8	1	0	1
1971	16	8	8	1	0	1
1972	14	7	8	0	0	0
1973	14	7	7	1	0	1
1974	14	7	7	1	0	1
1975	18	9	9	1	2	3
1976	18	9	9	1	0	1

We begin by assuming that in 1966 the firm started with just the necessary amount of capital stock, that is, machinery valued at $5 million. This means that for every dollar of water heater sales (column 1), the required stock of capital is 50¢. In other words, for any level of sales, we can find the required stock in machines simply by dividing the level of sales by 2.

Let's see what happens when sales increase by $2 million, as they did from 1966 to 1967. The required stock in machines increases by $1 million. Therefore, in addition to an assumed replacement investment of $1 million a year to take care of depreciation in machines (column 5), the A & B Water Heater Company will have to invest an extra $1 million in new machines (column 6). That means that gross investment, which is replacement investment plus net investment (column 7), will be $1 million plus $1 million, or $2 million. So far so good. Now notice that the level of sales increases by

another $2 million per year from 1967 to 1968 and from 1968 to 1969 but that gross investment remains constant at $2 million per year. This is a demonstration of the acceleration principle. Gross investment is a function of the *rate* of change of sales. If that rate of change is constant, then gross investment will also be constant.

Now look what happens when sales decline from $16 million to $14 million per year as they did from 1971 to 1972. The required capital stock falls by $1 million, but the actual capital stock on hand is still $8 million. It is not necessary to add new capital equipment, nor is it necessary even to pay for depreciation. Therefore, we see that for 1972 the replacement investment is zero, net investment is zero, and, consequently, the total gross investment is also zero. In other words, if the rate of capital formation is a function of the rate of change of sales, a decline in sales can lead to a zero amount of gross investment (and in some cases, negative net investment).

We can also see that changes in sales result in magnified percentage changes in planned investment. For example, from 1966 to 1967 sales went up by 20 percent but gross investment went up by 100 percent. From 1974 to 1975 sales increased by 28.57 percent whereas gross investment increased by 300 percent.

The Interaction between the Accelerator and the Multiplier

Investment is a key determinant of the level of income in the model we are using in this unit. If the rate of planned investment follows the accelerator principle, this could explain, to some extent, the swings in business activity. After all, any change in investment, according to our theory in Chapter 9, leads to a multiple change in equilibrium income and employment.

Economists see this as a distinct possibility. Nobel Prize laureates Paul Samuelson and Sir John Hicks have both shown that the accelerator principle, combined with the multiplier, may produce the business fluctuations that are experienced in the real world.[1]

The combination would work as follows. We assume that the economy is moving toward full employment, national income is rising, and sales are expanding at an increasing rate. Because of the acceleration principle, this increase in growth results in a relatively high level of planned investment. Furthermore, because of the multiplier, this relatively high level of

planned investment provokes even greater increases in national income. Thus the accelerator and the multiplier tend to reinforce each other, resulting in a strong upward movement in national income. This is the expansion phase of the business cycle.

Eventually, however, the economy nears some level of full employment. That is to say, since we have only a certain amount of labor, land, and other factors of production, it is impossible to continue increasing national income at the extraordinarily rapid rate which was experienced during the recovery period of the business cycle. At some point, growth has to slow down. Sales too will not increase forever at the same fast rate—rather, they will begin to increase at a slower rate. This slowdown means that the rate of growth of planned investment is going to turn down abruptly, just as it did, for example, when sales of the A & B Water Heater Company maintained themselves at $16 million a year. However, because of the multiplier effect, this decrease in planned investment will lead to a magnified or multiplied decrease in the equilibrium level of income. The reduction in the rate of growth of national income will mean a further reduction in the rate of sales growth, leading to a further reduction in gross investment, and so on. Eventually, the economy will run into a recession.

At some point, the capital stock of firms gets into line with those firms' reduced sales rates. This is what happened between 1972 and 1973 for the A & B Water Heater Company. Now the stage is set for another upturn, another recovery, and the interaction again of the accelerator and the multiplier.

You will note that the multiplier-accelerator theory of the business cycle is one in which business cycles are self-starting and self-terminating. Each phase of the business cycle automatically leads into the next.

[1]Paul A. Samuelson, "The Interaction between the Multiplier Analysis and the Acceleration Principle," *Review of Economics and Statistics*, May 1939, pp. 75–78; and John Hicks, *A Contribution to the Theory of the Trade Cycle*, London: Oxford, 1950.

Fiscal Policy

Adding the Government Sector

The government sector in our economy is large indeed. Government purchases of goods and services account for a full one-fourth of GNP and total government spending, more than 40 percent. The difference between total government spending and government purchases of goods and services is what we call **transfer payments.** Social Security and unemployment compensation fall in this category. You'll remember that transfer payments include any payment the government makes to households or businesses for which no goods or services are concurrently rendered.

In this chapter we will add the government sector to our model of income and employment. We will consider the effects of changes in government purchases of goods and services on the equilibrium level of income and employment. We will also learn the effects of changes in taxes on equilibrium income. This can all be done by using the multiplier analysis we developed in the last chapter.

Adding Government Purchases to Aggregate Demand

In Chapter 5 we talked about the role of government spending in our economy and how it is financed. Although it perhaps would be appropriate here to consider the determinants of the rate of government purchases of goods and services, such consideration is beyond the scope of this text. What we will do for our macroeconomic model is assume the level of government purchases to be determined by political processes outside the economic system under study. In other words, we will consider G to be autonomous, just as, in the last chapter, we considered I, for simplicity's sake, to be autonomous.

Let's take the aggregate demand function from Chapter 9 and add $100 billion of government purchases of goods and services. We do this in Figure 10-1. The new aggregate demand curve is labeled $C + I + G$.

We started out in equilibrium at point E. That is to say, aggregate demand was equal to aggregate supply at an equilibrium level of $1.6 trillion per year in national income. Then we added $100 billion of autonomous government spending. This shifted the aggregate demand line vertically by $100 billion to become $C + I + G$. The new aggregate demand curve crosses the aggregate supply curve at point E'. And the equilibrium level of national income has gone up to $2.1 trillion.

How did the equilibrium level of national income increase by $500 billion when we added only $100 billion worth of government purchases? The answer is that new government spending had a multiplier impact on the equilibrium level of national income. Remember from Chapter 9 that the multiplier can be found by taking the reciprocal of the marginal propensity to save. Because we are still assuming a marginal propensity to consume of 0.8, the marginal propensity to save is 0.2 or 1/5. The reciprocal of 1/5 is 5, so our multiplier in this situation is still 5. Since we had an autonomous increase in spending by the government of $100 billion, we know that the equilibrium level of national income will increase by $100 billion times 5, or $500 billion.

We can use this new addition to our income and employment determination model to show how an increase in government purchases can

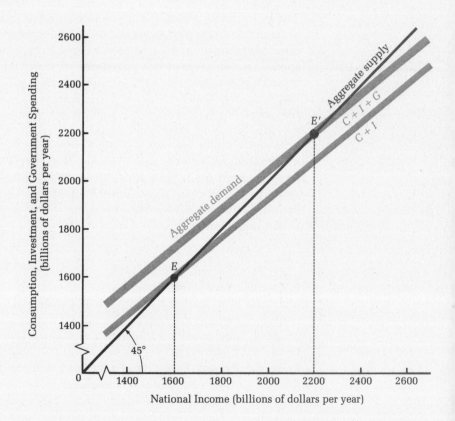

FIGURE 10-1 Adding Government to the Picture

If we add $100 billion of new government spending to the aggregate demand schedule we used in the last chapter, we get a new aggregate demand labeled $C + I + G$. The former equilibrium, without government spending, is labeled E, at an equilibrium level of national income per year of $1.6 trillion. When we add government, we get an increase in the equilibrium level of national income by $500 billion to $2.1 trillion per year, at point E'. In this case, as before, the multiplier is 5 because the marginal propensity to consume is assumed to be 0.8.

fill in the deflationary gap we mentioned in Chapter 9. That is, in a situation where the equilibrium level of income is below the full-employment level of income, an increase in government purchases of goods and services may be able to raise the equilibrium level toward the full-employment level.

Filling the Deflationary Gap

Look at Figure 10-2. Here we start out with the same $C + I + G$ or aggregate demand curve as in Figure 10-1, and the equilibrium level of national income is $2.1 trillion. However, the full-employment level of national income is greater than that—in our example, it is $2.3 trillion. The obvious gap between aggregate demand at the $2.3 trillion per year level of output and aggregate supply is what we have labeled the "deflationary gap" on this diagram. To fill the deflationary gap, which in this particular example is $40 billion, we increase government purchases of goods and services, and we do so by the full $40 billion. That raises the $C + I + G$ line to $C + I + G'$, where G' is now $40 billion greater than G. The new equilibrium level of national income is now at the intersection E', where aggregate supply now equals the

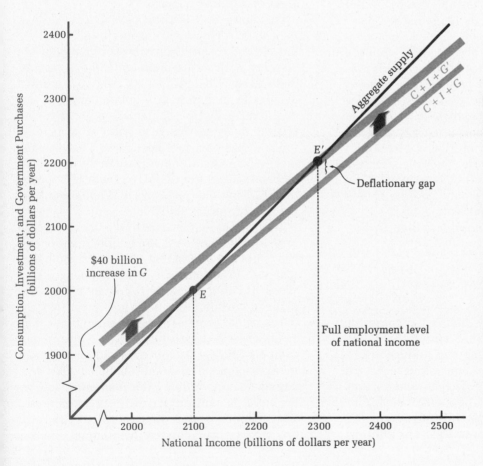

FIGURE 10-2 Plugging the Deflationary Gap with Increased Government Spending
If we start with an equilibrium level of national income of $2.1 trillion per year with a full-employment level of national income $2.3 trillion per year, we have a deflationary gap. It is labeled as the vertical distance between the aggregate supply schedule and the aggregate demand schedule at the full-employment level of national income. If we increase government spending from G to G' by exactly the amount of that deflationary gap—$40 billion —we will move the aggregate demand schedule upward so that it intersects the aggregate supply schedule at the full-employment level of national income at point E'.

new, greater aggregate demand, and the equilibrium level of national income is also the full-employment level.

Notice that this $40 billion increase in government spending led to a $200 billion increase in equilibrium national income. That's exactly what we would expect by the assumptions in this model. The multiplier is 5, and 5 times $40 billion equals $200 billion.

Reducing the Inflationary Gap

What if the situation in Figure 10-2 was reversed? What if $2.1 trillion was the full-employment level of national income and $2.3 trillion the equilibrium level of national income? Then we would have, as we labeled in the previous chapter, an "inflationary gap," which would be the same size as the deflationary gap described above. Now opposite measures would be needed. Government purchases of goods and services could be reduced by $40 billion so that the equilibrium level of national income would fall by $200 billion, that is, five times the reduction in G. The upward direction of the arrows in Figure 10-2 would now be reversed, and also, the labels for the two aggregate demand curves would be switched. The top one would now be $C + I + G$ and the bottom one would be $C + I + G'$, where G' was $40 billion less than G.

The Effects of Changing Taxes

We have been looking at only one aspect of government fiscal policy, that is, purchases of goods and services. What about the other aspect: taxation? What happens to the equilibrium level of national income when taxes are increased or decreased? The answer is that basically the same thing happens which happened when we altered the rate of government purchases of goods and services. The equilib-

rium level of national income changes by a multiple as taxes are changed, but it changes in the opposite direction. A reduction in personal income taxes, for example, gives consumers more take-home pay. And since disposable income is now increased, consumption spending, according to the consumption relationship, also increases. In other words, the C line shifts upward when taxes are reduced. That will also move the $C + I + G$, or aggregate demand schedule, upward also. The opposite occurs when there is an increase in personal income taxes. The consumption function shifts downward, bringing down with it the aggregate demand curve. A shift in the aggregate demand curve changes by a multiple the equilibrium level of national income.

In Figure 10-3 we change the full-employment level of national income to $2.1 trillion but leave the equilibrium level of national income at E, or $2.3 trillion, with the aggregate demand curve being $C + I + G$. The government decides to eliminate this inflationary gap. Its decision, in this particular example, is to increases taxes so that disposable income will fall and consumers will spend less. The ultimate result will be a shift downward in the aggregate demand schedule to $C' + I + G$, where C' is less than C. Now the question is "What should be the size of the tax cut?"

It turns out that the size of the tax cut necessary to eliminate the $40 billion inflationary gap is not $40 billion, but $50 billion. How can that be? Well, let's see what happens when taxes are increased. If taxes go up by $1, planned consumption falls, not by $1, but by the marginal propensity to consume times that $1 decrease in disposable income. Since in our example MPC = 0.8, for every dollar increase in taxes, planned consumption falls by 80¢ and planned saving falls by the remaining 20¢. In the initial spending round after the tax increase, then, planned consumption falls not by the full tax increase but only by MPC times the in-

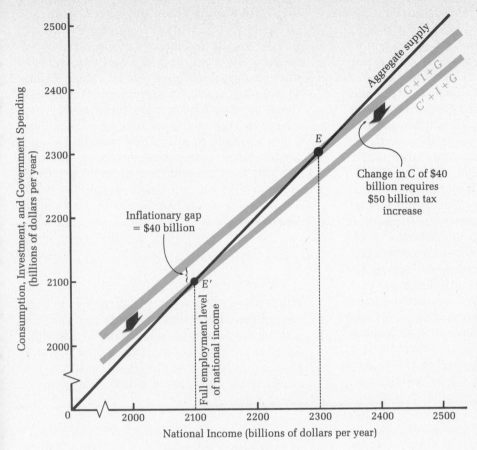

Consumption, Investment, and Government Spending (billions of dollars per year)

National Income (billions of dollars per year)

Aggregate supply

C + I + G

C' + I + G

E

Change in C of $40 billion requires $50 billion tax increase

Inflationary gap = $40 billion

E'

Full employment level of national income

FIGURE 10-3 **Taxing Away an Inflationary Gap**
We start at an equilibrium level of national income of $2.3 trillion, which exceeds the full-employment level of national income. The inflationary gap is $40 billion. To eliminate that inflationary gap, we need a tax increase of $50 billion. (Why?)

crease. In other words, the change in autonomous consumption due to a tax increase is equal to the marginal propensity to consume times the tax change. Thus, in our example, the change in C of $40 billion requires a $50 billion tax cut because 0.8 × $50 billion = $40 billion.

How much of a tax decrease would be necessary to move the equilibrium level of national income from $2.1 trillion to $2.3 trillion? The answer, of course, would be a tax cut of $50 billion. This level of tax decrease would elicit a $40 billion increase in consumption, which would shift the aggregate demand schedule

upward so that it intersected the aggregate supply schedule at $2.3 trillion.

What happens when we change taxes and government purchases of goods and services in the same direction and by equal amounts? Since the taxation multiplier T is lower than the G multiplier, when the two are changed by equal amounts, we get what is called the "balanced-budget multiplier."

The Balanced-Budget Multiplier

Having included changes in government spending and changes in taxes in our simple multiplier model, we can now present a somewhat startling theorem that Keynesian economists developed using this analysis. Suppose that government spending goes up by $20 million and taxes are raised by that same amount. What happens to total spending? You probably think that spending remains the same since the change in government purchases seems to be just offset by an equal change in government taxation. However, the taxation multiplier is smaller than the government multiplier. If government spending goes up by $20 billion, total spending will increase by a multiple of that. When our marginal propensity to consume is 0.8, the multiplier is 5, so income will be expected to rise by $100 billion. Now we take away from disposable income by taxing $20 billion. Since the taxation multiplier is less than the government multiplier, the reduction in total spending due to increased taxes will be smaller than the increase in total spending due to increased government expenditures. In fact, the **balanced-budget multiplier** will be exactly equal to 1, which happens to be the algebraic summation of the government multiplier and the tax multiplier. If G is increased by $20 billion and taxes are too, income will also increase by $20 billion!

Notice that this analysis assumes something very important. We said that people's consumption decisions depend upon their disposable incomes. But when government expenditures come into the picture, there may be an influence on C when G changes. For example, if the new government expenditures consist of providing milk to children whose parents were already paying for the milk, the parents' consumption expenditures on milk will fall by approximately the same amount as the government increase in spending. If this is the case, then, the balanced-budget multiplier will equal zero. In fact, the balanced-budget multiplier can range from zero to a number even greater

than 1, depending upon the nature of the increase in government spending. If it is a *substitute* for private investment or consumption that would have taken place anyway, then the balanced-budget multiplier will be definitely less than 1. If government spending makes people desire to spend more than they would have otherwise, the multiplier will be greater than 1. An example of stimulated spending would be increased government spending on flood control; as a consequence of such spending, some people will not desire to save as much for the rainy day when they're flooded out of house and home.

Fiscal Policy

We just described the effects of changes in both government purchases of goods and services and in the level of taxes on the equilibrium level of national income. Changes in G and T that are legislated by Congress constitute the major areas of what is called *discretionary fiscal policy*.

Discretionary Fiscal Policy

Fiscal policy is usually associated with government spending and taxing activities. Discretionary fiscal policy results from the deliberate actions of Congress and, to some extent, the executive branch.

If we were to follow exactly the model presented in the preceding chapter, we would see that the "appropriate" discretionary fiscal policy during periods of less than full-employment levels of national income would be to increase government spending or reduce taxes, or employ a combination of the two. This is called *expansionary fiscal policy*. In periods when there are inflationary pressures on the economy and we are operating at or close to full capacity, the "appropriate" discretionary action, again assuming our model is correct, would be the opposite: reduce government spending and/or increase taxes. This is called *contractionary fiscal policy*.

Other fiscal programs in our economy occur automatically; that is, neither the Congress nor the President cause them to happen. These are called "automatic" or "built-in" stabilizers.

Automatic Fiscal Policy

In Chapter 5 we showed the 1976 personal income tax schedule. As taxable income went up, the marginal tax rate also increased—to a maximum of 70 percent. Or we can say that as taxable income decreased, the marginal tax rate went down. Think about this now for the entire economy. If the nation is at full employment, personal income taxes may yield the government, say, $375 billion per year. Now suppose that, for whatever reason, business activity suddenly starts to slow down. When this happens, workers are not allowed to put in as much overtime as before. Some workers are laid off, and some must change to jobs that pay less. Some workers and even some executives might take voluntary pay cuts. What happens to taxes when wages and salaries go down? Taxes are still paid but at a lower rate than before since the tax schedule is progressive. For example, a person who makes $15,000 taxable income a year is in the 39 percent marginal tax bracket. Now if this individual suddenly drops to only $10,000 taxable income a year and into the 32 percent marginal tax bracket, average taxes paid as a percentage of income also fall. And as a result of these decreased taxes, disposable income—the amount remaining after taxes—doesn't fall by the same percentage as before-tax income. The individual, in other words, doesn't feel the pinch of

recession as much as we might think if we ignored the progressive nature of our tax schedule. The *average* tax rate falls when less is earned.

Conversely, when the economy suddenly comes into a boom period, peoples' incomes tend to rise. They can work more overtime and can change to higher paying jobs. However, their disposable income does not go up as rapidly as their total income because their average tax rates are rising at the same time. Uncle Sam ends up taking a bigger bite. In this way, the progressive income tax system tends to stabilize any abrupt changes in economic activity. (Actually, the progressive tax structure simply magnifies any stabilization effect that might exist. Proportional taxation could stabilize also since its yield varies directly with GNP.)

Unemployment compensation works in the same direction as the progressive income tax: to stabilize aggregate demand. Throughout the business cycle, it mitigates changes in people's disposable income. When business activity drops, most workers who are laid off automatically become eligible for unemployment compensation from the state government. Their disposable income, therefore, remains positive, although certainly it is less than when they were working. During boom periods, there is less unemployment and, consequently, fewer unemployment payments made to the labor force. Less purchasing power is being added to the economy because few unemployment checks are paid out.

The key stabilizing impact of these two aspects of our taxing and transferring system is their ability to mitigate changes in disposable income. Many economists believe that disposable income—take-home pay—is the main determinant of how much people desire to spend and, therefore, is a key activator of general economic activity. It is felt that if disposable income is not allowed to fall as much as it would otherwise during a recession, the recession will be automatically cut off before it becomes a depression. On the other hand, it is felt that if disposable income is not allowed to rise as rapidly as it would otherwise during a boom, the boom will not get out of hand, causing prices to rise, among other things. The progressive income tax and unemployment compensation therefore provide automatic stabilization to the economy.

Fiscal Policy and a Full-Employment Budget

We earlier discussed the government increasing expenditures, but we did not discuss how those expenditures would be financed. If we assume no increase in taxes, we can conclude that when the government spends more it ends up with a **deficit.** If the government is already running a deficit, it will have an even larger one. Active fiscal policy has therefore been associated with **deficit spending** on the part of the government. Fiscal policy advocates point out that an increase in the deficit stimulates the economy, whereas a decrease in the deficit has the opposite effect. The government can also run a **surplus.** That is, it can take in more revenues than it spends. An increase in the government's budget surplus is supposed to have a depressing effect on the economy, just as would a decrease in government expenditures or an increase in taxes. The existence of, or increase in, the government budget surplus presumably reduces total aggregate demand and thereby depresses economic activity.

The government and many economists currently do not like to look at the government's *actual* deficit or surplus. They do not think it is useful to look at current levels of taxes and expenditures or the current budget deficit or surplus that results. Consider for a moment the following situation. Suppose the economy is at

full employment and the government budget is in balance—no deficit and no surplus. Then the economy goes into a recession, and incomes fall. The government, however, does nothing. Spending on its part, *G*, remains the same; but, since some taxes, *T*, are based on income, government revenues fall. A formerly balanced budget goes into deficit since *G* is now greater than *T*. The budget deficit should certainly not be regarded here as an active stimulating policy decision on the part of the government. It is a *result* of the recession, not a counter-recessionary move. Therefore, economists now make calculations to determine whether *at full employment* the government budget would be in a deficit or a surplus position. The result is called the **full-employment deficit or surplus.** In Figure 10-4 the results of such calculations are presented for the years 1955 to 1975.

Economists now talk in terms of a *stimulating full-employment deficit* or a *depressing full-employment surplus.* The actual budget deficit may be $56 billion, as it was in fiscal 1975, but the full-employment deficit was much less. Many economists therefore maintained that the deficit was stimulating but not as *over*-stimulating as it would first seem because at full employment the deficit would have been much smaller.

Fiscal Policy and the Budget

Much of the content of fiscal policy debates is concerned with the advisability of actual federal budget deficits or surpluses or with the advisability of full-employment budget deficits or surpluses. Many economists, however, believe that in the long run the federal budget should be balanced. This is considered a "conservative" position because it requires that any deficits occurring during recessions be matched by surpluses at other times.

More recently, however, the notion of a

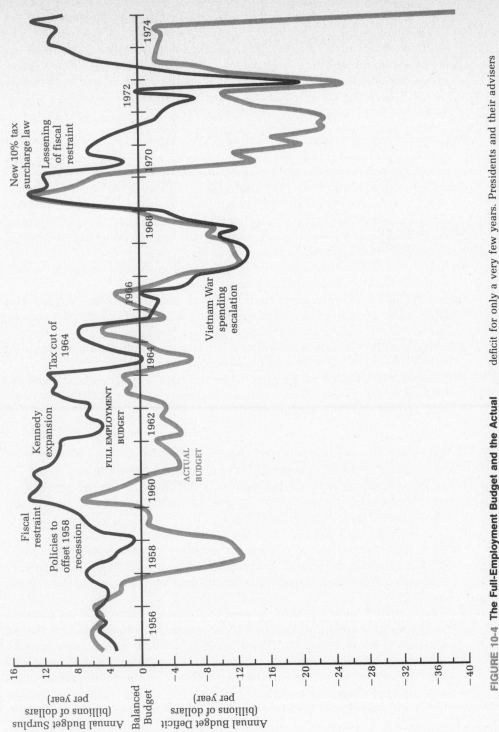

FIGURE 10-4 The Full-Employment Budget and the Actual Budget

Here we have drawn the actual budget of the United States government from 1955 to 1975. We have also put in the full-employment budget. We see that, for the most part, the federal budget has been in deficit for almost the last two decades. However, the full-employment budget has been in deficit for only a very few years. Presidents and their advisers like to talk in terms of the full-employment budget. (*Source: A. M. Okun and Nancy H. Teeters, "The Full Employment Surplus Revisited," in Brookings Papers on Economic Activity, no. 1 (Washington, D.C.: The Brookings Institution, 1970); and Council of Economic Advisers, Economic Report of the President, (Washington, D.C.: U.S. Government Printing Office, 1975).*)

long-term fiscal policy that is related to a full-employment balanced budget has caught favor with a number of policy prescribers. For example, the Committee for Economic Development, an organization of business leaders and some economists, has come out strongly in favor of a long-run, full-employment balanced budget. If this were indeed to become the overall policy of the federal government throughout the business cycle, and if that cycle were symmetrical, the actual federal budget would become balanced in the long run.

Definitions of New Terms

Transfer Payments: Payments made to households that are not made in exchange for concurrently rendered goods or services. Unemployment compensation and Social Security benefits are examples.

Balanced-Budget Multiplier: The multiplier resulting from equal changes in both government spending and taxes. Under the most simplified assumptions, the balanced-budget multiplier is 1, meaning that an equal increase in both taxes and government spending will lead to an equal increase in the equilibrium level of income.

Deficit: The difference between government revenues and government spending (usually expressed in annual rates).

Deficit Spending: Government spending in excess of government tax yields.

Surplus: The excess of government revenues over government spending (usually expressed in annual rates).

Full-Employment Government Budget: What government revenues *would* be if the economy were at full employment.

Full-Employment Deficit or Surplus: The difference between actual government spending and what government revenues would be if the economy were operating at full employment.

Chapter Summary

1. When we add government spending to our model, the equilibrium level of output rises by a multiple of that government spending.
2. In the simplified model of this chapter, a deflationary gap can be reduced by increased government spending, and an inflationary gap can be reduced by decreased government spending.
3. The taxation multiplier is less than the investment or government multiplier. Thus, to eliminate a given inflationary or deflationary gap via a change in taxes, the change would have to be greater than the necessary opposite change in government or investment spending of equivalent impact.
4. The balanced-budget multiplier, simply stated, indicates that an increase in government spending matched by an increase in taxes will lead to an increase in the equilibrium level of national income by the same amount.
5. Automatic stabilizers include personal and corporate income taxes and unemployment insurance. Automatic stabilizers automatically counter ups and downs in business activity.
6. It is usually inappropriate to regard the actual government deficit or surplus as a policy variable. After all, if the government budget is balanced and,

for some reason, there is a recession, government receipts will fall and there will result a budget deficit. But budget deficits are usually associated with stimulative government fiscal policy. In this case, the deficit is purely passive. To take account of this possibility, economists have devised a concept called the full-employment budget.

7. The full-employment budget is the level of government revenues that would prevail if the economy were at full employment. Similarly, the full-employment surplus or deficit is the difference between actual government expenditures and the government revenues that would occur if the economy were operating at full employment.

Questions for
Thought
and Discussion

1. Analyze the early 1975 debate on the usefulness of a $20 billion to $60 billion tax cut. Use the diagrammatic tools we have developed in this and preceding chapters.

2. If all expenditures for defense were cut out, what alternative programs would you want the government to undertake to maintain full employment?

3. Taxes were raised during the Great Depression in an attempt to balance the federal budget. If you had been an economist at that time, would you have agreed with that policy?

4. Discuss the rationale underlying the 1975 tax rebate.

5. What do you think is the best method for financing the government deficit during a recession?

6. Can you think of any problems that the President might run into when he wants to change taxes?

7. In this problem, equilibrium income is $1,100 billion and full-employment equilibrium is $1,450 billion. The marginal propensity to save is 1/7. Using these data, answer the following:

   (a) Is there an overfull employment gap or an underful employment gap? What is the size of the gap?
   (b) What is the multiplier here?
   (c) What is the MPC?
   (d) By how much must new investment or government spending increase to bring the economy up to full employment?
   (e) What is the tax multiplier in this problem?
   (f) By how much must government cut personal taxes to stimulate the economy to the full-employment equilibrium?

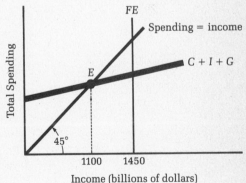

Income (billions of dollars)

Selected
References

Economic Report of the President, Washington, D.C.: U.S. Government Printing Office, published annually.

Heller, Walter W., *New Dimensions of Political Economy,* New York: W. W. Norton, 1967.

Thurow, Lester C. (ed.), *American Fiscal Policy,* Englewood Cliffs, N.J.: Prentice-Hall, 1967.

The Economic New Frontiersman

WALTER W. HELLER

**Former Chairman, Council of
Economic Advisers**

During the 1971 to 1972 academic year at the University of Minnesota, Walter Heller removed his own book, *New Dimensions in Political Economy,* from the introductory economics reading list. Heller quietly commented on why his book was no longer appropriate to the economic scene: "We were so pleased then [1966] to have accomplished the intellectual revolution of the 1960s. But we were expecting more than economics could deliver."

Walter Heller was one architect of the successful "new economics" of the Kennedy years. A combination of Keynesian economics and the social goals of the New Frontier, Heller's economic philosophy placed the federal government in a planning and channeling role that was completely different from the reserved, noninterventionist Eisenhower policies.

Heller first entered government service in 1942 as senior economic analyst for the Treasury Department. There he helped initiate the withholding tax system. During the 1940s and 1950s, he shuttled back and forth between his teaching job at the University of Minnesota and Washington, where he held several advisory jobs. In 1961, he was appointed chairman of the Council of Economic Advisers (CEA) by President Kennedy.

Under Heller's leadership of the CEA, more than advice in economics was given to the President. Heller also made statements to the press and various congressional subcommittees regarding housing, education, and other matters that eventually affect the economy. His approach was to stimulate economic growth rather than to balance budgets and keep prices stable: "Let's invest in education and scientific research and so forth. Let's get a defense establishment that will restore our position. Let's get an investment in space exploration. Then, if there's an inflation problem, by all means raise taxes and take the other necessary measures to curtail inflation."

Much of the impact Heller had was through his taxation plan. He viewed many taxes as potential economic levers and believed in selective programs to boost lagging sectors of the economy. In 1964, while still chairman of the CEA, Heller drafted an extensive revenue-sharing plan, a plan based on the belief that the Internal Revenue Service is a highly efficient tax-collecting device which could be used more effectively if it were to assume some of the tax-collection burdens now carried by the states. Moreover, Heller viewed the high interstate mobility of

corporations and citizens as a weakening influence on local tax bases, a weakness that would be offset by a central taxation clearinghouse.

Heller has been a vocal critic of the economic policies of Republican administrations since leaving government service in 1964. By the end of the 1960s, Heller, through his writings and speeches, was urging President Nixon to institute wage and price guidelines to slow down the inflationary pattern. At President Ford's economic "summit" conference in September 1974, Heller criticized the restrictive monetary policies of the Federal Reserve Board, and he was one of the liberal economists who encouraged Ford to accept a budget deficit and promote a substantial decrease in taxes. A designer of Johnson's successful 1964 tax cut, Heller, in early 1975, advocated a tax cut of over $25 billion annually to bring the country out of recession. "If we really want to reverse things," he said, "let's mainline it."

With the exception of the times he has worked in Washington, Heller has taught in the University of Minnesota economics department since the 1940s. He approves of the close ties between business and academia in the department, and he feels that the school offers a centralized position—both intellectually and geographically—that is particularly useful. As one of his colleagues commented: "His vision is of a great land-grant institution at one end of a boulevard and a state capital at the other, with an inevitable interplay of information between them."

PUBLIC SERVICE EMPLOYMENT PROGRAMS

Traditional vs. Nontraditional Fiscal Policy

In Chapter 10 we looked at traditional fiscal policy measures: changes in government spending *(G)* and changes in taxes *(T)*. Recently, the adequacy of such traditional policies has been questioned by many economists and politicians because of the persistently high inflation rates accompanied by significant amounts of unemployment. The cry in some circles has been that we need a new policy tool, one that is nontraditional and effective. The Emergency Employment Act of 1971 has provided just such a tool. The act provides for public service employment (PSE) and thereby not only adds fiscal stimulus to the economy but at the same time reduces the rate of unemployment.

Congress, at least, seemed sufficiently pleased with the results of the 1971 act to expand it with the comprehensive Employment and Training Act of 1973. Since then, massive expansions in the amount of money that can be provided for public jobs under the 1973 act have been requested by various senators and presidents.

The Position in Favor of PSE

Numerous economists are in favor of expanded PSE, including Harvard's John Kenneth Galbraith and the University of Minnesota's Walter Heller. And Yale Professor William Fellner was quoted, before he joined the Council of Economic Advisers, as saying that PSE ''[is] not utopia, but it's at least a second-best solution for achieving low unemployment with price stability.''

Of course, not everyone wants increased public employment. Dr. Ezra Solomon, while a member of the Council of Economic Advisers, remarked that ''We already have an awful lot of public employment in this country—one in every five or six jobs. I'm not sure the outcry for more public services is as great as some assume.''

Why PSE Is So Popular

To be sure, this nontraditional approach to fiscal policy has been tried in the past. During the Great Depression of the 1930s, there were numerous public service employ-ment programs. The one that is now in effect, however, seems to differ from the typical old-style Works Progress Administration (WPA) programs. The jobs created by the new-style PSE are supposedly for services needed by the community. There has never been any talk of hiring workers to dig holes and then fill them up again, as is alleged to have taken place under the WPA.

Also, the net government budget costs of PSE are relatively low because every dollar budgeted goes directly into a job—presumably one that is filled by an unemployed person, thus saving unemployment insurance and welfare dollars.

Proponents of PSE go one step further. They see expanded PSE as a way to improve the incomes of disadvantaged workers and achieve a shift in output toward the public sector, thus helping to meet some of society's unmet ''needs.''

The Problem of Federal Fund Usage

If we look at the results of the various PSE programs, we find that the job-creating potential has not been completely fulfilled. We find, for example, that many state and local governments obtaining federal funds to create public service employment have simply substituted these funds for their own payroll budgets. They have then used the savings to reduce state and local taxes or to purchase additional buildings, computers, and the like. Estimates of the amount of federal money substituted for state and local money range from 40 percent to as high as 90 percent. This use of federal money means that the employment-creating effect of expanded PSE is not as great as its proponents contend.

The Multiplier at Work

However, even if this substitution does take place, the money that does go into job creation might have a multiplier effect on output, income, and employment. Various economists and congressional staffs have used the multiplier analysis presented in the previous chapters to estimate the actual net cost to the Treasury of creating a certain number of jobs by expanded PSE, assuming that output and income will rise. They do this by first calculating the number of PSE jobs to be created and then reducing this number by an estimate of the substitution discussed above. The effective number of new jobs created is multiplied by some estimated government-spending multiplier. The multiplier, you will remember, comes into play because the wages paid to the new workers hired under PSE sets off a chain of additional consumer spending that further increases the demand for goods and services, which, in turn, leads to an increase in employment in that sector.

Using this type of multiplier analysis, Congressman Richard Vander Veen (Dem., Mich.), predicted that an additional 2 million jobs could be created at a net cost to the Treasury of only $4.6 billion. This would mean that in the mid-1970s the unemployment rate could be reduced by over 35 percent at a net cost totaling less than 1½ percent of the federal budget.

Such estimates are not without their critics, however. Robert I. Lerman, a former staff member of the Congressional Subcommittee on Fiscal Policy of the Joint Economic Committee, pointed out that such estimates unrealistically assume that federal funds substitute for state and local payroll expenditures only to the extent of zero to 15 percent. Moreover, he contended that it was also unrealistic to presume that half the PSE jobs would go to persons who

otherwise would be on unemployment or welfare.[1]

Do the Disadvantaged Get Help?

One of the major aims of PSE programs is to expand employment without adding to inflation. This is presumably accomplished by hiring disadvantaged persons who would otherwise remain unemployed. And, since these disadvantaged persons are hired, it is not necessary to bid up the wage rates of other workers. However, an analysis of the Emergency Employment Act of 1971 shows that only 17 percent of workers hired met the official criterion of "disadvantaged." Further analysis shows that those hired had a higher

[1]Robert I. Lerman, "The Public Employment Bandwagon Takes the Wrong Road," *Challenge*, January–February 1975, p. 12.

average educational level than the average of all workers in private employment.

It is not surprising that PSE seems attractive to other than disadvantaged workers. Most of the proposals for PSE call for jobs paying $7,000 and $8,000 per year. This is a salary level that exceeds the earnings of between 10 and 20 million full-time workers in the United States.

PSE and Fiscal Policy in the Future

Will PSE be expanded and become a major tool of fiscal policy in the future? It has been suggested by a number of economists that PSE be "triggered" automatically at predetermined levels of unemployment, thus hitting the problem immediately by providing new jobs. We have seen, however, that the total employment effect of PSE may not be as great as might be expected because of the substitution of federal funds for otherwise committed state and local expenditures. Moreover, we can be less than sanguine about the percentage of those newly employed who are actually "disadvantaged."

These criticisms, however, do not mean that PSE is necessarily ineffective or that it should be eliminated as a fiscal tool. Additional studies will undoubtedly be done to measure the impact of PSE on the equilibrium level of output, income, and employment.

Whatever the results of these studies, public service jobs provided by the federal government must be paid for out of government monies. In some cases (and, recently, in all cases) this involves increasing the federal government·budget deficit. What is the effect of an increase in the budget deficit on the economy? We look at this topic in the next issue.

Questions for Thought and Discussion

1. What is the difference between traditional fiscal policy and PSE programs?
2. For fiscal policy to be effective, does it matter which sectors of the economy are stimulated?
3. What do the old Works Progress Administration and the new PSE programs have in common?

Selected References

Barnes, Peter, "Bringing Back the WPA," *New Republic,* Mar. 15, 1975, pp. 19–21.
Lerman, Robert I., "The Public Employment Bandwagon Takes the Wrong Road," *Challenge,* January–February 1975, pp. 10–16.

Economics in the Public Mind

PAUL A. SAMUELSON

**Economist, Massachusetts
Institute of Technology**

"They don't give Nobel Prizes for writing textbooks," commented Paul Samuelson, the 1970 Nobel Laureate in economics. Nor are Nobel prizes given for writing magazine columns, giving newspaper interviews, making congressional testimonies, or the many other activities by which this prominent American economist is known to millions of people outside academia.

Paul Samuelson was America's first Nobel prize winner in economics; he was awarded the prize for his work in applying mathematics to broad questions of static and dynamic equilibrium and for "raising the level of analysis in economic science." This statement, which appeared in the Stockholm press, is deceptively simple. During the 1940s and 1950s, Samuelson began to synthesize economic methodology on the basis of mathematical models of almost universal applicability. He was foremost in developing mathematical model building and in expanding quantitative analysis and prediction.

Samuelson has authored many books, including *Economics: An Introductory Analysis* (1948), *The Foundations of Economic Analysis* (1948), *Linear Programming and Economic Analysis* (1958), and a two-volume collection of articles (1967).

Of his own work, Samuelson said in his presidential address to the American Economics Association in 1961: "My own scholarship has covered a great variety of fields. And many of them involve questions like welfare economics and factor-price equalization; turnpike theorems and oscillating envelopes; non-substitutability relations in Minkowski-Ricardo-Leontief-Metzler matrices of Mosak-Hichs type; or balanced budget multipliers under conditions of balanced uncertainty in locally impacted topological spaces and molar equivalences. My friends warn me that such topics are suitable merely for captive audiences in search of a degree—and even then not after dark." Samuelson has been a popular spokesman for the economic profession. The wide circulation of his views on current economic policy, by way of his column in *Newsweek* magazine and his testimony before congressional committees, has made him a most public "private citizen."

Although he has never held a major government economic policy post, Samuelson—true to his belief that economists should be concerned with social issues—served as adviser to both John Kennedy and Lyndon Johnson. Kennedy appointed Samuelson to head an economic task force which was to recommend means of reversing the business slump of that period. Samuelson suggested a temporary 3 or 4 percent tax cut, improved unemployment compensation, defense spending, foreign aid, federal aid to education, urban renewal, health and welfare, but no large-scale emergency public works program. All was accepted by Kennedy, except the tax cut. Samuelson later worked on the Johnson task force that developed his Great Society program.

Samuelson was a harsh and consistent critic of the policies of the Nixon administration, and the economic programs of President Ford did not escape his disapproval. "If you turn this recession upside down," Samuelson commented in early 1975, "you will read clearly on its bottom, 'Made in Washington.'" The reason for it, he said, was that Nixon and Ford wanted to bring two-digit inflation to an end. Now, to bring the country out of recession, Samuelson favored a larger income tax cut to more than offset a stiff energy tax and an expansion of the money supply. "If economic conditions are deteriorating, what the economy needs is an infusion of purchasing power from a contrived higher deficit. You cannot take $30 billion in energy taxes from the American people and rebate some $16 billion in income taxes and thereby do anything except worsen the recession." When recovery was ensured, Samuelson predicted that "inflation will again be our primary concern."

Is There a Burden of the Public Debt?

THE LONG-RUN EFFECTS OF DEFICIT FINANCING

Operating in the Red

Everybody knows that if a business ends up in the red, year in and year out, it will eventually go bankrupt. It should follow from this that the United States government too cannot spend more than it receives year in and year out. The fact is, however, that it can and does. Moreover, the government hasn't yet gone bankrupt, and it never will. When the government spends more than it collects in taxes, it runs a budget deficit. That is to say, when G exceeds T, the government is running a deficit, and the national debt is thereby increased. It should be made clear that the national debt is a stock concept. The increase in the national debt due to federal government deficits exceeding surpluses is a flow concept.

Much of the deficit is made up by the government selling bonds to the public. In the process it increases this public or national debt—a debt made up of all the loans people made to the government by buying bonds. Many people think that an increase in the **public debt** imposes a burden

on future generations. In this issue we will examine some of the arguments concerning the so-called **burden of the public debt.**

Growth of Public Debt

It is true that the public debt has grown continuously for many years. However, the total public debt is not what we should look at to analyze the burden of the debt. Let's consider the per capita public debt as shown in Table I-12.1.

We see that in 1945 the nominal public debt (expressed in current dollars) per capita was $1,849. In 1970 it was less than that, about $1,806. When we look at the *real* public debt per capita (that is, the public debt corrected for inflation), the decrease in recent years is even more drastic. Look at Figure I-12.1. Here we see that the real public debt per capita has actually fallen by more than one-half since 1945. Thus, although the total may be rising, the amount per capita is falling, and certainly the real amount per capita is falling rather noticeably.

Gross and Net Debt

We must also distinguish between the **gross public debt** and the **net public debt.** We will define net public debt as follows:

$$\begin{matrix} \text{Net} \\ \text{public} \\ \text{debt} \end{matrix} = \begin{matrix} \text{gross public debt} \\ - \text{ all intergovernmental} \\ \text{agency borrowing} \end{matrix}$$

Let's look at one example of interagency governmental borrowing. Suppose the Treasury is running out of money to pay the government bills. The Treasury decides to sell a $100,000 bond that the Social Security Administration has agreed to buy. The issuance of the bond by the Treasury and the purchase of it by the Social Security Administration will increase the gross public debt by $100,000. However, it will not increase the *net* public debt.

How Do We Measure the Burden?

We need to establish some method of measuring the so-called burden of the public debt. It is not sufficient to say merely that future generations will be worse off because they have to pay more taxes to cover the interest on the increased debt. Taxes may very well have to be raised by, for example, 10 percent over 25 years

Table I-12.1

The Public Debt of the Federal Government, 1915 to 1975

Here we show the gross public debt and the gross public debt per capita. Notice that per capita debt reached a peak in 1945 in terms of nominal dollars—that is, current dollars without correction for inflation. The gross public debt per capita was about the same in 1970 as it had been 25 years earlier.

YEAR	TOTAL (IN BILLIONS)	PER CAPITA
1915	$ 1.2	$ 12
1920	24.3	228
1925	20.5	177
1930	16.2	132
1935	28.7	226
1940	43.0	325
1945	258.7	1,849
1950	257.4	1,697
1955	274.4	1,660
1960	286.3	1,585
1961	289.0	1,573
1962	298.2	1,598
1963	305.9	1,615
1964	311.7	1,622
1965	317.3	1,631
1966	319.9	1,625
1967	326.2	1,637
1968	347.6	1,728
1969	353.7	1,741
1970	370.9	1,806
1971	409.5	1,978
1972	437.3	2,094
1973	468.4	2,226
1974	486.2	2,290
1975 (est.)	525.0	2,472

Source: U.S. Office of Management and Budget

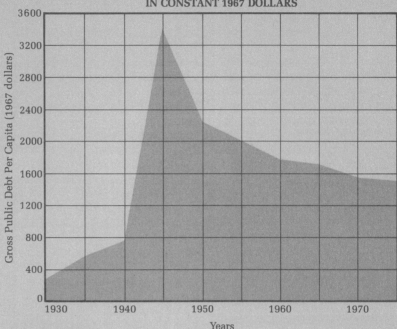

FIGURE I-12.1

Here we have plotted the per capita gross public debt in the United States after correcting for inflation. We see that it jumped drastically during World War II but since then has fallen by more than 50 percent. (Source: U.S. Department of the Treasury.)

to handle the increased interest payments on a larger public debt. But this simply means that although people pay higher taxes, many of them (that is, United States citizens who are holders of government bonds) are receiving those monies as interest payments on money lent to the government.

Changes in Capital Stock

Let's instead describe the burden of future generations by looking at the size of the **capital stock** they will inherit from the present generation.

The capital stock consists of buildings, machines, and the like—all those things that help provide for future consumption by contributing to the production of future goods. If an increase in the public debt forces the present generation to hand down a smaller capital stock (wealth) to future generations, then we will say that these future generations are worse off; they are shouldering a burden.

Alternatives to Debt

What are the alternatives to increasing the public debt? Certainly, the government doesn't increase the public debt merely for the fun of it. The government seeks additional borrowing only if it has to make expenditures that are not covered by tax revenues. Now, if the public debt is increased only to cover expenditures, then the government has a choice. It can finance its expenditures either by taxation or by increasing the public debt—that is, by borrowing. (It can also finance its expenditures by what is called "money creation," but we'll cover this topic in the following chapter.) Let's compare the alternatives of taxation and increased government debt.

Taxation vs. Borrowing

To determine the burden of the public debt, we want to know whether a switch from taxation to government borrowing will decrease the wealth (capital stock) that our generation will pass on to the next. We shall assume that the economy is operating at full employment and that government expenditures are as productive as private expenditures.

When the government switches from taxation to debt financing, it increases the *future* tax liabilities of the nation because more government interest payments will be made to holders of new government bonds. Whether or not the nation takes full account of this increase in future tax liabilities is crucial in determining whether it will pass on a diminished capital stock. Suppose the present generation ignores the fact that it will have to pay more taxes in the future; the increased public debt will cause

people today to feel wealthier because they will own more bonds. As a result, they will consume more, save less, and therefore there will be less investment. This will result in a lower capital stock in the future, less wealth bequeathed by the present generation to future ones. Future generations will indeed suffer a burden of the public debt.

Suppose, however, that the present generation is fully aware of its future tax liabilities. It will not feel wealthier merely because it holds more bonds. In fact, people will want to save enough extra to pay for the increased tax liabilities in the future. There will be no change in the *net* investment of the community. In this particular case, investment and consumption will be the same whether the government taxes people or sells bonds. Future generations will inherit a capital stock that has not been diminished, and, by our definition they will suffer no burden of the public debt.

Borrowing from Abroad

Thus far, we have been concerned with the *internal* public debt. If part of it is held by foreigners, then it is no longer true that "we owe it to ourselves." Increased taxes for paying the interest on increased public debt will no longer be paid to ourselves. Currently, about 0.18 percent of the national debt is owned by foreigners. Far from being a burden, however, an increase in the public debt sold to foreigners can prove to be a boon to future generations.

Assume we are at full employment. It is impossible for us to in-

crease either investment or consumption. We could, however, change the mix by altering savings behavior. Borrowing resources from abroad by selling public debt to foreigners can allow us to increase consumption today and also increase investment. Future generations must pay the interest that allows for this increased consumption today, but they will end up with a larger capital stock. Future generations will be better off if the additional income from the larger capital stock more than pays the interest owed to foreigners. If not, they will in fact be burdened by the increased **external public debt.**

How Big Is the Interest Payment on the National Debt?

Let's consider the size of the interest payments on public debt (the value of federal government bonds outstanding). In our Figure I-10.2 we show interest payments as a percentage of GNP. Even though interest payments have been rising steadily since before World War II, as a percentage of GNP, they have not gone much above 2 percent for the last two decades. Apparently, then, we are not getting future generations deeper and deeper into debt, relative to what their income is expected to be.

Redistribution of Income

It has been argued that the existence of a public debt on which interest

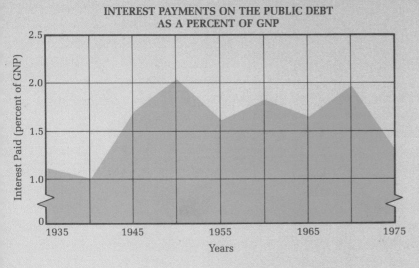

INTEREST PAYMENTS ON THE PUBLIC DEBT
AS A PERCENT OF GNP

Years

FIGURE I-12.2

Here we see that the interest payments
on the public debt vary between 1 and
2 percent as a percentage of GNP.
(Source: U.S. Department of
Commerce.)

is paid to bondholders tends to redistribute income. This presumably
is true to the extent that those who
receive interest are other than those
who pay the taxes from which those
interest payments are made. Whenever a situation exists where one
group of heavily taxed taxpayers
holds no bonds but another group
of lightly taxed taxpayers does hold
federal government bonds, there will
be a net transfer of income from the
first group to the second group. In
other words, a minor redistribution of
income might occur.

There is another effect of the
public debt that is, perhaps, even
more subtle than redistribution of
income. The existence of a public
debt requires taxes to be levied on
American citizens. Most of these
taxes, at least at the federal level,
are in the form of taxes on income.
If a larger public debt requires higher
taxes to pay the higher interest costs
of that debt, then Americans will pay
higher rates of income taxation. But

higher rates of taxation are an incentive for individuals to work less
because the opportunity cost of *not*
working falls as the rate of taxation
increases. Thus, even if income were
not transferred from one American
group to another, there could still be
a burden in the sense that the higher
tax rate needed to pay the interest
payment on the public debt would
lead individuals to choose more leisure (that is, to work less hard for
shorter periods). We say in such a
situation that the allocation of resources is distorted.

Note, of course, that debt financing really only *postpones* the tax
burden. Basically, the financing decision is between present or future
taxes.

Conclusions

It is impossible to determine exactly
what type of burden might be be-

stowed upon future generations by
increasing the national debt. First of
all, we have to know whether we are
talking about the gross or the net
debt. Then we have to know whether
individuals are going to discount
correctly the increased future tax
liabilities implicit in an increased
public debt. Next we can determine
whether investment will be altered
and, therefore, whether the capital
stock handed to future generations
will be the same as it would be in
the case of, say, taxation-financed
spending. One thing is sure: We
should be wary of editorials that
decry the horrible, bankrupting increases in our national debt when,
on the next page of the newspaper,
an ad tells us to contribute to the
public debt by buying U.S. Savings
Bonds.

We should also note that there is
much public outcry against the public debt, but no similar concern is
expressed about private debt. Check
the balance sheet of any company

in the United States, and you will undoubtedly find that the company is in debt. This is a normal business practice. Part of the capital structure of a company is made up of debt, and part of it is made up of equity—that is, shares of stock. Company managers and investors will get concerned if the interest payments on the debt of a company get close to the operating income of that company, but no such problem has ever occurred in the federal government. Similarly, the interest on the public debt uses up a very small part of the total revenues collected.

Definitions of New Terms

Public Debt: The market value of all federal government securities outstanding.

Burden of the Public Debt: Expansion of the public debt will supposedly be a burden to future generations. This burden will be caused by our increasing the debt in this generation. More precisely, the burden will occur when future generations inherit a lower capital stock (wealth) than they would have had public debt not been expanded.

Gross Public Debt: The market value of all outstanding securities of the federal government, including those held by federal government agencies.

Net Public Debt: The gross public debt minus all interagency holdings. All debt concepts refer to a stock measured at a moment in time.

Capital Stock: The sum of all buildings, machines, and the like in the United States. Capital stock allows us to produce more in the future—that is, to provide more future consumption.

External Public Debt: Public debt owed to foreigners, as opposed to internal public debt, which is owed to ourselves.

Questions for Thought and Discussion

1. Some economists have likened the public debt to robbing Peter to pay Paul. Are they right?
2. Why can the federal government be forever in the red?
3. Adam Smith once said: "What is prudence in the conduct of every private family can scarce be folly in that of a great kingdom." Take out the words "that of a great kingdom" and insert "the United States." Was he right concerning the public debt?

Selected References

Anderson, William H., *Financing Modern Government,* Boston: Houghton-Mifflin, 1973, chaps. 22–29.

Bowen, William G. et al., "The Public Debt: A Burden on Future Generations?", *American Economic Review,* September 1960, pp. 701–706.

Okun, Arthur (ed.), *The Battle against Unemployment,* rev. ed., New York: W. W. Norton, 1972, parts II and IV.

Money and the Banking System

If someone were to ask you "How much money do you make?", you might answer so many dollars per week or per year. In this context, the term "money" really means income or the ability to purchase goods and services—in fact, the term money is most generally used to mean income. But in this sense it is being used incorrectly. Only counterfeiters and banks "make money." What you make is income. In this chapter and throughout the rest of the text, we will use the term money to mean only that which we use as our medium of exchange. Money is most often thought of as those pieces of paper and coins you have in your wallet, purse, or buried in the back yard. Our money supply, however, includes more than currency. At the very minimum, your checking account balance can be considered a medium of exchange because you can use it in exchange for the things you want to buy.

In this chapter we will examine the functions that money serves, the different types of money which are in existence today, the banking system, and how the supply of money in circulation is controlled.

Types of Monetary Standards

In the United States today we have a **fiduciary monetary system.** This means that the value of our currency rests upon the public's confidence in it. "Fiduciary" comes from the Latin *fiducia*, which means trust or confidence. In other words, in our monetary system the currency is not convertible into a fixed quantity of gold or silver.

Prior to the existence of a fiduciary currency, a **commodity currency** was used. A commodity currency is one in which a commodity such as cigarettes, beads, salt, or other items has a use other than as a medium of exchange.

Before money was used, transactions or exchanges took place by means of **barter.** Barter is simply a direct exchange—no intermediary good called money is used. Economic historians often suggest that the switch from bartering to the use of money allowed for the economic growth of the Western world since increased specialization was then possible. It was extremely costly (that is, the transactions costs were high) to make all exchanges via barter. Imagine the difficulty you would have today if you had to exchange your labor directly for the fruits of someone else's labor. Imagine the many exchanges that would have to take place for you to get from a position of owning, for example, 25 pairs of shoes to a position where you owned only two pairs but now also had bread, meat, a pair of pants, and so on. The use of money facilitates exchange, allowing for increased specialization and therefore higher material standards of living. (Remember, we are talking about money and *not* income.)

The Functions of Money

There are three traditional functions of money. The one most people are familiar with and the one we referred to above is as a medium of exchange. However, money also serves as a unit of accounting and as a store of purchasing power.

Money As a Medium of Exchange

As a medium of exchange, money allows individuals to specialize in any area in which they have a comparative advantage, receiving money payment for the fruits of their labor that can then be exchanged for the fruits of other people's labor. The usefulness of money as a medium of exchange therefore increases with the amount of a country's trade and specialization. Money would not be as important in self-suf-

ficient family units, for example, as it is in modern commercial economies.

For money to serve as a medium of exchange, it must first be generally accepted as a means of payment for all market exchanges. The fiduciary currency in our country works as a medium of exchange because it is accepted in payment for all debts and obligations. In fact, in the United States, individuals are required to accept our currency as ". . . payments for all debts public and private. . . ."

Money As a Unit of Accounting

As a unit of accounting, money is actually the common denominator that allows individuals to compare the relative value of different goods and services in our economy. In colonial times, our unit of account was not the dollar but the British pound sterling. Spanish pesos were also circulated, but prices were generally quoted in terms of pounds. The dollar became the official unit of account in 1792.

Money As a Store of Value

As a store of value, money is an asset that accounts for part of one's wealth. Wealth in the form of money can be exchanged later for other assets. Although it is not the only form of wealth that can be exchanged for goods and services, it is the one most widely accepted. This attribute of money is called **liquidity.** We say that an asset is liquid when it can easily be acquired or disposed of without high transactions costs and with relative certainty as to its value. Money is by definition the most liquid asset there is. Just compare it, for example, to a share of stock listed on the New York Stock Exchange. To buy or sell that stock, you must call a stockbroker who will place the buy or sell order for you. This must be done during normal business hours. You have to pay a percentage commission to the broker. Moreover, there is a distinct probability that you will get more or less for the stock than you originally paid for it. This is not the case with money. You can exchange a dollar for a dollar and exchange it for other assets at any time of the day or night. Therefore, most individuals hold at least a part of their wealth in the form of this most liquid of assets, money.

However, when we hold money, we pay a price for this advantage of liquidity. That price is the interest yield that could have been obtained had the asset been held in another form, for example, in the form of a savings and loan account. In other words, the cost of holding money (its opportunity cost) is measured by the alternative yield obtainable by holding some other form of asset.

The Distinction between Money and Credit

The distinction between money and credit is sometimes not very clear. Credit is funds or savings that are made available to borrowers. In other words, the credit market is basically a market where those who are willing to wait to have purchasing power provide funds at a cost (the interest rate) for those who want to have purchasing power now and are willing to pay a price to have it. It is through the interaction of supply (lenders) and demand (borrowers) in the credit market that saving provides funds for investment.

This is not the case with money per se. Money is merely the most liquid asset in which people choose to hold part of their wealth. We will see, however, that the ultimate amount of money supply is determined by credit expansions and contractions by banks. To *not* confuse money with credit, you should think of credit as a loan and money as that part of a person's wealth which is completely liquid.

Defining the Money Supply

There is not complete agreement about what should and what should not be included in the money supply. If we define money, functionally by its three roles: medium of exchange, unit of account, temporary store of purchasing power, then currency and checking account balances, which are also called demand deposits, should obviously be included. Currency has been defined as paper notes and coins. Demand deposits are accounts in commercial banks that can be transferred or converted into currency on demand—in other words, you can write a check at any time on your checking account. The most narrow definition of money includes demand deposits and currency in the hands of the nonbanking public. This total of currency and demand deposits held by the nonbanking public has been labeled M_1. Throughout the remainder of the macro portion of this text, we will talk in terms of M_1, even though there are broader measures of liquidity that could be used.

A second definition of money includes M_1 plus time deposits in commercial banks. Time deposits are savings account balances and small certificates of deposit held by commercial banks. They are called time deposits because, in principle, the bank can require notice of your intent to withdraw from your savings account. This second definition of money has been labeled M_2.

So, M_2 is circulating currency, plus demand deposits, plus time deposits in commercial banks. If we extend our definition of money even further to include deposits in noncommercial bank thrift institutions, such as passbook shares in savings and loan associations, then we obtain M_3. This M_3 is our broadest measure of the money stock. You can see in Figure 11-1 that there is a distinct difference between M_1, M_2, and M_3. However, we will talk only in terms of M_1 for the rest of this unit.

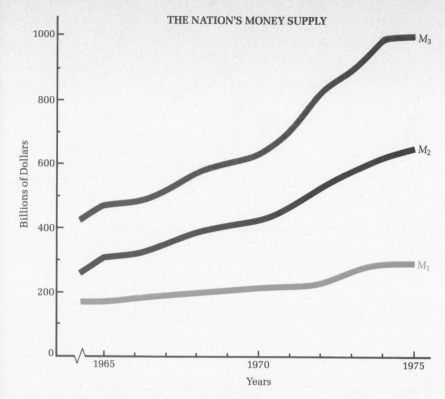

THE NATION'S MONEY SUPPLY

Billions of Dollars

M_3

M_2

M_1

1965   1970   1975

Years

Table 11-1 shows the components of M_1 for selected years. Although demand deposits account for over 75 percent of the money supply, even this figure underestimates their importance. Demand deposits are used for 95 percent of the dollar volume of all *C, I,* and *G* purchases in our economy.

Currency accounts for the remainder of M_1, but its percentage importance over time has been rising. Some observers contend that this shift toward a larger percentage of money being held as currency is the result of a rise in illegal activities. Since currency cannot be traced, illegal transactions demand the use of currency. And as more illegal transactions are undertaken, a higher percentage of the money stock will be demanded in the form of currency. Also, currency is used to conceal income from the IRS.

How does currency get into circulation? Who provides it? Who watches over the money supply? The answer is our central bank, which we call the Federal Reserve, or the Fed for short.

Table 11-1 **Components of M_1 (in Billions of Dollars)**

COMPONENT	1920	1950	1975 (MAY)
Demand deposits	18.66	90.20	219.48
Currency	4.49	25.00	69.52
Money supply (M_1)	23.15	115.20	289.0

Source: Board of Governors of the Federal Reserve System

The Federal Reserve System

Our central bank was established by the Federal Reserve Act, signed on December 23, 1913, by President Woodrow Wilson. The act was the outgrowth of recommendations from the National Monetary Commission, which had been authorized by the Aldridge-Vreeland Act of 1908. Basically, the Commission had attempted to find a way to counter the periodic financial panics that had occurred in our country. The Fed was set up to aid and supervise banks and also to provide banking services for the U.S. Treasury.

Organization of the Federal Reserve System

Figure 11-2 shows the Federal Reserve organizational chart. Basically, it consists of a Board of Governors, which is composed of seven salaried full-time members appointed by the President with the approval of the Senate. There are 12 Federal Reserve banks, which have a total of 24 branches. Additionally, there is the very important Federal Open Market Committee (FOMC), which decides the policy course for the Fed in future days and weeks. That committee is composed of the members of the Board of Governors plus five representatives of the Federal Reserve banks who are rotated periodically. The FOMC determines by its actions the future growth of the money supply and other important variables.

Member Banks

Of the 14,000 or so commercial banks in the United States, about 5700 are members of the Federal Reserve System. This is in contrast to

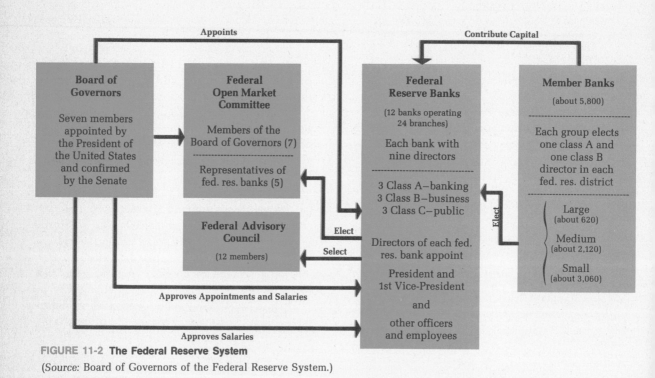

FIGURE 11-2 **The Federal Reserve System**
(*Source:* Board of Governors of the Federal Reserve System.)

the almost 7000 banks that were members of the system at the end of World War II. There has been an increasing movement of commercial banks away from membership in the Federal Reserve System to state bank status. All national banks have to be members of the system, but those banks that prefer to be regulated by state rules can, upon successful application, change their membership.

Banks belonging to the Fed do obtain significant privileges and prestige. They can borrow from the Federal Reserve banks and they can also obtain currency, information, and advice from those same banks. They can also use the check-clearing facilities of the Fed and transfer funds over the Federal Reserve's teletype wires.

There is, however, a cost for these privileges. The cost is that they must forgo certain profitable investment opportunities because of the higher requirements for non-income-producing assets, or "reserves" as they are called, which member banks must keep available in the form of vault cash or on deposit with the local Federal Reserve branch. State banks can keep a smaller proportion of their total assets in such non-income-producing reserves than can national banks in the Federal Reserve System.

Let's go into more detail now about the reserve system we have and see how it is used as a tool by the Fed to control the nation's money supply. In the process, we will see how the money supply can be expanded and contracted.

Reserves

Member banks of the Federal Reserve System are required to maintain a specified percentage of their customer deposits as reserves. If the required level of reserves is 20 percent and the bank has $1 billion in customer deposits, then it must have at least $200 million between the cash in its vault and the money in its account at the local Federal Reserve branch. Actually, the average required reserve level now is around 15 percent. Table 11-2 shows the reserve requirements that have been in effect since February 1975. Notice that there are lower reserve requirements for time deposits than for demand deposits and that there is a legal range within which the Fed's requirements must stay. That range has been legislated by Congress. To change it, new legislation would have to be passed.

Assets and Liabilities

Since required reserves are less than 100 percent of demand deposits, we have what is called a **fractional reserve banking system**—that is, only a fraction of customer account balances must be kept in reserve by banks. Note that a checking account balance, from a bank's point of view, is a liability since you own it, not the bank. However, the reserves the bank has in a Federal Reserve branch are part of its assets, and the Fed's liabilities.

We can see in Table 11-3 that the assets of member banks consist in large part of loans to customers and of securities such as stocks and bonds. On the other hand, their liabilities consist mainly of demand deposits and time deposits. These are liabilities because the banks must pay the former on demand and the latter essentially on demand. Table 11-3 is a composite or consolidated balance sheet, lumping all commercial banks together. The one term you may not be familiar with is *net worth*. This is the difference between assets and liabilities. It is put in the liabilities column because it is owned by the stockholders in the bank.

Excess Reserves

Member banks often hold reserves in excess of what is required by the Federal Reserve System. This difference between actual reserves and required reserves is called **excess**

Table 11-2 Reserve Requirements of Member Banks

Here we see the reserve requirements of all member banks. Notice that the reserve requirements for time deposits are less than for demand deposits.

| EFFECTIVE DATE | NET DEMAND DEPOSITS | | | | | TIME DEPOSITS | | |
| | | | | | | | Other Time Deposits | |
	Under $2 Million	$2–10 Million	$10–100 Million	$100–400 Million	Over $400 Million	Savings Deposits	Over $5 Million	Under $5 Million
In Effect Feb. 13, 1975	7½%	10%	12%	13%	16½%	3%	3%	5%
Present legal requirements: Minimum Maximum			10% 22%				3% 10%	

Source: Board of Governors of the Federal Reserve System

reserves. Excess reserves can be negative as well as positive. Negative excess reserves indicate that banks do not have sufficient reserves to meet their legal requirements. Excess reserves are an important determinant of the rate of growth of the money stock for it is only to the extent that banks have excess reserves that they can expand their deposits by lending money to firms and individuals. Since reserves produce no income, banks have an incentive to minimize any excess reserves. They use them either to purchase income-producing securities or to make loans on which they earn income through interest payments. But we will see that the Fed itself is the primary determinant of the level of reserves in the banking system.

Table 11-3 Consolidated Balance Sheet of Member Banks, January 1975 (in Billions of Dollars)

ASSETS		LIABILITIES AND NET WORTH	
Total reserves	$ 36.95	Demand deposits	$180.95
Loans	414.40	Time deposits	316.70
Securities	135.80	Borrowings from Federal Reserve	0.39
Other assets	89.75	Other liabilities	130.12
		Net worth	48.74
Total	$676.90	Total	$676.90

Source: Federal Reserve Bulletin

The Supply of Money

What determines the number of dollars in circulation in the form of currency and demand deposit balances? We know that commercial banks must be an important part of our analysis because they hold the bulk of the money supply as liabilities in the form of demand deposits. We also know that the central bank, the Fed, must be an important part of the analysis because of its control over the commercial banks. What we will see is a very clear-cut relationship between the level of reserves and the level of demand deposits and hence the total money supply. We will see that whatever affects reserves affects the money supply.

Let's first talk about how the Fed affects the level of reserves in the most direct manner possible, and then we will discuss the process by which a change in the level of reserves causes a multiple change in the total money supply. We will begin with the Federal Open Market Committee since its decisions essentially determine the level of reserves in the system.

Federal Open Market Committee

Open-market operations involve the buying and selling of United States government securities in the open market (the private bond market). Most government bonds except U.S. Savings Bonds are negotiable. If the Open Market Committee decides that it wants the Fed to sell bonds, it instructs the trading desk at the New York Federal Reserve Bank to do so. Since the bond market is very well developed, this can be accomplished immediately. If the Committee decides it wants to buy bonds, it instructs the trading desk to buy.

But what happens when the trading desk of the New York Federal Reserve buys a $10,000 bond? How does it pay for it? To buy the bond, the New York Federal Reserve writes a check on itself. The person or bank selling the bond receives the check and deposits it in its own account. The depository bank gives it to the Fed and the Fed writes $10,000 in the reserve account of that particular bank. Therefore, if the Fed buys a bond, it expands reserves by the amount of the purchase. Conversely, if the Fed sells a bond, the person or bank buying the bond writes a check, and the Fed reduces the reserves of the bank on which the check was written. In other words, when the Fed sells bonds, it reduces the reserves in the banking system. It reduces the reserves of the commercial member bank by the amount of the sale. When the Fed buys bonds, the opposite occurs. We see, therefore, that open-market operations on the part of the Fed can increase or decrease commercial member bank reserves.

The Relationship between Reserves and Total Deposits

To show the important relationship between reserves and total deposits, we'll first look at a single bank. A single bank can make loans, that is, create deposits, only to the extent that it has excess reserves to cover those new deposits. Thus, the isolated individual bank can in no way alter the money supply. However, the banking system as a whole can. This will become obvious as we work through a set of what are called T *accounts,* showing the assets and liabilities of an individual bank and those of the banking system as a whole.

We'll begin by making some assumptions that will make the problem much easier to handle:

1. The required reserve ratio is 20 percent for all demand deposits.
2. Demand deposits are the bank's only liabilities, whereas reserves and loans are the bank's only assets. (Loans are pieces of paper promising that the bank will be paid back in the future or I.O.Us.) Net worth, therefore, is zero.

3. Banks desire to keep their excess reserves at a zero level.

Now look at the initial position of our representative bank. Liabilities consist of $1 million in demand deposits, and assets consist of $200,000 in reserves, either in the form of vault cash or in the account of the Federal Reserve branch, plus $800,000 in loans to customers. Assets of $1 million therefore equal liabilities of $1 million.

Bank 1	Assets		Liabilities	
Total reserves		$ 200,000	Demand deposits	$1,000,000
Required reserves		(200,000)		
Excess reserves		(–0–)		
Loans		800,000		
Total		$1,000,000	Total	$1,000,000

Now a new customer comes to the bank and deposits a check for $1 million. Demand deposits in our individual bank increase by $1 million; at the same time, total reserves increase by $1 million, leaving an excess reserve of $800,000. Reserves increase when the representative bank deposits the check it receives in its account at its local Federal Reserve branch.

Look at excess reserves. They used to be zero and now they're $800,000—$800,000 worth of non-income-earning assets. Our third assumption, however, was that the bank desires to have zero excess reserves. So, in this simple world, the bank will make additional interest-earning loans totaling $800,000. Now loans increase to $1.6 million, total reserves fall to $400,000, and excess reserves are again zero.

We see, then, that for any individual bank the amount of reserves it has is directly related to the amount of deposits it receives. In this example, a person came in and deposited an

Bank 1	Assets		Liabilities	
Total reserves		$1,200,000	Demand deposits	$2,000,000
Required reserves		(400,000)		
Excess reserves		(800,000)		
Loans		800,000		
Total		$2,000,000	Total	$2,000,000

Bank 1	Assets		Liabilities	
Total reserves		$ 400,000	Demand deposits	$2,000,000
Required reserves		(400,000)		
Excess reserves		(–0–)		
Loans		1,600,000		
Total		$2,000,000	Total	$2,000,000

additional $1 million that became part of the reserves of that bank. Since excess reserves now exceeded zero, further loans were possible, and these were made in order to earn interest.

There is no overall deposit creation (that is, money creation) because the $1 million check brought in to open a new account was probably written on another bank, which means that while this bank had its deposits and reserves increased and was therefore able to expand its loans, another bank was doing just the opposite.

Now let's look at the banking system as a whole and see the primary method by which the actual money supply is expanded. We do this by seeing how banks respond to an increase in reserves in the system, that increase being due to Federal Reserve actions.

The Money Supply Expands

We begin by making another assumption: The $1 million check deposited by the bank client was written not on another commercial bank but on a Federal Reserve bank. We'll further assume that this depositor obtained that $1 million check because the FOMC decided it wanted to purchase a $1 million bond from a private individual. When it did so, it gave the

individual a check written on itself.

Let's go back now to our individual bank, Bank 1, and look again at the third T account, in which both liabilities and assets have been increased by $1 million and loans have been expanded from $800,000 to $1.6 million. Because of our new assumptions, the money supply has also been increased. The money supply increases by $800,000 when the bank expands its loans.

The process does not stop here. Let's assume that the additional $800,000 loan was given to a firm wishing to purchase a MacDonald's franchise. This firm takes the $800,000 check and deposits it in its bank account at bank 2. For simplicity, we'll ignore the assets and liabilities in that bank and concentrate only on the T account changes resulting from this new deposit. We add a plus sign to indicate that we are looking only at changes in the T accounts. We see that for bank 2 this new deposit becomes an increase in reserves. Since the required reserves are 20 percent or $160,000, excess reserves are $640,000. But, of course, excess reserves earn no income, so bank 2 will eliminate them by making loans, which do earn income, as shown. These loans increase the money supply again—by $640,000.

Bank 2

Assets		Liabilities	
Total reserves	+ $800,000	Demand deposits	+ $800,000
Required reserves	(160,000)		
Excess reserves	(640,000)		
Total	+ $800,000	Total	+ $800,000

Bank 2

Assets		Liabilities	
Total reserves	+ $160,000	Demand deposits	+ $800,000
Required reserves	(160,000)		
Excess reserves	(–0–)		
Loans	+ 640,000		
Total	+ $800,000	Total	+ $800,000

But we can't stop here. We assume that another firm has taken the $640,000 loan from the bank in anticipation of buying into an oil drilling fund later. This fund has a bank account at bank 3. Now look at bank 3's simplified T account, where again we look only at changes in the account.

When the depositor pays the $640,000 to the fund managers who bank in bank 3, total reserves go up by that amount. Required reserves are 20 percent, or $128,000, and excess reserves are $512,000. Bank 3, too, will want to lend out these non-income-earning assets. When it does, total reserves fall to $128,000, excess reserves become zero, and loans, increasing by $512,000, add the same amount to the money supply.

Bank 3

Assets		Liabilities	
Total reserves	+ $640,000	Demand deposits	+ $640,000
Required reserves	(128,000)		
Excess reserves	(512,000)		
Total	+ $640,000	Total	+ $640,000

Bank 3

Assets		Liabilities	
Total reserves	+ $128,000	Demand deposits	+ $640,000
Required reserves	(128,000)		
Excess reserves	(–0–)		
Loans	+ 512,000		
Total	+ $640,000	Total	+ $640,000

This process goes on and on and on. Each bank gets a smaller and smaller increase in deposits and each bank makes a correspondingly smaller amount of loans.

But what happened to the total money supply? In this simple model, the money supply was increased by the $1 million the Fed gave to the private individual in exchange for a bond; it was increased also by the $800,000 deposit in bank 2; and it was increased again by the $640,000 deposit in bank 3. Eventually, in fact, the money supply will be increased by a total approaching $5 million! This can be seen in Table 11-4, which is graphically represented by Figure 11-3.

The key to understanding how the money supply can be increased in this manner is remembering that the original new deposit in bank 1 was in the form of a check written on the Federal Reserve and therefore represented new reserves to the banking system. Had that check been written on another bank, bank 5 for example, nothing would have happened to the total amount of demand deposits and hence to the total money supply, for what one bank gained another bank would lose. This is not the case when the additional deposit that forms additional reserves comes from the Federal Reserve System itself. The commercial banking system, then, can increase the money supply primarily because excess reserves are created by the Federal Reserve System.

Table 11-4 The Maximum Potential Effects on the Money Supply of an Increase in Reserves of $1 Million with a 20% Required Reserve

BANK	NEW DEPOSIT	POSSIBLE LOANS (= EXCESS RESERVES)	REQUIRED RESERVES
Bank 1	$1,000,000	$ 800,000	$ 200,000
Bank 2	800,000	640,000	160,000
Bank 3	640,000	512,000	128,000
Bank 4	512,000	409,600	102,400
Bank 5	409,600	327,680	81,920
Bank 6	327,690	262,140	65,540
Bank 7	262,140	209,710	52,430
Bank 8	209,710	167,760	41,950
All other banks	838,870	671,110	167,760
Total	$5,000,000	$4,000,000	$1,000,000

The Expansion Multiplier

We can now make a generalization about the extent to which the money supply will increase when the banking system's reserves are increased. If we assume that no excess reserves are kept and that all loans are spent and deposited in other banks in the system, then the following equation applies:

$$\text{Maximum deposit expansion multiplier} = \frac{1}{\text{required reserve percentage}}$$

In our example, the required reserve level was 20 percent, or 1/5. Therefore, the maximum deposit expansion multiplier was 5, and that's exactly what we show in Table 11-4 and Figure 11-3: A $1 million increase in reserves due to a Federal Reserve purchase causing a $5 million increase in demand deposits and hence in the money supply.

The deposit expansion multiplier equals the maximum potential change in the money supply due to a change in reserves. Notice we use

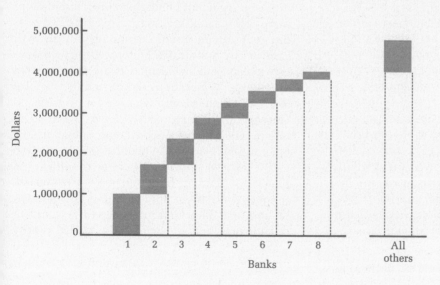

FIGURE 11-3 The Multiple Expansion in the Money Supply Due to $1 Million in New Reserve

The banks are all aligned in decreasing order of new deposits created. This is merely a graphical representation of Table 11-4.

the word "change" rather than "increase" because reserves can also be reduced by the Fed (when, for example, it sells a bond in the open market), and in that case we would see a multiple contraction in the money supply.

It may be easier to see this multiple expansion and contraction by picturing a monopoly bank that takes care of all banking services in the United States. In this case, an individual would deposit the proceeds from a bond sale to the Fed in the monopoly bank. The monopoly bank, since it receives all deposits and grants all loans, could immediately lend a multiple of its excess reserves, producing a 5 to 1 expansion in bank deposits, because every loan it made, whether spent or put into a checking account, would ultimately return to the monopoly bank, which would never lose reserves to any other bank. The T account of a monopoly bank would look the same as the consolidated balance sheet for all banks in the system.

Note that we made a number of simplifying assumptions to come up with the maximum potential deposit expansion multiplier. In the real world, however, the expansion (or contraction) multiplier is considerably smaller. Several factors account for this.

Leakages The entire loan from one bank is not always deposited in another bank. Rather, some borrowed funds remain in circulation, as cash or currency. As a result, the expansion multiplier is smaller than the maximum.

Excess Reserves Banks do not always keep excess reserves at zero. And to the extent that they want to keep positive excess reserves, the deposit expansion multiplier will be smaller. To test your understanding, go back to the example we used and find the multiplier, assuming required reserves of 20 percent and excess reserves of 5 percent at all times.

The Desire to Borrow We have implicitly assumed that individuals and businesses want to borrow whatever the banks want to lend. However, whenever or not this is the case, the deposit expansion multiplier will be lower. Borrowers, for whatever reason, may not want to borrow.

The actual relationship between the total money supply (which includes currency) and reserves is definitely smaller than its potential maximum.

The Tools of Monetary Policy

Monetary policy in the United States is carried out by the Federal Reserve System. We have already discussed one of the major tools of that monetary policy: changes in excess reserves by open-market operations. Now, we will go into more detail about open-market operations and discuss the other two major policy tools used by the Fed. In all cases, these policy tools are aimed at altering the supply of money in the United States.

Open-Market Operations

We have seen that if the Fed purchases a United States government bond, the money supply will increase by a multiple; similarly, if the Fed sells the government bond, the money supply will contract by a multiple. Federal Reserve monetary policy is concentrated in its open-market operations. When the Fed, through the Federal Reserve Open Market Committee, desires to "loosen up," it instructs the New York Fed to buy United States government bonds in the open market. When the Fed decides to "tighten up," it instructs the New York Fed to sell United States government bonds in the open market. In these ways, the supply of money is expanded or contracted. A multiple change (expansion or contraction) in the level of the money supply occurs with any change in the level of total reserves. Most changes in our money supply

TIME 3:15
TEMPERATURE 57
PRIME INTEREST RATE 11.75

Drawing by Bernard Schoenbaum; © 1974
The New Yorker Magazine, Inc.

are due to open-market operations like this.[1]

Member-Bank Borrowing and the Discount Rate

If a commercial bank wants to increase its loans but has reached the limit of its reserves, there

is only one way it can expand its deposits, and that is by borrowing reserve funds. One place it can borrow reserves is from the Fed itself. (This is another way the money supply is expanded.) The commercial bank member goes to the Federal Reserve Discount Window and asks for a loan of a certain amount of reserves. The Fed does not have to lend reserves to requesting member banks because it is not required to do so by law. Reserve borrowing by the member banks is a privilege—not a right. In any event, the Fed charges these member banks for any reserves that it lends them. The rate that the Fed charges used to be called the

[1]Actually, since Sept. 12, 1968, the Federal Reserve open-market operations do not work as simply as this. On that date, some new rules were put into effect. The most important one was that the current week's required reserves were to be calculated on the basis of average daily deposits 2 weeks *earlier*.

"rediscount rate," but now it is typically called the **discount rate.** In Canada and England, it is called the *bank rate.* When the newspapers report that the Fed has increased the discount rate from 7 percent to 8 percent, you know that the Fed has increased its charge for lending reserves to member banks. Note, however, that the discount rate is *not* the charge that banks must pay when borrowing money to lend you. The discount rate is applied to a very small percentage of total bank reserves.

Member banks actually do not often go to the Fed to borrow reserves because the Fed will not lend them everything they want. In addition, the Fed can always refuse to lend money to member banks even when the commercial banks need the money to make their reserve account meet legal requirements. There are, however, alternative sources for the banks to tap when they want to expand their reserves or when they need reserves to meet a requirement. If a commercial bank, for example, discovers that its required reserves are $200 million but that it only has $190 million in actual reserves, it can go to the **Federal Funds Market.** Since some banks are at the same time probably going to have excess reserves, banks wanting to borrow reserves can do so in that market. In fact, almost all reserve borrowing is done in the Federal Funds Market. Usually, the borrowing is for overnight only.

Reserve Requirement Changes

Another less-often used but still very important method by which the Fed can alter the money supply is to change reserve requirements. Previously, we assumed that reserve requirements were given. Actually, these requirements are set by the Fed within limits established by Congress. In Table 11-2 those limits were given along with the current reserve requirements.

What would a change in reserve requirements from 10 to 20 percent do (if there were no excess reserves)? We already discovered that the deposit expansion multiplier was the reserve requirement percentage turned upside down. If reserve requirements are 10 percent, then the deposit expansion multiplier *in principle* would be the reciprocal of 1/10, or 10. If, for some reason, the Fed decided to double reserve requirements to 20 percent, then the deposit expansion multiplier would equal the reciprocal of 1/5, or 5. The deposit expansion multiplier is therefore inversely related to reserve requirements. If the Fed decides to increase reserve requirements, then we will see a decrease in the deposit expansion multiplier. With a given level of reserves, the money supply will therefore contract.

Let's take a simple example. Suppose that the deposit expansion multiplier is in fact 10, and that reserves are $100 billion. We know then that the money supply is going to be $1 trillion. If the Federal Reserve decides to change member bank reserve requirements from 10 to 20 percent, we expect the money supply eventually to fall to only $500 billion because the deposit expansion multiplier will fall from 10 to 5 (if there are no excess reserves). What happens is that, as reserve requirements are raised, banks find they are in the red with the Fed. They must call in loans, for example, to increase their reserves to the new required level. When all banks attempt to do this, there will be a multiple contraction in the money supply.

Notice the difference between this method and the first two methods the Federal Reserve has for changing the total money supply in circulation. When the Fed makes open-market purchases or sales of bonds, it directly alters the bank reserves. When the Fed decides to lend more money at the discount window, it again directly alters the bank reserves. (Recall that the change in the money supply is equal to the change in the bank reserves times the deposit expansion multiplier.) When the Fed alters reserve requirements, however, it does not change the bank reserves as we have defined it. Rather, it changes the deposit expansion multiplier. When the Fed changes the deposit expansion multiplier without any offsetting change in the bank reserves, a change in the money supply will result.

However, open-market operations allow the Federal Reserve to control the money supply much more precisely than do changes in reserve requirements. A small change in reserve requirements will result in a very large change in the money supply, if there are no changes in the bank reserves. That is why the Federal Reserve does not change reserve requirements very often. When requirements are changed, they are changed in very small steps. Usually the Fed will also offset at least part of the change in the money supply by engaging in open-market operations to change the monetary base in the direction opposite the expected money supply change.

The Dynamics of Monetary Policy

We live in a world of change. We live in a world of rising incomes and rising population. The money supply grows as the economy around us grows and monetary policy changes. The Fed is continually changing the rate of growth of the money supply. For example, the money supply may be growing at 6 percent a year when the Fed decides to "tighten up." Then, by its open-market operations, the Fed may cause the money supply to grow at only a 4 percent rate per year. Thus, when we talk about contractionary monetary policy, we are usually referring to decreasing the rate of growth in the money supply. When we talk about an expansionary monetary policy, we are usually referring to increasing the rate of growth in the money supply. The dynamics of monetary policy, however, do not essentially change the analysis we have given. Understanding the dynamic nature of monetary policy should pose no problems in later chapters.

Definitions of New
Terms

Fiduciary Monetary System: A system in which currency is issued by the government, and its value is based uniquely on the public's *faith* that the currency represents command over goods and services.

Commodity Currency: A money supply composed of actual commodities, such as cigarettes or bottles of cognac. These commodities are used in place of bills and checking accounts.

Barter: A system where goods and services are exchanged without the use of a medium of exchange, or money.

Liquidity: A characteristic of any asset, it describes the degree to which the asset can be acquired or disposed of without much danger of any intervening loss in nominal value and without relatively high transactions costs. Money is the most liquid asset.

Fractional Reserve Banking System: A system of banking whereby member banks keep only a fraction of their deposits on reserve.

Excess Reserves: The difference between a member bank's actual reserves and the reserves required by law.

Discount Rate: The interest rate the Federal Reserve charges for reserves it lends to member commercial banks. Sometimes referred to as the rediscount rate or, in Canada and England, the bank rate.

Federal Funds Market: A private market (made up of member commercial banks) from which banks can borrow reserves from other banks that want to lend them. Federal funds are usually lent for overnight.

Chapter Summary

1. It is important to distinguish between money and income. Income is what you earn; money is a form in which you hold your wealth.

2. We use money as a medium of exchange and therefore do not use a barter system. Our monetary system is fiduciary in the sense that the currency is issued by the government, and its usefulness depends on the public's faith in its command over goods and services.

3. Money also serves as a unit of accounting and a store of value.

4. The money supply can be defined in many ways. Usually it is defined as currency in the hands of the public plus demand deposits or checking account balances in commercial banks. This definition is often labeled M_1. If we add time deposits in commercial banks, we get M_2. If we further add deposits in noncommercial banks and thrift institutions, we get M_3.

5. Our central bank is the Federal Reserve System, created by the Federal Reserve Act of December 23, 1913. The Federal Reserve is an independent agency of the federal government composed of a Board of Governors and 12 Federal Reserve banks, which have a total of 24 branches.

6. Members of the Federal Reserve System are required to keep reserves equalling a certain percentage of their deposits. Since this percentage is not 100 percent, we have a fractional reserve banking system.

7. A change in the reserves in the banking system will lead to a multiple change in the total money supply outstanding. The maximum increase is given by the deposit expansion multiplier, which is merely the reciprocal of the reserve requirement. However, the maximum deposit expansion multiplier is rarely reached because of leakages, excess reserves, and changing desires to lend and borrow.

8. The three tools in monetary policy are open-market operations, changes in the discount rate, and changes in reserve requirements. Open-market operations are by far the most important monetary policy tool.

Questions for Thought and Discussion

1. Do you think that actual reserves would fall to zero if there were no legal requirements?

2. Why would some people prefer that banks be required to hold 100 percent reserves?

3. Would you prefer to live in an economy without money? Why?

4. What is the difference between the money multiplier given by the reciprocal of the reserve requirement and the actual money multiplier? Why is there this difference?

5. How can banks get away with holding reserves equal only to a fraction of their total deposits?

6. If you ask a banker if he can create money, he will definitely tell you no. In fact, he is right; as an individual banker he cannot. Why is it, then, that the banking system taken as a whole can create money?

7. Since reserves earn no interest, why would a bank ever want to hold excess reserves?

8. Problem:

Multiple Money Supply Creation

Round	Deposits	Reserves	Loans
Bank 1	$1,000,000	$ _____	$ _____
Bank 2	$ _____	$ _____	$ _____
Bank 3	$ _____	$ _____	$ _____
Bank 4	$ _____	$ _____	$ _____
Bank 5	$ _____	$ _____	$ _____
All other banks	$ _____	$ _____	$ _____
Totals			

Bank 1 has received a deposit of $1,000,000. Assuming the banks retain no excess reserves, answer the following:

(a) The reserve requirement is 5 percent. Fill in the blanks. What is the money multiplier?

(b) Now the reserve requirement is 25 percent. Fill in the blanks. What is the money multiplier?

Selected
References

Angell, N., *The Story of Money*, Philadelphia: Stokes, 1929.

Board of Governors of the Federal Reserve System, *The Federal Reserve System: Purposes and Functions*, 5th ed., Washington, D.C.: U.S. Government Printing Office, 1963; see chaps. 1 and 4 in particular.

Chandler, Lester V., *The Economics of Money and Banking*, 6th ed., New York: Harper & Row, 1973.

Maisel, Sherman J., *Managing the Dollar*, New York: W. W. Norton, 1973.

Ritter, Lawrence S. and William L. Silber, *Money*, 2d ed., New York: Basic Books, 1973.

Robertson, D. H., *Money*, 6th ed., New York: Pitman, 1948.

Doctor of High Finance

ARTHUR BURNS
**Chairman, Federal Reserve
Board of Governors**

Photo by Dennis Brack, from Black Star

Shortly after becoming chairman of the Federal Reserve Board of Governors, Arthur Burns was conducting a meeting of the Federal Open Market Committee. The staff members had prepared two alternative proposals for consideration by the full committee, as is standard procedure. Burns listened carefully to the presentation and then quietly pulled a third proposal out of his pocket. Long known for his independent thinking, Arthur Burns has been an influential economist for more than 20 years, especially during the Republican administrations of Eisenhower, Nixon, and Ford.

Burns first came into prominence in 1930 when he joined the staff of the National Bureau of Economic Research, an organization founded to provide factual background for the exploration of economic issues. There he began his study of business cycles, a field in which he is now considered an expert. In 1945 he became director of NBER.

Dwight Eisenhower brought Burns to

Washington when he appointed him chairman of the Council of Economic Advisers (CEA) in 1952, partially to restore the council's prestige, which had suffered during Truman's administration. Burns also served as chairman of the Advisory Board on Economic Growth and Stability during the Eisenhower years.

Burns' close association with Richard Nixon began in the early 1950s and was solidified during the 1960 presidential election campaign, when Burns correctly predicted the business slowdown that worked against Nixon's chances for election. During the Kennedy years, Burns returned to the National Bureau of Economic Research and taught at Columbia and Stanford. He returned to active political work as adviser on economic matters during Nixon's campaign in 1967 and 1968. After his election, Nixon created an advisory position in the Cabinet just for Burns.

The decision to move Burns from the White House to the Federal Reserve Board in 1970 was much more than an admiring gesture by a President who wanted to honor his close friend and trusted adviser. At that time, the Federal Reserve Board was a body appointed primarily by Democrats, and Nixon wanted his own man in charge.

Governments see themselves as having primarily two means of affecting the economy: changing the growth rate of the money supply as controlled by the Federal Reserve Board and using fiscal policies enacted by Congress. Burns' predecessor, William McChesney Martin, had resented the burden the Federal Reserve Board was forced to assume when Congress did not raise taxes to fund the Vietnam conflict. Burns was determined to avoid such a bind. He developed his own congressional contacts and emphasized that the Fed could not solve the country's economic problems by itself.

Like many of the President's appointees, Burns did not always see eye to eye with Nixon. In 1971, Burns publicly criticized Nixon's economic policies, which led Nixon in turn to threaten to expand the composition of the Federal Reserve Board. Burns was an early advocate of a wage-price review board because he felt that conventional fiscal and monetary tools were ineffective in combating inflation and unemployment.

Inflation has been Burns' driving preoccupation as chairman of the Federal Reserve Board. In June 1974, he warned that "the future of our country is in jeopardy" if inflation were not brought under control. At that time he imposed an even more restrictive monetary policy in the hope that this would return the country to an era of relative price stability. What was needed, for stability, he said, was a long period of slow growth to curb inflation.

During the Ford administration, Burns had come under increasing attack from both conservatives and liberals for his policies regarding the 1974 to 1975 recession. Since Burns became chairman of the Federal Reserve Board, the United States experienced its worst peacetime inflation and its worst slump since the Depression. Many economists argue that this is partially the result of Burns' policies—first, pumping too much money into the economy and then restricting the money supply too abruptly. Worried by the dangers of another Depression, critics of Burns have said the Federal Reserve Board, during a recession like that in 1974 to 1975, should expand the supply of money more rapidly and act more forcefully to lower interest rates.

Burns, whose term does not expire until 1984, has long since grown accustomed to criticism from all sides. "One of the functions of the Federal Reserve Board," he remarked, "is to be criticized."

Should Commercial Banks be Subsidized?

BORROWING FROM THE FEDERAL RESERVE

Looking at the Discount Rate from a Different Perspective

We pointed out in the last chapter that Federal Reserve member banks can, at the discretion of the Federal Reserve, borrow reserves from it at the discount rate to make up any deficiencies in required reserves. Or the bank in need of reserves can go to private sources where it must pay whatever is the going market rate. The primary source of additional reserves in the private market is the so-called Federal Funds Market, which we also discussed in the previous chapter.

In Table I-13.1 we present the average yearly Federal Funds Market rates from 1962 through 1975, along with the respective average discount rates posted by the New York Fed. Notice that there is a difference between the discount rate and the Federal Funds rate for many of the years. The difference has often been one in which the Fed has charged a lower rate of interest for reserves than has the private Federal Funds Market.

The Subsidy Aspect of the Discount Window Operations

Whenever a bank is allowed to borrow reserves from the Fed at an interest rate below the next best alternative, which is generally the Federal Funds Market, that bank is receiving a very definite subsidy. We can measure the actual amount of the subsidy by figuring the difference between the Federal Funds rate and the discount rate and multiplying that difference by the amount of the reserve loan. For example, if the Federal Funds rate is 10 percent per year and the discount rate is 7 percent per year, the difference is 3

Table I-13.1

The Difference between the Federal Funds Rate and the Discount Rate

Anytime the Federal Funds Rate exceeds the Discount Rate, any bank borrowing reserves from the Fed is obtaining an implicit subsidy equal to the interest saved.

YEAR	AVERAGE FEDERAL FUNDS RATE (PERCENT PER YEAR)	AVERAGE DISCOUNT RATE AT NEW YORK FED (PERCENT PER YEAR)
1962	2.68	3.00
1963	3.18	3.50
1964	3.50	4.00
1965	4.07	4.50
1966	5.11	4.50
1967	4.22	4.50
1968	5.66	5.50
1969	8.21	6.00
1970	7.17	5.50
1971	4.66	5.00
1972	4.44	5.50
1973	8.74	6.00
1974	10.51	8.00
1975 (January)	7.13	7.25

Source: Board of Governors of the Federal Reserve System

percent. Hence, for every $1 million loan the Fed makes through its discount window, the recipient member bank will receive an implicit subsidy at the rate of $30,000 per year. That means that if a bank were able to keep a Federal Reserve loan outstanding for 1 month, it would receive a subsidy equal to 1/12 × $30,000 or $2,500 per month for every $1 million borrowed. To get a better idea of the actual implicit subsidy given to the banking system as a whole, look at Table I-13.2. Here we take the difference between the Federal Funds rate and the discount rate as presented in Table I-13.1. Then we apply that difference to the average amount of Federal Reserve loans outstanding per year. You will notice, for example, that in 1974 the banking system as a whole obtained

an implicit subsidy of $50 million. This is not an insignificant sum.

This type of subsidy to the commercial banking system is something relatively new in the history of banking. If we look, for example, at the difference between the Fed's discount rate and the Federal Funds rate for years prior to the 1960s and 1970s, we find much less of a difference. In fact, when discounting first started, the Fed generally set the discount rate at a level that was slightly higher than alternative market rates. Any member bank that chose to go to the Fed for a loan was essentially punished by having to pay a higher rate of interest.

The question then remains, "Why is the Fed subsidizing member commercial banks today, and is such subsidization desirable from a policy

point of view?" The best way to find answers is to look at one of the best-known examples of the Fed using its power to help an individual bank.

A Case History of Subsidization

In 1974 the nation's twentieth largest bank, Franklin National, on Long Island, got into serious trouble. It had engaged in extensive foreign currency speculations and had lost money. There were also apparently other reasons why it had been mismanaged. In any event, the bank was in trouble. Some of its depositors started to sense impending doom and pulled out many of their deposits. This meant that Franklin started losing reserves at an alarming rate.

Table I-13.2

The Implicit Subsidy to Member Banks by the Fed

(1) YEAR	(2) DIFFERENCE BETWEEN AVERAGE FEDERAL FUNDS RATE AND AVERAGE DISCOUNT RATE	(3) AVERAGE AMOUNT OWED BY MEMBER BANKS TO THE FED (IN MILLIONS OF DOLLARS)	(4) IMPLICIT SUBSIDY (COLUMN 2 × COLUMN 3) (IN MILLIONS OF DOLLARS)
1962	−.0022	304	− 0.67
1963	−.0032	327	− 1.05
1964	−.0050	243	− 1.22
1965	−.0043	454	− 1.95
1966	+.0061	557	+ 3.40
1967	−.0028	238	− 0.67
1968	+.0012	765	+ 0.92
1969	+.0221	1,086	+24.00
1970	+.0167	321	+ 5.36
1971	−.0034	107	− 0.36
1972	−.0106	1,049	−11.12
1973	+.0274	1,298	+35.57
1974	+.0251	2,050	+51.46
1975 (Jan.)	+.0012	390	+ 0.47

Source: Board of Governors of the Federal Reserve System

It had to go heavily into debt to make up these lost reserves. When it looked as if the bank might go under, the Federal Reserve stepped in and lent Franklin, through the Fed discount window, approximately $1.5 billion. The loan was made at the current discount rate of 7½ percent per year. At this same time, the Federal Funds rate ranged from 10.5 percent to 12.9 percent. The difference, and hence the implicit subsidy, was thus around 3 to 4 percentage points per year on whatever loans were made available. Since Franklin was given about $1.5 billion, the implicit subsidy was about $1 million per week! It should be noted that this subsidy was not voted on by Congress. It was given at will by the Fed.

This subsidy was provided to Franklin to prevent its demise; it was feared that if Franklin National went under, the banking system as a whole might suffer. The subsidy notwithstanding, however, Franklin

National was eventually forced into bankruptcy proceedings and was immediately taken over by another bank. It is interesting, nonetheless, to examine this reasoning that a large bank should be prevented from failing because of the potentially deleterious effect its failure would have on the entire banking system and hence on the economy in general.

Protecting the Banking System

A bank can fail for a variety of reasons. Today, however, a bank fails usually because of poor management. There is no difference in theory between operating a bank and operating a clothing store or a record shop. All three are profit-seeking enterprises. The main function of a bank is to provide checking and savings account services to its clients and to provide loans. Additionally, banks buy interest-earning securi-

ties. The business of running a bank involves choosing an appropriate portfolio, as it is called, of different types of earning assets. In the case of Franklin National, certain officers of the bank apparently felt that more earning assets should be held in the form of foreign currency balances which they hoped could be sold later at a higher price than they had paid. When instead the price dropped, the bank suffered a loss rather than a profit. This situation is actually no different from the bank making loans to customers who don't pay them off. If the bank makes too many "bad" loans, it may suffer a loss in its loan operations. Sound management of a bank requires the weighing of potential risks against potential gains. In the case of Franklin National and other banks that have failed, sound management did not prevail.

The above is merely a rundown of how a bank is managed and what can go wrong. What we are trying to understand is how one bank's demise might lead to a collapse in the entire banking system. In the early 1930s, at the beginning of the Great Depression, banks began failing right and left; when one bank failed, it would trigger the failure of another as depositors got cold feet and tried to withdraw all their funds. As an increasing number of depositors attempted to withdraw their bank deposits, an ever-increasing number became insolvent. If that were possible today, we could indeed understand the case for subsidizing banks with reserves from the Federal Reserve discount window at a below market rate of interest. However, times have changed, and the reason they have changed is because we now have federal deposit insurance, which protects depositors from the loss of their deposits even if the bank fails completely. It all involves the Federal Deposit Insurance Corporation.

The Federal Deposit Insurance Corporation

The Federal Deposit Insurance Corporation (FDIC) was established during the Depression in 1934. Its principal purpose was to insure commercial bank deposits. The establishment of deposit insurance has been considered by banking historians as perhaps the most significant banking legislation since the creation of the Federal Reserve System itself in 1913.

All member banks of the Federal Reserve System are required to belong to the FDIC, and most non-member banks also have joined. Presently, the FDIC insures the deposits of each individual or firm in each bank up to $40,000. Banks that have insurance must pay an annual premium equal to one-twelfth of 1 percent of their total deposits.

The FDIC has come to the rescue of depositors in a number of small bank failures, as well as in a number of more spectacular large ones. The number of banks that actually fail in any given year, however, is extremely small—on the order of 2 to 10. In most cases, depositors receive close to 100 percent of the funds they had in the bank. Generally, the FDIC will force the failing bank to merge with a more liquid bank.

The FDIC, in addition to providing almost complete insurance to individual depositors, also provides a

psychological barrier against a banking panic or a collapse because depositors no longer need fear the possible loss of their deposits. And since in all practicality there never again will be a general run on banks because of the existence of FDIC, many students of our banking system contend that there is little need to subsidize failing banks. They point out that if such subsidization con-

tinues as it has in the past couple of decades, the competitive control mechanism that weeds out bad management in banks will be seriously weakened. If bad management does not lead to the total collapse of a bank because the Fed steps in and props it up, then there is less incentive to minimize bad management; or rather, there is less of a check on the improper handling of a bank's portfolio, and bank managers will rationally opt for greater profit at excessive risk in their investment decisions.

The Pros and Cons Summarized

Should banks be subsidized by loans made at below market interest rates? Those who favor subsidization contend that banks in trouble should be at least temporarily bailed out to maintain confidence in the banking system as a whole and the economy in general. Additionally, those who favor subsidization feel that it provides for the smooth functioning of the banking system because it prevents precipitous collapses in individual banks.

Opponents of bank subsidization, however, contend that it is impossible for us ever to have a run on banks because the FDIC insures deposits. Therefore the subsidization of banks in trouble merely reduces the cost of bad managers to the bank's stockholders and leads to an inefficient use of our banking resources.

Perhaps you can think of other pro and con arguments. What conclusions can you draw from your arguments?

Questions for Thought and Discussion

1. "The banking system is the cornerstone of the American economy. The banking system must be preserved at all cost." Analyze this quote.
2. What is the difference between the Federal Funds rate and the Federal Reserve discount rate?
3. Member-bank borrowing from the Fed's discount window is considered a privilege and not a right. Does this have any effect on how much member banks feel they can use the discount window?
4. Why does lending money to member banks at a below market rate of interest constitute a form of subsidization?

Selected Reference

O'Bannon, Helen B. et al., *Money and Banking: Theory, Policy, and Institutions,* New York: Harper & Row, 1975, p. 356ff.

Money in a Keynesian Model

In Chapter 3, we discussed the elements of basic supply and demand. In the last chapter, we discussed what determines the supply of money. In this chapter we will discuss what determines the demand for money. Then we will integrate a simplified demand for money relationship into the income and employment determination model (generally considered a Keynesian model) used in Chapters 9 and 10.

The Demand for Money or Cash

Why do people want to hold money, rather than, for example, invest it in bonds, or savings and loan shares, or houses, or any of the other myriad assets that can replace money? One way of looking at the determinants of the demand for money is to look at the motives behind holding money. The British economist John Maynard Keynes outlined three motives: transactions, precautionary, and speculative.

Transactions Demand for Money

This is probably the most widely understood motive for holding money. It hinges on the use of money as a medium of exchange. Individuals desire to use money in order to handle the ordinary, day-to-day transactions in their lives. Without money, such transactions would be costly indeed. The amount of money desired for transaction purposes generally depends on the volume of purchases to be made per unit time. The amount needed will also depend on the frequency of income payments—that is, the more frequent the payments, the smaller the average amount of money needed to finance transactions.

Precautionary Demand for Money

The precautionary motive for holding money is related to the use of money's function as a temporary store of value. Money provides individuals with protection against certain risks. In other words, having completely liquid balances provides a cushion against abrupt reductions in income due to illness, accident, or unemployment. Businesses may need money or complete liquidity to meet unexpected payments for increased costs and also to take advantage of unanticipated opportunities for a quick expansion of profits.

The Speculative Demand for Money

Money provides individuals with the liquidity necessary to shift rapidly into other assets. This motive is called the speculative motive because it involves outguessing the movements in the prices of alternative assets such as bonds or stocks. If, for example, it is anticipated that bond prices will fall in the future, individuals may well want to hold more money today to take advantage of lower bond prices in the future.

In the remainder of this chapter we will concentrate on the speculative demand for money. For us to completely understand it, however, we must understand the role of interest rates in our economy and know the relationship between movements in the general level of interest rates and in the market value of bonds.

Interest Rates: An Introduction

The concept of interest dates back to the time of the Romans, when the laws stated that the defaulting party to a contract had to pay his creditor some sort of compensation. During medieval times, lawyers used the legal tactic of *damna et interesse* to extract such compensation. Thus, *interesse* became a charge for the use of money under the guise of indemnity for failure to fulfill a contract.

Indeed, interest rates have played a very special role in much of macroeconomic theory. The investment schedule is negatively related to the rate of interest. Actually, every specific lending market has its own interest rate. The bond market where the Federal Reserve sells and buys government bonds has its own interest rate. The housing (mortgage) market has its own interest rate and so do savings and loan associations. There is a particular interest rate for every type of market lending instrument.

Interest Rates and Bond Prices

Suppose you bought a bond for $1,000 which had an infinite lifetime—that is, it could never be turned in to the original issuer for the $1,000 face value. (You could, of course, sell it to another person.) In compensation for your loan of $1,000 to the bond issuer, you would get a large number of coupons that had the years 1977, 1978, 1979, and so on written on them, along with the following inscription: "Send this in on December 31 and you will get back $100 in the mail." The "coupon rate" on your **consol** (a bond with no maturity date) would, therefore, be 10 percent per year because you would get $100 interest per $1,000 invested every year. (Although consols exist in the United Kingdom, they are not used in the United States. We will use them in our own example only to simplify the analysis.) Let's say at the time you bought this $1,000 bond, with a coupon rate of 10 percent, other bonds of equal risk also yielded 10 percent per year. Assume also that *there had never been inflation in the past and that none was expected in the future.*

Now suppose, for some reason, prices suddenly started to rise at a rate of 10 percent a year and are expected to continue rising forever at that rate. Now would anybody pay you $1,000 for a bond with a coupon rate of 10 percent? Probably not because now $100 a year would just cover the loss in purchasing power of the bond you were holding. Most people would require an inflationary premium of 10 percent in addition to some real compensation for lending the money in the first place. That means that interest rates in the economy would rise from 10 to, say, 20 percent. The value of *your* bond would now be only $500 since that would make the $100 coupon give the current interest yield of 20 percent on a $500 investment. If you tried to sell your bond, you would get no more than $500. Notice that *the interest rate and the price of the bond are inversely related.* In fact, we have a formula for bonds with an infinite life; this formula is also approximately correct for bonds with very long lives. The value of $1 in interest payments per year *forever* is equal to $1 divided by i, where i is the nominal rate of interest:

$$\text{Value today of \$1 in interest payments forever} = \frac{\$1}{i}$$

In this example, $100 was paid out per year. With a market rate of interest of 10 percent, our formula tells us that the price of the bond was $100 divided by 0.10, or $1,000. When the market rate of interest rose to 20 percent, the market value of the bond equaled $100 divided by 0.20, or $500. Even if you could be absolutely sure of getting all your interest payments, you can never be certain that the price of the bond will equal what you paid for it. Any time market interest rates in the economy rise, the price of existing bonds fall. And of course, if interest rates fall, the price of your fixed-income-producing bond will rise.

The Demand for Money and the Interest Rate

In a simplified Keynesian analysis, we assume that people's demand for money—cash balances—depends mainly upon the cost of holding that money. What is the cost of holding money? The cost equals the earnings you could have had if you had invested that money. You have the opportunity, for example, to buy bonds with your money. If the interest rate on bonds is 10 percent per year and you decide to hold your cash rather than buy bonds, then the cost of holding that cash is 10 percent per year. We would expect that the higher the cost of holding money, the less money would be demanded. We can therefore construct on a graph a downward sloping demand function for money with the nominal interest rate on the vertical axis. We have done just that in Figure 12-1. The horizontal axis measures the quantity of money in billions of dollars; the vertical axis measures the interest rate yield on bonds. As interest rates go up, the quantity of money demanded falls. As interest rates go down, the quantity of money demanded rises. This is a demand schedule just like any other demand schedule except that the product in question happens to be the medium of exchange and the price happens to be the opportunity cost (interest rate) of holding that medium of exchange.

Keynes liked to call this the **liquidity preference function.** As we saw in Chapter 11, the most liquid asset around is money. You can purchase whatever you want with it, and it never loses its *face* value. A dollar is a dollar, today or tomorrow. The next most liquid asset might be savings deposits. You can take your passbook to the bank and get cash fairly rapidly.

Since money is the most liquid of all assets, the demand schedule for money can be thought of as the liquidity preference schedule. You show your preference for complete liquidity—

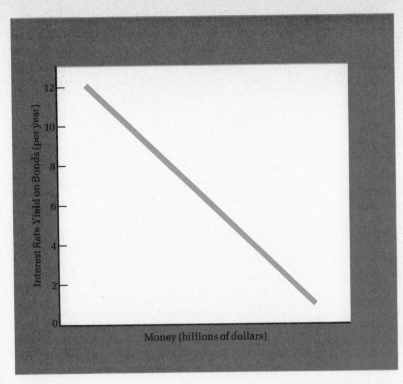

FIGURE 12-1 **The Liquidity Preference Function: The Demand for Money**

Here we show the liquidity preference function. The quantity of money demanded increases as the interest rate decreases. That is because the interest rate is the opportunity cost of holding money. As the opportunity cost falls, the quantity of money demanded will rise.

holding money—in accordance with the opportunity cost of holding it.

Another way to look at the liquidity preference function is to consider a person's *speculative motive* for holding money. Let's assume that the only alternative to holding money is buying bonds. Remember, there is an inverse relationship between the price of a fixed-income bond and the interest rate prevailing in the economy. If you are holding a bond and, for some reason, interest rates rise in the economy, you will suffer a capital loss. The value of that bond will depreciate. However, if you are holding the bond and interest rates fall, you will experience a capital gain; the value of the bond will rise. Think about how you might react to historically low interest rates in the economy. You might expect that the probability of interest rates falling is smaller than the probability of their rising. Therefore, you would not want to invest in bonds because you do not want to suffer a capital loss as interest rates rise. You would hold your speculative balances in money instead of bonds. At the other end of the spectrum, if interest rates prevailing in the economy are historically high, you might expect that the probability of interest rates falling is greater than the probability of their rising. Therefore, instead of holding your speculative balances in money, you would switch to bonds. Your demand for money would be smaller than it was at lower interest rates. Thus, the liquidity preference function slopes downward, as we have drawn it in Figure 12-1.

Adding the Money Supply

Now let's add the policy variable that can be used by the government—changes in the money supply. We can add the money supply to our liquidity preference diagram merely by drawing a vertical line wherever the money supply happens to be. Let's say the money supply is at M_s. We have drawn a vertical line at M_s in Figure 12-2. What we have in this figure is a demand schedule—liquidity preference function—and a supply schedule, which happens to be a vertical line. This means that the *supply* of money is completely insensitive to the interest rate. It is exogenous, assumed to be determined solely by the Federal Reserve. With a supply schedule and a demand schedule, we should be able to find an equilibrium point. As expected, the equilibrium is at the intersection of the supply schedule and the demand

schedule, or point E in Figure 12-2. At point E, the equilibrium interest rate happens to be 10 percent. This is the interest rate that equates the quantity of money demanded with the quantity of money supplied.

Excess Supply

If interest rates were somehow 11 percent, the quantity of money demanded would be less than the quantity supplied. Excess cash balances would be floating around. People would take those excess cash balances and buy bonds, but the increased demand for bonds would cause the price of bonds to rise. Remember, though, that there is a negative relationship between the price of bonds and the interest rate. As the price of bonds rises, the interest rate falls. In other words, when more people try to

FIGURE 12-2 Putting Together the Demand and Supply of Money

The demand schedule, *DD*, is downward sloping; the supply schedule is not only upward sloping, it is vertical at some given quantity of money supplied by the monetary authorities. The equilibrium rate of interest is at 10 percent. An interest rate of 9 percent could not prevail for very long because the quantity of money demanded would exceed the quantity supplied. For people to try to get more money, they would have to sell bonds, for example. But when they sell bonds, they must lower their price. They must offer higher yields to prospective buyers in order to get rid of the bonds; the interest rate would rise. Conversely, the interest rate couldn't last for long at 11 percent because there would be an excess supply of money. In the process of buying bonds, people bid up the price. When the price of bonds goes up, the interest rate falls because there is an inverse relationship between the price of a bond and the yield on it. The interest rate would fall to the equilibrium rate of 10 percent.

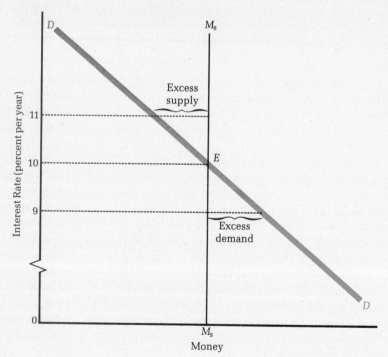

buy bonds, the only way they can do so is by accepting a lower yield—that is, a lower interest rate. Thus, when the interest rate is above the equilibrium level, the excess supply of money is translated into an increased demand for bonds, which in turn raises the price of bonds, thus lowering the interest rate.

Excess Demand

If the interest rate is lower than 10 percent or the equilibrium rate, there will be an excess demand for money. People will sell their bonds in an attempt to make up the deficiency between actual cash balances and desired cash balances; they will want to make up the deficiency between actual liquidity and desired liquidity. As people reduce their demand for bonds, the price of bonds falls. That is, the interest rate rises. Another way of looking at it is that since the demand for bonds has fallen, the only way people can be induced to hold them is by being offered higher yields—that is, higher interest rates. Hence, when the interest rate is below the equilibrium level, there is an excess demand for money that translates itself into a decreased demand for bonds; this causes the price of bonds to fall and the interest rate to rise until it reaches equilibrium.

Completing the Keynesian Model

How do we relate the monetary sector of this aspect of the Keynesian model to the rest of the model? Remember in Chapter 8 when we talked about the investment schedule? We drew it as a function of the interest rate and it sloped downward. We recreate that investment schedule in Figure 12-3. But the equilibrium interest rate has already been established by the liquidity preference function and the money supply in Figure 12-2. It is 10 percent. So we go from

the 10 percent equilibrium interest rate in Figure 12-2 to find out how much investment there is at that particular interest rate. As shown in Figure 12-3, the desired investment is $200 billion. We can now find out what equilibrium income will be given at that level of investment. We go to the $C + I + G$ diagram that we have drawn in Figure 12-4. C and G are already given. We add $200 billion worth of investment to get the $C + I + G$ schedule as shown in the figure. Equilibrium income turns out to be $2.0 trillion.

Transmitting Monetary Policy

You should now have some idea of how monetary policy works in a simplified Keynesian system. We assumed that the money supply was an exogenous variable, under the control of the Federal Reserve System. Suppose now that, for some reason, equilibrium income is less than full-employment income. Suppose, as shown in Figure 12-4, that the $C + I + G$ schedule intersects the 45 degree line (where total spending always equals total income) at only $2 trillion when the full-employment level of income is $2.125 trillion. We shall assume that the government decides monetary policy is the appropriate tool to use in stimulating the economy up to its full-employment level. The government decides therefore to increase the money supply; it goes out into the open market and buys government bonds. When the government buys bonds, it increases the reserves of banks. Those banks will not want to keep the excess reserves in the Federal Reserve banks; they will therefore start lending money. A chain reaction starts, whereby the money supply expands in a multiple of the change in reserves. If the money multiplier happens to be 3, then the money supply will expand by three times the original purchase of bonds by the Federal Reserve.

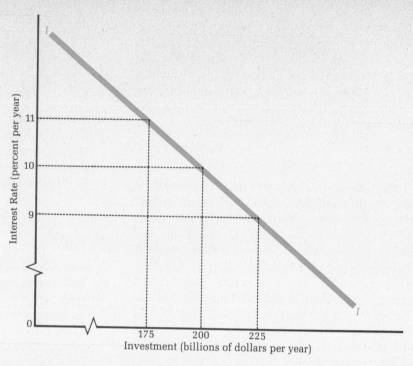

FIGURE 12-3 **The Investment Schedule**

The investment schedule represents the demand for investment. It slopes downward like all demand curves. The price, though, is not in terms of dollars but in terms of the interest rate measured on the vertical axis. At an 11 percent rate of interest, the investment schedule tells us there will be $175 billion worth of investment. At a 10 percent interest rate, there would be $200 billion, and, at a 9 percent interest rate, there would be $225 billion worth of investment.

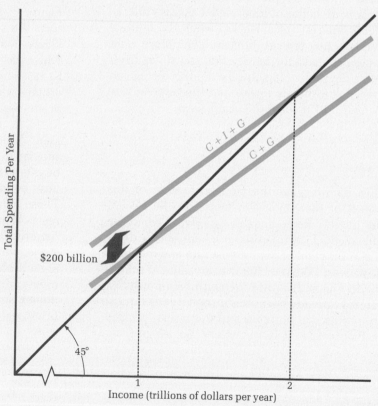

FIGURE 12-4 **Finding the Equilibrium Level of Income**

Without investment, the $C + G$ schedule intersects the 45 degree spending-equals-income line at $1 trillion. We take the $200 billion of investment from Figure 12-3 and add it vertically to the $C + G$ line to get $C + G + I$, which now intersects the 45 degree line at an equilibrium income of $2 trillion. Here we have assumed, as always, that the multiplier is 5 because the marginal propensity to save is assumed to be 0.2 or 1/5.

How do we show that on our graph for the demand and supply of money? In Figure 12-5, we have drawn the original supply curve of money as M_s, the vertical line. Now we increase M_s to M'_s and draw another vertical line to represent the larger money supply. But, at the same interest rate as before (10 percent), there is an excess supply of money in circulation. According to this particular Keynesian theory, people will therefore attempt to buy bonds with their excess money balances. When they all attempt to buy bonds with their excess money balances, they will bid up the price of those bonds; that is, the interest rate will fall. Obviously, it will fall to the point of equilibrium, where the liquidity preference function (demand for money curve) and the vertical supply of money function intersect. In our particular example, that happens to be at an interest rate of 9 percent.

Looking back at our investment schedule in Figure 12-3, we find that a decrease in the interest rate from 10 percent to 9 percent causes an increase in investment of $25 billion. We add that $25 billion of investment to our $C + I + G$ schedule in Figure 12-6 to get $C + I' + G$, which is $25 billion higher than the old schedule. Now look at where the new $C + I' + G$ schedule intersects the 45 degree line. If we assume that the marginal propensity to consume is 0.8, then the marginal propensity to save is 0.2 or 1/5. The multiplier is the reciprocal of the marginal propensity to save, or 5. A $25 billion increase in investment will eventually lead to a $125 billion increase in income, which is shown in Figure 12-6. Equilibrium income has been raised to a full-employment level of $2.125 trillion. As we can see, expansionary monetary policy has been successful in this particular model.

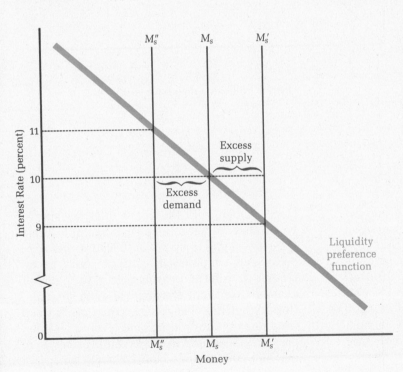

FIGURE 12-5 **Effects of Changes in the Money Supply**

If the money supply starts out at M_s, the equilibrium interest rate will be 10 percent. If the monetary authorities increase the money supply to M'_s, then at the old interest rate of 10 percent, there will be an excess supply of money. People's attempts at getting rid of this excess supply of money will cause the equilibrium interest rate to fall to 9 percent. That is, as people buy bonds with their excess supplies of money, they will drive up the price of bonds and thereby lower the interest rate. On the other hand, if the monetary authorities contract the money supply to M''_s at the old equilibrium interest rate of 10 percent, there will be an excess demand for money. As individuals sell their bonds to get into equilibrium, they will be forced to accept a lower price for those bonds. That is, they will be forced to pay a higher interest rate to get rid of the bonds. The equilibrium interest rate will rise to 11 percent.

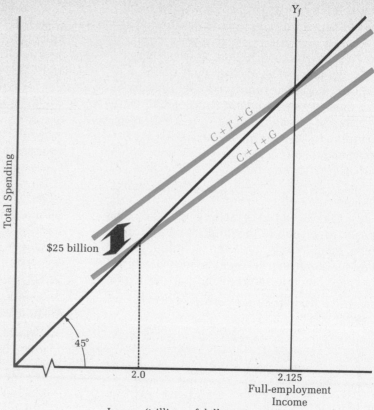

FIGURE 12-6 **Effective Monetary Policy**

Suppose that the economy finds itself in an underemployment situation where income is only $2.0 trillion. That is at the point where the $C + I + G$ curve intersects the 45 degree spending = income line. The Fed then decides to use monetary policy to increase equilibrium income and reduce unemployment. In a simplified Keynesian world such as we have outlined in this chapter, the Fed would increase the money supply by buying bonds in the open market. Having an excess supply of money, the public will demand more bonds. As it demands more bonds, the interest rate falls. As the interest rate falls, investment increases from I to I', where I' is greater than I by $25 billion. The $C + I + G$ schedule now shifts up to $C + I' + G$. Equilibrium income, that is, the intersection of $C + I' + G$ with the 45 degree spending = income line, is now at $2.125 trillion or full-employment income.

Closing the Inflationary Gap

To increase your understanding of the monetary mechanism in a Keynesian model, assume the economy is operating at more than full employment. Redo Figure 12-6, now labeling $2 trillion as the full-employment level of national income per year. Draw the $C + I + G$ line such that there is an inflationary gap. Assume that the equilibrium level of national income is $2.125 trillion. What should the monetary authorities do in this situation?

The Transmission Mechanism

One problem with the above analyses should be pointed out here. In our first example, there were no changes in prices because we were below *full* employment. Output could be increased without increasing prices. In the other example we were starting out with an inflationary setting. Therefore, when we moved from one equilibrium income level to another, prices changed, and in our example prices were the only things that could change since we started at full employment. It must be realized, therefore, that we weren't strictly correct in discussing all our variables in *nominal* terms. We probably should have talked about changes in the real money supply—that is, the nominal money supply divided by the price level. Also, we probably should have made the distinction between real and nominal interest rates. We can, however, forget about those problems for the moment and recapitulate the transmission mechanism of monetary policy in our model:

The transmission mechanism = a change in the money supply → a change in the interest rate → a change in investment → a change in income → a change in employment and/or price level

This transmission mechanism says nothing about the magnitude of a change in investment due to a change in the interest rate. In other words, we have to know something about the interest elasticity of the demand for investment. There is a general consensus among Keynesian economists that this interest elasticity of investment demand is not great. In other words, a change in the interest rate may indeed cause an increase in the rate of planned investment, but the increase will be rather small. In the extreme case, if the investment schedule in Figure 12-3 were completely vertical, monetary policy could have no effect; all it would do is change the interest rate. There would be no resulting change in investment and hence no change in income and employment.

When Monetary Policy Doesn't Work

In his *General Theory*, Keynes mentioned the possibility of a situation in which changes in monetary policy would have no effect whatsoever. Let's see whether we can analyze the situation he suggested. Imagine a period when interest rates are historically very low. Let's say

that the interest rate is only 2 percent. You might think that the probability of interest rates rising was much greater than the probability of interest rates falling. If so, you would probably not want to put your money into bonds because you would try to avoid a consequent capital loss. You would reason that there is a high probability that the value of those bonds will decrease. After all, there is an inverse relationship between the prevailing interest rate in the economy and the value of any fixed-income bonds you might be holding. If interest rates fall, you're better off. The value of your bonds will rise. But if interest rates rise, you're worse off. The value of your bonds will fall. We might expect, therefore, that at very low interest rates, people would be unwilling to exchange money—cash balances—for bonds.

This is the crux of what Keynes called the **liquidity trap.** He reasoned that at a particularly low interest rate, nobody would be willing to buy any more bonds. Therefore, increases in the money supply would be merely stashed away. There would be no mechanism by which an increase in the money supply would lead to a decrease in interest rates, thereby leading to increases in investment and output.

In Figure 12-7, we find that the liquidity preference function has changed shape. At a 2 percent interest rate, it becomes completely flat or horizontal. In other words, the demand for money at a 2 percent interest rate is infinite. This means that when bonds are yielding only 2 percent, nobody will be willing to buy any more. People will merely keep additional money in cash balances. This has very serious implications for the efficacy of monetary policy.

Imagine, as in Figure 12-7, that the money supply was at M_s. The interest rate is established by the intersection of the demand for money and the supply of money. In this case the equilibrium interest rate happens to be 2

FIGURE 12-7 **The Liquidity Trap**

The liquidity preference function is the normal shape until it reaches a 2 percent interest level. Then it becomes horizontal. At 2 percent the demand for money is infinite. Nobody is willing to buy any more bonds. Any money that is injected into the economy goes into people's cash balances. If the money supply is at M_s, the equilibrium interest rate will be at 2 percent. An increase in the money supply from M_s to M'_s leads to no lowering of the interest rate because the liquidity preference function is horizontal at 2 percent. The new intersection with the new larger money supply is at the same interest rate as the old intersection with the smaller money supply. In this particular case it is impossible for the unyielding interest rates to stimulate investment and thus increase output and employment. In short, monetary policy is ineffective in this model.

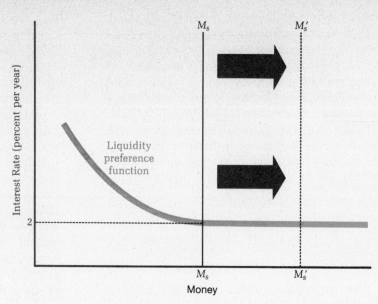

percent. Now suppose that the economy is languishing; there is unemployment. The government decides to use expansionary monetary policy. It therefore increases the supply of money by buying government bonds in the open market. There is a multiple expansion in the money supply. M_s moves out to M'_s, the dashed vertical line in Figure 12-7. We know, however, that the demand for money is already in the liquidity trap. We are at an interest rate of 2 percent, and nobody wishes to buy any more bonds. All the extra money injected into the economy by the Federal Reserve is merely kept in checking accounts and in cash by the people who receive it. Nobody bothers to trade it in for bonds. The equilibrium interest rate remains at 2 percent because here is where we find the new intersection of M'_s and the liquidity preference function. *There will be no change in investment and no change in income or employment.* We're stuck in the liquidity trap. Monetary policy is useless. The only thing that can help out is fiscal policy—that is, increases

in government spending or decreases in taxes. So goes the most simplified theory of the liquidity trap.

However, you should be warned that few serious Keynesians today believe the liquidity trap has ever existed. Keynes himself never said he saw it. It turned out to be a cute analytical exposition of a possibility that never became a reality. Economists have not even found evidence that a liquidity trap of this kind existed during the depths of the Depression.

Other Views on the Subject

The way we have analyzed the role of money in this simplified income and employment determination model is certainly not the only way to handle its effects. We will see in the following chapter that there are significant disagreements among economists concerning the function of money supply changes in our economy.

Consol: A bond with no maturity date.

Liquidity Preference Function: A relationship between the opportunity cost of holding money and the quantity of money demanded—otherwise stated as the quantity of liquidity preferred.

Liquidity Trap: That part of the liquidity preference function which is horizontal. If the economy is in the liquidity trap—as the theory is most simply postulated—an increase in the money supply will not lower interest rates. People's demands for money or for perfect liquidity will be infinite. All increases in the money supply therefore will go into their pockets or into their checking accounts rather than into an increased demand for bonds.

Chapter Summary

1. Keynes outlined three different motives for demanding money or cash balances: the transaction demand, the precautionary demand, and the speculative demand.

2. The price of a bond and the prevailing interest rate in the economy are inversely related.

3. The interest rate is the opportunity cost for holding money. The liquidity preference function shows the relationship between the cost of holding money and the quantity of money demanded. It is otherwise called the demand for money function. It is negatively sloped; at lower rates of interest, more money is demanded.

4. Another way of viewing the demand for money function is that, at least in part, it is determined by people's speculative motives. They may wish to hold money because they think interest rates will rise in the future, in which case it would be better for them to wait to earn higher returns later and also to avoid a capital loss. If the market rate of interest rises while you are holding a bond, the value of that bond will fall. At low interest rates you expect that the probability for market interest rates rising would be relatively high. Therefore, you wish to hold money instead of bonds to avoid the possibility of a capital loss. The converse holds for high interest rates.

5. In our simplified model we assumed that the supply of money is completely exogenous. In our graphs it is a vertical line determined by the monetary authorities. The equilibrium level of interest is found at the intersection of the liquidity preference function and the vertical supply of money curve. At the equilibrium level of interest there is neither an excess demand nor an excess supply of money.

6. We can go from the equilibrium level of interest established in the money market by the intersection of the demand and supply schedules of money to find out what the equilibrium level of investment will be. We look at our downward sloping investment schedule to find out what the level of investment will be at the given equilibrium interest rate. Then we carry

over this amount of investment to our standard 45 degree line $C + I + G$ diagram to find out what the equilibrium level of income will be with that amount of investment. Remember, there is a multiple expansion in equilibrium income for any given increase in investment. The multiplier in our examples has always been 5.

7. In the model we have presented, monetary policy is transmitted through changes in the interest rate. If, for example, we're at less than full employment, the Fed might wish to engage in expansionary monetary policy. It would increase the money supply, thereby creating an excess supply of money. Individuals' attempts to rid themselves of those excess supplies will cause the interest rate to fall. That is, they attempt to buy bonds; in their attempt, they will bid up the price of bonds, which means the interest rate will fall. When the interest rate falls, the level of investment will increase. There will be a multiplier effect from the increase in the level of investment. Equilibrium income will go up by a multiple of that increase in I. Monetary policy can also be used to quell over full employment or inflation.

8. In our model the transmission mechanism of monetary policy goes from a change in the money supply to a change in the interest rate to a change in investment to a change in income to a change in employment and/or price level.

9. There are certain theoretical situations in which monetary policy doesn't work. One of them is the liquidity trap. The liquidity trap is the horizontal section of the liquidity preference function where the demand for money is infinite. The interest rate cannot be lowered by expansionary monetary policy. An increase in the money supply will not lead to a lowering of interest rates. Therefore, investment will not expand and neither will equilibrium income.

1. During the Great Depression, the Federal Reserve stated that it could make sure there were enough reserves in banks to make money available to commerce, industry, and agriculture at low rates. However, the Fed stated that it could not make people borrow and it could not make the public spend the deposits that resulted when banks made loans and investments. Do you agree with that statement? Why or why not?

2. Can you think of any other reasons for wanting to hold money besides a liquidity preference or a speculative reason? (*Hint:* What do you use money for?)

3. What if the investment schedule were completely exogenous? (That is, it was not determined by the interest rate.) How would monetary policy work then?

4. Monetary policy has been criticized as being ineffective in the fight against inflation. One of the reasons is that "you can pull on a string but you can't push on it." Why would you expect monetary policy to be effective in increasing employment but ineffective in decreasing inflationary pressures? What is the string we are talking about?
5. Interest rates today are much higher than they were during the Great Depression. Does that mean that the possibility of the liquidity trap is less today?

Selected References

Bach, G. L., *Making Monetary and Fiscal Policy*, Washington, D.C.: The Brookings Institution, 1971.

Mayer, Thomas, *Elements of Monetary Policy*, New York: Random House, 1968.

Nichols, Dorothy M., *Modern Money Mechanics*, rev. ed., Chicago: Federal Reserve Bank of Chicago, 1971.

Ritter, Lawrence S. and William L. Silber, *Money*, 2d ed., New York: Basic Books, 1973.

The Role of Money: Other Views

We saw in the last chapter that in the most simplified of Keynesian models, monetary policy works through the mechanism of changes in excess reserves affecting the money supply altering the rate of interest; this then has an effect on the level of planned investment and hence on the equilibrium level of income and employment. The liquidity preference function was at the heart of this analysis. There are, however, many other ways of viewing the role of money in an income and employment determination model. In this chapter we briefly look at a variety of these views as outlined by macroeconomists who tend to call themselves monetarists because of their belief that changes in the money supply are the primary influence on the level of employment, output, and prices in the short run. That is not to say that the nonmonetarists, or Keynesians, as most would prefer to be called, who do not accept such a strong view of the role of money, believe that money does not matter. On the contrary, just about all economists talk in terms of both monetary and fiscal policy. Congress is important as it determines the level of government spending and taxation, and hence the size of the budget deficit or surplus, but so too is the Federal Reserve in its capacity as the controller of the money supply and hence the interest rates and economic activity that result from changes in it.

Stressing the Transactions Demand for Money

Rather than stress the speculative demand for money, or the liquidity preference function as Keynes preferred to call it, one alternative view puts more emphasis on the transactions motive. If individuals desire to hold a certain percentage of their income in cash, then as their income changes, their demand for cash balances will too. Moreover, if individuals with a certain level of income have larger cash balances than normal at that level, they will attempt to rid themselves of the excess. They do this by spending more than their current income. In the opposite situation, to build up their cash balances, they would spend less than their current income.

Although each of us can determine our own holding of cash, altogether we must hold the nation's money supply, by its definition. If, for example, the Federal Reserve buys United States government bonds and thereby increases the total amount of money in circulation, we, as the public, would be the holders of that increase in cash balances. The question is, in this case, what do we do with this increase?

In Chapter 12 it was hypothesized that the excess amount of cash balances would be an inducement to individuals to purchase bonds—the speculative demand. Looking at the situation from another viewpoint, that of the transactions demand, we could hypothesize that any increase in the money supply over that quantity demanded at the current level of income will cause households and firms to spend more than their current income. We can show this in our standard $C + I + G$ diagram by shifting the $C + I + G$ line upward by whatever amount autonomous investment and consumption expenditures increase due to an increase in the money supply. This is what is done in Figure 13-1.

We can now outline the transmission mechanism for this monetarist view of the role of money and income determination models.

The Transmission Mechanism

Let's suppose the quantity demanded and quantity supplied of money are equal, and

equilibrium exists. Now the Federal Reserve decides to buy bonds; in doing so, it increases the reserves of member commercial banks. Member banks then lend their excess reserves, causing a multiple expansion in the money supply. Now the money supply is greater than it was before, but the quantity of money demanded is less than this new, larger quantity supplied. According to the monetarists, people will attempt to get rid of their excess money balances. They will spend their money on a whole spectrum of possible assets—bonds, stocks, houses, cars, and myriad goods and services. The trade-off, then, is not just between money balances and bonds but between money balances and all possible avenues of spending. The monetarists, therefore, believe that the effect on interest rates is small—much smaller than the Keynesians expect. Certainly, part of the excess money balances will go into buying bonds, which will raise the price of bonds and thus lower the interest rate. However, the main influence is on income and employment, which are affected directly by people spending their excess cash balances on a variety of assets and goods and services. The monetarists maintain that spending will increase until income is such that the demand and supply of money are again in equilibrium. Equilibrium occurs when nominal income has risen sufficiently to cause people to want to hold all cash balances made available by the monetary authorities.

The Monetarists' Explanation of an Inflationary Recession

For a period of several years after the 1969 to 1970 recession, there were both high levels of unemployment and increasing prices. The United States experienced a phenomenon called an **inflationary recession.** We can use the monetarist theory presented above to explain this, if we add to it a little information

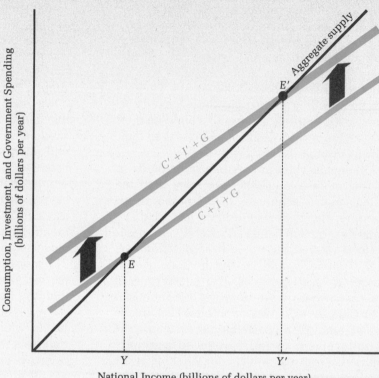

FIGURE 13-1 **The Effects of an Increase in the Money Supply**

This is one possible transmission mechanism for monetary policy. It is assumed that an increase in the money supply directly increases aggregate demand by increasing the autonomous component of planned consumption and/or planned investment and thus moves the aggregate demand function, $C + I + G$, up to a new aggregate demand function, $C' + I' + G$. The equilibrium level of national income moves from Y to Y'.

The vertical axis of the figure is labeled "Consumption, Investment, and Government Spending (billions of dollars per year)" and the horizontal axis is labeled "National Income (billions of dollars per year)". The lines are labeled "Aggregate supply", "$C' + I' + G$", and "$C + I + G$", with equilibrium points E and E'.

about the formation of expectations—on the part of both workers and business people.

In early 1960, we were at a period of under full employment. There were unemployed workers and there were machines that were not being used. The monetarists point out that, at this time, the rate of expansion of the money supply increased from 1.7 percent to 3.8 percent (see Figure 13-2). As people attempted to get rid of their excess cash balances, they spent more than their current income. As they spent more money for goods and services, they were increasing nominal aggregate demand. As people demanded and bought more, producers produced more because we were not at full employment. Prices rose hardly at all. By 1965, however, we were straining our available capac-

ities. The unemployment rate was 4.5, the lowest it had been in 8 years. But, at that time, the monetary authorities increased the rate of expansion of the money supply from less than 4 percent to about 7 percent per year except for a brief pause in 1966. As the private sector attempted to rid itself of the increased excess cash balances, the only thing that could go up were prices. The monetary authorities continued to increase the money supply until December 1968. Then there was an abrupt cutback in the rate of expansion of the money supply.

Using almost any demand for money relationship, we would now expect that the private sector would desire greater cash balances than it actually had, and this is what occurred. It was just the opposite of the situation in the

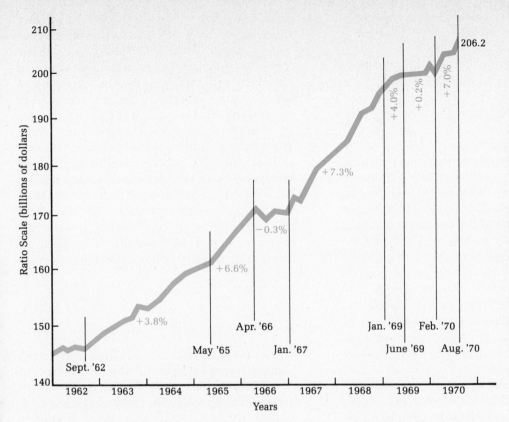

FIGURE 13-2 **The Money Supply during the 1960s**
Starting in September 1962, the growth of the money supply increased to 3.8 percent. Then in May 1965, it jumped up to 6.6 percent increase per annum. There was a temporary pause during the latter part of 1966. Then it shot off again, now at a higher rate of 7.3 percent. It finally slowed down at the end of 1968. Percentages are annual rates of change for periods indicated. (Source: Federal Reserve Bank of St. Louis.)

previous few years. To make up deficient cash balances, people spent less than they received. Total nominal aggregate demand fell.

Since prices increased when we were at full employment, when the situation was reversed, why didn't prices fall? Why did total output fall rather than prices? Why did we end up with continued rising prices and falling employment—that is, rising unemployment? The answer lies in the way workers and business people formulate their expectations about future prices and wages.

Expectations

From 1965 through 1968, workers found that every increase in their nominal wages was eaten up by increasing prices. In fact, blue collar workers experienced a slight drop in real income during that period. The purchasing power of their paychecks was actually smaller in 1968 than it had been in 1965. Workers had been continuously fooled into accepting wage increases they thought would compensate for rising prices but that, in the end, did not. Their expectations of how prices would change in the future were based on the experiences of past years. Workers refused to believe that prices were going to stop rising in the future, even when it was pointed out to them that the monetary authorities had switched to contractionary monetary policy. Due to their expectations, workers demanded increases in nominal wages not only to make up for *past* decreases in the real purchasing power of their paychecks but also as a hedge against anticipated price increases in the future.

In the beginning of the recession, business people were willing to give in to such wage demands because they too had experienced several years of being fooled. Every year they raised their prices but were still able to sell more than they had anticipated. That is, at the end of each year, they had smaller inventories than they felt were optimal. They sold more than predicted, even with the higher prices. Business people felt they could pass the increased labor cost on to the consumer and still make as much profit as before. They had no idea that total nominal aggregate demand had permanently shifted down, due to the restrictive action of the Federal Reserve. The rate of growth of nominal aggregate demand had fallen because the rate of growth of the money supply had fallen, thus inducing people to reduce their desired spending to get back to their desired level of cash balances.

We can now understand the monetarist analysis of the inflationary recession. Total aggregate demand fell because of restrictive monetary policy. However, prices did not fall but continued to rise due to *expectations* of rising prices that were built into the decisions of unions and business people. One can blame neither unions nor business people for their actions. They had no way of knowing that, in fact, the growth rate of aggregate demand had fallen.

Resulting Unemployment

The result was unemployment. Workers demanded higher wages and got them. Employers felt they could pass on the increased labor costs in higher prices, but they found that the demand for their products did not increase as they had expected. Inventories began to pile up, and workers were laid off as production slowed.

Output fell, but workers did not immediately accept lower wage offers because they did not believe the decrease in the demand for their services was permanent. So we see that, in some sense, the expectation of higher prices led to continuing increases in prices. However, sooner or later, the wage-price spiral had to peter out as unemployment grew and grew and grew. Workers eventually got the message, and employers refused to grant ever-increasing wages. We did not expect the price level to start falling, but we did expect the *rate* of increase of prices to fall, which is exactly what happened in 1970 when the rate of inflation finally peaked. As shown in Figure 13-3, the Fed continued its restrictive monetary policy, although at varying rates.

The Phillips Curve

When introducing the Phillips curve, in Chapter 7, we pointed out that it has been quite unstable over time; that is, the trade-off between inflation and unemployment hasn't remained constant. Professors Mary Hamilton and Albert Rees have commented upon the relationship: "We regard the construction of a plausible Phillips curve from annual data for a long period of time as a *tour de force* somewhat comparable to writing the Lord's Prayer on the head of a pin, rather than as a guide to policy."

Since 1965, the maintenance of a given unemployment rate has required higher and higher rates of inflation. The trade-off between unemployment and inflation has become increasingly worse.

The Importance of Expectations

The monetarists believe that, in fact, there can be no long-run trade-off between unemploy-

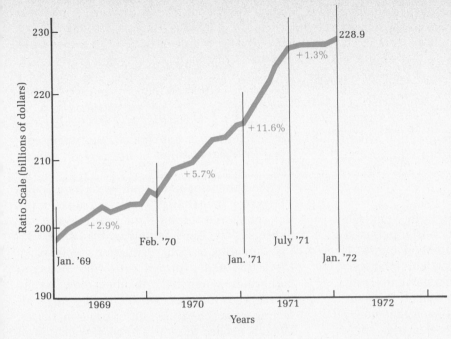

FIGURE 13-3 **Restrictive Monetary Policy**

In January 1969, restrictive monetary policy set in. From January 1969 to February 1970, the money supply increased at only 2.9 percent per year, compared to the 7.7 percent rate at which it had increased in the previous 2 years. Then the rate of growth picked up somewhat to 5.7 percent; it went crazy from January to July 1971 when it grew at 11.6 percent, and then became very restrictive between July and the end of 1971 when it grew at only 1.3 percent. *(Source: Board of Governors, U.S. Federal Reserve System.)*

ment and inflation. They don't believe that increasing the rate of inflation can forever "buy" less unemployment. Their reasoning relates to the fact that the original Phillips curve analysis completely ignored people's *expectations of future changes in prices.* Changes in the *expected* as opposed to the *actual* rate of inflation have an important impact upon the so-called trade-off between unemployment and inflation.

Ask yourself why inflation could reduce the level of unemployment in the first place. This assertion can be justified by assuming that workers always lag behind in their requests for higher wages. Employers are able to raise prices continuously and thereby make higher profits. Workers' anticipations of future increases in prices are not consistent with actual increases. Therefore, workers demand wage rates that fall behind actual increases in the cost of living (the price level). What, then, is the real wage rate

employers have to pay employees? The real wage rate is the money wage rate divided by the price level. If the price level goes up but the money wage rate does not go up proportionately, then the real wage rate falls. Since this is what employers actually look at in terms of their costs of labor, we would expect that, when the real wage rate falls, the quantity of labor demanded will rise. Therefore, unemployment will be decreased.

Full Anticipation

Now ask yourself what would happen if the rate of inflation were fully anticipated at every moment in time. Workers wouldn't be fooled; their demands for higher wage rates would take into account any expected inflation. Since the real wage rate would not fall, employers would not demand more workers; more workers would not be employed and output would not be increased. Therefore, any change in nominal aggregate demand due to, say, expansionary monetary policy would have very little effect on *real* output. The only thing that could be affected is nominal income. It would go up because prices would rise. Any change in the rate of expansion of the money supply would simply translate itself into a change in the rate of inflation. The growth in real output would remain the same as its long-run equilibrium.

Short-Run Effects

The monetarists contend that, in the long run, when the actual rate of inflation is anticipated, real output as opposed to nominal output is independent of the rate of growth of the money supply or of nominal aggregate demand. However, there can be short-run effects if there are abrupt changes in the growth of the money supply and nominal aggregate demand. There can be important effects on both output and employment. According to the monetarists, there can be temporary fluctuations in output and employment that are the results of unfulfilled expectations occurring during periods of adjustment to a new, previously unanticipated rate of inflation.

Suppose the Fed suddenly increased the money supply at a pace that was faster than it had been in the past. According to the monetarists, people would find themselves with excess cash balances. In their attempts to rid themselves of these excesses, they would cause nominal aggregate demand to rise. Businesses would find their inventories running low and would increase their production rates. New workers would be hired. In general, workers would find that they were able to find jobs faster than usual, even at the wage rates they had been used to asking. In short, a change in the rate of growth of the money supply would change the amount of employment, and, even-

tually, there would be an increase in prices as we approached full employment. This, however, is not a long-run trade-off between inflation and unemployment because expectations will eventually adjust to reality. Any stable rate of growth of nominal aggregate demand will permit the *equilibrium* rate of inflation to be fully anticipated. According to the monetarists, when inflation is anticipated, the unemployment rate will stabilize at its long-run natural rate.

Monetarists maintain that, to keep an unemployment rate below its long-run natural level, the actual rate of inflation must exceed the expected rate. Expectations will, however, adjust to reality; thus, to maintain a gap between the actual and expected rates, the monetary authorities would have to inject new money into the economy at ever increasing rates, affecting an accelerating rate of price increases. *What is needed to reduce unemployment is an accelerating inflation that is always underestimated.* We can translate the monetarist view of the Phillips curve into graphic analysis.

Graphic Analysis

In Figure 13-4, we see two curves similar in appearance to the standard Phillips curve. On the horizontal axis we measure unemployment; on the vertical axis we measure the *actual* rate of inflation. The Phillips curves, however, are drawn for two different levels of *expected* rates of inflation. The first one is drawn for an expected rate of inflation of 3 percent; the second one is drawn for an expected rate of inflation of 6 percent. The vertical line labeled U^* represents the so-called natural rate of unemployment, which we will assume to be 4 percent.

The monetarists assume that the unemployment rate will eventually settle at U^* when the future inflation rate is correctly anticipated—that is, when the actual rate of change

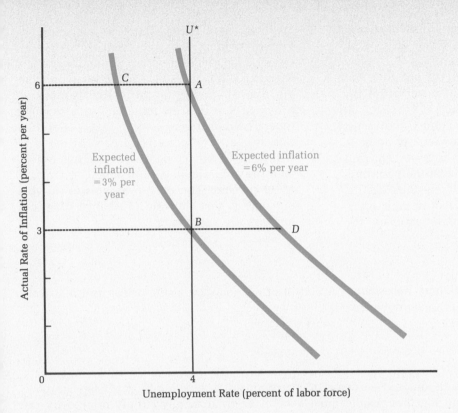

FIGURE 13-4 **Hypothetical Phillips' Curves**

Here we show two Phillips' curves. On the horizontal axis, the unemployment rate is measured. On the vertical axis is the rate of inflation. We assume that the "natural" or long-run level of unemployment is at U^*, or 4 percent of the labor force. There are two separate Phillips' curves: One is for an expected rate of inflation of 6 percent per year, and the other is for an expected rate of inflation of 3 percent per year. If the expected rate of inflation is 6 percent per year and the actual rate of inflation (which is measured on the vertical axis) is also 6 percent per year, then the long-run equilibrium unemployment level will be maintained at point A. However, if the expected rate of inflation remains at 6 percent per year, but the *actual* rate of inflation is only 3 percent per year, we will find ourselves at point D, where there is excess unemployment—that is, unemployment over and above the normal long-run U^* of 4 percent. Here we see that an actual rate of inflation less than the expected rate of inflation leads to unemployment. Now take the innermost curve, where the expected rate of inflation is 3 percent per year. If the actual rate of inflation is also 3 percent, then there will be no excess unemployment—that is, unemployment will be at its "normal" long-run level of 4 percent. We will be at point B. Suppose, however, that the actual rate of inflation is 6 percent. We will find ourselves at point C. We will be at over full employment—that is, unemployment will be less than its long-run or normal level of 4 percent. At point C, individuals *underestimate* the actual rate of inflation. Contrast this with point D, where individuals *overestimate* the actual rate of inflation. The underestimate causes unemployment rates to fall below U^*. The overestimate causes unemployment rates to be greater than U^*.

in prices is equal to the expected rate of change in prices. This would occur either at point A, if the actual rate of inflation was 6 percent, or point B, if the actual rate of inflation was 3 percent. Look at point C, however. Here, the anticipated rate of inflation is 3 percent, but the actual rate is 6 percent. Point C represents "over full" employment. Now look at point D. The actual rate of inflation is 3 percent, but the anticipated rate is 6 percent. Unemployment exceeding the natural rate thus occurs.

If the monetarists are correct in their interpretation of the Phillips curve analysis, the monetary authorities cannot be successful in forever keeping unemployment down by increasing the rate of inflation. If the monetarists are correct, it matters little in the long run what the rate of growth of the money supply is, provided that the rate remains stable through time. The monetarists believe that a continual rate of change of prices of 4 percent per year will yield the same long-run level of unemployment as a continual rate of change of prices of 10 percent. The only prerequisite for this outcome is that the rate of change of prices be correctly anticipated.

Definition of New Term

Inflationary Recession: A period of concomitant rising prices and relatively high unemployment.

Chapter Summary

1. Individuals in the economy determine their own holdings of cash balances, but together people must accept the total money supply offered by the monetary authorities.

2. Modern monetarists view the demand for money as part of the demand for all assets. Money is just one particular asset. Monetarists therefore maintain that the demand for money depends upon nominal income, the rate of return on alternative assets, and the rate of inflation. The rate of inflation is a determinant of the demand for money because it is equal to the rate of depreciation of cash balances. The faster cash balances depreciate, the more expensive they are to hold.

3. Monetarists and Keynesians alike predict that at full employment, any increase in the money supply will be translated into a rise in the price level. There will be no increase in output because that is impossible at full employment.

4. Expectations play a key role in monetarist analysis. Expectations, according to the monetarists, were responsible for the 1969 to 1970 inflationary recession. Workers demanded higher wages because of past inflationary experience; employers gave them higher wages, expecting to be able to raise prices without losing any business. However, since there was a drop in the rate of growth of nominal aggregate demand, at higher prices, employers could not sell all the goods they thought they could. Inventories built up; workers were laid off; unemployment and a recession resulted.

5. Monetarists maintain that there is no long-run trade-off between unemployment and inflation. They state that the Phillips curve will shift according to the expected rate of inflation. If inflation is fully anticipated, they maintain that there will be no employment effect from rising prices. It is only when the rate of inflation is completely unanticipated that it will have an employment effect.

Questions for
Thought
and Discussion

1. On the average, how much cash do you keep? (Remember to count not only the cash in your wallet but your checking account balances as well.) Do you think you would hold more cash if your part-time income or your scholarship or the money your parents send you were to double?
2. How can you increase your cash balances? How can you decrease your cash balances?
3. Why does the public have to accept the total money supply offered by the monetary authorities?
4. Do you think you would want to hold more or less cash if the rate of inflation increased from 5 percent per year to 500 percent per year?

Selected
References

Federal Reserve Bank of Boston, *Controlling Monetary Aggregates,* Boston: Federal Reserve Bank of Boston, 1969.

Friedman, Milton, *Dollars and Deficits,* Englewood Cliffs, N.J.: Prentice-Hall, 1968.

Meiselman, David, Testimony before the Subcommittee on Fiscal Policy of the Joint Economic Committee, Congress of the United States, Oct. 13, 1969.

The Iconoclast As Institution

MILTON FRIEDMAN

Economist, University of Chicago

Milton Friedman has played a unique role in the continuing battle over the role of government in the economy. He has never held a major government post, but he has heard his ideas soundly condemned by the "new economists" of the early 1960s, eventually—if cautiously—adopted by the "gamesmen" of the Nixon administration, and then ignored shortly thereafter. Throughout, Friedman has hounded the economic watchmen about uselessly attending to invalid fiscal indices while ignoring what he considers the one crucial factor: fluctuation in the money supply.

One of America's major conservative economists, Friedman defends the modern "quantity" theory of money: changes in the amount of money in circulation shape short-run economic events. In his testimony before the Joint Congressional Economic Committee in 1959, Friedman said that the Federal Reserve Board, instead of tightening money during booms and loosening money during recessions (which doesn't work because of the lags), should simply increase the supply of money at a steady rate of 4 percent, "month in and month out, year in and year out."

An ideal economy, according to Friedman, is based on a free-market model; government's role should be little more than the maintenance of optimal competitive conditions. This concept has two important corollaries, both of which stand solidly in opposition to "liberal" economic thought in this country: (1) the obligation of the business community is the maximization of profit with direct responsibility to the stockholder, and (2) the economy is not a tool of social betterment, to be manipulated by the government in pursuit of social-welfare goals. Friedman explained, in "The Social Responsibility of Business is to Maximize Profit" (*New York Times Magazine,* 1970), that the use of corporate profits for environmental protection, safety and quality-control devices, and so on represents a direct tax on the stockholder; a board of directors that "levies" such a tax is acting as a legislative body. The way certain companies have timidly received the demands of consumer groups is, to Friedman, completely at odds with the valid economic role of the corporation. "When I hear businessmen speak eloquently about the 'social responsibility of business in a free enterprise system,' I am reminded of the wonderful line about the Frenchman who discovered at the age of 70 that he had been speaking prose all his life."

In Friedman's view, it is dangerous to regard the economic sector as a cure for social problems. It drives economists into roles of oracles and social magicians. As Friedman stated: "I believe that we economists in recent years have done vast harm—to society at large and to our profession in particular—by claiming more than we can deliver."

Friedman would, nonetheless, like to apply many of his free-market concepts to other areas of the society. He opposes protective tariffs, feeling that America has a good deal to gain by encouraging imports. "If Japan exports steel at artificially low prices, it is also exporting clean air. Why shouldn't we take it?" Other aspects of Friedman's approach are his distaste for subsidies (especially farm) and price supports and his dislike of government mandates for safety equipment in automobiles. He has advocated abandoning Social Security and welfare, to be replaced with a negative tax (a cash subsidy for those citizens in the lowest income group).

During Senator Barry Goldwater's unsuccessful bid for the presidency in 1964, Friedman served as chief economic adviser. Friedman also advised Nixon on economic matters during his campaign for the presidency in 1968, but Nixon broke with Friedman's theories when he instituted the wage and price freeze. In the first year of the Ford administration, Friedman advocated a substantial tax cut coupled with an equal cut in government spending. To cut income taxes without reducing government spending, Friedman argued, only means increased taxes later or higher inflation rates if the increased budget deficit is partly or wholly financed by the Fed.

Whether the American economy will ever turn in the direction Friedman proposes is perhaps not as important as Friedman's advocacy role in the economics establishment. Paul Samuelson said a few years ago: "To keep the fish that they carried on long journeys lively and fresh, sea captains used to introduce an eel into the barrel. In the economics profession, Milton Friedman is that eel."

Is Short-Run Stabilization Possible?

POLICYMAKERS' PROBLEMS

Keeping the Economy on an Even Keel

You have just been presented with the rudiments of income and employment determination models. One is characteristically labeled "Keynesian," the other "monetarist." Whichever model is used, the goal is the same: to understand and predict how our economy works. You should be aware that macroeconomic modeling, as it is sometimes called, is not done merely as an exercise in intellectual tinkering. Rather, we are in an era of applied macroeconomics, where policymakers rely on the results of sometimes simple and sometimes complicated macroeconomic models. How do they rely on those models? They use the models to make predictions of what will happen to the economy in the future; then they alter certain policy variables such as the rate of government spending, the rate of government taxation, or the rate of growth in the money supply in order to effect a desired change in future economic activity. Such policymaking is generally called short-term macroeconomic stabilization, since

it is concerned with changes in economic activity expected to occur over the subsequent 12-month period.

Short-run stabilization policymaking was virtually unheard of prior to the Great Depression. For one thing, the consensus among economists in those days was that the economy was self-regulating. For another, the importance of fiscal policy—changes in government spending and taxation—didn't really gain a foothold until after the publication of Keynes' *General Theory*.

At the end of World War II, Congress made explicit the federal government's "responsibility" to stabilize economic activity in the short run. The Employment Act of 1946 proclaimed:

The Congress hereby declares that it is the continuing policy and responsibility of the Federal Government to use all practicable means consistent with its needs and obligations and other essential considerations of national policy, with assistance and cooperation of industry, agriculture,

labor and State and local governments, to coordinate and utilize all its plans, functions, and resources for the purpose of creating and maintaining, in a manner calculated to foster and promote free competitive enterprise and the general welfare, conditions under which there will be afforded useful employment opportunities, including self-employment, for those able, willing, and seeking to work and to promote maximum employment, production, and purchasing power.

Economic activism by the federal government was and continues to be the reality of the day.

However, is a proclamation that declares the federal government "responsible" for promoting maximum employment, production, and purchasing power sufficient to guarantee that the ups and downs in economic activity will in fact be smoothed out? Are there any reasons why short-run stabilization policies may work sometimes but not other times? Does the income and employment model used in predicting economic activity determine the success or failure of the policies based thereupon? These are the questions to which we address ourselves in this issue.

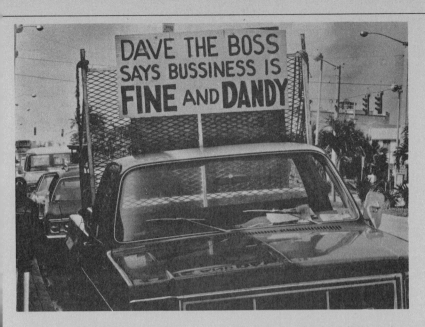

How Do We Define Full Employment?

Given the tenor of what is often called the "Full" Employment Act of 1946, it seems appropriate to start our discussion with a query—just what is meant by full employment? You might get an idea by reading the reports from certain government economists. They might define full employment these days as an employment situation where 5 percent —or even more—of the active labor force declares itself unemployed when surveyed by the Bureau of Labor Statistics. Presumably, that 5 percent level represents frictional unemployment which is "optimal" because of the transactions costs that exist in the real world labor market. However, if you refer back to statements by government officials, say, a period of 10 years ago, full employment was defined as 4 percent unemployment, and if you

go back even further, full employment was 3 percent unemployment.

Obviously, there is no objective way to come up with a definition of full employment. How much unemployment can we call frictional? There is no way of telling. The full employment level of unemployment has been defined in a very ad hoc manner and has been raised in recent years. Nonetheless, for any certain period of time, policymakers do accept, and work with some definition of full employment. Then, if their current definition is, for example, 5 percent unemployment and the unemployment rate rises to 6½ percent, policymakers can react to what is considered an unacceptably high rate of unemployment.

Deciding What to Do

Given the policymakers' tool kit, consisting primarily of the monetary

and fiscal policies we have discussed throughout this entire unit, how is the decision made that a particular policy should be put into play? Generally the decision is based on an admixture of data on the current economic scene: the current rate of inflation, the current level of unemployment, the current level of business capital formation, and so forth. Predictions about future economic activity based on current and past data will also be added. These predictions are not difficult to obtain for there are hundreds of business-forecasting organizations, both private and public. The government has, at its disposal, models employing elements of what you have learned in this unit that give projections on a monthly, quarterly, and yearly basis about future values of aggregate economic variables. The numerical values in these models are obtained by feeding past data into a computer that is programmed according to whatever the income and employment determination model in use indicates is appropriate. The subdiscipline used in this instance is called **econometrics,** which is basically the application of mathematics and statistics to the measurement of economic relationships. The models involved are called econometric models. They give predictions of future economic activity. However, ultimately, of course, theories are devised by economists. Therefore, when a particular econometric model doesn't work, that is, when the model doesn't predict well, it is rarely the fault of the computer. (In fact, there is a common saying among those people who use computers: Garbage in, garbage out.)

We mentioned already the first problem of policymaking—defining full employment. We now see a second difficulty—predicting with some accuracy the future course of economic activity. To a large extent this ability depends on using an income determination model that takes account of all the relationships necessary to do the job. Moreover, it depends on the availability of current accurate data on key aggregate variables. Models, for example, that use changes in inventories as a variable often go awry because the data on business inventory changes never seem to be right the first time they are collected. There are nearly always changes 3 or 6 months later.

The problem of information forms part of the larger problem called "time lags."

Time Lags for Short-Run Policies

Have you ever suddenly realized you had a cold when retrospect would indicate that you had felt it coming on for some time? In other words, have you ever experienced a time lag between displaying the first symptoms of a cold and your recognition of them? Short-run stabilization policymakers face not only a time lag like this but several others as well.

The Information Time Lag

Before any policy can be made, there must be information on the current state of the economy. However, we don't know concurrently what is happening to the rate of capital formation, the unemployment rate, changes in prices, and so on until after the fact and after a time lag. It is crucially important for us to obtain accurate information as quickly as possible, but sometimes accurate information about the entire economy doesn't come for months. In other words, it's possible that we will not recognize we are in a recession until, say, 6 months after it starts. This is often called the "recognition lag."

Another problem, one that particularly concerns fiscal policy, also faces policymakers.

The Action Time Lag

Once we discover we are indeed in a recession, a long period can sometimes elapse before any policy is put into effect. This is particularly true of tax cuts and tax increases that are desired for stabilization purposes. A tax cut was first suggested in the Kennedy administration in 1961. It didn't pass until 1964, a lag of 3 years. Monetary policy does not suffer the same action lag because the Board of Governors of the Federal Reserve System meet 13 times a year and can, almost instantaneously, put into effect any policy it decides upon. It must simply instruct the trading desk at the New York Fed how to proceed. The action lag, then, can be long and variable for fiscal policy but will generally be relatively short for monetary policy.

An effect lag also faces policymakers.

The Effect Time Lag

Even if there were no information lag or action lag, there would still be an effect lag because even the most perfect economic policy variable change will not have an immediate impact upon the economy. An increase in government spending, for example, takes time to work itself out; a change in taxes does too. A change in the rate of growth of the money supply may not have an effect for several months or several years. Economists have spent countless years attempting to estimate this effect lag. Some say that for fiscal policy the lag can draw out over several years. The initial lag in monetary policy, on the other hand, may be only months although it can draw out for several years after.

Taking Lags into Account

Now you can see the problems inherent in trying to stabilize the economy in the short run. Assume you are a policymaker and you have just discovered that the economy is going into a recession. You try to get taxes changed to counter that recession. What kind of problems will you encounter? First of all, we may have already been in a recession for 6 months or 1 year before you detected it. Secondly, it may take another year or two to get Congress to put the tax-change package into effect, and thirdly, it may take another year until the major effect of that fiscal policy change is felt in the economy. By that time, the economy may have already turned around and be on the upswing. Your fiscal policy change will then be inappropriate and only add fuel to a booming inflationary fire.

The long and variable lags in-

A monetary rule would require the money supply to grow at a fixed annual rate that would not be altered by the Federal Open Market Committee or anyone else for that money. In fact, that Committee would have no function if a monetary rule were instituted.

On the fiscal policy side, there are numerous advocates of a long-run commitment to a balanced full-employment budget. Essentially, there would be no discretionary fiscal policy to change the direction of economic activity in the short run.

Note that the adoption of a monetary rule and a long-run commitment to a balanced full-employment federal budget would, to a large extent, lessen the importance of macroeconomic models as a basis for short-run stabilization policies.

Coordination

Since stabilization policy can be instituted by using fiscal tools as well as monetary tools, there would seem to be a problem of coordination. What if the fiscal authorities—the President and Congress—decide on one policy, and the monetary authorities—the Fed—decide on another? As a matter of fact, we have observed occasionally conflicting policies being carried out by monetary and fiscal authorities. In 1968, for example, a fiscal policy of restraint was adopted by the Congress in the form of a temporary income surtax. Soon after that surtax went into effect, however, the monetary authorities began what would have to be considered an expansionary policy. It seems, therefore, that unless all

volved in short-run stabilization policy have prompted some critics of such policies to recommend essentially that no short-run stabilization attempts be made at all, either from a monetary or a fiscal policy point of view. The most outspoken proponent of stable, or nondiscretionary, monetary policy is Milton Friedman of the University of Chicago. He has been a proponent of the so-called monetary rule for many years now.

policymaking is put under one roof, so to speak, the problem of coordination will at times be serious enough to negate policies that might otherwise help stabilize our economy.

Policymaking and the Public

A relatively new school of macroeconomic thought is developing that, if right, will have serious repercussions on policymaking. This school of thought skirts completely the issue of monetary versus fiscal policy, or Keynesianism versus monetarism. In other words, according to this school, the debate between the effectiveness of monetary versus fiscal policy and the debate between the Keynesians and the monetarists about the role of money in income determination is irrelevant. To adherents of this school, the only way that short-run stabilization policy works is for the public to be temporarily fooled because if the public knew exactly what was going to happen, then it would be able to capitalize on that information and effectively negate it. This is similar to the argument that public information about a company is useless to an individual wishing to invest in that company because the information, if accurate, will already have been used by someone else and therefore the current price of the company's stock will reflect the information. If we look specifically at the trade-off expressed by the Phillips curve, we can apply the same argument. The employment effect depicted in the Phillips curve results from fooling individuals about the future rate of inflation.

If the same argument can be used for the economy as a whole, then government policymakers can suc-

ceed only to the extent that they are able to fool the public. However, somebody once said that you can't fool all the people all the time. Thus, the public will eventually catch on to what government policymakers are doing, and a new policy will have to be devised to have any effect. We can even extend this analysis to its ultimate conclusion; that is, even if policymakers use extremely complicated econometric models to make predictions on which to base their policies, economic agents in our society will find it profitable to decipher the models being used. Then they will be useless as prediction devices,

no matter how many equations or how long the computer works on them.

Such a view of economic policy is disconcerting to those who believe we can do better than essentially doing nothing, but, according to these critics, doing nothing really involves long-run stable monetary and fiscal policies such as those mentioned above—a monetary rule and a long-run balanced full-employment budget. If it is impossible to stabilize in the future, we may be better off doing nothing since then at least we won't exacerbate the ups and downs in business activity.

The Final Word

Economic debates sometimes go on for years. The debates on monetary versus fiscal policy and Keynesianism versus monetarism continue to occupy much of the time of numerous economists. However, a new debate has begun to surface that threatens to overshadow anything else which has come before. The debate concerns not only the appropriateness of short-run stabilization policy but the possibility that it is virtually impossible; that is, there is no way the federal government can do better than a stable long-run monetary and fiscal policy. The majority of economists and policymakers probably still believe strongly in our ability to dampen fluctuations in business activity. They can point to the longest peacetime expansion in United States history, which occurred in the 1960s under a regime of relatively active short-run stabilization policymaking. They can compare the ups and downs in business activity after the Employment Act of 1946 to what happened before that time and thereby demonstrate that the business cycle has not been as erratic as it was previously. For many years to come, you and I will be reading about government attempts to keep the economy on a fairly even keel. Now, however, you should have a good understanding of the macroeconomic models that form the basis for many of those government policies.

Definition of New Term

Econometrics: The measurement of economic variables and the use of statistics in economic model building for the purpose of explaining and predicting what happens in the economy.

Questions for Thought and Discussion

1. What goals are there in our economy besides full employment?
2. Do you know how to define full employment?
3. "You can fool some of the people all the time and all the people some of the time, but. . . ." Does this famous quote have anything to do with short-run stabilization policy?
4. Why are lags important in policymaking?

Selected References

McMillan, Robert A., "A Re-examination of the 'Full Employment' Goal," *Economic Review*, March–April 1973, pp. 3–17; pub. by the Federal Reserve Bank of Cleveland.
Miller, Roger LeRoy and Raburn M. Williams, *Unemployment and Inflation: The New Economics of the Wage-Price Spiral,* St. Paul, Minn.: West Publishing, 1974, chap. 8.

FOUR

THE INTERNATIONAL SCENE

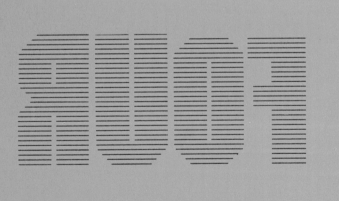

Benefiting from Trade among Nations

Most people regard trade as a gain when they are able to buy cheaper foreign products but as a loss when they see workers put out of jobs because of foreign competition. In this chapter, we hope to ferret out the real issues involved in international trade. It is certainly true that you as a consumer gain from cheaper foreign products. It is also true that employees and stockholders of industries hurt by foreign competition end up losing. The question is: "Are the gains from trade worth the costs?"

Putting Trade in Its Place

Trade among nations must somehow benefit the residents of each nation by more than it costs them. The volume of world trade has been increasing at a compound growth rate of between 5 and 10 percent per year for quite a while. In 1800, world trade was a mere $1.3 billion in terms of current purchasing power; just before the Great Depression, it reached almost $70 billion. That figure was again reached in 1950. Today, as seen in Figure 14-1, world trade on the average exceeds $300 billion a year. For the most part, the transactions involved take place voluntarily among individual citizens in different countries.

Table 14-1 shows that the size of international trade in different countries varies greatly when measured as a percentage of GNP. Some countries export and import more than one-third of their GNP. The United States ranks at the bottom of the list. In fact, the United States is the Western country that would suffer the least if foreign trade were completely stopped. The change, however, would not go unnoticed.

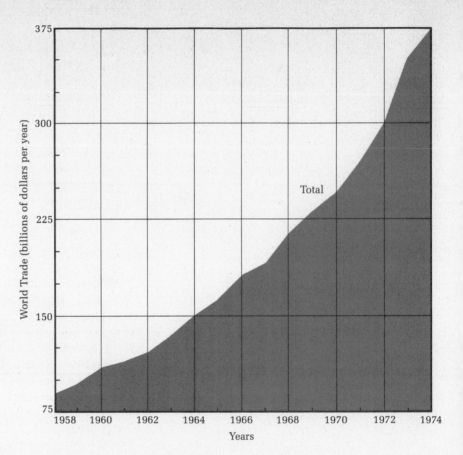

FIGURE 14-1 **World Trade Per Year**

World trade has grown rapidly over the last decade or so. In 1974, it had reached the $300 billion mark. *(Source:* U.S. Department of Commerce.)

If Foreign Trade Stopped

If imports stopped, tea and coffee drinkers would have to switch to Postum or Pero. Chocolate would be out of the question; you'd have to switch to carob. You would have no bananas, no pepper, no Scotch whiskey.

Many of our raw materials come from other countries. Over 90 percent of the bauxite from which we make aluminum is of foreign origin. All our chrome, cobalt, and the greater part of our nickel, platinum, tin, and asbestos are imported. If the world's trade stopped, we wouldn't be able to drink French wine; we wouldn't see Italian movies; and we wouldn't drive VWs.

Exports

Imports, of course, are only half the story. We pay for imports either by exports or through an extension of credit by other countries. Much of our employment comes from export industries. Twenty percent of our cotton, 25 percent of our grains, and 25 percent of our tobacco are shipped abroad. A third of our sulfur and a fifth of our coal is sold in foreign countries. Over 14 percent of our auto production, 25 percent of our textile and metal work machinery, and 30 percent of our construction and mining machinery are exported. And there are perhaps 35 other industries in which at least 20 percent of the output is regularly sold

Table 14-1 **World Trade in Different Countries**

Here we show the amount of world trade in different countries expressed as a percentage of their GNP. The United States, where world trade represents only 9 percent, is the lowest on the list. The Netherlands, on the other hand, where world trade is a whopping 44 percent of GNP, is at the top of the list.

COUNTRY	% OF GNP
Netherlands	44
Belgium-Luxembourg	37
Sweden	26
Canada	21
West Germany	19
United Kingdom	16
Italy	15
Japan	12
United States	9

Source: U.S. Department of Commerce

abroad. All told, there are 3 to 4 million jobs involved in the production of exports.

Of course, if world trade ceased to exist, all those jobs wouldn't be lost and all the imported goods wouldn't vanish from our shelves—we would simply alter our own production to take account of the situation. New industries would spring up to provide substitutes for the imported goods. Workers who lost their jobs in export industries would probably get jobs later as we readjusted.

Voluntary Trade

We engage in foreign trade for only one reason: We benefit from it. All trade is voluntary, and a voluntary exchange between two parties has to benefit both of them. Otherwise the exchange would not take place. The reasoning behind this argument is so simple that it often goes unnoticed by politicians who complain about for-

eigners "underselling" us by offering relatively cheap goods.

Demand and Supply of Imports and Exports

Let's explore the mechanism that establishes the level of trade between two nations. First we will need to develop a demand schedule for imports and a supply schedule for exports.

Imports

We will try to calculate graphically how many gallons of wine Americans will desire to import every year. We do this by deriving the **excess demand schedule** for wine. The left side of Figure 14-2 shows the usual supply and demand curves for wine in the United States. We draw consecutive price lines starting at equilibrium and going down. At the equilibrium price of $2 per gallon, there is no excess demand or excess supply for United States wine. In the right-hand portion of the figure, we again show that at the price of $2, *excess* demand is zero. If $2 were the world price of wine, there would be no net imports of wine. (In our two-country model, we're assuming the world is comprised of France and the United States.) In other words, at $2 per gallon, no wine trade would take place between these two countries.

But what about prices lower than $2? At a price of $1, there is an excess demand for wine in the United States. This is represented by the quantity (horizontal distance) between the domestic supply curve and the domestic demand curve at that price. We take that distance (indicated by the heavy arrow) and transfer it, at that price level, to the right-hand side of the figure. Here we draw the excess demand for wine at a price of $1 (the amount of wine represented by the length of the arrow).

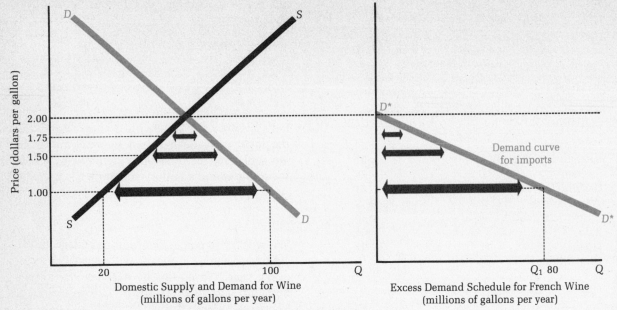

FIGURE 14-2 **Derivation of Import Demand Schedule for the United States**

On the left-hand side of the diagram, we draw the domestic supply and demand schedules for wine. The demand schedule is *DD*; the supply schedule is *SS*. The equilibrium price is $2. At $2 per gallon, there will be no excess demand for wine; therefore, the demand for imports will be zero. However, at a price of $1, there will be an excess demand for wine. The excess demand is represented by the longest arrow. We transfer that arrow to the right-hand graph to show the excess demand for wine at a price of $1. *D*D**, the excess demand for wine is, in other words, the demand for imports of wine. If the world price were $1, we would demand the quantity Q_1 of imported wine. The excess demand curve for French wine slopes down, starting at the domestic equilibrium price of wine—in this case $2.

The length of the arrow is the same on both sides of the graph. If we could continue doing this for all the prices below $2, we will come up with an *excess demand schedule for wine*. Whatever the world price is, we can find out how much the United States will import. If the price is established at $1, for example, we will bring in imports equal to Q_1. As we would expect, the excess demand schedule for imports is downward sloping, like the regular demand schedule. The lower the world price of wine, the more imports we will buy.

Exports

What about the possibility of the United States exporting wine? Europe, in fact, is starting to drink California wines. The situation is depicted graphically in Figure 14-3, where we derive the **excess supply schedule.** Let's look at prices above $2. At a price of $3, the *excess supply* of wine is equal to the amount represented by the distance between the demand curve and the supply curve (again represented by the bold arrow). The excess supply curve

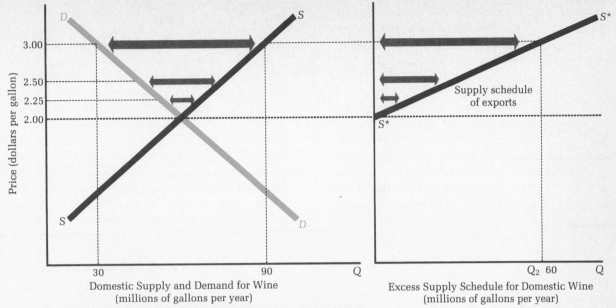

FIGURE 14-3 Derivation of Export Supply Schedule for the United States

The domestic demand and supply of wine is shown in the left-hand side of the figure. At an equilibrium price of $2, there is no excess demand or excess supply of domestic wine. In the right-hand graph, we show the excess supply of wine. At prices higher than $2, there is an excess supply of wine. The excess supply is represented by the bold arrows. We transfer these bold arrows over to the right-hand graph to derive the quantity of excess supplies that can be used for exportation purposes. In this manner, we derive the supply schedule of exports, S^*S^*. It slopes upward like all supply schedules. If the world price of wine were $3, we would export the quantity Q_2 to other countries.

is shown on the right side of the figure. The supply curve of exports slopes up, like all supply curves. At a price of $2, there are no net exports from the United States. At a price of $3, however, there are exports. The amount of these exports is represented by the length of the heavy arrow. Thus, if the world price rises above $2, the United States would become a net exporter of wine. The higher the world price, the more wine we would export. The lower the world price, the less wine we would export. Below a price of $2, we would start importing. The **zero trade point,** then, is $2. At

a world price of $2, we will not engage in world trade. (Note that the world price is established by the interaction of total world demand and world supply.)

The Quantity of Trade in a Foreign Country

We can draw the graph for France, our trading partner, in a similar manner. However, we have to establish a common set of measurements for the price of wine. Let's do this in terms of dollars, and let's say that the exchange rate is

20¢ for 1 franc. We place the excess demand schedule for imports and the excess supply schedule for exports on the same graph. Figure 14-4 shows a standard supply and demand schedule for French wine in terms of dollars per gallon. The equilibrium price of French wine is established at $1 per gallon. At a world price of $1 per gallon, the French will neither import nor export wine. At prices below $1, the French will import wine; at prices above $1 they will export wine. We see in the right-hand portion of Figure 14-4 that the excess supply schedule of French wine slopes up starting at $1 per gallon. The excess demand schedule for imports of wine slopes down, starting at $1 per gallon.

International Equilibrium (in a Two-Country World)

We can see the quantity of international trade that will be transacted by putting the French and the American export and import schedules on one graph. The zero trade point for wine in America was established at $2 per gallon, whereas in France it was established at $1 a gallon. We see in Figure 14-5 that the excess supply schedule of exports in France intersects the excess demand schedule for imports in the United States at point E with an equilibrium world price of wine of $1.50 per gallon and an equilibrium quantity of trade of 10 million gallons per year. Here we see how much and

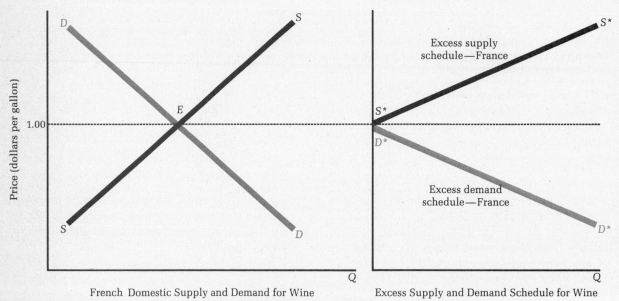

FIGURE 14-4 **Derivation of Excess Demand and Supply of Wine for France**
The left-hand side of the graph shows France's domestic demand and supply curve for wine. The domestic equilibrium price of wine in France, at an exchange rate of 20¢ per franc, translates into $1 per gallon. At $1 per gallon, France will have neither an excess demand nor an excess supply of wine. At higher prices, it will have an excess supply—that is, it will export wine. At lower prices it will have an excess demand—that is, it will import wine. On the right-hand side of the graph, we have drawn France's excess supply schedule and excess demand schedule. The export schedule is S*S*, and the import schedule is D*D*.

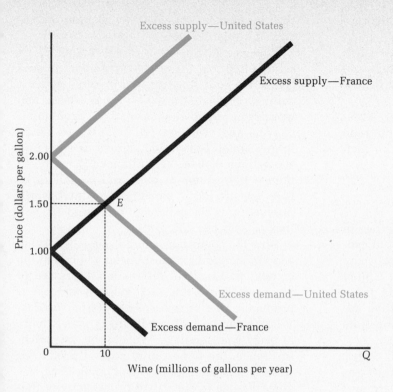

Price (dollars per gallon)

Excess supply—United States

Excess supply—France

2.00

1.50 .... E

1.00

Excess demand—United States

Excess demand—France

0   10   Q

Wine (millions of gallons per year)

FIGURE 14-5 **International Equilibrium**
We plot France's excess demand and supply
schedule along with the United States' excess
demand and supply schedule. France's excess
supply schedule intersects our excess demand
schedule at point E, which establishes an
equilibrium world price of wine. That world
price is $1.50, which will be the price of wine
everywhere. America will import 10 million
gallons of wine at that price and France will
export 10 million gallons of wine.

the terms under which trade takes place. The
amount is determined by the excess demand
and supply schedules in each country and the
point at which they intersect each other. If the
tables were turned and America's no-trade
point was below France's no-trade point, then
America would be exporting wine and the
French would be importing it.

The free-trade international equilibrium
price will never fall below $1 per gallon, nor
will it rise above $2 per gallon in this example.
Moreover, you should realize that the equilibrium price in this example turns out to be $1.50
because of the particular way the curves were
drawn. If we were to do the example differently, we might come out with a somewhat
different equilibrium price—although it would
still lie between $1 and $2 per gallon.

The Gains from Trade

We can once again mention that there are gains
to be made from trade between the United
States and France. Let's look at the United
States first. After we started trading with
France, the price of wine fell from $2 per gallon
to $1.50 per gallon and the quantity demanded
increased. Additionally, domestic wine production fell and the resources released when
those firms went out of business could be used
elsewhere. The increased satisfaction we received from the additional wine was *greater*
than the cost to us in resources forgone. We
are better off.

So, too, are the French. Their *consumption*
of domestic wine fell, but their domestic *production* increased. The difference went to the

United States in the form of exports. With those exports the French could now purchase United States imports, the value of which to the French will be *greater* than the resources forgone to make additional wine for export to the United States.

Both countries gain in the free-trade situation. If, however, both countries had a no-trade point at the same price, there would, in fact, be no net imports or exports.

Comparative and Absolute Advantage

The reason there are gains from trade lies in one of the most fundamental principles of economics: A nation gains by doing what it can do best relative to other nations. The United States benefits by *specializing* in only those endeavors in which it has a **comparative advantage.** Let's take an example to demonstrate this concept.

Let's look at France and the United States. We show in Table 14-2 the comparative costs of production of wine and beer in terms of person-days. This is a simple, two-country–two-commodity world where we assume that labor is the only factor of production. As you can see from Table 14-2, in the United States it takes 1 person-day to produce 1 gallon of wine and the same for 1 gallon of beer. In France it takes 1 person-day for 1 gallon of wine, but 2 person-days for 1 gallon of beer. In this sense, Americans are more productive

than the French: They have an **absolute advantage** in producing beer.

However, trade will still take place. Let's assume first that there is no trade and no specialization and that the work force in each country consists of 200 workers. These 200 workers are divided equally in the production of wine and beer. We see in Table 14-3 that, in the United States, 100 gallons of wine and 100 gallons of beer are produced per day. In France 100 gallons of wine and 50 gallons of beer are produced per day. The total world production is 200 gallons of wine and 150 gallons of beer per day.

Now the countries begin to specialize. What can France produce most cheaply? Look at the comparative costs of production expressed in person-days in Table 14-2. What is the cost of producing 1 gallon more of wine? 1 person-day. What is the cost of producing 1 gallon more of beer? 2 person-days. We can say, then, that, in France, the opportunity cost of producing wine is less than that of producing beer. We allow France to specialize in the activity that has the smallest opportunity cost. In other

Table 14-3 **Daily World Output before Specialization**		
UNITED STATES		
100 workers on wine	=	100 gallons of wine
100 workers on beer	=	100 gallons of beer
FRANCE		
100 workers on wine	=	100 gallons of wine
100 workers on beer	=	50 gallons of beer

World total = 200 gallons of wine, 150 gallons of beer.

Table 14-2 **Comparative Costs of Production in Person-Days**		
	UNITED STATES	FRANCE
Wine (1 gallon)	1	1
Beer (1 gallon)	1	2

words, France specializes in her comparative advantage, which is the production of wine.

According to Table 14-4, after specialization, the United States produces 200 gallons of beer, and France produces 200 gallons of wine. Notice that the total world production per day has gone up from 200 gallons of wine and 150 gallons of beer to 200 gallons of wine and 200 gallons of beer per day. This was done without any increased use of resources. The world is better off when countries specialize in their comparative advantage and then trade, because world output is larger.

Finding One's Comparative Advantage

It is important to understand the difference between the concept of comparative advantage, which we covered before in Chapter 1, and the notion of absolute advantage. Any time a country can produce a product with fewer person-hours of labor than another country, we say that it has an absolute advantage over the other in the production of those products. You, for example, may have an absolute advantage in doing a large variety of jobs. This does not mean, of course, that you divide your time equally among all these jobs. What you do is discover your area of comparative advantage and specialize in that area.

In general, people discover their own area of comparative advantage by contrasting the return from doing one job with the return from doing another job. An executive in a large corporation may have an absolute advantage in doing 15 different tasks for that company. For example, he may be able to type better than all his secretaries, wash windows better than any of the window washers, file better than any of the file clerks, and carry messages better than any of the messengers. His comparative advantage, however, lies in being an executive. He knows this because he is paid more for being an executive than he would be for any other job. The company willingly pays his salary as an executive because the value of his output in that job is at least as large as the salary paid to him. They would not pay him the same amount if he wanted to be a typist. In fact, they might be able to pay 10 or more typists the amount of his salary.

The key to understanding comparative advantage lies in realizing that total resources are fixed at any moment in time. You have only so much time in a day. A nation has only so many workers and machines. An individual, a company, or a nation must decide how it will allocate its available resources at a given moment. No one can use a resource in two different jobs at the same time. Even if companies or nations are *absolutely* better at doing everything, they will still specialize in only those tasks in which they have a comparative advantage because in that specialization they maximize the returns for the use of their time and resources. The United States may have an absolute advantage in producing computers and roller skates in the sense that we can produce both goods with fewer person-hours of labor than any other nation in the world. However, we let other countries produce roller skates

Table 14-4 **Daily World Output after Specialization**		
UNITED STATES		
200 workers on beer	=	200 gallons of beer
FRANCE		
200 workers on wine	=	200 gallons of wine
World total = 200 gallons of beer, 200 gallons of wine		

because our comparative advantage lies in producing computers. We might be 25 percent more efficient in the production of roller skates but 60 percent more efficient in the production of computers—so we specialize in computers. We gain by exchanging the computers we produce for the roller skates that other countries produce.

Comparative Advantage and Opportunity Cost

We can also relate the concept of comparative advantage to the concept of opportunity cost. In fact, understanding comparative advantage will give you an important insight into all relationships involving exchange among individuals or among nations. Comparative advantage emphasizes the fact that cost means opportunities that must be forgone. If the United States decides to produce roller skates, it forgoes part of its opportunity to produce computers because the time and resources spent in producing roller skates cannot be used simultaneously in producing computers. The basic reason for the existence of comparative advantage among individuals, companies, and countries lies in the fact that opportunity costs vary. It costs less for different parties to engage in different types of economic activities. Opportunity costs for different countries vary just as they vary for different individuals. Let's examine some of the reasons why opportunity costs and, hence, comparative advantages differ among nations.

Differing Resource Mixes

We know that different nations have different resource bases. Australia has much land relative to its population, whereas Japan has little land relative to its population. All other things being equal, one expects countries with relatively more land to specialize in products that require more land. One expects Australia, for example, to engage in sheep raising but not Japan because the opportunity cost of raising sheep in Japan is much higher. Since land in Japan is scarce, its use represents a higher opportunity cost.

There are also differences in climates. We do not expect countries with dry climates to grow bananas. The limitations of a resource base, however, do not always prohibit a country's actions. Watermelons require tremendous amounts of water; they are, nonetheless, grown in Arizona. (The federal government subsidizes water to watermelon growers in that state.)

Advantageous Trade Will Always Exist

Since the beginning of recorded history, there have been examples of trade among individuals. Since these acts of exchange have usually been voluntary, we must assume that individuals generally benefit from the trade. Individual tastes and resources vary tremendously. As a consequence, there are sufficient numbers of different opportunity costs in the world for exchange to take place constantly.

As individual entities, nations have different collective tastes and different collective resource endowments. We would expect, therefore, that there will always be potential gains to be made from trading among nations. Furthermore, the more trade there is, the more specialization there can be. In most instances, specialization leads to increased output and—if we measure well-being by output levels—to increased happiness. (Indeed, we are using the term *well-being* very loosely here.) Self-sufficiency on the part of individuals undeniably means that they forgo opportunities to consume more than they could by not being self-sufficient. Likewise, self-sufficiency on the part of a nation will lower its consumption possibilities and, therefore, will lower the real-income level of its inhabitants. Imagine life in Delaware, if that state were forced to become self-sufficient!

Costs of Trade

Trade does not come without cost. If one state has a comparative advantage in producing agricultural crops, other states may not be able to survive as centers of agricultural production. Farm workers in states that are losing out will suffer decreases in their incomes until they find another occupation.

As tastes, supplies of natural resources, prices, and so on change throughout the world, different countries may find their area of comparative advantage changing. One example of this is the United States' production of steel. Japan has become increasingly competitive in steel products, and United States steelmakers are being hurt. The stockholders and employees in United States steel companies are feeling the pinch from Japan's ability to produce steel products at low prices.

Japanese Miracle

Japan is a good example of how a nation can benefit from exploiting its comparative advantage and engaging in a large volume of world trade. Japan's recovery from World War II has been called miraculous. Real income in that country has been growing at an average rate of about 10 percent a year. Foreign trade has grown at an even faster rate. While real incomes doubled between 1952 and 1960, exports from Japan more than tripled. During the early 1960s, Japan's exports were doubling almost every 5 years. Japan has used its comparative advantage in manufacturing to expand its export markets in cameras, automobiles, and steel products. One wonders how Japan can become a net exporter of steel products without already hav-

ing the raw materials needed to make them, but Japan's comparative advantage is in the machining of the steel and not in the exploitation of raw resources to make it. Japan, therefore, imports iron ore and exports cold rolled steel.

Obviously, you can see that many American steel producers would want to fight to *restrict* Japanese imports into the United States. Some industrialists claim that Japan has an absolute advantage (in the sense of person-hours consumed to produce a good) in the production of electronic equipment and steel products. Even in those areas where Japan must consume more person-hours than the United States to produce goods, the lower wage rates paid in Japan may still permit Japanese producers to undercut the prices of American producers. In any event, complaints about increased Japanese competition with American industries have produced pressures for hindering free trade among nations. We will discuss a few of the arguments against free trade here.

Arguments against Free Trade

The numerous arguments against free trade all have merit. However, most of the time, these arguments are incomplete. They mainly point out the costs of trade, but they do not consider the benefits or the possible alternatives for mitigating costs while still reaping benefits.

Infant Industry Argument

A nation may feel that, if a particular industry were allowed to develop domestically, it could eventually become efficient enough to be competitive in the world. Therefore, if some restrictions were placed on imports, native producers would be given the time needed to develop their efficiency to the point where they would be able to compete in the world market without any restrictions on imports. This **infant industry argument** has some merit and has been used to protect a number of American industries in their infancy. Such policy can be abused, however. Often the protective import-restricting arrangements remain even after the infant has matured. The people who benefit from this type of situation are obviously the stockholders in the industry that is still being protected from world competition. The people who lose out are the consumers, who must pay a price higher than the world price for the product in question.

National Security

It is often argued that we should not rely on foreign sources for many of our products because in time of war these sources may well be cut off and we would have developed few if any substitute sources. A classic example of this involves oil exploration. For national defense reasons (supposedly), President Eisenhower instituted at first a voluntary, and then a mandatory, oil-import **quota** system, thereby restricting the amount of foreign oil that could be imported into the United States. The idea was to create an incentive for more exploration of American oil; thus, in time of war we would have a ready and available supply of oil for our tanks and ships and bombers.

However, restricting the amount of foreign oil imported merely served to raise the price of oil in the United States. The people who benefited were, obviously, the stockholders in oil corporations; the people who lost out were the consumers of oil products. It has been estimated by various government officials that the oil-import quota program cost the consumer a staggering $7 billion a year in the form of higher oil product prices. Also, it was the poor who paid more, relatively, than the rich since the poor spend a larger proportion of their income on petroleum products than do the rich. And finally, it was absurd to think that restricting the amount of foreign oil imported would allow us to have more oil for a national emergency. Obviously, using more of our own would lead only to less for a national emergency.

Stability

Many people argue that foreign trade should be restricted because it introduces an element of instability into our economic system. They point out that the vagaries of foreign trade add to the ups and downs in our own employment level. However, if we follow this argument to its logical conclusion, we would restrict trade among our various states as well. After all, the vagaries of trade among particular states sometimes cause unemployment in other states. Things are sorted out over time, but workers suffer during the adjustment period. Nonetheless, we don't restrict trade among the states. In fact, there is a Constitutional stricture against taxing exports among the states.

As regards the international sphere, though, people somehow change their position. They feel that adjusting to the vagaries of *international* trade costs more than adjusting to the vagaries of domestic *interstate* trade. Perhaps people believe foreign trade really doesn't benefit us that much, and thus they argue against it, claiming that the stability of aggregate economic activity is at stake.

We should note one difference between the domestic and international situations, however, that lends some truth to this argument. Labor is mobile among our states, but it is not mobile among nations. Immigration laws prevent workers from moving to countries where they can make the most money. Therefore, the adjustment costs to a changing international situation may, in fact, be higher than the adjustment costs to a changing domestic situation.

"As Adam Smith so aptly put it . . ."

Protecting American Jobs

Perhaps the most often heard argument against free trade is that unrestrained competition from other countries will eliminate American jobs because other countries have lower-cost laborers than we do. This is indeed a compelling argument, particularly for Congresspersons from an area that might be threatened by foreign competition. For example, a Congressperson from an area with shoe factories would certainly be upset about the possibility of constituents losing their jobs because of competition from lower-priced shoe manufacturers in Spain and Italy. This argument against free trade is equally applicable, however, to trade among the several states. After all, if labor in the south is less expensive than labor in the north, southern industry may put northern workers out of jobs; but, again, we do not, and constitutionally cannot, restrict trade (at least not overtly) among states.

This is a sufficiently important topic for us to spend the next issue on it. There are numerous ways to hinder free trade, and there are even more arguments in favor of restrictions on trade. Which of the arguments is most meaningful from your particular point of view?

Definitions of New Terms

Excess Demand Schedule: A demand schedule for imports derived from the difference between the quantity of a product supplied domestically and the quantity demanded at prices *below* the domestic no-trade equilibrium price.

Excess Supply Schedule: A supply schedule of exports derived from the difference between the quantity of a product supplied domestically and the quantity demanded at prices *above* domestic no-trade equilibrium prices.

Zero Trade Point: The point on an excess demand and supply diagram at which there is no foreign trade. At this price the domestic demand and supply schedules intersect.

Comparative Advantage: An advantage arising out of relative efficiency, which follows from scarcity of resources. As long as the opportunity costs of doing the same job differ for different people or different countries, each will have a comparative advantage in something.

Absolute Advantage: The advantage that a person or nation has over other people or nations in the production of a good or service. If you have an absolute advantage in doing something, you can do it better than anybody else—absolutely.

Infant Industry Argument: An argument in support of tariffs: Tariffs should be imposed to protect from import competition an industry that is trying to get started. Presumably, after the industry becomes technologically efficient, the tariff can be lifted.

Quota: A specified number of or value of imports allowed into a country per year.

Chapter Summary

1. In terms of current purchasing power, trade has expanded from a mere $1.3 billion in the year 1800 to over $300 billion in 1975. Trade rates differ among nations. The United States has one of the smallest amounts of world trade (which is expressed as a percentage of GNP). Trade represents only 9 percent of our GNP, whereas it represents 44 percent of the GNP of the Netherlands.

2. Although it only represents 9 percent of GNP, we would, nevertheless, notice a substantial change in our life-style if we were to cease trading with other countries.

3. Trade is always voluntary among nations and among people. Therefore, it must benefit everyone concerned.

4. We can draw an excess demand schedule for foreign goods by looking at the difference between the quantity demanded and the quantity supplied domestically at prices below our domestic equilibrium price.

5. The excess supply schedule of domestic goods is found by looking at the difference between quantities supplied and quantities demanded at prices above our domestic equilibrium price. The excess supply schedule is our supply schedule of exports.

6. The equilibrium price and quantity traded are established at the point where one country's excess demand schedule intersects another country's

excess supply schedule. As long as the zero trade points of two countries are at different prices, there will be trade (in the absence of restrictions).

7. It is important to distinguish between absolute and comparative advantage. A person or country that can do everything better than every other person or country has an absolute advantage. Nevertheless, trade will still be advantageous because people will specialize in the things that they do relatively best. They will take advantage of their comparative advantage.

8. An individual's comparative advantage lies in that activity for which she or he is best paid. Comparative advantage follows from different relative efficiencies and from the fixed nature of our resources at a point in time.

9. Along with the gains, there are costs from trade. Certain industries may be hurt if trade is opened up. There are numerous arguments, therefore, against free trade.

10. There is also a national security argument for tariffs and import quotas. For example, the oil-import quota was imposed in the name of national security; presumably by keeping out cheap foreign oil, we increase the incentive for domestic exploration of oil resources. Therefore, in time of war we would have a sufficient amount of gas to put in our bombers and ships.

Questions for Thought and Discussion

1. Do you ever make trades in which you don't benefit? Why do you make them?

2. "Cheap foreign labor is ruining jobs for Americans. Therefore, we should stop all trade with other countries." Evaluate this statement.

3. If you believe in free trade among nations in reference to goods and services, do you also believe in the free movement of human resources? That is, do you think all immigration laws should be repealed?

4. If every state in the union had exactly the same productivity and efficiency, would there be any trade? Why?

5. Is it possible for a country to lose its comparative advantage in the production of a specific good or service? What happens then?

6. Why would you expect a newly discovered continent to have a comparative advantage in the production of food?

Selected References

Kenen, Peter B. and Raymond Lubitz, *International Economics,* 3d ed., Englewood Cliffs, N.J.: Prentice-Hall, 1971.

Pen, Jan, *A Primer on International Trade,* New York: Random House, 1967.

Snider, Delbert A., *Introduction to International Economics,* 5th ed., Homewood, Ill.: Richard D. Irwin, 1971.

Does International Competition Pose a Threat?

THE QUESTION OF JOB PROTECTION

The Tenets of Protectionism

. . . This bill would discourage American business investment abroad and limit the flow of imports into this country. We can no longer afford to export American jobs and technology at the expense of our own industry all in the name of "free trade". . . .

Such were the words contained in the preamble to one of the most talked about bills introduced into Congress in this decade: the Burke-Hartke Foreign Trade and Investment Proposal. The preamble went on to state that the statute under consideration was to be interpreted as attempting to "ensure that the production of goods which have historically been produced in the United States is continued and maintained." Moreover, "to the extent that production of such goods has been transferred abroad, it is the intent of Congress that this production be encouraged to return to the United States."

Such words seem to be at odds with the underlying principles of economics. We talked, in Chapters 1 and 14, about the virtues of trade. Specialization by people and countries in their area of comparative advantage, coupled with trade, presumably allows for increased standards of material well-being. Why, then, would Senators Burke and Hartke want to stifle free trade? How could other senators introduce numerous other bills along the same lines, that is, putting restrictions on the flow of goods and services between our nation and other countries? We already briefly touched on this phenomenon. It concerns protection—mainly what is called "job protection"—for those in industries hurt by foreign competition.

Getting Hurt from Free Trade

We have never said that free trade benefits everyone. What we did say on several occasions was that free trade allows for a higher *overall* material standard of living. This says nothing about how individuals may fare. Let's take a specific example.

Suppose you are a worker in a shoe factory in Massachusetts. Suppose, also, that the industrialization of Spain allows them to produce shoes at a lower cost per pair than is possible in Massachusetts. In other words, given the relatively lower wage rate in Spain, shoes can be produced there at a lower per-unit cost. The importation of these low-cost Spanish shoes into the United States might seriously threaten the profitability of the shoe manufacturing company for which you work. Suppose, in fact, there is no way for your Massachusetts company to effectively compete with the Spanish shoe imports. In this case, your company will go out of business. You, as a worker in that company, will suffer a loss of job. You will be upset and annoyed that "unfair" competition from "cheap" labor in Spain has taken away what was "rightfully yours."

This is the crux of the argument against free trade, and it is the backbone of such bills as the Burke-Hartke one mentioned. Free trade does put some Americans out of work. In a dynamic world where tastes change, resource bases change, technologies change, and everything else changes, the comparative advantages of individuals as well as states and nations will change.

How Trade Can Be Hindered

There are many ways that international trade can be stopped, or at least partially stifled. These include, among other things, quotas and taxes—the latter are usually called tariffs when applied to internationally traded items. Let's talk first about quotas.

Quotas

In the quota system, countries are restricted to a certain amount of trade. Until 1973, we set a quota on the importation of oil into the United States. Let's look at Figure I-15.1. Here, we present the standard supply and demand graph for the product in question. The horizontal line, P_w, represents the world price line; this line also represents the world's supply of oil to the United States. We draw this line horizontally because we assume (somewhat unrealistically) that the United States buys only an extremely small fraction of the total world supply; therefore, the United States can buy literally all the oil it wants at the world price. In the absence of world trade, the price will be at the intersection of the domestic supply and demand schedules. The quantity demanded will be determined at that intersection also. With world trade opened up, Americans will buy 4 billion barrels of oil in total; domestic oil producers will provide 3.5 billion barrels of this total. The difference between 4 billion and 3.5 billion represents the imports. This is an equilibrium situation. The supply curve is the domestic one below the price P_w but becomes the horizontal P_w line at the price of P_w.

The fact, for example, that the United States has historically been a provider of high technology goods for the rest of the world does not mean that the United States' comparative advantage hasn't and won't change in the future toward some other good or service. This is essentially what has happened with the United States, Japan, and Germany. Historically, the United States has had a comparative advantage in high technology goods, but in recent years that comparative advantage has been eroded by the increasing sophistication of such countries as Japan and Germany. Naturally, jobs have suffered in the United States. But, this is what we call a *sectoral effect*. It affects a specific sector and not the entire American economy.

How We Pay for Imports

Strange as it may seem, if we reduce imports into the United States, we will also reduce exports out of the United States for we must ultimately pay for imports with exports. After all, the rest of the world is not interested in providing us with charity in the form of their exports (our imports). They want something in return. What they want in return ultimately is American goods and services. During certain periods of time, the rest of the world may be content to take, in exchange for the goods and services they provide the United States, such things as dollar bills, United States treasury bonds, and other financial assets. But ultimately, the rest of the world will want to exchange whatever liquid or illiquid United States assets they hold for United States goods and services. Thus, we know that the balance of payments must balance, and also that, in the very long run, the balance of trade must balance. Hence, if we stifle imports, we will, in effect, stifle exports. We will treat these topics in detail in the next chapter.

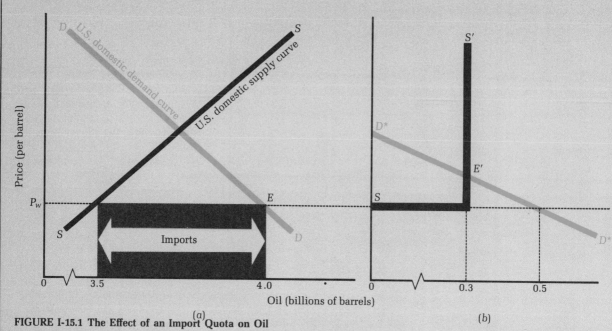

FIGURE I-15.1 The Effect of an Import Quota on Oil

The world price of oil is established at P_w. We assume that the United States buys a very small part of the total world supply of oil. The United States can buy all the oil it wants at the world price. The supply curve faced by the United States, in effect, is P_w. Our domestic supply curve is SS in the left-hand portion of the graph, and our domestic demand curve is DD. At the world price of P_w, we will reach equilibrium at E. This means we will consume 4 billion barrels of oil, of which 3.5 billion will be produced domestically. The difference is represented by imports. In the right-hand portion of the figure, we show the excess demand for oil as D^*D^*. That is, D^*D^* represents the demand curve for oil imports. At the world price of P_w, the quantity demanded will be 0.5 billion barrels of oil. The government, however, steps in and imposes an import quota of only 0.3 billion barrels. The supply curve remains P_w until it hits the quota line of 0.3 billion barrels. Then it becomes vertical. The new supply curve is then SS'. The new supply curve, SS', intersects the demand curve for imports, D^*D^*, at a new equilibrium of E'. The consumers of oil will end up paying the higher price represented by the vertical distance to E'. The stockholders in domestic oil-producing companies will benefit, however.

The intersection of the combined supply curve and the domestic demand curve is at E, where it will stay if there are no restrictions.

Let's now look at the right-hand portion of the graph. We draw the excess demand for imports. We put in the world price line, P_w, and we come up with the 0.5 billion barrels of oil imported at the world price.

Now we want to see what happens when a quota is instituted. Instead of allowing 0.5 billion barrels of oil to be imported, the government says that only 0.3 billion barrels may be brought into the United States. We draw a vertical line at 0.3 billion barrels per year. The supply curve effectively becomes the world demand price line until it hits the import

quota restriction at the vertical line. The supply curve then follows the vertical line up; it is now SS'. The new equilibrium point is at E', the intersection of the new supply schedule with the excess demand for imports. We see that at point E', however, there is a higher price for all oil consumed in the United States. This indicates that something in the situation has to change. Indeed— the price Americans must pay has to change. You, the consumer, lose. The importers (who get the quotas) and the import-substituting industries gain.

Tariffs

We can use our graphic technique to analyze the effect of a tariff. A tariff raises the price of a product—in this case oil—both foreign and domestic to United States residents.

Let's assume that the tariff is 10 percent of the price of the oil entering this country. In Figure I-15.2, we show the domestic supply and demand schedules for oil, with the world price at P_W. Now we add a

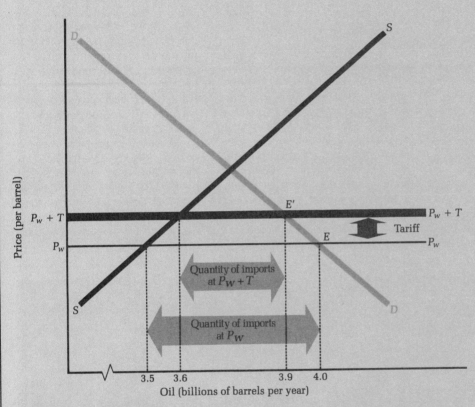

FIGURE I-15.2 An Import Tariff

The domestic supply curve for oil is SS. The domestic demand curve is DD. At a world price of P_W the United States can buy all the oil it wants. Equilibrium is established at E where the quantity demanded is 4 billion barrels. The quantity supplied domestically is 3.5 billion. The difference is imports, or 0.5 billion barrels. Now the government puts on a tariff, T dollars per barrel. The price at which Americans can buy oil now is equal to P_W plus the tariff. This shifts the effective horizontal supply curve up to the heavy solid line, $P_W + T$. Now, at this higher price the quantity demanded is at E', or 3.9 billion barrels. The quantity supplied domestically increases to 3.6 billion barrels. Imports, therefore, fall from 0.5 billion barrels to 0.3 billion barrels, as in the arbitrary example used for the import quota set at 0.3 billion barrels. However, in this particular case, it is the U.S. Treasury that reaps the benefits of restricting the supply of imports. In the case of import quotas, it was the stockholders in oil companies who benefited.

tariff. The tariff, T, is equal to the difference between the world price, P_w, and the heavy horizontal line above it $(P_w + T)$. Domestic demanders of oil must now pay the world price plus the tariff. They cannot get oil any cheaper because producers know that everyone must pay the tariff; no one can escape it. The quantity of oil demanded falls from 4 billion barrels to 3.9 billion barrels because of the higher price. The quantity supplied domestically rises from 3.5 billion barrels to 3.6 billion barrels. The level of imports decreases from 0.5 billion barrels to 0.3 billion barrels, as it did in the quota system we discussed. However, there are differences. Although in both cases the price is higher, the quantity demanded is smaller, and the domestic quantity supplied is greater. In this case, *the government is now in possession of tariff revenues.* These revenues can be used to reduce taxes or to increase government expenditures on public goods and services. These revenues did not result from the oil-import quota program. There, the beneficiaries of the higher oil price were the stockholders in oil corporations, not the United States Treasury. The United States has had a history of widely varying tariff rates as we can see in Figure I-15.3.

What the Future Holds

To be sure, the future will see a continuation of special interest groups lobbying for protection from international competition. It is difficult, though, for these groups to use the same arguments they have in the past—economic reality changes much too fast. For many years the cry of "cheap Japanese labor" was heard, particularly from the United States labor movement. Lower-paid Japanese workers were undercutting American workers, and, in essence, we were exporting jobs to Japan.

Japanese wages today, however, are far from being "slave" wages.

What we must realize is that every economic action has a cost. It is indeed rare when everybody can be made better off by some policy. But any time trade is stifled, there are gainers and losers. Economic analysis tells us that general material well-being will be reduced any time there are restrictions on trade. However, by the same token, specific groups will benefit by restrictions on foreign competition. It is impossible to argue, from a purely economic point of view, whether certain types of foreign trade should be restrained because to do so would require ultimately a value judgment as to who should benefit or gain from a particular policy. One thing is fairly certain, though: Free traders win all the arguments, but protectionists win all the votes. Do not be surprised, then, if some form of a highly restrictive Burke-Hartke bill is eventually passed in Congress.

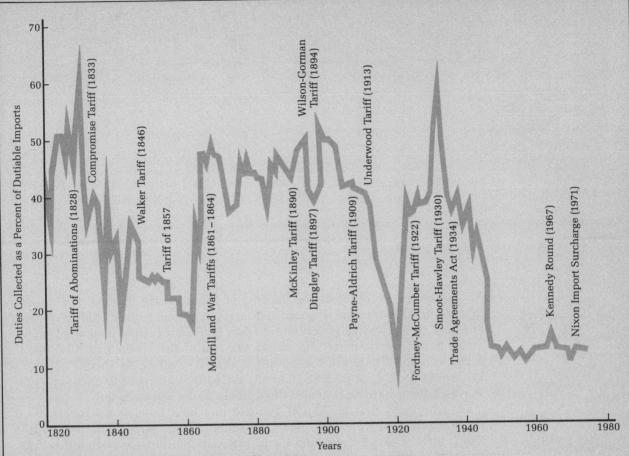

FIGURE I-15.3 Tariff Rates in the United States Since 1820

Tariff rates in the United States have bounced about like a football, and, indeed, in Congress, tariffs do represent a political football. Import-competing industries prefer high tariffs. In the twentieth century, the highest tariff we have had was the Smoot-Hawley Tariff of 1930, which was almost as high as the Tariff of Abominations in 1828. (*Source:* U.S. Department of Commerce.)

Questions for Thought and Discussion

1. What do we mean when we say that foreign trade is eliminating American jobs?
2. Is it possible for international trade not to create benefits for some and costs for others?
3. What is the argument in favor of a quota as opposed to a tariff?

Selected References

Adams, Walter, "The New Protectionism," *Challenge,* May–June, 1973.
Meier, Gerald M. *Problems of Trade Policy,* New York: Oxford University Press, 1973.

Financing World Trade

In Chapter 14 we outlined the benefits of trade among nations. We talked in terms of the movement of goods and services. We made very little reference, however, to the way in which world trade is financed. How does the United States pay for its imports? How does the rest of the world pay for United States exports? These are the questions that we will cover in this chapter. We will be looking at an area generally called *international finance*—an area in which there have been major disruptions in the last decade.

Let's begin by first looking at a world in which there is no government intervention in international monetary affairs. To an extent, this is the case today; there is less intervention in the international finance system than has occurred in many years. The 1970s have seen a more or less unrestricted international monetary market.

Flexible Exchange Rates

When you decide to buy foreign products—French wine, for example—you have only dollars with which to pay the French winemaker. However, that individual would be hard pressed to pay his workers in dollars. They're French; they live in France, and they need francs to buy goods and services. Obviously, then, there has to be some way of exchanging dollars for the francs the winemaker will accept. Normally, a **foreign exchange market** specializing in exchanging francs and dollars—that is, establishing a **foreign exchange rate**—would develop. In fact, these kinds of markets did develop very early in the game of international trade.

To get the Bordeaux wine you want, you go to the foreign exchange market.

Your desire to buy the wine therefore provides a supply of dollars to the foreign exchange market, and, at the same time, you demand francs. Every transaction concerning the importation of foreign goods constitutes a supply of dollars and a demand for some foreign currency and vice versa.

To simplify, we shall again consider only two countries: the United States and France. We will not worry about other currencies. We shall also assume only two goods are being traded: French wine and American bluejeans. The American demand for French wine creates a supply of dollars and a demand for francs. In France, the demand for American bluejeans creates a supply of francs and a demand for dollars. In the absence of restrictions—that is, in a freely floating exchange rate situation—these supplies and demands are going to reach an equilibrium level. The equilibrium level will be the equilibrium *exchange rate*, which tells us how many francs a dollar can be exchanged for (that is, the dollar price of francs).

Equilibrium Foreign Exchange Rate

We can easily demonstrate what the equilibrium exchange rate will be. The idea of an exchange rate is not different from the idea of paying a certain price for something you want to buy. If you like to buy cigarettes, you know you have to pay something like 70¢ a pack. At one time, cigarettes cost around 25¢. Usually, at such lower prices, you would demand more cigarettes. Therefore, the demand schedule of cigarettes expressed in terms of dollars slopes downward.

Demand Schedule of Francs

Now think about the demand schedule for francs. Let's say that today it will cost you 20¢

to purchase 1 franc. This is the exchange rate between dollars and francs. If you have to pay 25¢ tomorrow to buy that same franc, then the exchange rate has changed. When the dollar price of francs is higher, you will probably demand fewer of them. The demand schedule in terms of dollars for francs also slopes downward.

The easiest way to understand the derived demand (derived from the demand for final product) for francs is to take a simple numerical example. Below is the quantity of French wine demanded per week by, say, a representative wine drinker.

DEMAND FOR FRENCH WINE IN THE UNITED STATES PER WEEK

Price Per Liter	Quantity Demanded
$10	1 liter
8	2 liters
6	3 liters
4	4 liters

If the price per liter of wine in France is 20 francs, we can now find the quantity of francs needed to pay for the various quantities demanded above.

Quantity Demanded	Francs Required to Purchase Quantity Demanded
1 liter	20
2 liters	40
3 liters	60
4 liters	80

If the exchange rate is 1 franc = 50¢, then a bottle of French wine costing 20 francs in France would cost $10 in the United States. The quantity imported would be 1 liter. If the exchange rate is 1 franc = 40¢, then a 20-franc bottle of wine would cost $8 and the quantity imported would rise to 2 liters per week. At an exchange rate of 1 franc = 30¢, the United States price would be $6 and 3 liters would be imported. And finally, at an exchange rate of 1 franc = 20¢, a bottle would cost $4 and 4 liters would be imported.

Now we can obtain the derived demand for francs in the United States with which to pay for imports of wine.

DERIVED DEMAND FOR FRANCS IN THE UNITED STATES WITH WHICH TO PAY FOR IMPORTS OF WINE

Price of 1 Franc	Quantity Demanded
50¢	20 francs
40¢	40 francs
30¢	60 francs
20¢	80 francs

As can be expected, as the price of francs falls, the quantity demanded will rise. The only difference here from standard demand analysis is that the demand for francs is derived from the demand for a final product called French wine.

We show an aggregate version of the demand for French francs in Figure 15-1. It represents the demand for francs or, in our hypothetical situation, the demand for all foreign currency. The horizontal axis represents the quantity of foreign exchange—the number of francs. The vertical axis represents the exchange rate—the price of foreign currency (francs) expressed in dollars (cents per franc). At the foreign currency price of 25¢, you know it costs 25¢ to buy 1 franc. At the foreign currency price of 20¢, you know that it costs 20¢ to buy 1 franc.

FIGURE 15-1 **The Demand and Supply of French Francs**

Here we have drawn the demand curve for French francs. It is a derived demand schedule—that is, a schedule derived from the demand by Americans for French wine. We have drawn the supply curve of French francs, which results from the French demand for American bluejeans. The demand curve, *DD*, slopes downward like all demand curves, and the supply curve, *SS*, slopes upward. The foreign exchange price, or the U.S. dollar price of francs, is given on the vertical axis. The number of francs, in millions, is represented on the horizontal axis. If the foreign exchange rate is 25¢—that is, if it takes 25¢ to buy 1 franc—then Americans will demand 80 million francs. The equilibrium exchange rate is at the intersection of *DD* and *SS*. The equilibrium exchange rate is 20¢. At this point 100 million French francs are both demanded and supplied.

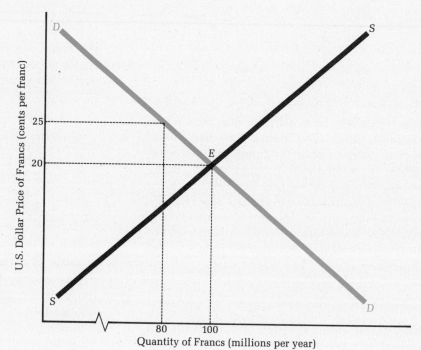

Supply Schedule of Francs

We now need to draw the supply relationship between French francs and their price in dollars. Obviously, the French want dollars in order to purchase American goods. When the dollar price offered for francs goes up, the French should be willing to supply more because they can then buy more American goods with the same quantity of francs. Let's take an example. A pair of bluejeans in the United States costs $10. If the exchange rate is 25¢ for 1 franc, the French have to come up with 40 francs to buy a pair of bluejeans. However, if the rate of exchange goes to 50¢ for 1 franc, they must come up with only 20 francs, thus inducing more purchases of bluejeans than before. Therefore, the supply schedule of foreign currency (francs) will be upward sloping.[1]

Equilibrium

As in all supply and demand diagrams, an equilibrium price will be established for the good in question—an exchange rate at which the French are happy to supply just the number of francs the Americans want to buy. The good in question here is foreign currency (French francs). The equilibrium price is established at 20¢ for 1 franc. This equilibrium is not established because Americans like to buy francs or the French like to buy dollars. Rather, the equilibrium exchange rate depends upon how many bluejeans the French want and how much wine Americans want (given their respective incomes, tastes, and the relative prices of wine and bluejeans).

[1]Actually, the supply schedule of foreign currency will be upward sloping if we assume that the demand for American imported bluejeans on the part of the French is price elastic. If the demand schedule for bluejeans is, however, price inelastic, the supply schedule will be negatively sloped. In the case of unitary elasticity of demand, the supply schedule for francs will be a vertical line. Throughout the rest of this chapter, we will assume that the demand schedule is elastic.

A Shift in Demand

Assume that a successful advertising campaign by American wine importers has caused the American demand (schedule) for wine to double. Americans demand twice as much wine at all prices. Their demand schedule for wine has shifted out and to the right. (Can you draw this?)

The increased demand for French wine can be translated into an increased demand for francs. All Americans clamoring for bottles of Bordeaux wine will supply more dollars to the foreign exchange market while demanding more French francs to pay for the wine. Figure 15-2 presents a new demand schedule, $D'D'$, for French francs; this demand schedule is to the right and outward from the original demand schedule. If the French do not change their desire for bluejeans, the supply schedule of French francs will remain stable. A new equilibrium will be established at a higher exchange rate. In our particular example the equilibrium is established at an exchange rate of 30¢. It now takes 30¢ to buy 1 French franc whereas it took 20¢ before. This is translated as an increase in the price of French wine to Americans and a decrease in the price of American bluejeans to the French.

Constant and Floating Exchange Rate

With *flexible* or *floating exchange rates*—that is, no regulations on the exchange rates—the number of francs demanded is always equal to the number supplied. Otherwise, the price will change until the quantities demanded and supplied are equal. With a floating exchange rate, there will always be equilibrium in the foreign exchange market. Actually, however, the foreign exchange market is merely a reflection of American desires for French wine and French desires for American bluejeans.

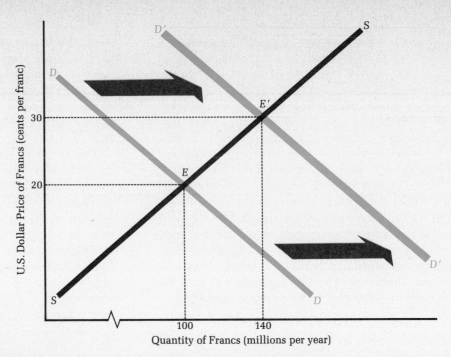

FIGURE 15-2 A Shift in the Demand Schedule
Americans experience a shift in their taste for French wine. The demand schedule for French wine shifts to the right, causing the derived demand schedule for francs to shift to the right also. We have shown that shift is a movement from *DD* to *D′D′*. We have assumed that the French supply schedule of francs has remained stable—that is, their taste for bluejeans has remained constant. The old equilibrium foreign exchange rate was 20¢. (It cost 20¢ to buy 1 franc.) The new equilibrium exchange rate will be at the intersection of *D′D′* and *SS*—or, *E′*. The new exchange rate will be higher than the old one. It will now cost 30¢ to buy 1 franc. The quantity of francs demanded is greater even at this higher price because the demand schedule has shifted out. The higher price of francs will be translated into a higher price for French wine.

In the above example, we assumed that Americans' taste for wine had shifted. Now let's assume that an inflation in France has caused the prices of everything there to double. The French now have to pay more for their wine. To Americans, prices in France have risen by 100 percent, while the price of bluejeans in the United States has remained constant. What would happen if exchange rates remained constant in such a situation? The price of French wine would rise relative to the price of American bluejeans in both countries. At the fixed exchange rate, the increase in French wine prices would reduce the supply of dollars in

the foreign exchange market because American citizens would buy less French wine at the new higher dollar price. The demand for dollars would increase because the French would want to buy more bluejeans that are now cheaper relative to French wine.

If we assume a *free* or floating foreign exchange market, this disequilibrium situation cannot last. What happens is that the exchange rate falls by 50 percent. We see in Figure 15-3 that the supply schedule for francs will shift to the right. (The demand schedule, for simplicity, is shown to be stable. However, this will occur only with a unitary demand schedule for

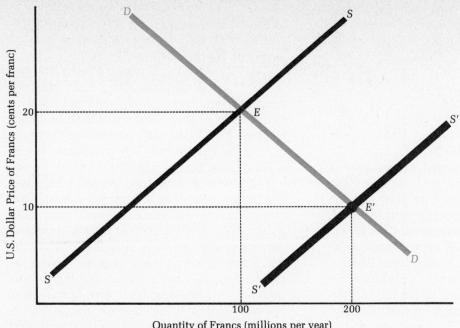

FIGURE 15-3 **Free Foreign Exchange Market**

An inflation in France causes prices there to double. As a result, Americans demand fewer francs than before and the French demand more dollars. (American prices are now cheaper relative to higher French prices.) A disequilibrium situation cannot last in a free or floating foreign exchange market, however, and the exchange rate falls. Now 10¢—rather than 20¢—will buy 1 franc. The supply schedule for francs will shift to the right. After the exchange rate adjustment, the amount of francs demanded will be 200 million. Thus, changes in prices due to inflation in one country bring about compensating changes in the foreign exchange rate so that the total amount of trade (measured in goods) remains the same.

exports.) The new equilibrium will be established at an exchange rate of 10¢. That is, 10¢ will now buy 1 franc, whereas before the rise in the price of wine, it took 20¢ to buy 1 franc. After the exchange-rate adjustment, twice as many francs will be demanded and sold as before. Notice the key point of this analysis: Changes in prices due to inflation in one country bring about *compensating* changes in the foreign exchange rate so that the total amount of trade remains the same.

This analysis did not hold in the first example because we assumed American tastes for wine had changed. Suddenly Americans were

willing to pay more for their wine than they had before. We ended up with a higher exchange rate and a larger quantity of francs being demanded and supplied. That is, the change in American tastes for foreign trade elicited an increase in foreign trade. In the present example, however, there is no change in tastes or in the underlying demand schedules for wine and bluejeans. Rather, there is an increase in the price of French wine relative to the price of American bluejeans at a fixed exchange rate. The final adjustment occurs in the foreign exchange market only. Our **balance of trade**—the value of goods bought and sold in the world market—remains constant. It remains in balance. The balance of payments also remains in balance because the exchange rate adjusts so that it will.

Balance of Payments

The **balance of payments** is a more general term used to reflect the value of *all* transactions made between nations, usually for a period of 1 year. Aside from buying and selling goods, we transact other business, such as investing and borrowing, with foreign nations. In our particular example, the balance of trade was equal to the balance of payments. The value of the transactions we had with France was equal to the value of the transactions France had with us. However, when a balance-of-payments deficit occurs (as it has in the United States for almost 20 years), it means that the value of our transactions with other countries is such that they are sending us more things than we are sending them. These "things" include all possible types of services, investments, and so on. Something very special is necessary for a balance-of-payments deficit to exist since with freely floating exchange rates, the balance of payments will, by definition, always be in balance. In fact, with a freely floating exchange rate it is meaningless to talk about a balance of payments since there can be no deficit or surplus.

How We Measure the Balance of Payments

Unfortunately for the beginning students, the balance of payments can be measured in a number of ways. In Table 15-1, we list six of the most common measures applied to the United States for various years over the last decade. These measures are described below.

Merchandise Trade Balance   This is merely the difference between our exports and imports of tangible items. For the better part of the last

30 years, the United States had a surplus in its merchandise trade account. However, the situation reversed in the 1970s, and we started importing more than we exported.

Goods and Services Account   The goods and services account is the same as the merchandise trade balance except that services and intangible items have been added. These are the invisibles; they include shipping insurance, tourist expenditures, and income from foreign investments. Note that these items are net in the sense that they represent the difference between what foreigners purchase here and what we purchase abroad. Thus the investment income aspect of the goods and services account tells us the difference between income received by Americans from investments abroad and the income received by foreigners from investments here. We see, for example, when we compare lines 1 and 2 in Table 15-1, that in the year 1961 the service balance in our balance-of-payments account was zero. Since then it has grown, primarily due to the growth in income from direct United States investment in other countries.

Table 15-1 **Our Foreign Accounts**

	1961	1966	1971	1975
Merchandise trade balance (goods)	5.6	3.8	−2.7	7.4
Goods and services	5.6	5.2	0.7	13.4
Current account	3.1	2.3	−2.8	8.6
Basic balance (current account and long-term capital)	0	−1.7	−9.4	−1.9
Net liquidity balance	−2.3	−2.2	−22.0	12.3
Official settlements balance	−1.3	0.2	−29.8	−12.9

Source: Federal Reserve Bank of St. Louis, *U.S. Balance of Payments Trends,* 1975 data are preliminary

Current Account This balance differs from the one in line 2 by the inclusion of net government and private transfers. In other words, it includes extension of foreign aid by the United States to other countries, charity to those living in other countries, and military expenditures.

Basic Balance (Current Account and Long-Term Capital Flows) The difference between the basic balance and the current account given in line 3 is the inclusion of long-term capital balances. Long-term capital flows relate to, for example, the purchase of foreign long-term bonds by Americans or the purchase of United States long-term bonds by foreigners.

Net Liquidity Balance Whenever there is a deficit or surplus in the basic balance, the difference must be made up by what are called short-term private capital flows and government actions. This is where we get the net liquidity balance. It tells us how much short-term debt (that is, debt investments having a maturity date of less than 1 year) we had to sell abroad to make up our basic balance (or vice versa).

Official Settlements Balance This balance differs from the net liquidity balance in that it includes private liquid-capital flows. In other words, it includes dollars that are accumulating in foreign banks (for example) instead of being spent in the United States because the United States has a balance-of-payments deficit.

The United States Deficit

However you look at it, the United States was running a balance-of-payments deficit at the beginning of this decade. Obviously, this is not possible in a freely floating exchange world, but at that time we weren't in a freely floating exchange world; rather, we were using **fixed exchange rates,** more or less, when transacting

international business. To understand the adjustment mechanism for fixed exchange rates, we first have to consider a hypothetical world that is on a gold standard.

The Hypothetical Pure Gold Standard

Assume that many years ago, the world was on a pure **gold standard** and every nation's currency was tied directly to gold. Nations operating under this gold standard agreed to redeem their currency for a fixed amount of gold upon the request of any holder of that currency. Although gold was not necessarily the means of exchange for world trade, it was the unit to which all currencies under the gold standard were pegged. And since all currencies in the system were linked to gold, exchange rates between those currencies were fixed. Let's once again confine our discussion to two countries. Also, let's again assume that Americans buy French wine, and the French buy American bluejeans.

The value of a United States dollar is pegged to gold at a rate of $1 per 1/20th of an ounce of gold. The French have pegged their franc at a rate of 1 franc for 1/100th of an ounce of gold. Therefore, the exchange rate between francs and dollars is fixed at 1 franc for 20¢. Let's also assume that this is the equilibrium exchange rate at which the quantity of foreign exchange demanded is equal to the quantity supplied.

Inflation in France

Suppose an inflation raises French prices by 100 percent. At the fixed exchange rate, Americans will find wine is priced higher than before, and they will demand a smaller amount. Americans will supply fewer dollars to the foreign exchange market and demand fewer francs. On the other hand, the relative price of bluejeans will be lower for the French. (Everything they buy in France has gone up in price, but American bluejeans have not.) Wanting more bluejeans, the French will supply more francs to the foreign exchange market and demand more dollars.

Now, instead of an adjustment in the exchange rate, the exchange rates are fixed under the gold standard. There will be a balance-of-payments problem. France will run a deficit with respect to the United States, and the United States will run a surplus with respect to France. At the fixed exchange rate, the value of bluejeans sent to France is greater than the value of wines sent to America. This is a disequilibrium situation, and something has to give. Disequilibrium in the foreign exchange market (balance-of-payments imbalance) cannot last forever. Americans will find they have more and more francs, which, in themselves, are useless. Francs are only good if they can be exchanged for something. But French wine is too expensive, so Americans don't want to buy as much as before.

Rise in American Prices

Under the gold standard, the Americans can exchange their francs for French gold. Americans do this, and for every 1 franc they get 1/100th of an ounce of gold. The French are forced to ship the gold to America.

But what good is gold? Under our hypothetical gold standard, gold at that time was in circulation; it was used as money, as a medium of exchange. Thus, gold could be sent from France, and the Americans receiving it could spend it on goods and services. An increase in the supply of gold in the United States under the hypothetical gold standard, however, results in an increase in our money supply. In a full-employment situation, prices in the United States rise. As United States prices go up, French wine at the fixed exchange rate becomes increasingly attractive. Even though the cost of French wine is higher than before, the price of French wine to a United States buyer remains the same (at least for a while) because of a fixed exchange rate. French wine therefore becomes less expensive *relative* to everything else in the United States, and Americans start to demand more.

Fall in French Prices

The French now see the price of bluejeans going up and up as United States prices rise. They start demanding fewer bluejeans. And since gold is leaving France, the money supply falls there and deflation ensues—falling prices. Eventually prices in the United States rise and prices in France fall to levels that induce French and American buyers alike to purchase the old quantities of bluejeans and wine. There would be equilibrium again in the foreign exchange market. The quantity of dollars supplied and francs demanded would just equal the quantity of dollars demanded and francs supplied.

With a fixed exchange rate under the gold standard in a full-employment situation, the adjustment mechanism is by way of changes in *internal prices*—not by changes in the exchange rate. How would the gold standard work in an under full employment situation? According to one analysis, it would work through adjustments in *real income*.

Real-Income Adjustment Mechanism

Let's assume the United States is experiencing unemployment. As gold flows in, people find they have excess supplies of cash balances. To rid themselves of these cash balances, they spend more than they receive. Desired expenditures rise. There is increased total aggregate demand, which results in an increase in output. Prices don't have to rise because unemployed people and resources are used to meet the increased demand. The increase in output can be translated to an increase in real income. Now, realizing that people's demand for goods and services is a positive function of their income, we know that, as incomes go up, more will be demanded even at the same price. The price of French wine in America would not fall. But the gold flow would result in increased real income, which would eventually cause Americans to demand more wine even at higher prices. As Americans demand more wine, they supply more dollars to the foreign exchange market and demand more francs. Eventually equilibrium is established when output rises high enough for Americans to want to buy the same quantity of wine they had purchased at a lower price. When equilibrium in the foreign exchange market is established, there ceases to be any more gold flows.

We have not considered the money supply, the price level, or the output in France. To test your understanding, analyze the situation at the same time in France as she loses gold. You will see that an offsetting situation establishes itself which also brings the foreign exchange market back to equilibrium.

Pure Gold Standard in Theory

Under the hypothetical pure gold standard outlined here, no country's money supply could be insulated from international balance-of-payments problems. Any difference between exports and imports alters a country's money supply. A country whose prices are relatively high in the world market at a fixed exchange rate will experience a decrease in her gold stock (money supply) and prices will fall. A country whose prices are relatively low in the world market will experience an increase in her gold stock (money supply) and prices will rise. Monetary control, as defined by alterations in the money supply, would not be under domestic control by domestic central banks. Such a situation would never be tolerated. Even a modified gold standard would fall apart sooner or later—as it did in the 1930s.

Monetary Policies Come into Play

During the 1930s, nations asserted their independence from the fixed-exchange-rate discipline. Nations refused to allow any excess demand or supply of their currencies in the foreign exchange markets to affect their own domestic money supplies. They would no longer give balance-of-payments problems the slightest priority over domestic economic considerations. What happens to a system of fixed exchange rates when there are not many shipments of gold? National governments, through their central banks, stabilize exchange rates by entering the foreign exchange markets themselves.

Let's take our two-country example again. Suppose the price of bluejeans has gone up. Suppose, in fact, there is a general rise in prices for everything in the United States. The French now will buy fewer bluejeans than before. They supply fewer francs to the foreign exchange market and demand fewer dollars at the fixed exchange rate. But Americans continue to demand French wines. In fact, they will demand more because, at the fixed exchange rate, the relative price of French wines has fallen. Americans will now supply more dollars in the foreign exchange market and demand more francs. As in Figure 15-4, the demand curve for francs will shift to D'D'. In the absence of any intervention by central banks, the exchange rate will change. The price of French francs in terms of dollars will go from 20¢ per franc to 25¢. That is, the value of a dollar in terms of francs will go down. The dollar will suffer a **depreciation** in its value relative to francs, and the franc will experience an **appreciation** in its value in terms of dollars. But the United

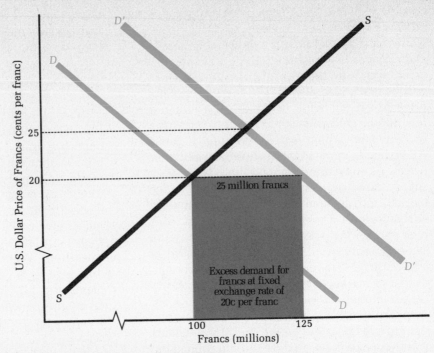

FIGURE 15-4 Supporting the Value of the Dollar in the Foreign Exchange Market

If there is inflation in the U.S., all prices go up. However, prices remain constant in France, so French goods become cheaper for Americans. The demand schedule for French goods shifts to the right as does the derived demand schedule for French francs, from *DD* to *D'D'*. Without exchange rate controls, the exchange rate would rise to 25¢—it would now cost 25¢ instead of 20¢ to buy a franc. The U.S. government, however, is committed to supporting the price of the dollar. Instead of allowing the dollar to equal 4 francs, the government maintains the price of a dollar at 5 francs—it keeps the price at 20¢ per franc. But at that exchange rate there is an excess demand for francs at the fixed exchange rate of 25 million. The U.S. government must step in and supply 25 million francs from its coffers in order to support the dollar in the foreign exchange market.

States government is committed to maintaining a fixed price of dollars in the foreign exchange market. When the French take their excess dollars and throw them onto the foreign exchange markets, the American central bank—the Federal Reserve—will be forced to go into the foreign exchange market and buy up those excess dollars. The Federal Reserve has to have foreign currency to buy up the excess dollars. That is, it has to have a reserve of francs in its coffers to get the dollars that the French want to sell. It must supply 25 million francs, as seen in Figure 15-4, to keep the exchange rate fixed. In the process, the money supply in the United States will fall because the dollars that left the country ended up with the Fed rather than in domestic circulation.

Just to make the process clearer, let's review it briefly.

A Recap

1. Prices in the United States have gone up.
2. French wine becomes a better deal for Americans at the fixed exchange rate;

American bluejeans become a worse deal for French buyers at the fixed exchange rate.

3. Americans buy more wine than before; the French buy fewer bluejeans than before.
4. At the fixed exchange rate, the value of American imports (French wine) exceeds the value of American exports (bluejeans). This is a trade deficit for the United States.
5. Americans send dollars abroad that are only partly returned as the French buy American bluejeans.
6. The French end up with excess dollars—those dollars are no longer in circulation in the United States.
7. The Federal Reserve buys up, with francs, those excess dollars in the foreign exchange market to support the price of the dollar; it now has dollars in its coffers.
8. The dollars in the coffers of the Federal Reserve do not constitute part of the money supply in the United States; therefore, the money supply falls.

Thus, we can see there are money supply alterations even without the gold standard if countries attempt to stabilize the price of their currency in the foreign exchange market.

Many countries finally tired of letting their money supplies be dictated by these balance-of-payments adjustments made in order to stabilize the fixed exchange rate. Instead of allowing the money supply to fluctuate, however, countries engaged in **sterilization policies.** A drop in the money supply due to a balance-of-payments deficit, for example, was made up by expansionary monetary policy.

In the last example, the money supply fell when there were more imports than exports because the Federal Reserve bought surplus dollars on the foreign exchange market in order to support their price. The Fed does not have to sit back and watch the money supply fall, however. It has the option of increasing the

money supply by open-market operations. Therefore, every time the money supply falls because of a *deficit* in our balance of payments, the Fed can sterilize that fall by buying bonds from the commercial banks, thereby putting back in circulation all the dollars that flowed out of the country and into the coffers of the Federal Reserve as it stabilized the price of the dollar. This is essentially how each individual central bank can insulate its own money supply from the vagaries of world monetary events, when it does not opt for flexible exchange rates.

Currency Crisis

Notice that the only way for the United States to support the price of the dollar was to buy up excess dollars with foreign reserves—that is, with French francs (or with gold). But the United States might eventually run out of the francs (or gold). It would then no longer be able to stabilize the price of the dollar, and a **currency crisis** would ensue. A currency crisis occurs when a country can no longer support the price of its currency in foreign exchange markets. Many such crises have occurred in the past several decades. Deficit countries ran out of the wherewithal to stabilize foreign exchange rates.

Internal Policies

Deficit countries do have the option of following internal policies that will reduce the deficit in their balance of payments. This can be done by somehow lessening the demands for goods from other countries. Causing a deflation or reducing people's real incomes (belt tightening) are two possible actions. Surplus countries, on the other hand, can allow an inflation. Most countries, however, find this type of internal price and income adjustment to international payments problems too costly, although England has followed such policies on many occasions—much to the chagrin of most English citizens.

Devaluation

Another alternative is to unilaterally *devalue*. When this happens, a country states that it will now support the price of its currency at a lower value than before. Devaluation is exactly what would happen in a freely floating exchange-rate situation. With fixed exchange rates, though, it happens only after there has been a long period of balance-of-payments deficits—that is, only after the country has exhausted all the possible ways to support the price of its currency in the foreign exchange market.

There are several other possibilities that we have yet to discuss. One of these involves borrowing from abroad; others are using gold, "paper gold," or special reserves in the International Monetary Fund. We shall discuss these last three methods in the following issue. For now, we shall examine the alternative of borrowing abroad.

Financial Assets

In addition to buying and selling goods and services in the world market, it is also possible to buy and sell financial assets. There is really no difference in terms of the foreign exchange market. If, on the one hand, Americans decide to buy stocks in French companies, the demand for French financial assets will create a derived demand for francs and a supply of dollars. On the other hand, if the French decide they want to buy AT&T corporate bonds, that demand will result in a derived demand for American dollars and a supply of francs.

Suppose that, at the fixed exchange rate, there is a balance-of-payments deficit in the United States; the value of our imports exceeds the value of our exports to France. What happens if the American government gets the French government to purchase American financial assets? What if Americans somehow get the French to lend back some of those excess dollars? If we are successful, then the value of our imports at the fixed exchange rate can be made equal to the value of our exports including the export of debt—financial assets—to the French. This is one way of making up the difference between the value of imports and the value of exports.

If Americans have to cajole the French central bank into lending back dollars, then at present interest rates in the United States, *individual* French citizens will not find our financial assets attractive enough to purchase. If they did, it would alleviate the balance-of-payments problem. Their demand as *individuals* for our financial assets would provide a demand for United States dollars and a supply of francs so that equilibrium could be maintained in the foreign exchange market. The fact that it is not individuals but foreign central banks which lend us back our money by buying our financial assets indicates that these are *involuntary* loans. Germany and Japan have run a surplus with the United States for many years. Apparently, the Japanese and German citizenry has been "involuntarily" lending us back our dollars for a number of years. We can draw this conclusion because it is the central banks of those countries that have been buying our bonds to help our deficit with them.

There are ways, of course, to make our financial assets more attractive to foreigners. The easiest way is to increase the yield on those assets—that is, make the interest rate higher through monetary and fiscal policies. Thus, the government can temporarily get itself out of a balance-of-payments deficit by increasing its interest rates.

The Multiplier

Let's now try to analyze the output and employment effect of changes in exports or imports by using the multiplier analysis from past chapters. We now add to our $C + I + G$ schedule a **net export** factor. Let's call net exports X, so that

$$\text{Net } X = \text{exports} - \text{imports}$$

If X is negative, we are importing more than we are exporting; we're running a deficit in our balance of trade. If X is positive, we're exporting more than we're importing, which means we're running a surplus in our balance of trade. A change in our balance of trade will have a multiplier effect on output and employment.

Let's redraw our $C + I + G$ schedule to include net exports, X, which are considered to be autonomous, like G and I. There is also a **net export multiplier** of the same magnitude as the government multiplier and the investment multiplier. The reasoning behind this follows. With a positive X, foreigners demand more of our goods while we continue to demand the same quantity of their goods. There is an increase in net exports, and American exporters receive "fresh" income from the outside world. They pay this income to their workers (in part). Their workers save part of it and spend part of it. People who receive what these workers spend also save part and spend part, and so it goes. Thus, there is a multiple expansion in national income from any increase in exports without a concomitant increase in imports.

Look at our $C + I + G + X$ schedule in Figure 15-5. If X goes up, we have a new line, $C + I + G + X'$, which is higher by the amount of the increase in X, net exports. The increase in income, however, is a multiple of the increase in X. If our marginal propensity to consume is 0.8, the increase in NNP will be five times the increase in X.

Using this Keynesian analysis, we can see that the government would desire to increase exports relative to imports so as to have an increase in income. Also, the government would be concerned if there were an increase in imports over exports because it would fear a decrease in income and employment. In other words, using Keynesian analysis, one would predict that a rising balance-of-trade deficit (or a shrinking surplus) would lead to a reduction in output and employment. But corresponding changes in investment, government purchases, transfers, or taxes could compensate for any reduction in net exports, X.

Sectoral Effects

All economists readily agree that shifts in world trade will have effects on different sectors of the economy. For example, if Japan becomes more price competitive in the world market with her automobiles, Americans will demand more Japanese automobiles. The stockholders in General Motors and Chrysler will be hurt. Employment in the automobile industry in the United States will be lower than it would be otherwise. Workers who are laid off in that industry will experience the costs of unemployment even if it's temporary. If, however, IBM becomes more competitive in the world market, stockholders and workers in that company will be better off. Thus, whenever our balance-of-trade position worsens vis-à-vis the rest of the world, government officials become concerned because certain sectors of the economy suffer. Any time America's international competitive position weakens, the export sector as well as the import-competing sector will suffer. Any time America's world position in trade improves, the export- and the import-competing sectors will benefit (but there will still be offsetting changes in the nontraded goods sector).

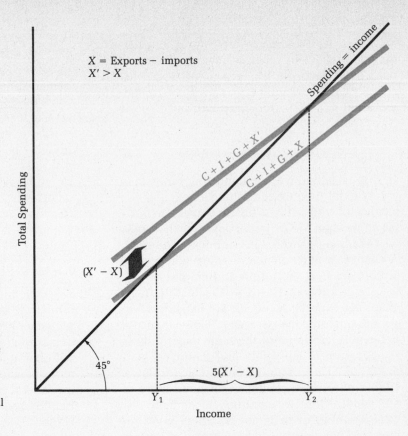

X = Exports − imports
X' > X

Spending = income

C + I + G + X'

C + I + G + X

Total Spending

(X' − X)

45°

5(X' − X)

Y_1 Y_2

Income

FIGURE 15-5 The Export Multiplier

Here is our usual multiplier graph. Income is measured on the horizontal axis; total aggregate spending, on the vertical axis. The 45 degree helper line is where total spending equals total income. We have added an X factor to our C + I + G line. X equals exports minus imports, or net exports. We start out in equilibrium with the C + I + G + X line intersecting the 45 degree spending-equals-income line at an income of Y_1. Now there is an increase in net exports. The schedule shifts up to C + I + G + X', where X' is greater than X. The vertical shift in the schedule is the difference between X' and X. However, the new equilibrium income, if we assume a multiplier of 5, is going to be equal to the old equilibrium income of Y_1 plus five times the new increase in net exports, or $Y_1 + 5 (X' − X)$. The new equilibrium will be at Y_2.

Definitions of New Terms

Flexible Exchange Rates: Exchange rates that are allowed to fluctuate in the open market in response to changes in supply and demand. Sometimes called free exchange rates or floating exchange rates.

Foreign Exchange Market: The market for buying and selling foreign currencies.

Foreign Exchange Rate: The price of foreign currency in terms of domestic currency, or vice versa. For example, the foreign exchange rate for francs is 25¢. This means that it takes 25¢ to buy 1 franc. An alternative way of stating the exchange rate is that the value of the dollar is 4 francs. It takes 4 francs to buy $1.

Balance of Trade: The value of goods and services bought and sold in the world market.

Balance of Payments: The value of goods, services, financial assets, military transactions, and all other transactions in the world market.

Fixed Exchange Rate: A system of exchange rates that requires government intervention to fix the value of each nation's currency in terms of each other nation's currency.

Gold Standard: In its purest form (which is only hypothetical), an international monetary system in which gold plays a prominent part. Nations fix their exchange rates in terms of gold. Thus, all currencies are fixed in terms of each other. Any balance-of-payments problems could be made up by shipments of gold.

Depreciation: A lessening of the value of a domestic currency in terms of foreign currencies. Depreciation occurs in a freely floating foreign exchange market when there is an excess supply of the currency in question. In a fixed exchange market, depreciation can occur if the government allows it. Then it is called *devaluation*. Devaluation is an official lessening of the value of a domestic currency in terms of other currencies.

Appreciation: The increasing of the value of a domestic currency in terms of other currencies. This occurs in a freely floating exchange market when the demand for a currency exceeds the supply. In a fixed exchange-rate market, appreciation cannot occur naturally; it must be done officially. Then it is called *revaluation*.

Sterilization Policies: Central bank policies designed to mitigate or completely eliminate money supply changes due to the central bank's foreign exchange transactions. These transactions are necessary now and then to maintain a fixed exchange rate.

Currency Crisis: A situation in the international money market that occurs when a country no longer has the wherewithal (foreign exchange, gold, credit, and so on) to support the price of its currency. A currency crisis brings forced devaluation.

Net Exports: The difference between exports and imports.

Net Export Multiplier: The factor by which an increase in net exports will increase national income. Similar to the government and investment multipliers we discussed in previous chapters.

Chapter Summary

1. To transact business internationally, it is necessary to convert different domestic currencies into other currencies. This is done via a foreign exchange market, which specializes in exchanging different foreign currencies. If we were trading with France only, French producers would want to be paid in francs since they must pay their workers with francs. American producers would want to be paid in dollars since American workers are paid in dollars.

2. An American's desire for French wine is expressed in terms of a supply of dollars, which in turn is a demand for French francs in the foreign exchange market. The opposite situation arises when the French wish to buy American bluejeans. Their demand for bluejeans creates a demand for American dollars and a supply of French francs. We put the demand and supply schedules together to find the equilibrium foreign exchange

rate. The demand schedule for foreign exchange is a derived demand—derived, that is, from the demand for foreign products themselves.

3. With no government intervention, there will exist an equilibrium foreign exchange rate that clears the market. After a shift in demand or supply, the exchange rate will change so it will again clear the market.

4. Suppose Americans increase their demand for French wine. The demand schedule for French wine shifts outward to the right. The derived demand for francs also shifts outward to the right. The supply schedule of francs, however, remains stable because the French demand for American bluejeans has remained constant. The shifted demand schedule intersects the stable supply schedule at a higher price (the foreign exchange rate increases). This is an appreciation of the value of French francs (a depreciation of the value of the dollar against the franc). It now costs 25¢ instead of 20¢ to buy 1 franc. This causes the price of wine to Americans to rise and the price of bluejeans to the French to fall.

5. To take another example, assume there is an inflation in France. The price of all French goods goes up. The relative price of French goods increases, and American demand for French goods falls. French demands for American goods rise, however. In a freely floating exchange market, the supply curve will shift right so that a new equilibrium in the exchange market occurs. The new equilibrium will be at a lower price for French francs; the value of the French franc falls and the value of the American dollar in terms of francs rises. With freely floating exchange rates in this situation, the equilibrium quantity of trade remains the same while the exchange rate falls to take account of the inflation in France.

6. The balance of trade is defined as the value of goods bought and sold in the world market, usually during the period of 1 year. In the last example, it remained constant. The only thing that changed was the exchange rate. The balance of payments is a more inclusive concept since it includes the value of all transactions in the world market. In a world of freely floating exchange rates, it is impossible to have a balance-of-payments deficit or surplus. That is, the value of transactions in one country must equal the combined value of transactions in all the other countries it deals with. In essence, in a world of freely floating exchange rates, there is no such thing as a balance-of-payments imbalance.

7. With fixed exchange rates, however, there can be balance-of-payments deficits or surpluses. That is, the value of foreign transactions at the fixed exchange rate may be greater in one country than in another country. A deficit or surplus arises. One way to understand the fixed exchange rate is to go back to a hypothetical pure gold standard.

8. In a hypothetical pure gold standard situation, the American value of the dollar is pegged to gold at the rate of, say, $1 per 1/20th of an ounce. The French peg their franc to gold at the rate of 1 franc for 1/100th of an ounce. The fixed exchange rate, then, is 1 franc for 20¢. If there is inflation in France, a deficit in France's balance of payments results. American goods are more attractive at the fixed exchange rate. The French buy more American goods than Americans buy French goods. However, the French deficit means that Americans end up with surplus francs. Having no use for these francs, Americans ship them back to France and demand gold. Gold is shipped to America and is used as money, thereby increasing the money supply. In a full-employment situation, prices rise in America. In France the money supply falls and prices fall. Internal prices change so that equilibrium comes about again even at the fixed exchange rate.

9. It is also possible in a gold standard situation to have changes in real income. Such changes would lead to a contraction in the French demand for American products and an expansion in the American demand for French products. Equilibrium would be established again.

10. The pure gold standard has very high internal domestic adjustment costs and was, therefore, rejected long ago. Countries wanted to pursue their own independent monetary and fiscal policies. They sterilized money supply changes resulting from balance-of-payments problems and from their attempts to support a constant or fixed exchange rate for their currencies. Eventually, countries experiencing chronic deficits ran out of the foreign exchange or gold that they could use to support the price of their currencies in the world foreign exchange market. They experienced a currency crisis and were then forced to devalue. England has done this many times.

11. Americans purchase financial assets in other countries, and foreigners purchase American financial assets, such as stocks on a stock exchange or bonds in our bond markets. The buying and selling of foreign financial assets has the same effect on the balance of payments as the buying and selling of goods and services.

12. We can use a multiplier analysis to show the effects of a change in net exports. Net exports are defined as exports minus imports. Keynesian multiplier analysis indicates that an increase in net exports will increase income more than proportionally to the increase in net exports. In fact, there will be a multiple expansion. If the multiplier is 4, an increase in net exports of, say, $2 billion will equal an increase in income of $8 billion.

1. What is the case for flexible exchange rates?
2. What is the case for fixed exchange rates?
3. Why have we had a balance-of-payments deficit for such a long period of time?
4. Is America as a nation better off if it has a balance-of-payments deficit? If so, is there anybody who is worse off?
5. Why aren't there balance-of-payments problems between New York and California, or, for that matter, between any two states in the United States?
6. Do you think that devaluation or revaluation should be used as a stabilizing policy to influence income and employment in the United States?

Selected
References

Economic Report of the President, various issues, Washington, D.C.: U.S. Government Printing Office.

Evans, John W., *U.S. Trade Policy,* New York: Harper & Row, 1967.

Friedman, Milton and Robert U. Roosa, *The Balance of Payments: Free versus Fixed Exchange Rates,* Washington, D.C.: American Enterprise Association, 1967.

Mikesell, Raymond F., *Financing World Trade,* New York: Thomas Y. Crowell, 1969.

Snider, Delbert, *International Monetary Relations,* New York: Random House, 1966.

Issue I-16

Can Flexible Exchange Rates Halt Worldwide Inflation?

THE CHANGING WORLD OF INTERNATIONAL FINANCE

Inflation—A Worldwide Problem

Inflation is a problem in the United States and throughout the world. We show in Table I-16.1 the inflation rates for some industrialized countries. Inflation in the United States during the first half of the 1970s was

Table I-16.1

The Various Rates of Inflation in the World, 1970–1974

All industrialized nations have suffered inflation in this decade at rates equal to or greater than the United States.

COUNTRY	ANNUAL RATE OF INFLATION
Belgium	7.6
Canada	6.6
France	8.2
Germany	5.8
Italy	10.8
Japan	11.4
Netherlands	8.3
Switzerland	7.8
United Kingdom	10.5
United States	6.6

Source: Federal Reserve Bank of St. Louis

bad, but it certainly was not as severe as that of the other countries listed. There are, of course, many theories about what caused this worldwide inflation. We went into some of these theories in Chapter 7, and we also mentioned the monetarists' ideas concerning the importance of changes in the money supply in determining the long-run rate of inflation. In this issue, we will look at the relationship between inflation and the international monetary system.

Several years ago there was a great upheaval in the international monetary system. In 1973, world trade essentially began to take place on a flexible exchange rate basis. At that time there also occurred a great upsurge in our own rate of inflation. The natural conclusion seemed to follow—a switch to flexible exchange rates caused inflation. However, not all economists agreed. In fact, there was—and still is—a large group of international economic experts who firmly believe that a shift to flexible exchange rates will allow the world to reduce its high rate of inflation.

Before we discuss the pros and cons of this argument, let's look at the historical development of the

flexible exchange rate system that started in 1973.

The International Monetary Fund

In 1944, representatives of the world's capitalist nations met in Bretton Woods, New Hampshire, to create a new international payments system to replace the old gold standard that had collapsed during the 1930s. In 1944, Western Europe had been devastated by war and needed large amounts of imported capital—machines and raw materials—to rebuild its productive capacity. Also at that time, Western European countries were running large deficits with the United States. At the fixed exchange rates existing then, we were shipping more goods abroad than foreigners were shipping to us.

Lord Keynes—Head of British Delegation

At the head of the British delegation to the conference was John Maynard Keynes. He advocated a payments mechanism that would require surplus nations (the United States) to finance the deficits of other nations by lending them foreign exchange. The only other alternative was for the devastated Western European countries to reduce their imports so as to eliminate their trade deficits. Such a drastic measure would have made the recovery from war agonizingly slow. Lord Keynes rightly contended that if surplus nations were forced indefinitely to lend their foreign exchange to deficit nations, fixed exchange rates could be maintained. No country running a deficit would face a currency crisis. Any country could support the price of its currency with the foreign exchange lent to it by surplus nations.

Harry White—Head of American Delegation

The American delegation was headed by Harry Dexter White, who vigorously fought Keynes' proposal. America was the largest surplus nation in the free world, owning most of the world's gold stock. Keynes' proposal would have forced the United States into lending foreign exchange at a zero interest rate, thus forcing the country to continue subsidizing Europe for a long period to come. Harry Dexter White made a counterproposal that was finally adopted, and the **International Monetary Fund** (IMF) was created to help facilitate world financial exchanges.

The IMF Quota System

White's counterproposal called for fixed exchange rates but only a limited obligation to lend to deficit nations. The obligation was in the form of providing reserves for the International Monetary Fund. Upon becoming a member of the fund, each country was assigned a reserve quota. This quota was set according to a formula that took into account the economic importance of the country, its trade volume, and so on. The quota was paid to the IMF in a country's own domestic currency and in gold. The IMF was then able to lend foreign currency to any country that needed it in order to maintain a stable exchange rate.

When a country first borrowed from the IMF (within 25 percent of its quota), approval was given automatically. After the first borrowing, further borrowings were conditional. The IMF typically required deficit countries to take certain corrective measures (which would have occurred automatically under the gold standard) such as reducing their internal rate of inflation to make their goods more attractive internationally. In any event, the maximum amount a country could borrow was twice the quota assigned to that country. The unused portion of each country's automatic borrowing rights was called its **reserve position** in the IMF. Thus, America's limited obligation to lend to deficit nations was equivalent to the size of its quota in the IMF and no more.

Marshall Plan

The United States later solved Western Europe's deficit problems by voluntarily lending large quantities of dollars to Europe under the Marshall Plan. These loans enabled European countries to finance their imports from the United States. Consequently, the problem that Keynes feared concerning United States ability to finance imports was solved by voluntary loans from Uncle Sam.

The United States Develops a Deficit

Beginning in the late 1950s, the United States became chronically deficient in its balance of payments. Instead of a "dollar shortage," there was a "dollar surplus." By 1960 it was necessary for the United States to favor some arrangement whereby surplus nations, such as Germany and Japan, would be forced to lend exchange to deficit nations like the United States—just as Keynes had proposed in 1945.

The United States supported the creation of IMF Special Drawing Rights (SDRs), or "paper gold," that would enable deficit nations to borrow from surplus nations. A modified United States proposal was finally enacted and became effective January 1, 1970. The SDRs are different from the regular quota; they are a new international means of payment that has been *created* by the IMF. The original proposal was modified to give European nations a veto on the use of these pieces of paper gold. This, in effect, made the loans *voluntary* rather than obligatory on the part of the surplus countries.

Dwindling Gold Stock

Under IMF rules, the dollar was pegged to gold. The United States was obliged to redeem dollars in gold at $35 an ounce, if so requested by foreign holders of dollars. In effect, we were pegging dollars to the price of gold. Since foreigners had the right to demand gold for their excess dollars, we saw large outflows of gold during our period of balance-of-payments deficits. In Figure I-16.1

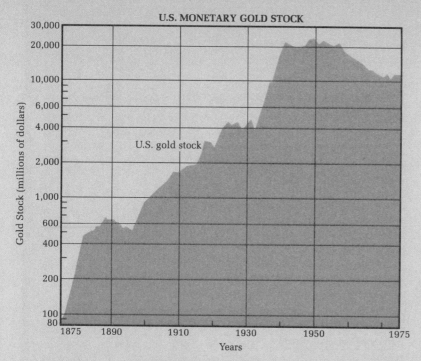

U.S. MONETARY GOLD STOCK

Gold Stock (millions of dollars)

30,000
20,000

10,000

6,000
4,000

U.S. gold stock

2,000

1,000

600
400

200

100
80

1875   1890   1910   1930   1950   1975

Years

FIGURE I-16.1

By the middle of World War II, we had amassed more than $20 billion worth of gold at the official price of $35 an ounce. By 1970, we had a little more than $10 billion worth of gold. Our chronic balance-of-payments deficit was responsible for this drain. *(Source: Federal Reserve Bulletin.)*

we see that our gold stock dwindled from $22 billion just after World War II to $11 billion in 1970. Many Americans were very distressed about our loss of gold.

In any event, during the 1960s, practically every Secretary of the Treasury spent part of his time trying to persuade foreign central banks to buy American financial securities rather than trade in their excess dollars for gold. In other words, we wanted surplus nations to lend back our dollars so we could continue our balance-of-payments deficit without altering our exchange rate and without cutting back our imports. Many countries went along with the American request, particularly West Germany. Other countries did not. We

had much trouble with de Gaulle when he was in power in France because he kept turning in his excess dollars for gold.

A Two-Tiered Gold System

Finally, in March 1968, the United States announced it would no longer sell gold to foreign private holders of dollars. A two-tiered price system of gold developed. There was a private market (no central banks participated) in which the United States did not support the price of gold. Theoretically, however, we continued to sell gold to foreign central banks at $35 an ounce. From 1968 until August 1971, we lost very little of our gold. The reason for this was that we had made it clear to other

nations that we would not allow a run on our gold. Essentially, we told other nations that they could buy gold from us at $35 an ounce, provided they did not ask for any.

A Rise in the Official Price of Gold

Although we were neither buying nor selling gold, the United States changed its official price for gold first from $35 to $38 an ounce, and then to $42.42 an ounce in February 1973. Throughout the world at that time there was a widespread adoption of floating exchange rates. This is not to say that the world financial community saw exchange rates moving up and down in response to the pure forces of supply and demand. Rather, governments entered foreign exchange markets to prevent changes in certain exchange rates, but the government intervention merely made the situation one of a **"dirty" float**. It did not, in effect, put us back onto the fixed exchange-rate system that had existed since the formation of the International Monetary Fund.

How would a floating exchange-rate situation affect a nation's rate of inflation? This is the basic question of this issue; we now turn our attention to it.

Exchange Rates and Monetary Policy

As we pointed out in Chapter 15, in a world of fixed exchange rates, a central bank can intervene any time there are forces that would alter the exchange rate from its pegged level. If, for example, there is pressure for an exchange rate to fall (depreciation), a central bank can enter the foreign exchange market and prevent such a fall by buying the currency with foreign exchange reserves. Normally, this would cause a contraction in the money supply and, in the long run, a reduction in the rate of inflation. However, a central bank, throughout the periods of large balance-of-payments deficits, prevents such a contraction in the money supply by expansionary open-market operations. On the other side of the picture, whenever there is pressure for a currency to go up in value (appreciate), then a central bank can enter the picture and prevent such a rise in value by selling its own domestic currency in the foreign exchange market. Normally, this would lead to an increase in the domestic money supply because the central bank merely creates its own domestic currency for sale in the exchange market. This would have a tendency to cause an increase in the price level—at least in the long run.

Opponents of fixed exchange rates point out that during the period of rapidly rising prices in Europe and Japan, which started in the early 1970s, these surplus nations made a concerted effort to prevent the appreciation of their currencies and rapidly expanded their money supplies. However, the inevitable result was higher rates of inflation. Thus,

Table I-16.2

Percentage Rate of Change in Money Supply in Selected Countries*

DATE	MONEY
1960	9.94
1961	13.54
1962	12.02
1963	13.73
1964	9.43
1965	11.26
1966	8.83
1967	8.77
1968	9.24
1969	9.94
1970	9.74
1971	17.47
1972	17.31
1973	13.05
1974	10.10

*Weighted averages of data from France, Germany, Japan, United Kingdom, Italy, Belgium, Netherlands. *Source: The Phenomenon of Worldwide Inflation*, David I. Meiselman and Arthur B. Loffer (eds.), Washington, D.C.: American Enterprise Institute, 1975, p. 86.

according to these same observers, switching to the system of floating exchange rates allows all nations to pursue independent monetary and fiscal policies without worrying about balance-of-payments problems because by definition they cannot exist in a world of floating rates. If we look at the data in Table I-16.2 in terms of changes in the money supply in selected countries, we do see some

evidence to support this position. We also see some evidence to support the position that worldwide rates of inflation did slow down when flexible rates became the rule rather than the exception in world financial dealings.

The United States Experience

The United States experience was somewhat different from that of Europe. When we essentially went on a system of free exchange rates, the dollar depreciated in world currency markets. We had to pay more for our imports than before—that is, we had to deliver more exports to pay for the same physical quantity of imports. Hence, depreciation of the dollar resulted in a decline of aggregate productivity and output. There is little doubt that the strong depreciation of the dollar in the early 1970s had an inflationary impact on the United States. However, the question is, "Will that inflationary impact be continuous and long lasting?" Or was it once and for all? Those who believe the former argue that we should go back to an international monetary system based on fixed exchange rates and in which the United States would be the world's central bank. Perhaps by the time you read this, more evidence will be available to support or refute such a view. Have worldwide rates of inflation finally slowed down in a world of flexible exchange rates? Or, does the argument in favor of an unrestricted international monetary system seem at odds with recent data?

Floating Exchange Rates and Oil Prices

Proponents of floating exchange rates point out that severe restrictions on oil production by leading oil exporters, particularly in the Middle East, and the resulting higher prices of oil, would, under a system of fixed exchange rates, have led to international monetary chaos. In fact, we can be fairly certain that if oil importing nations had attempted to maintain fixed exchange rates during the period when the Middle East oil-exporting countries effectively quadrupled the price of oil, there would have been recurrent currency crises. Flexible exchange advocates point with pride to the way in which the international monetary system was able to handle the perhaps unprecedented shock given to it by Persian Gulf oil politics.

Definitions of New Terms

International Monetary Fund (IMF): An institution set up to manage the international monetary system. It came out of the Bretton Woods Conference in 1944, which established, more or less, fixed exchange rates in the world.

Reserve Position: The unused portion of the automatic borrowing rights of IMF member countries.

"Dirty" Float: A freely floating exchange system that involves governments stepping in occasionally to prop up the value of their currency. To be contrasted with a "clean" float, where there is no government intervention in the foreign exchange market.

Questions for Thought and Discussion

1. "Fixed exchange rates impose the discipline necessary to keep the worldwide rate of inflation down." Evaluate this statement.
2. What does the IMF do today?
3. Does the official price of gold matter?

Selected References

Aliber, Robert Z., *The International Money Game*, New York: Basic Books, 1973.

Behrman, Jack N., "The Futility of International Monetary Reform," *Challenge*, July–August 1973, pp. 23–31.

Manne, Henry G. and Roger LeRoy Miller (eds.), *Gold, Money, and the Law*, Chicago: Aldine Publishing, 1975.

Stevens, Robert Warren, *A Primer on the Dollar in the World Economy*, New York: Random House, 1972.

Triffin, Robert, *Our International Monetary System: Yesterday, Today and Tomorrow*, New York: Random House, 1968.

Weil, Gordon L. and Ian Davidson, *Gold War: The Story of the World's Monetary Crisis*, New York: Holt, Rinehart and Winston, 1970.

Development of the Less-Developed Countries

The world consists of the haves and the have-nots. In this chapter we'll look at some of the problems facing these have-nots—the so-called less-developed countries, or LDCs. Then in the issue following we will look at the question of whether or not foreign aid can actually help the LDCs to become more developed, that is, richer.

How Do We Define an LDC?

The term *less-developed country* doesn't have a very definite meaning—what does "less developed" mean as opposed to "more developed?" The answer, of course, is relative. We usually define this term by comparing the per capita incomes of different countries and arbitrarily classifying those with a per capita income of around $500 or less as "less-developed countries." Look at Table 16-1. Here we show countries classified by the level of their per capita income: those with per capita income in excess of $1,000; those with per capita income between $501 and $1,000; and those with per capita income of $500 or less. Notice that the final category fits our definition of LDCs. It includes most of the Middle East and southeastern Europe, all Africa except South Africa, all Asia except for a few countries, and most of Latin America.

The Problems of the Information Explosion

The LDCs today are not as content with their economic lot as they were in the past. One of the reasons for this is that information about how the inhabi-

Table 16-1 Level of Per Capita Income in Selected Countries in Three Categories

Here we see which countries are classified as developed and which are classified as less developed by arbitrarily separating those countries with per capita incomes in excess of $1,000 from those countries where per capita income is less than $500. In between these two figures are countries that are in the process of development.

PER CAPITA INCOME OVER $1,000	PER CAPITA INCOME OF $501 TO $1,000	PER CAPITA INCOME OF LESS THAN $500
Australia	Argentina	Most of Latin America
Austria	Chile	All of Africa (except South Africa)
Canada	Cuba	All of Asia (except for a few
Czechoslovakia	Greece	countries)
East Germany	Most of the Middle	Mexico
Denmark	East and Southeast	Panama
Finland	Europe	Poland
France		Portugal
Ireland		Spain
Italy		Rumania
Japan		
Netherlands		
New Zealand		
Norway		
Sweden		
Switzerland		
United States		
U.S.S.R.		
Venezuela		
West Germany		

Source: Statistical Office of the United Nations

tants of rich countries live is now known in even the remotest villages of the most backward nation. Everybody knows about the comforts of modern Western living. The relative poverty of the world's masses is not as accepted as it used to be. These masses know that a better life exists elsewhere, and this is the life they are striving for. What do they want? They want all the good things in life: better health conditions, better housing, a more equal distribution of the wealth, perhaps starting with land reform, and so on.

And the poor people of the world are demanding that their governments do something about poverty and substandard living conditions. The governments, on the other hand, are relying on various political and economic theories to determine which policies will be the most appropriate to achieve these desired ends. But before we look into this matter, let us first take a look at why living standards are different throughout the world. Why, in other words, do some nations develop, but other nations do not?

Geographical Theories of Economic Development

One of the earliest and most simplistic theories of growth concerns geographical location. This might also be called the north/south theory of economic development. Nations that are in the colder climates will be more developed than nations in the warmer climates. This north/south theory works in some places today. In the United States, the north is more developed than the south. (However, this was not the case before the Civil War and might not be the case now had the institution of slavery been *gradually* abolished.) In Italy too, the north is more developed than the south; and the same is also true in France. It is not the case, however, in other countries.

In addition, if this theory had any relevance or validity, it should apply also to the past. It doesn't. Some of the first civilizations were in the southern, hot regions of the world. Look at the Mayas in Central America and all the great civilizations in the Mediterranean area and the Near East. The Germans and the Saxons were far behind the Greeks in development, even though the Greeks endured a warmer climate.

As an offshoot of this north/south theory, some economists have hypothesized that the geographical distribution of natural resources is important: where the oil and ore deposits are, where the best soil is, where the most useful rainfall is, and so on. However, although this may have had some validity in the past when trade was not as widespread as it is today, Japan, Denmark, and Israel demonstrate successful counterexamples of this theory.

The Race Theory of Development

Even more simplistic and certainly less easily defended is the race theory of development. Prosperity, according to this theory, is a matter of race: the whiter the race, the more productive the economy. There are so many counterexamples to this theory that they cannot all be mentioned here. The incredible success of the Japanese population in raising its standard of living is the most currently obvious example. However, the great development of the Egyptian, Greek, and Indian cultures, as well as the development of ancient China, also contradict this theory. Ethiopia too developed to a relatively high degree on its own. Race per se does not seem to be a very useful device for explaining why or predicting where prosperity will occur in the world economy.

More Modern Theories

More modern and more sophisticated theories of development are presented by today's economists. One of the most widely discussed concerns the need for balanced growth.

Balancing Industry with Agriculture

One characteristic of most developed countries is their high degree of industrialization. In general, nations with relatively high standards of living are more industrialized than countries with low standards of living. Some economists have taken this to mean that industrialization can be equated with economic development. The policy prescription is then obvious: So-called backward nations in which a large percentage of the total resources are devoted to agricultural pursuits should attempt to obtain a more balanced growth; they should industrialize.

Although the theory is fairly acceptable at first glance, it leads to some absurd results. We find in many LDCs with steel factories and automobile plants that the people are actually worse off because of this attempted industrialization. The reason is not hard to find. Most LDCs currently do not have a comparative advantage in producing steel or automobiles. They can engage in such industrial activities only by a heavy subsidization of the industry itself and by massive restrictions on competitive imports from other countries. For example, in India a steel mill may produce steel at two or three times the resource cost that would be required if the steel were imported. It seems quite apparent that the country is worse off, not better off, because of the steel mill. It may have the national prestige of owning a large, smoke-producing factory, but its citizens get less economic value out of their given resources than they would otherwise. This circumstance occurs throughout the entire less-developed world. Import restrictions abound, preventing the purchase of foreign, mostly cheaper, substitutes for the industrial products that the country itself produces in a usually subsidized environment. Sometimes the subsidization is not grossly obvious, but it usually exists in one form or another. In general, when an industry must be subsidized to exist, the subsidy leads to a misallocation of resources and a lower economic welfare for the country as a whole. The owners in the subsidized industry and the workers with skills specific to that industry are obviously better off. But the consumer ends up paying a higher *total* cost for the domestically made goods, and the total output of the nation remains less than it could be if the resources were reallocated.

The Stages of Development

If we look at the development of modern nations, we find that they go through three stages. First there is the agricultural stage, when most of the population is involved in agriculture. Then there is the manufacturing stage, when much of the population becomes involved in the industrialized sector of the economy. And finally there is a shift toward services. That is exactly what is happening in the United States: The so-called tertiary or service sector of the economy is growing by leaps and bounds, whereas the manufacturing sector, and its percentage employment, is declining.

However, it is important to understand the need for early specialization in one's comparative advantage. We have continuously referred to the doctrine of comparative advantage, and it is even more appropriate for the LDCs of the world. If trading is allowed among nations, a nation is best off if it produces what it has a comparative advantage at producing and imports the rest. This means that many LDCs should continue to specialize in agricultural production.

Agriculture Subsidized

There is a problem here, to be sure, and it is that modern Western countries have continually subsidized their own agricultural sectors to allow them to compete more easily with the comparative advantage that LDCs might have in this area. If we lived in a world of no subsidization, we would probably see much less food being produced in the highly developed Western world and much more being produced in the less-developed nations of the rest of the world. They would trade food for manufactured goods, and we would do the opposite. It would appear, then, that one of the most detrimental aspects of our economic policy for the Third World has been the continued subsidization of the American farmer. The United States, of course, is not alone; Germany, France, and England do exactly the same thing.

Even with this situation, however, a policy of balanced growth, or increased industrialization, in the LDCs of the world may lead

to more harm than good. Industrialization is generally only beneficial if it comes about naturally—that is, when the economic market conditions are such that the countries' entrepreneurs freely decide to build factories instead of increasing farm output.

Planning for Development in the LDCs

In many LDCs the governments have established specific development plans with specific targets and goals for the economy. In all cases, the purpose of these plans is to allocate resources so as to achieve a more rapid rate of economic growth. Capital, for example, may be allocated for specific purposes to encourage the development of well-defined sectors of the economy such as industry, education, or agriculture.

Development plans, however, should be carefully scrutinized before a decision is made as to their value. Some plans, for example, are merely window dressing. They are not based on careful investigation and some are not even actually put into effect. Other planning depends on such tools of modern economic analysis as linear programming and input-output analysis. These tools have been used extensively in certain situations and have been considered successful by some observers. However, their importance should not be exaggerated. No matter how good a plan is, it must be put into effect in a realistic and useful manner. Some of the

LDCs that have experienced the most development have tended to put aside their early development plans. Planning in these particular countries has become either modest or nonexistent. And although this is not to say that planning cannot help in development, nevertheless, some countries may find it difficult to formulate realistic plans and put them into effective action.

Property Rights and Economic Development

If you were in a country where bank accounts and businesses were periodically expropriated by the government, how willing would you be to leave your money in a savings account or to invest in a business? Certainly you would be less willing than if such things never occurred. A good rule of thumb is: The more certain private property rights are, the more capital accumulation there will be. People are more willing to invest the money that they do not spend in endeavors which will increase their wealth in future years. They have property rights in their wealth that are sanctioned and enforced by the government. In fact, some economic historians have attempted to show that it was the development of well-defined private property rights which allowed Western Europe to increase its growth rate after many centuries

of stagnation. The degree of ability and certainty with which one can reap the gains from investing also determines the extent to which businesspersons in *other* countries will invest capital in LDCs. The threat of nationalization that hangs over many Latin American nations probably prevents a great amount of the foreign investment which might be necessary to allow these nations to become more developed.

What Hope Is There for LDCs?

We have no perfect plan or theory for development. There have been few spectacular examples of development in the last 25 years—that is, few countries have shifted from the less-developed to the developed category. Israel is one that has. But there is no guaranteed model of economic development—no guaranteed process by which LDCs can become developed.

The future, however, may be different. Economists may become better attuned to the actual determinants of growth in different situations so that specific models can be made and applied in specific situations. The economics of development and growth is perhaps one of the least well-defined disciplines in the entire study of economics, despite the large number of books written on the subject. Economists still have many deep disagreements regarding a theory of economic development.

Chapter Summary

1. There are numerous theories of why nations grow. Some of the most simplistic are the north/south theory, the race theory, the natural resources theory, and so on.

2. One of the modern theories is that of balanced growth—agriculture and industry should grow in a balanced manner for the whole nation to develop. However, this often involves heavy subsidization of industrial projects against the dictates of comparative advantage, thus leading to reduced total output of the nation.

3. Modern Western nations have continuously subsidized their own agricultural sectors, thus putting a crimp in the apparent comparative advantage that LDCs might have in agricultural pursuits.

Questions for
Thought
and Discussion

1. It is often said that the rich are getting richer and the poor poorer. Do you agree?
2. Why do you think there is so much disagreement about what LDCs should do to grow faster?
3. Do you think that the prestige value of industrial development is so important as to negate certain economic arguments against that development?
4. Some people have stated that since we have given LDCs death control, we have a moral obligation to help them out today. Do you agree?

Selected
References

Bauer, Peter T., *Dissent on Development: Studies and Debates in Development Economics,* Cambridge, Mass.: Harvard University Press, 1972.

Elkan, Walter, *An Introduction to Development Economics,* Middlesex, England: Penguin Books, 1973.

Gill, Richard T., *Economic Development: Past and Present,* Englewood Cliffs, N.J.: Prentice-Hall, 1973.

Myrdal, Gunnar, *Challenge of World Poverty: A World Poverty Program in Outline,* New York: Pantheon Books, 1970.

Ranis, Gustav (ed.), *The United States and the Developing Economies,* rev. ed., New York: W. W. Norton, 1973.

The Economist as Evangelist

BARBARA WARD

English Economist

Photo by V. Sladon, W. W. Norton & Co., Inc.

At the age of 26, Barbara Ward was named honorary secretary of the Sword of the Spirit movement, the purpose of which she said was "to remind English Catholics of the fifth precept of Pope Pius' encyclical which inveighed against the division of the world into have and have-not nations." The year was 1940 and Ward was already well launched on what has become a distinguished career devoted to bridging the gap between rich lands and poor. She had already written her first book, a study of the colonial question, titled *The International Share-Out*. The same year she was made foreign editor of *The Economist*. By 1949, having written two more books, worked for the British Ministry of Information during World War II, and served on the staff of the BBC, she was awarded an honorary degree at Smith as "one of the most widely read and most influential persons in the entire Western world."

Born in England and educated in France, Germany, and England, Ward was named Albert Schweitzer Professor of International Economic Development at Columbia University in 1968 and is now president of the International Institute for Environment and Development. She is the author of numerous books on economic development and the necessity for aid to poor countries, including *The West at Bay* (1948), *Policy for the West* (1951), *Faith and Freedom* (1954), *The Interplay of East and West* (1957), *Five Ideas that Change the World* (1959), *India and the West* (1961), *Nationalism and Ideology* (1966), *Spaceship Earth* (1966), *The Lopsided World* (1968), and with others, *The Widening Gap* (1971).

In one of her most influential books, *The Rich Nations and the Poor Nations* (1962), the popular development economist draws on themes from her earlier work. Noting that communism provides a coherent and appealing program for development, Ward urges the Western industrialized nations to formulate a cooperative strategy of their own toward developing nations. She calls for a spiritual revival of the Marshall Plan and proposes that each country contribute 1 percent of its annual income to foreign aid. The gap between the rich lands and the poor is widening, she says, because the nations of the West have already achieved a "momentum of sustained growth" while the poor countries—because they are poor—have not been able to accumulate sufficient capital "to get off the ground."

Since the thirst for modernization, as well as many current dilemmas in the poor countries are directly attributable to the impact of the "Western colonial system," Ward argues that it is therefore the responsibility of the capitalist nations of the "Atlantic arena" to finish the task of development. A foe of the haphazard nature of most foreign aid programs, she criticizes the colonial system of

the past and foreign aid programs of the present for creating only partial modernization, when what is needed is enough capital to transform the entire economies of the poor nations. "All parts of the economy have to change if the economic pattern as a whole is to change," she says.

In recent years Ward has become more critical of the private enterprise system and economic nationalism. She has become increasingly involved in projects and commissions of the United Nations, and she emphasizes the need for planning and international cooperation in economic development. Though still concerned with the gap between rich lands and poor that endangers political and economic stability, and still critical of Western foreign aid programs, Ward has broadened her scope to include the ecological consequences of different strategies of development.

In her latest book, *Only One Earth* (1972), written with microbiologist René Dubos and based on the United Nations Conference on the Human Environment, Ward and Dubos ask what would happen if all the world's peoples lived like Europeans or Japanese. If the rates of energy use, consumption of foodstuffs and raw materials, urbanization, and population continue their present degree of acceleration, "the natural system of the planet upon which biological survival depends" will be altered "dangerously and perhaps irreversibly." Outlining the major worldwide "external diseconomies" that "pass on a hidden and heavy cost to the community," Ward and Dubos conclude that economic growth is still imperative but feasible in the long run only if more vigorous and conscious planning is exercised. They call for a new vision of unity, based on the realization that all nations and all peoples are interdependent and that such unity is necessary for human survival.

Issue I-17

Can Foreign Aid Help Less-Developed Countries?

CAN DEVELOPMENT ASSISTANCE WORK?

The Rationale behind Foreign Aid

The United States and other countries have been giving assistance to less-developed countries for many years now. Why? Four basic reasons are usually given to justify this assistance, which can be in the form of grants, food, military supplies, or technical expertise. We will look at these reasons now.

Security

Foreign aid during the 1950s was provided by the United States principally under the amended Mutual Security Act of 1951. It was justified primarily as a national security measure needed to strengthen allies and to build up low-income countries to make them less vulnerable to communist invasion or takeover. Throughout the 1960s, the long-term security argument remained the underpinning of the official rationale. Basically, America wanted allies and lots of them. Economic aid was, so to speak, a down payment on a military alliance with a less-developed country. Through such alliances, the

United States obtained foreign bases that could be used for military intelligence gathering and for United States forces. In the age of intercontinental ballistic missiles, Trident submarines, and spy satellites, however, the importance of such bases has seriously diminished, and although the United States may want military allies, it certainly is less in need of foreign bases for its own internal security.

Economics

Economically, extending foreign aid to help develop other countries can be good business. Developing other countries presumably widens the market for American exports and also provides new opportunities for international investment by American capitalists. In addition, lower-cost sources of raw materials can also be developed. Really poor LDCs tend to be unreliable sources of raw materials. However, if they can be developed, then both reliability and quantity supplied may grow.

Also, higher levels of production and trade in LDCs will strengthen international trade and international

financial transactions. Countries with undiversified, weak economies are often feeble members in the network of international trading institutions on which all nations must ultimately rely for international trade.

Politics

It used to be thought that development assistance would have an obvious political payoff in that it would help win friends for the United States. Although not completely dead, such a view is certainly highly discredited today. In its place is a longer-range view of the world political situation. If we help develop, then the world will have greater order and the international political climate will be improved. In this sense, foreign aid is only one of many tools that are helping fashion an international environment that will be less polarized and less divisive.

Humanitarianism

The humanitarian argument in support of foreign aid remains a strong and potent rationale. In the United States itself, the problem of poverty has not gone unnoticed. If we feel that our citizens should not starve or live in despicable conditions, then we can justify foreign aid by merely extending these humanitarian views to the rest of the world. One might say that our world has become too small for feelings of kinship between individuals to be stopped at political frontiers.

In its most elementary form, the humanitarian appeal is quite clearly a plea for the relief of suffering. At this level then, aid would be for consumption only rather than for investment. But immediate consumption relief is only a short-run palliative and not a cure. The humanitarian rationale would be better served in the long run if aid were in the form of investments in industry, agriculture, and education.

A Brief Rundown of American Foreign Aid

Look at Table I-17.1. Here we show the total amount of economic and military aid that the United States has extended to other nations. We also break down that aid into its military component and its economic components consisting of grants and loans. The numbers are given in constant dollars, with 1967 as a base year. One thing strikes us immediately: Foreign aid, in real terms, has been falling dramatically over the last several decades.

To get a better idea of how much aid each individual country receives, we show in Table I-17.2 the net receipts of economic aid per capita for the years 1960 to 1965. Note that these are current dollars rather than constant dollars. In any event, we see that many countries have received minute amounts of aid in terms of aid per person per year.

Table I-17.1

Foreign Economic and Military Aid Program, 1949–1975 (In Billions of 1967 Dollars)

In the last 2½ decades, the amount of foreign aid, both military and economic, has trended downward, if we express it in constant 1967 dollars.

YEAR	TOTAL AID	YEAR	TOTAL AID
1949	8.8	1964	3.9
1950	5.1	1965	3.5
1951	4.6	1966	3.8
1952	4.5	1967	3.2
1953	7.6	1968	2.6
1954	6.8	1969	2.1
1955	5.2	1970	2.1
1956	5.4	1971	2.9
1957	4.4	1972	3.0
1958	4.7	1973	2.2
1959	4.6	1974	2.6
1960	4.0	1975	2.5
1961	3.8		
1962	4.4		
1963	4.6		

Source: Statistical Abstract of the United States

Table I-17.2

Receipt of Economic Aid Per Capita in Selected Countries

Here we show the net receipts of economic aid per capita from 1960 to 1965 for selected countries. If we were to correct for inflation, the amount of aid per person would be much smaller.

COUNTRY	PER-CAPITA AID RECEIVED (DOLLARS PER YEAR)	COUNTRY	PER-CAPITA AID RECEIVED (DOLLARS PER YEAR)
Argentina	1.6	Mexico	1.3
Ceylon	1.6	Pakistan	3.6
Chile	13.2	Peru	1.8
Colombia	3.7	Philippines	1.7
Egypt	8.7	Spain	1.3
Greece	5.5	Taiwan	6.3
India	2.0	Thailand	1.4
Israel	46.2	Venezuela	2.5
Malaya	2.1	Yugoslavia	6.1

Source: OECD

The Marshall Plan

After World War II, American financial assistance to other countries in the world became quite impressive. The United States financed approximately three-quarters of the United Nations Relief and Rehabilitation Program, which extended $4 billion worth of food, clothing, and medical services to war-ravaged European economies. In fact, in the 3 years following the end of the war, the United States provided about $17 billion in aid to Europe. That, however, did not seem to be enough.

By 1948 it became clear to Secretary of State George Marshall that more was needed to stimulate the European economies. In a famous address at Harvard University in June 1948, Marshall outlined a plan to speed Europe's recovery—and so we got the Marshall Plan. The plan established the European Recovery Program, which granted over $10 billion in foreign assistance to Europe. Most of this $10 billion was in the form of outright grants. Many observers contend that the Marshall Plan was instrumental in allowing Europe's productive capacity to grow dramatically during the late 1940s and early 1950s.

A Shift in Emphasis

After European economies got back on their feet, United States foreign aid began to go to LDCs. About one-third of this was military aid and the other two-thirds was nonmilitary aid. Much of it, however, was in the form of loans or grants of money that were "tied"—that is, the aid had to be spent on American goods and services. In other words, much of it was a form of subsidy to American

"A trillion-dollar economy is all right with me, but will it buy happiness?"

Drawing by Alan Dunn; © 1970
The New Yorker Magazine, Inc.

exporters rather than purely and simply aid for other nations.

We also gave aid under Public Law 480, which allowed for the transfer of "surplus" commodities, such as wheat, to selected countries. India, for example, obtained more than $3.3 billion worth of agricultural surplus commodities during the period 1953 to 1956. Public Law 480, however, has been greatly criticized. We'll look at these criticisms shortly.

The Case of India

It is interesting to examine the foreign aid situation of a country where such aid has accounted for a large percentage of that nation's gross national product. Take the case of India. In 1951, foreign assistance was about 1 percent of GNP. By 1958 such assistance had risen to 2.7 percent, and by 1970 it had increased to over 4 percent. We have given India surplus wheat and other aid in the form of grants and loans. Other Western countries, international agencies, and communist-bloc countries, have also given aid to India. Almost all noncommunist aid to India has been channeled through the Aid India Consortium. This consortium is composed of Canada, Japan, the United States, the United Kingdom, Belgium, France, West Germany, Italy, Holland, and others. India has also received long-term loans at preferential interest rates from Japan, Germany, the United Kingdom, and other countries.

Problems with Assistance to Less-Developed Countries

We have now given over $100 billion total in foreign aid to Europe and LDCs. The Marshall Plan seemed to show all involved that foreign aid could be extremely effective. However, critics of foreign aid pointed out that the Marshall Plan's apparent success could not be duplicated in other countries. Under the Marshall Plan, money was given to countries who already had advanced economic organizations, skilled labor forces, and experienced, as well as relatively efficient, government bureaucracies. Hence, the Marshall Plan was essentially an aid system to help restore or replace physical plants and equipment destroyed during the war. Proponents of the Marshall Plan, who saw its success as justification for further foreign aid, must agree that perhaps the major factor in that success was the United States' provision of the one ingredient—physical resources—missing from an economic environment ready to generate its own recovery.

The Situation in Less-Developed Countries

The LDCs in the world today cannot be compared to those war-torn European countries at the end of World War II. The modernization of LDCs is a much more complicated task than the restoration of postwar Europe. There are many barriers to economic growth: a lack of technical skills and capacities, poorly organized markets, political and social elites who are unreceptive to change, non-growth-oriented foreign trade policies, and so on.

If we look back at Table I-17.2, we see that the foreign aid impact on per capita income in recipient countries has been small, both in absolute terms and relative to existing levels of per capita income. Israel, for example, received approximately $29.10 in aid per capita from the United States in 1968, but the country's 1968 per capita income was over $1,000. The contribution of foreign aid to per capita income has to be quite small.

Critics of foreign aid contend that the only countries in which foreign aid may have caused a substantial percentage increase in national income are those countries where military and political motives dominated. These countries include Taiwan, Laos, Jordan, Libya, and Liberia.

The Rate of Return on Investment

Even if we assume that every dollar given as foreign aid is put into an investment in a less-developed country, the end result is still not that significant. Much research has been done on the rate of return on invest-

ments in underdeveloped countries, and at the most, we are talking in terms of a 10 percent annual figure. Although such a rate of return is not bad, given the per capita levels of foreign aid we are talking about, we cannot expect miracles from our foreign aid dollars.

Destroying Relative Prices

We have talked throughout the microeconomic section of this book about the role of relative prices. Relative prices indicate the relative scarcity and desirability of the various goods and services available in our economy and throughout the world. Relative prices will also determine the amount of resources that will go into producing a particular good or service. If the relative price of one good goes up and everything else remains the same, generally the profitability of increasing production of that good will go up also. This is the notion of a long-run competitive equilibrium, where economic profits are competed away by new producers entering the industry when the going market price yields a higher than normal rate of return.

Critics of foreign aid have pointed out that Public Law 480 has in many instances hurt countries like India more than it has helped them. Why? Simply because when we give our "surplus" food products to another nation, we destroy the system of relative prices that is supposed to signal individual farmers or would-be farmers in such countries that increased production would be profitable in the future. Think about it this way: When there is a reduction in the supply of agricultural commodities during any one year for whatever reason—drought, pestilence, or whatever—the relative price of agricultural commodities will rise. When the relative price rises, the profitability of engaging in agricultural pursuits rises also. More individuals will go into the farming sector of the economy, and those already in that sector will expend more energy and resources to provide food for the future. However, if, when there is a reduction in agricultural supplies due to some natural calamity, the United States or any other nation ships large quantities of food products to the stricken nation, then the relative price of food products will not rise as abruptly. The incentive to put more resources into the farming sector will be destroyed. In the short run, those recipients of "free" surplus food commodities from the United States will be better off. In the long run, however, the agricultural sector will not expand as much as it would have otherwise, and the nation will be worse off.

A Final Note

A former president of the International Finance Corporation, Robert L. Gardner, has succinctly stated the probable impact of foreign aid:

> Over the post-war period immense sums have been made available to the developing areas. Some of these funds have been well applied and have produced sound results, others have not . . . if [foreign aid] is applied to uneconomic purposes, or if good projects are poorly planned and executed, the result will be minus, not plus. The effective spending of large funds requires experience, competence, honesty and organization. Lacking any of these factors, large injections of capital into developing countries can cause more harm than good. The test of how much additional capital is required for development is how much a country can effectively apply within any given period, not how much others are willing to supply.

The game of foreign aid is indeed a difficult one. It has not been and will not be enough for the United States and other more developed countries merely to transfer funds to countries in need. Foreign aid can help, but only to a limited extent and only if it is applied wisely, as Gardner pointed out.

Questions for Thought and Discussion

1. Is foreign aid as essential today in the development of the LDCs as it was 50 years ago?
2. Some observers contend that the Marshall Plan was not the key to Western Europe's development after World War II. Rather, they assert it was the tremendous amount of human capital that already existed in Western Europe which allowed such rapid rebuilding after the war. Do you agree or disagree?
3. Several rationales for foreign aid were given in this issue. Can you think of others?
4. What do you think is the effect of "tied" foreign aid? (Tied foreign aid requires the recipient to spend the proceeds on United States products.)

Selected References

Bauer, Peter T., *Dissent on Development: Studies and Debates in Development Economics,* Cambridge, Mass.: Harvard University Press, 1972.
Bhagwati, Jagdish and R. S. Eckhaus (eds.), *Foreign Aid,* Baltimore: Penguin Books, 1970.
Raffaele, Joseph A., *The Economic Development of Nations,* New York: Random House, 1971.

17 Economic Growth

Economic growth is an important policy variable that concerns the governments of all nations. Today in the United States there is an increasing clamor to *reduce* our current economic growth rate. We will touch on this in greater detail in the following and final issue of this text. Here we will discuss the general theory of growth. Zero economic growth may seem desirable to many in the United States, but LDCs in the world today are struggling for higher standards of living and are therefore still interested in the problems of economic growth.

What Is the Meaning of Economic Growth?

Most of you probably have a general idea what the term *economic growth* means. When a nation grows, its citizens are in some ways better off—at least in terms of material well-being. A formal definition of economic wealth might be as follows:

Economic growth is the rate of change in an economy's real level of output over time.

Generally, economic growth is measured by the rate of change of some measure of output. In this nation, and in most other nations today, the most commonly used measure of economic output is gross national product (GNP). In discussing the rate of change of actual output, we have to correct GNP for changes in prices. When we do this, we get what is called *real GNP*. Hence, one measure of economic growth is the rate of change in real GNP over time. This measure may be misleading, however, if the population is growing rapidly at the same time that real GNP is growing. In this case, economic growth is measured by the rate of change in per capita real GNP over time.

Growth and the Production-Possibilities Curve

We can graphically show economic growth by using the production-possibilities curve presented in Chapter 2. Figure 17-1 shows the production-possibilities curve for 1977. On the horizontal axis are agricultural goods and on the vertical axis are manufactured goods. If there is economic growth between 1977 and 1980, then the production-possibilities curve

will shift outward to the heavy line. The distance that it shifts represents the amount of economic growth—that is, the increase in the productive capacity of the nation.

The Importance of Growth Rates

Look at the growth rates in per capita income for selected countries in Table 17.1. The difference between the growth rates of different countries is not large; generally it varies by only 1 to 3 percentage points. You might want to know why such small differences in growth rates are important. What does it matter, you could say, if we grew at 3 percent or at 4 percent per year?

It matters a lot—not for next year or the year after—but for the future. The power of com-

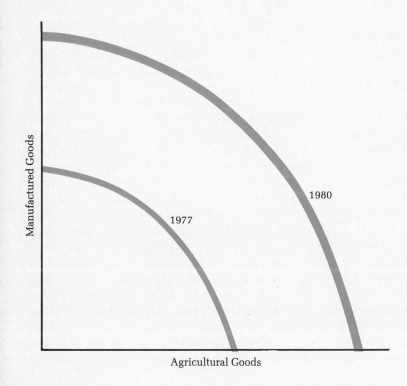

FIGURE 17-1 **Economic Growth**
We can see economic growth in terms of production-possibilities curves. If there is growth between 1977 and 1980, then the production-possibilities curve for the entire economy will shift outward from the line labeled 1977 to the heavier curve labeled 1980. The distance that it shifts represents an increase in the productive capacity of the nation.

Table 17-1 Per Capita Growth Rates—Various Countries

Here we show the average annual rate of growth of GNP per capita for various countries.

COUNTRY	AVERAGE ANNUAL RATE OF GROWTH OF INCOME PER CAPITA (1929–1970)
United States	1.9%
France	2.0
Italy	2.5
United Kingdom	1.7
Germany	3.0
Canada	2.1
Greece	5.2
Brazil	1.8

Source: Statistical Abstract of the United States and Statistical Office of the United Nations

pound interest is overwhelming. Let's see what happens with three different growth rates: 3 percent, 4 percent, 5 percent. We start with $1 trillion, which is approximately equal to the gross national product of the United States in 1971. We then compound or grow this $1 trillion into the future at these three different growth rates. The difference is huge. In 50 years, $1 trillion becomes $4,380,000,000,000 if compounded at 3 percent per year. Just one percentage point more in the growth rate—that is, 4 percent—results in a GNP almost double that amount. Two percentage points difference in the growth rate—that is, 5 percent per year—results in a GNP of $11,500,000,000,000 in 50 years. Obviously, there is a great difference in the results of economic growth for very small differences in growth rates. That is why nations are concerned if the growth rate falls even by a very small amount in absolute percentage terms.

It is often asserted that income and wealth in the United States are so great relative to other countries because we were endowed with such a large amount of valuable natural resources. This factor, however, is neither a necessary nor a sufficient condition for rapid economic growth.

Natural Resources and Economic Growth

A large amount of natural resources is not sufficient to guarantee economic growth. Many Latin American countries are fantastically rich in natural resources. However, they have not been overly successful in exploiting these resources. Natural resources must be converted to useful forms. Even in the United States, the Indians had more natural resources available to them than we have now, but they were unable to increase their standard of living or experience economic growth.

Only if we include people in the category of natural resources can we say that natural resources are required for economic growth; obviously, *people* must devise the methods by which other natural resources can be converted into useable forms. This is where the United States was more fortunate than other countries, particularly those with similar natural resources. (We also benefited from large capital investments from England and other Old World countries.) The founding fathers of our nation were a biased sample of the people at that time. Many of the "criminals" who were transported to the colonies were guilty of such crimes as religious heresy, being in debt, evading economic laws made by the government, and disagreement with the government itself. In other words, they were people who either wanted to or who were forced to escape the regimentation of a much more structured society. These are just the type of people who would attempt to devise new methods to utilize the natural resources in America. And that they did.

This is not to say, of course, that if we transplanted a cross section of Americans to some Latin American country, the growth rate in that country would suddenly take off. However, we can assert that the United States required more than just abundant natural resources to reach its current level of development; it required people who could devise ways to form those resources into something useful. Less-developed nations will also require this type of human resource.

Capital Accumulation

It is often asserted that a necessary prerequisite for economic development is a large capital stock—machines and other durable goods which can be used to aid in the production of consumption goods and more capital goods in the future. It is true that developed countries have larger capital stocks per capita than less-developed countries. It is also true that the larger the capital stock for any given population, the higher the possible level of real income. This fact is one of the bases of many foreign aid programs. The United States and other nations have attempted to add capital stocks to less-developed countries so that they, too, might grow. However, the amount of capital that we have actually given is, as we saw in Issue I-17, quite small.

What is the relationship between capital and a nation's growth rate?

Let's look at a production-possibilities curve for a country as a whole. We want to find the trade-off between goods today and goods tomorrow, or between present consumption and future consumption. Therefore, in Figure 17-2 we label the horizontal axis as present goods and the vertical axis as future goods. The pro-

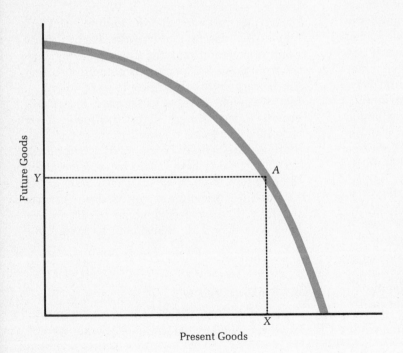

FIGURE 17-2 **The Trade-Off between Present Goods and Future Goods**

Here we show the production-possibilities curve between present goods and future goods. If we want to have more goods in the future, we have to sacrifice goods today. In other words, there has to be more saving if we are to have more future goods. At a point in time—for example, at point A—we could consume X present goods and still have Y future goods.

duction-possibilities curve, as you will remember, represents the *maximum* amount of each of the two goods that a nation can produce at any point in time. If, for example, we were at point A, we could, with our present resources, consume X amount of present goods and Y amount of future goods. By decreasing the amount of present goods, we can increase the amount of future goods. This means that if we consume less today, we will have more tomorrow. We have to sacrifice present consumption to have more future consumption.

All individuals, of course, are faced with this decision. It is a decision they must make with respect to how much they want to save. If they want a lot of future consumption, they cut back on current consumption; they save more. More income can go into a savings and loan association or into the stock market so that later, perhaps when they retire, they will be able to consume more than otherwise. In terms of the economy as a whole, the decision as to whether there should be present consumption or future consumption translates into a decision as to whether there should be more movies and food consumed today or more buildings and machines constructed today. When you decide not to consume but to save part of your income, you will perhaps put it in a savings and loan association. That money will then be available to borrowers for new housing. Or you might invest your savings in a new company or in the expansion of an old one. This way, the money you save provides the money capital for businesspersons to construct and purchase physical capital—machines and equipment.

Why Is Capital Important?

The size of the capital stock determines the maximum amount of income that can be produced at any point in time. Obviously, if very few machines can be used to make goods and

services, we will be able to make fewer and our income will be lower. The more machines there are, the more income can be generated. Therefore, the larger the capital stock, the larger the income pie. But how does the capital stock grow? It grows by people making the decision not to consume today but to save and invest. The more saving and investment there are as a percentage of total income, the higher will be the capital stock, and therefore, the higher will be possible future income. We can perhaps demonstrate this decision by again using our production-possibilities curve.

In Figure 17-3, we show a production-possibilities curve for 1984. The horizontal axis is again labeled as present consumption, but now the vertical axis is labeled capital goods. "Capital goods" is just another way of describing future consumption. We would expect that if our economy is operating at A, where there are relatively more capital goods being produced than at B, the production-possibilities curve in 1984 would be farther to the right than it would be if we were producing at B. We have labeled the outside curve AA and the middle curve BB. Obviously, the rate of growth starting from point A is greater than the rate of growth starting from point B. The pie gets potentially larger the more people are willing to save today. In fact, we might be able to increase the rate of growth in the United States drastically if we somehow increased the saving rate of the population. This could be done by government taxation. That is, taxes could be increased, and the proceeds from those increased taxes could be put into investment goods that, in turn, would yield increased income in the future. Let's now turn from investment to saving.

Saving Decisions

Saving decisions are based on many things. However, one key determinant is what we call

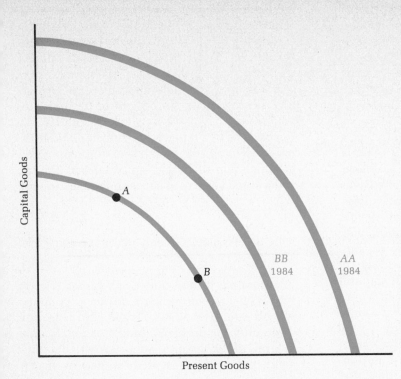

Capital Goods

Present Goods

A

B

BB
1984

AA
1984

FIGURE 17-3 **The Importance of Capital for Growth**

Here we show a production-possibilities curve with two points on it, *A* and *B*. At point *A* we are consuming less today and providing more consumption for tomorrow in the form of capital goods. At point *B* we are consuming more today and providing less in the form of future consumption. If we operate at point *A*, we may end up on a production-possibilities curve of *AA* in 1984. However, if we are at point *B*, we may end up at a production-possibilities curve of only *BB* in 1984. In other words, there will be less growth during the next decade if we consume more goods today instead of saving and investing in capital goods that provide for more future consumption.

a person's **personal discount rate.** If you just can't wait to consume all the income you make, you have a relatively high discount rate. If you are not so impatient and can wait longer, you have a relatively low discount rate. The lower your discount rate, the more you'll be willing to save at any given yield on those savings. Whenever your personal discount rate exceeds the yield you can get on savings, you will not save; you have to be offered a yield that is higher than your discount rate. Otherwise you'll be better off by consuming today. The saving behavior of economies taken as a whole depends therefore on the collective discount rate of the population and the average rate of return on saving. Note here that we are talking about the rate of saving—that is, how much of current income people put away per period of time.

Saving and the Poor

It is often stated that people in less-developed countries cannot save because they are barely subsisting. This is not actually true. Many anthropological studies—of villages in India, for example—have revealed that saving is in fact going on, but it takes forms that we don't recognize in our money economy. In some places, saving may involve storing dried onions. In any event, saving does take place even in the most poverty-stricken areas.

The Hard Facts

Look at it this way: Even if you are very, very poor and just barely making a living, you know that sometime in the future you will no longer be able to work. You will either reach mandatory retirement or you will become so debilitated and unproductive that nobody will be willing to hire you. Your income stream will be cut off. Unless there is a benevolent government or some charitable people (perhaps your family) who will take care of you, you will starve. There is a way out: You can have accumulated savings, the income and principal of which you can live on. Therefore, today you must make the decision as to how much of your current income you want to set aside for those retirement years, or for those years when you are sick or debilitated and cannot work. Unless it is literally true that you will starve if you reduce your current level of consumption, you probably will attempt to save a little bit out of your income. Most people are willing to reduce current consumption by a small amount to, at least, exist after they no longer can work. If this is not done, they face certain starvation when their income stream falls to zero.

Basically, then, saving is a method by which individuals can realize an optimal consumption stream throughout their expected lifetimes. Be careful. The word optimal here does not mean adequate or necessary or decent. It means most desirable from the *individual's* point of view.

Improving Technology

When people save, there has to be a profitable outlet for those savings so that the capital stock will grow and future incomes will be higher. Otherwise, saving would not lead to higher economic growth. One of the main ways that less-developed countries have been able to increase their capital stock and productivity in general is by adapting foreign techniques to their own situation. The most obvious and helpful technological advances that less-developed countries have been able to borrow from the developed world involve those in

agriculture—improved pesticides, hybrid seeds, improved irrigation techniques. One of the most striking examples of these technological breakthroughs that have aided less-developed countries is the development of "miracle" rice.

When we see the importance of technological progress in the growth of an underdeveloped country (or a developed country), we might come to a tentative conclusion that technological progress, along with the *associated* accumulation of human and material capital, is *the* crucial aspect of successful development.

Can We Tell Which Factor Is Most Important?

Is it possible to find out which factor is most important in determining a nation's economic growth rate? The answer is difficult. One way to simplify the problem, though, is to talk only in terms of the three economic growth determinants that can be measured—at least in theory:

1. Growth of capital stock
2. Growth of the labor force
3. Technological progress

Economists have found it relatively easy to measure the first two determinants. And in the past they have had a tendency to attribute any economic growth not accounted for by these determinants to technological progress. However, this is a very questionable procedure. In fact, recently economists have found that a large part of economic growth can be attributed to improvements in the labor force or, otherwise stated, improvements in human capital. This may also be true in the measurement of the capital stock. To the extent that the measurement of the growth in capital and labor does not take account of the growth in quality of these two factors, any residual measure of technological progress will be seriously biased upward.

Economic Growth—A Policy Objective

After World War II, governments throughout the world made economic growth a distinct policy objective. When, in the 1950s and early 1960s, American economists and politicians realized that the American rate of economic growth was slower than that of other nations, an explicit policy directive was issued by President Kennedy. He set a target of a 4½ percent annual increase in total real output during the 1960s. Presumably, government stimulation of

the rate of economic growth was necessary because of our political desire to stay ahead of the communist countries, the Soviet Union in particular. Economic growth was also considered important for national prestige as well as national defense. In addition, some economists, including John Kenneth Galbraith, pointed out that there was underinvestment in public sector spending. Hence, economic growth was called for to increase the funds available for public expenditures on urban renewal, hospitals, and public transportation.

Recently, political stress on increasing the rate of economic growth in the United States has greatly diminished. There are many economists who have pointed out that economic growth brings with it serious environmental problems in addition to depleting natural relevels. They point out that higher levels of economic growth may cause higher levels of congestion and noise in our cities and the destruction of our natural heritage. We will take up these very important problems in the following issue.

Definition of New Term

Personal Discount Rate: The rate at which you as an individual discount future pleasure or future consumption. If you have a high personal discount rate, you will want to consume a lot today because you don't want to wait until tomorrow. If you have a low personal discount rate, you will be willing to wait in order to have more consumption in the future. You will be willing to save more.

Chapter Summary

1. Just as there are different levels of per capita income in the world, there are different rates of growth. There seems to be no correlation between the level of per capita income and the rate of growth, however. It is the rate of growth that we are concerned with in this chapter.
2. A slight difference in the compound rate of growth can cause a tremendous difference in the per capita income or GNP many years in the future. For example, a jump from a 3 percent to a 5 percent per year rate of growth results in, at the end of 50 years, a difference in total income of almost 250 percent.
3. While natural resources are important for allowing economic growth, we must include in the concept of natural resources people and their productive services in order to come up with factors necessary for economic growth.
4. Even though people are important, so is capital accumulation or capital from other countries. We find that the more saving there is today, the larger is the capital stock and the larger will be the amount of possible future consumption. Hence, in economies where the people save a large percentage of their income, we would expect, *ceteris paribus*, a higher

rate of growth than in economies where people do not save as much. The use to which this capital is put is also important. If it is not used for investments that allow for future production and consumption, then the rate of growth may not be high even if the rate of saving is high.

5. Saving is a way to reach an optimal rate of consumption throughout one's life. Even poor people may want to save, to provide for future consumption when they are no longer working and making an income.

Questions for
Thought
and Discussion

1. Do you think Latin America is going to be better off by discouraging foreign investment through numerous nationalizations and expropriations of foreign property? Why?
2. Many less-developed countries put extreme restrictions on the purchase of imported luxury goods. Do you think this is a helpful policy for increasing the rate of growth in these countries?
3. If you were the economic policy adviser to a less-developed country, where would you suggest the government start investing? Why?
4. Many people contend that in most less-developed countries, the population is too poor to be able to save. Go back to our definition of saving as a way to distribute consumption optimally throughout one's lifetime. Do you think it is true that poorer people are unable to save as much as rich people in percentage terms? What is the relevant determinant of desired saving?

Selected
References

Baldwin, Robert E., *Economic Development and Growth*, 2d ed., New York: Wiley, 1972.

Fabricant, Solomon, *A Primer on Productivity*, New York: Random House, 1969.

Mansfield, Edwin, *The Economics of Technological Change*, New York: W. W. Norton, 1968.

Mishan, E. J., *Technology and Growth*, New York: Praeger, 1970.

Rostow, W. W., *The Stages of Economic Growth*, New York: Cambridge University Press, 1960.

Should Growth Be Stopped?

WHAT DOES THE FUTURE HOLD?

The Economic Problem

The economic problem occurs because we live in a world of scarcity. John Maynard Keynes, however, wrote an article in 1930 in which he concluded that "[a]ssuming no important wars and no important increase in population, the economic problem may be solved, or be at least within sight of solution within a hundred years."[1] Keynes felt that within 100 years, we would be eight times better off economically.

Keynes didn't see this opulence as such a good thing. In fact, he felt that "[for] the first time since his creation man will be faced with his real, permanent problem—how to use his freedom from pressing economic cares, how to occupy his leisure, . . . to live wisely and agreeably and well."

It would be nice if that were our only problem. Serious doubt has been expressed about Keynes' forecast by those who are worried that if we continue growing at the same

[1]John Maynard Keynes, "Economic Possibilities for Our Grandchildren," rep. in *Essays in Persuasion,* London: Macmillan, 1933.

rate we have in the past, the world will no longer be livable.

Stopping GNP Growth

We've noted some of the various theories that explain why nations grow, and we've shown some of the strategies less-developed nations might want to follow to increase their rate of economic growth so their inhabitants might enjoy higher standards of living. Recently, though, there has been a cry that economic growth should be stopped, at least in advanced areas of the world. Ecologically minded scientists, laypersons, academicians, and public officials have declared that we must end our fetish with GNP growth. They argue that growth in GNP should be stopped because it depletes our natural resources, pollutes our environment, and makes us into materialistic money grubbers. Furthermore, lurking somewhere in the future is a maximum limit that will be reached sooner or later. A fast growth rate in GNP just makes us reach it sooner. And when it is reached, then GNP will fall, and liv-

ing standards will go down instead of up.

To Zero Economic Growth enthusiasts, there is no hope. Those concerned with the environment attack GNP as a digital idol worshipped by materialistic gluttons. GNP measures, of course, only the output of goods and services. It ignores the pollution and industrial grime that growth generates.

So some maintain that there must be a limit to growth. In fact, in the hands of several scientists, the computer has shown that growth will reach a limit. An 18-month study sponsored by the Club of Rome arrived at this very conclusion. We will discuss it now.

The Limits to Growth

Look at Figure I-18.1. It's pretty wild, isn't it? But the conclusion, if those lines mean anything, is that food supplies are going to prove inadequate, even with ample natural resources, pollution controls, and a falling population. The question is: "Who drew those curves and how did they do it?" Several scientists at the Massachusetts Institute of Technology set up mathematical equations using information on what determines industrial output, food production, pollution, population,

THE LIMITS OF GROWTH

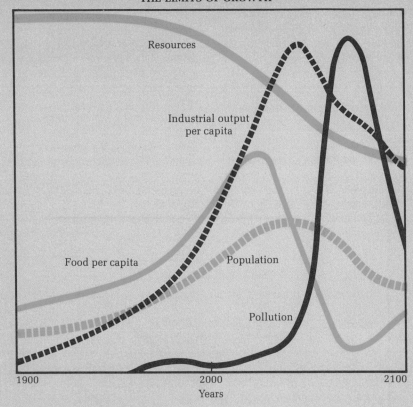

Resources

Industrial output
per capita

Food per capita   Population

Pollution

1900   2000   2100
Years

FIGURE I-18.1

Here we look into the twenty-first century. The prediction is that even though we will have ample natural resources, sufficient pollution controls, and better birth control, we will still run out of food. Malthus revisited. (*Source:* Potomac Associates.)

and so on, and the relationships between these factors. A computer was then used to calculate and project the behavior of each of these trends as they related to each other.

The M.I.T. computer forecast dramatic events for the world if the current trends in these variables continued. Before the year 2100, the world as a system would reach a point where the population could no longer be supported by existing resources. These grim findings apparently hold even if important advances are made in birth control and food production, in natural resources output and pollution control.

The equations show exponential (geometric) growth for everything except food production. Even breakthroughs in technology will not prevent the final collapse of the world. Take, for example, one computer run that the M.I.T. scientists experimented with. This is the one that actually underlies the curves shown in Figure I-18.1. These curves assume that recycling technology will reduce the input of raw material per unit of output to 25 percent of the amount now used. It is also assumed that birth control will eliminate unwanted children. Additionally, pollution will be 75 percent below its present level. What happens? Resources are sufficient; that's no problem. But the growth of industry is so great that higher output soon offsets the 75 percent decline in pollution. That is, even with the smaller amount of pollution per unit of output, the tremendous increases in output result in an overwhelming absolute amount of unwanted waste. Population, of course, even when all unwanted pregnancies are eliminated, gets out of hand so that there is a food crisis. Even increases in agricultural technology apparently will not save us. There will still be overuse of land, which will lead to erosion, causing food production to drop. This, at least, is what the computer predicted.

The M.I.T. authors of *Limits to Growth* point out that even if there are tremendous scientific breakthroughs, they must be matched by equally dramatic changes in the world's social institutions. Otherwise, these breakthroughs, whether they be birth-control devices or high grain yields, will not be effectively distributed to those in need of them. Needed changes, in other words, won't appear.

Changing the Equation

Not everyone was happy with the way in which the Club of Rome's first model of the future was put together. It seemed to have left out some critical variables. One of these was relative prices.

An economic fact that you are all aware of by now was completely forgotten in the model established by the scientist-authors. When specific resources become scarce, their price goes up. People are motivated to find substitutes or, if necessary, to do without the more expensive goods and services. That's something that many ecologists seem to forget, but it is an immutable economic fact of life. If a good becomes scarcer, the supply curve shifts inward. With a stable demand curve, we expect a rise in price. The quantity sold falls, as we see in Figure I-18.2. If timber becomes scarcer we

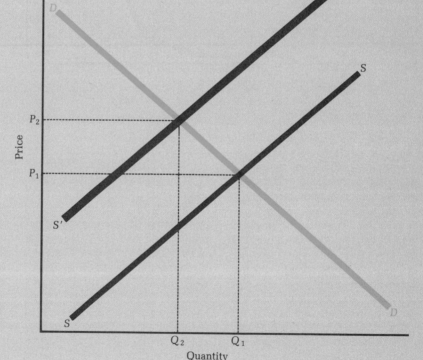

SCARCITY ALTERS PRICE

FIGURE I-18.2

If some particular resource becomes scarcer, its supply curve will shift from SS to $S'S'$ and its price will rise from P_1 to P_2. The quantity demanded and supplied will fall from Q_1 to Q_2. This change in the relative price of resources that become scarcer is something that modern-day doomsayers do not discuss.

expect its price to rise and substitutes to be found. The same holds for steel, coal, copper, and anything else. The history of any economy is in part a history of how changing relative prices reflect relative scarcity. Production and innovation respond to changes in relative prices. If the price of steel goes up because iron ore is becoming scarcer and more expensive, more attempts will be made at finding steel substitutes. Perhaps there will be an increased use of plastics. In any event, such is the way of the economic world.

A new study published in 1974 by the Club of Rome, *Mankind at the Turning Point,* did in fact take into account some changing relative prices. Aiming specifically at problems concerned with energy and the presumed lack of oil in the future, researchers compiling the new report found that a relative rise in the price of oil might, in the long run, help the economies of both the oil producers and the consuming nations. In the consuming nations, individuals would learn to use fewer petroleum products and alternatives would be found.

On the subject of food, the report points out that the only way to avoid a tragic situation where 500 million children starve by the year 2025 is for the developed nations to tighten their own belts and to invest heavily in building up the industries of poorer nations.

The Club of Rome's second report tells us, in other words, that with a concerted effort the world can devise solutions to its shortages of goods and excesses of people. Nonetheless, this second report still predicts horrifying scenarios of what might happen in the future if "something" isn't done.

The Problem with Gloom and Doom Projections

We have to be careful about projections into the future which tell us that the future of the world, the future of humankind, is one of mass starvation, overwhelming pollution, or total destruction. The *Economist* of London pointed out, for example, that

> ". . . if a Club of Rome has rightly forecast Britain's present quantum of travel, industry, and urban work force exponentially forward from 1850, it would have proved that this plague-ridden, industrial maimed nation must long since have disappeared beneath several hundred feet of horse manure."

We just cannot assume that things won't change in the future. It is possible to cite numerous examples of situations that have gotten better, not worse—such as the pollution level in London, which has been reduced by 85 percent in the last 15 years, doubling the hours of winter sunshine and adding 55 species of fish to the once mordant Thames. Concerning the problem of the psychological well-being of the human species, a University of Utah medical sociologist, Dr. John Collett, contends, based on the results of a massive study of urban stress, that the mental and physical well-being of city dwellers exceeds that of backwoodspersons and plainspersons.

Planning for Planning

In spite of a history of solutions to technological, sociological, and ec-

onomic problems, numerous concerned scientists, including economists, feel that the only way we can solve our problems in the future is by planning. In other words, instead of allowing unrestricted market forces to allocate scarce resources, we must institute planning on a massive scale never before considered in the United States. Planning would involve coordinating the use of resources in different critical areas in the economy to prevent bottlenecks and disrupting shortages. Planning, presumably, would also attempt to bring the rate of economic growth into line with the supposed reality of dwindling natural resource supplies.

Does the future of civilization require that planning take over the role that relative prices play in our market economy? Is planning required to reduce the rate of economic growth in this nation and elsewhere? Do we have to provide for the poorer nations of the world so that they can reach the level of material well-being that we in the United States have attained? These are important questions that we cannot attempt to answer here. A complete study of the pros and cons of a planned economy would require an examination of the success or failure of current planned economies, an analysis of why prices should not be used to allocate scarce resources, and whether a blueprint for the practical and operational aspects of planning is possible.

In the United States, perhaps a less-dramatic approach to these problems can be taken. Perhaps we can just redirect the growth equation so that it concerns itself with specific areas in the economy which we want to grow. Neither the United States' nor any other economy was built in a day. It seems inappropriate to talk about changing it overnight.

Questions for Thought and Discussion

1. Why is growth a problem today but wasn't a problem in the past?
2. Do you think that growth should be stopped?
3. Why are relative prices important in predicting what will happen to resources in the future?
4. Are predictions of the future demise of civilization new?

Selected References

Adelman, Morris A. et al., *No Time to Confuse,* San Francisco, Calif.: Institute for Contemporary Studies, 1975.

Barnett, H. and C. Morse, *Scarcity and Growth,* Baltimore: Johns Hopkins University Press, 1963.

Mishan, E. J., *The Cost of Economic Growth,* London: Staples Press, 1967.

Olson, Mancur and Hans H. Landsberg (eds.), *The No Growth Society,* New York: W. W. Norton, 1973.

Weintraub, Andrew et al. (eds.), *The Economic Growth Controversy,* White Plains, N.Y.: International Arts and Sciences, 1973.

Index

Numbers in **bold** indicate pages where terms are defined.

15 · 303